YALE ORIENTAL SERIES

BABYLONIAN TEXTS

VOLUME XIX

YALE ORIENTAL SERIES • BABYLONIAN TEXTS VOL. XIX

LEGAL AND ADMINISTRATIVE TEXTS FROM THE REIGN OF NABONIDUS

BY

PAUL-ALAIN BEAULIEU

NEW HAVEN AND LONDON, YALE UNIVERSITY PRESS

Published with assistance from the Yale Babylonian Collection

Designed by Ulla Kasten. Set in Bembo type.
Printed in the United States of America.

Library of Congress Cataloging-in-Publication Data

Beaulieu, Paul-Alain.
Legal and administrative texts from the reign of Nabonidus / by Paul-Alain Beaulieu.
p. cm. – (Yale oriental series. Babylonian texts ; v. 19)
Includes indexes.
ISBN 0-300-05770-9 (alk. paper)
1. Law–Iraq–Babylonia–Sources. 2. Babylonia–Politics and government–Sources. 3. Cuneiform tablets–Facsimiles. I. Title. II. Series.

KL2214.B43 2000
340.5 35–dc21 99–088525

The paper in this book meets the guidelines for permanence and durability of the Committee on Production Guidelines for Book Longevity of the Council on Library Resources.

10 9 8 7 6 5 4 3 2 1

A la mémoire de Vincent Hardy
(1955–1997)

Contents

Preface

The present project grew out of my Yale doctoral dissertation on the reign of Nabonidus, the last king of the Neo-Babylonian dynasty.* When Professor William W. Hallo and I agreed on my dissertation topic in 1983, he called to my attention the existence of a substantial body of unpublished texts dated to the reign of Nabonidus in the Yale Babylonian Collection and gave me a list of the museum numbers. Systematic research through the holdings of the Collection yielded more documents, accounting for 312 of the tablets herewith published in autographed copies. While I was able to discuss some of these texts in my dissertation, I soon realized that the entire group warranted separate treatment, and therefore we agreed that I should undertake the task of copying them for publication in a volume of the Yale Oriental Series – Babylonian Texts. The years 1986 to 1988 were mainly devoted to the preparation of this manuscript. Financial support during this period was provided by a postdoctoral fellowship from the *Conseil de Recherche en Sciences Humaines du Canada.* The Alexander Kohut Fellowship, awarded by the Department of Near Eastern Languages and Civilizations, Yale University, enabled me to complete the work. Special thanks go to Professor David B. Weisberg, of Hebrew Union College-Jewish Institute of Religion, Cincinnati, who made extensive comments on the copies and the indices.

* Published as P.-A. Beaulieu, *The Reign of Nabonidus, King of Babylon–556–539 B.C.* (YNER 10; New Haven/London, 1989).

Abbreviations

ADFU	Ausgrabungen der Deutschen Forschungsgemeinschaft in Uruk-Warka
ADOG	Abhandlungen der Deutschen Orient-Gesellschaft
AHw	W. von Soden, *Akkadisches Handwörterbuch*
AO	Département des Antiquités Orientales (Musée du Louvre)
ASJ	*Acta Sumerologica*
BIN	Babylonian Inscriptions in the Collection of J.B. Nies
BRM	Babylonian Records in the Collection of J. Pierpont Morgan
CAD	*The Assyrian Dictionary of the Oriental Institute of the University of Chicago*
CBCY	Catalogue of the Babylonian Collections at Yale
GCCI	Goucher College Cuneiform Inscriptions
HSM	Harvard Semitic Museum
IEJ	*Israel Exploration Journal*
JNES	*Journal of Near Eastern Studies*
MLC	Morgan Library Collection (Yale University)
NBC	Nies Babylonian Collection (Yale University)
N.A.B.U.	*Nouvelles assyriologiques brèves et utilitaires*
Nbn	J.N. Strassmaier, *Die Inschriften von Nabonidus, König von Babylon*
NCBT	Newell Collection of Babylonian Tablets (Yale University)
OA	*Oriens Antiquus*
OIP	Oriental Institute Publications
*Or*NS	*Orientalia,* Nova Series
RA	*Revue d'assyriologie et d'archéologie orientale*
RBC	Rosen Babylonian Collection (Yale University)
RGTC	Répertoire géographique des textes cunéiformes
TBER	*Textes babyloniens d'époque récente*
TCL	Textes cunéiformes du Louvre
YBC	Yale Babylonian Collection (Yale University)
YNER	Yale Near Eastern Researches

YOS	Yale Oriental Series, Babylonian Texts
ZA	*Zeitschrift für Assyriologie und vorderasiatische Archäologie*

Introduction

The reign of Nabonidus is the best documented of all first-millennium Babylonian reigns, both in respect to archival (viz. economic and administrative) and nonarchival (viz. monumental, historical, and literary) sources. According to the most recent survey of the evidence,[1] no fewer than 2,628 published archival cuneiform texts are dated to Nabonidus's reign, which, taken together with the 313 texts herewith published, amount to 2,941 texts, averaging nearly 175 texts annually for the years 556–539 B.C. Similar calculations for the preceding and following reigns reveal a steady increase in the number of documents from the end of the Assyrian dominion over Babylonia down to the accession of Nabonidus, whose reign represents the peak in the number of available documents. This is followed by a continuous decline starting with the downfall of the Neo-Babylonian empire. The annual average of texts known until now is 15 for the reign of Nabopolassar (626–605), the founder of the Neo-Babylonian dynasty, almost 40 for that of his son and successor Nebuchadnezzar II (605–562), and 60 for the short reigns of Amēl-Marduk, Neriglissar, and Lābâsi-Marduk (562–556). There is a yearly average of 100 texts for the reigns of the first two Persian rulers, Cyrus II (539–530) and Cambyses (530–522), and a little more than 40 for the long reign of Darius I (522–486).

Previously, 431 Yale texts dated to the reign of Nabonidus have been published, not counting the letters, almost all undated, which were published by Keiser and Clay in BIN 1 and YOS 3, respectively. Many of these letters can be shown to belong to this period on the basis of prosopographic data. Texts from the Yale Babylonian Collection proper (siglum YBC) were published by R.P. Dougherty (YOS 6, 1–246) and D.B. Weisberg (YNER 1, 3), from the Goucher College Collection (siglum GCBC) also by Dougherty (GCCI 1, 263–420 and GCCI 2, 342 and 396), from the Morgan Library Collection (siglum MLC) by A.T. Clay (BRM 1, 58–61), and from the Nies Babylonian Collection (siglum NBC) by Keiser (BIN 1, 3, 71, 97, 100, 104, 120, 135, 137, 161, 165, 174 and BIN 2 113, 117–19, 121–23, 127, and 133).

The present publication includes the remaining 312 Nabonidus texts found in the various collections housed at Yale. They are distributed as follows: 50 texts from the Yale Babylonian Collection, 108 from the Nies Babylonian Collection, 139 from the Newell Collection of Babylonian Tablets (siglum NCBT), 14 from the Morgan Library Collection, and 1 from the

1. M.A. Dandamaev, *Slavery in Babylonia—From Nabopolassar to Alexander the Great - 626–331 B.C.*, rev. ed., trans. by V.A. Powell, ed. by M.A. Powell and D.B. Weisberg (De Kalb, Ill.: Northern Illinois University Press, 1984), 10–12.

Rosen Babylonian Collection (siglum RBC). A survey of the unpublished material in the Goucher College Collection of Cuneiform Inscriptions, on deposit at Yale, has shown that all the Nabonidus texts in that collection were included by Dougherty in GCCI 1 and 2. Finally, one text from the Harvard Semitic Museum (siglum HSM) is included with the permission of Professor Piotr Steinkeller. All the texts included in this volume are previously unknown documents, with the exception of no. 100, which is a duplicate of YOS 6, 18.

Most of these texts are dated to Nabonidus's regnal years. Those that are undated or whose dates are partly lost or incomplete can be assigned to his reign on the basis of internal evidence. Undated letters nos. 103 and 104 were both sent by Bēl-šar-uṣur to Nabû-šar-uṣur. This Bēl-šar-uṣur can be identified as the son of Nabonidus, Belshazzar, who acted as regent during his father's sojourn in the Arabian oasis of Teima. His years of co-regency coincided with the incumbency of one Nabû-šar-uṣur as *bēl piqitti* official of the Eanna temple at Uruk, no doubt the recipient of these two letters.[2] A third letter, no. 105, also addressed to Nabû-šar-uṣur, contains several references to the crown prince (*mār šarri*), presumably again Belshazzar. Texts 180 and 268 have fully preserved dates, except that no king's name is mentioned. They can nevertheless be assigned to the reign of Nabonidus because they are dated to the intercalary month Ulūlu of the tenth year, and, as far as we know, only Nabonidus among Babylonian rulers of the first millennium had an intercalary Ulūlu in his 10th year. Texts 20 and 66 mention Nabû-šar-uṣur again as the acting commissioner (*bēl piqitti*) of the Eanna, an office he held from the first to the 13th year of Nabonidus. Texts 65 and 114 mention Zēriya as chief administrator (*šatammu*) of the Eanna, an office which he held under Nabonidus.[3] Finally, the same reasoning applies to text 86, in which Šum-ukīn appears as manager of the agricultural estates of the Lady-of-Uruk (*ša muḫḫi sūti ša Bēlti ša Uruk*), a distinction conferred on him by the king in his first regnal year and retained until the latter's return from Teima.

The great majority of these texts, specifically 239 of them, come from Uruk, as do most previously published Neo-Babylonian and Late Babylonian texts at Yale. The other groups of texts included in this volume are as follows: 21 documents drafted at Borsippa or in neighboring towns, 19 from Larsa and its region, 11 from Nippur and the surrounding communities, 4 from Babylon, 3 from Sippar, 2 from Marad, 1 each from Kish, Dilbat, Elammu, and Ṣidunu, and a small archive comprised of 10 documents possibly originating in Borsippa.

1. Texts from Uruk

The following texts come from Uruk or its region: 1, 2, 6, 9, 11–15, 18(?), 20, 24, 30, 31, 35, 40, 42, 51, 52, 56, 64–67, 71, 74–76, 78, 81–87, 90–95, 97–100, 103–30, 132–52, 154, 156–58, 160–251, 253–97, and 308–10.

2. On the career of Nabû-šar-uṣur, see G. Frame, "Nabonidus, Nabû-šarra-uṣur, and the Eanna Temple," *ZA* 81 (1991) 37–86.

3. On the career of Zēriya, see Beaulieu, *Reign of Nabonidus*, 125. Zēriya also held the same office from the second year of Amēl-Marduk until the first year of Neriglissar, so there is a possibility that texts 65 and 114 belong to that period.

Only the legal transactions specifically mention Uruk or neighboring localities. Administrative texts, letters, and letter-orders can be assigned to Uruk on the basis of internal evidence alone. Since all these texts were acquired from the antiquities market, their archaeological context is unknown. Therefore, although it can be confidently assumed that the vast majority of the texts from Uruk and its region originate in the archive of the Eanna temple, the possibility that some of the private transactions were found in private houses cannot be excluded completely. The following items are of special interest.

Text no. 1 records the acquisition by the Eanna temple of a house in exchange for 40 talents of bronze (or copper), 1 talent of tin, and 10 minas of wool. The transaction was witnessed by several high officials of the Eanna, including four individuals bearing the title "scribe of Eanna" (*ṭupšar Eanna*).[4] The title *ṭupšar Eanna* (often modified to *ṭupšar bīti*) was borne by one official at a time until the beginning of Nabonidus's reign, at which time the office seems to have lost its importance since the title was henceforth shared by several incumbents. This is confirmed by this document, the only one, to my knowledge, in which several "scribes of Eanna" are attested in this capacity at the same time. Also to be noted are the five beautifully preserved stamp seal impressions on the edges. The captions identify the owners of the seals as the five high officials of the Eanna who witnessed the transaction.

Texts 11 and 12 record leases of boats to the Eanna and are dated to the 4th and the 6th month of the 17th regnal year of Nabonidus, respectively. They should be considered in conjunction with text 94, dated to the 5th month of the same year, which records a deposition before an assembly of notables by a man who had carried a load of barley by boat to Babylon for the regular offerings to the Lady-of-Uruk, whose statue had been shipped to the capital because of the threat of a Persian invasion. As I have discussed elsewhere, the boats leased in texts 11 and 12, as well as in other such transactions dated to the 4th, 5th, and 6th months of Nabonidus's 17th year, were probably used to ship to Babylon the various commodities needed for the cult of Ištar.[5]

Texts 76, 78, 81, 82, 83, 85, and 86 document the activities of Kalbâ and Šum-ukīn as land managers and should be added to the large number of transactions related to the agricultural domains owned by the Eanna temple.[6]

Text 91 records a deposition before witnesses and Eanna officials concerning the legal status of the daughter of a temple slave. A woman named Ina-Esagil-bēlet had received from her

4. They appear in lines 42–46. These four scribes are known from other transactions as well; cf. H.M. Kümmel, *Familie, Beruf und Amt im spätbabylonischen Uruk* (ADOG 20; Berlin, 1979), 143–44. Ištar-mukīn-apli is generally known under the hypocoristic form Kīnâ; cf. *ibid.*, 144 and 115 s.v. Ištar-mukīn-apli 3. and n. 50.

5. See P.-A. Beaulieu, "An Episode in the Fall of Babylon to the Persians," *JNES* 52 (1993) 241–61, and on this type of text see G. Frame, "Some Neo-Babylonian and Persian Documents Involving Boats," *OA* 25 (1986) 29–50.

6. The main study is by D. Cocquerillat, *Palmeraies et Cultures de l'Eanna d'Uruk* (ADFU 8; Berlin, 1968). See also F. Joannès, *Textes économiques de la Babylonie récente* (Paris, 1981), 126–72. On the formulary of the *imittu* contracts see also G. Ries, *Die neubabylonischen Bodenpachtformulare* (Berlin: J. Schweitzer Verlag, 1976), 90–110.

father, as part of her dowry, a female slave named Bānītu-râmat, whom she had afterward dedicated as an oblate to the Eanna temple. While a temple slave, Bānītu-râmat bore two sons and one daughter named Gāmiltu. The nephew of Ina-Esagil-bēlet, one Bāniya, took Gāmiltu away from the temple and sold her for a sum of silver. The end of the text is damaged, but it seems that after having heard Ina-Esagil-bēlet's deposition relating the legal history of Bānītu-râmat and Gāmiltu, the assembly decided that the latter had been sold illegally and was to be returned to the temple. Text 91 confirms the evidence from other similar legal decisions that children born to female oblates remained the property of the temple. The social origins of individuals claiming a *zakītu* woman as ancestress is probably to be explained in light of that legal practice. Text 91 also contains a small item of historical interest: in lines 24–25 the 13th year of Nebuchadnezzar II is qualified as "the year of the *ḫuzirtu* insects" (MU.AN.NA *šá ḫu-zi-ra-tu*$_4$), probably indicating that Babylonia was afflicted with swarms of those insects that year. So far the insect *ḫuzirtu* has been attested only in lexical lists (*CAD* s.v.), and as a personal name in the Middle Assyrian period.[7]

Of all the texts published in this volume, no.110 is perhaps the most remarkable. It is an injunction issued by Kurbanni-Marduk, the *šatammu* of the Eanna, to an individual named Bēl-kāṣir, prohibiting him from revealing the contents of excerpt tablets (*liginnī*) to the temple slaves. This text was previously published in a separate article in which I argue that the injunction recorded in this document should be understood in light of statements sometimes found in the colophons of first-millennium scholarly texts prohibiting their dissemination outside a narrow circle of initiates.[8]

Text 112 consists of a list of fugitive temple slaves, all specified as being the offspring of various *zakītus* listed by name. This document should therefore be studied in conjunction with text 91.

Texts 113–15 concern assignments to the temple watch (*maṣṣartu*). Of these three documents, no.115 deserves special consideration. It consists of a list of teams of craftsmen assigned to the watch in various areas of the Eanna temple precinct. It is unfortunate that the last paragraph of the document is fragmentary, for it presumably spelled out the conditions under which the assignment was made. Nevertheless, the prohibitory tone of the remaining portions (cf. line 39: *la i-bi-it* "he shall not stay overnight"), as well as the wording of the heading (line 1: [^{lú}*um-ma-nu šá ana m*]*a-aṣ-ṣar-tú šá* É.AN.NA *sa-an-q*[*u*] "[These are the craftsmen who] were enlisted? for the watch of Eanna"), suggest that these craftsmen were assigned to their duties by order of the administrators of the temple. The text should therefore be compared with the "Craftsmen's Charter" of the Eanna, which enumerates some of the duties imposed by the temple administration on its dependent craftsmen.[9]

7. C. Saporetti, *Onomastica Medio-Assira* I (Studia Pohl 6; Rome, 1970), 227.

8. See P.-A. Beaulieu, "New Light on Secret Knowledge in Late Babylonian Culture," *ZA* 82 (1992) 98–111.

9. D.B. Weisberg, *Guild Structure and Political Allegiance in Early Achaemenid Mesopotamia* (YNER 1; New Haven/London, 1967), 5–12.

Text 116 records the consecration of a man named Nabû-aḫ-iddin as oblate of the Lady-of-Uruk and Nanaya by his son, his daughter, and his son-in-law.

Text 213 is an account of silver remaining at the disposal of various shareholders in the temple livestock industry. Of particular interest is the fact that the accounting covered transactions between the 1st and the 13th year of Nabonidus. Upon the king's return from Teima in the middle of his 13th year, a general turnover of officials took place in the Eanna temple. As a result, all the officials who were then in office were dismissed. It is therefore possible that text 213 is the only remnant of a general audit of accounts that was undertaken at that time.

Several texts published in this volume concern the use, care, and repair of sacred jewelry and cultic paraphernalia. Among them, texts 266 and 267 should be mentioned as well-preserved examples of a category of texts studied by F. Joannès that consist of detailed inventories of sacred vessels taken out of the treasury for cultic performances and stored again after inspection.[10]

2. Texts from Borsippa

Twenty-one texts come from the city of Borsippa; 16 of them are dated in that city (5, 10, 21, 26, 43, 45, 47, 60, 62, 72, 77, 79, 88, 89, 102, 313), and 5 more can be ascribed to Borsippa or its region on the basis of internal evidence (50, 58, 153, 159, 252). With the exception of nos. 26 and 313, all these texts belong to the archive of the families Ili-bani and Ea-ilūtu-bani, reconstructed by F. Joannès.[11] The combined archives of these two families extend over six generations, from the beginning of the seventh century to the end of the reign of Darius I. The economic activities of the families Ea-ilūtu-bani and Ili-bani were quite varied. We find in the archive, for example, transactions in real estate, documents related to the management of their agricultural domains, loans of silver, barley, and dates, and an interesting group of transactions documenting their involvement as contractors in the building works carried out by Neo-Babylonian rulers, Nebuchadnezzar II in particular, at Borsippa. The disappearance of the archive at the end of the reign of Darius I has sometimes been related to the upheavals of the first years of Xerxes' reign. If the Ezida temple suffered because of the repressive policy of Xerxes, this might explain the interruption of the archive, which was probably kept in storage in the temple itself, in a storeroom owned by the family. This correlation, however, remains hypothetical.[12]

10. F. Joannès, "Un inventaire de mobilier sacré d'époque néo-babylonienne," *RA* 75 (1981) 143–50.

11. A preliminary description of the archive was presented by F. Joannès, "Les archives d'une famille de notables babyloniens du VIIIe au Ve siècle av.J.C.," *Journal des Savants* (1984) 135–50. The main study is F. Joannès, *Archives de Borsippa: la famille Ea-ilūta-bani* (Hautes Études Orientales 25; Genève: Droz, 1989), which presents all the texts with transliterations, and some also with translations; for an index to transliterations and translations see pp. 439–40.

12. It is indeed far from certain that there is a correlation between the suppression of the Babylonian revolts by Xerxes and the sudden and near complete interruption of cuneiform documentation at Babylon and Borsippa at the beginning of his reign. The arguments are discussed most recently in reference to Babylon in M.A. Dandamaev, "Xerxes and the Esagila Temple in Babylon," *Bulletin of the Asia Institute* 7 (1993) 41–45. Joannès, *Archives de Borsippa*, 20, regards this correlation as hypothetical, and P. Briant, *Histoire de l'Empire Perse* (Paris, 1996), 560–61, as unfounded.

Also possibly coming from Borsippa is the small archive made up of texts 298–307. Most of them are receipts of barley to be converted to malt (ŠE.BAR *ana* BÙLUG+ŠE), presumably for brewing beer. The same individuals are involved in a majority of the transactions. Although the origin of the archive is unknown, the high frequency of theophoric names with Nabû, as well as the occurrence of the ancestral name Ilšu-abušu, characteristic of Borsippa,[13] lead one to believe that the texts may come from that city. More texts from the same archive but dated to the reign of Cyrus have been identified by the author while cataloguing the holdings of the Yale Babylonian Collection.

3. Texts from Larsa

First-millennium Larsa has yielded very little epigraphic material. Apart from the two building inscriptions of Nebuchadnezzar II and Nabonidus discovered in the foundations of the Ebabbar temple, only a handful of Neo-Babylonian and Late Babylonian documents drafted at Larsa have come down to us. The present volume makes a significant addition to the epigraphic material from Larsa, as it contains seventeen texts from that city and its region: 7, 27, 33, 39, 41, 44, 48, 49,[14] 53, 55, 59, 63, 69, 70, 73, 131 and 311, and two documents probably drafted at Larsa but with date formulas partly lost (68 and 213). Nine of them (7, 27, 33, 39, 44, 55, 59, 63, and 69), as well as one of the texts drafted at Uruk (no. 35), belong to the archive of one Itti-Šamaš-balāṭu, son of Lābâši, and his son Arad-Šamaš. This archive includes nearly a hundred texts preserved in various museums.[15] It covers a time range of slightly more than one generation, from the reign of Nebuchadnezzar II until the beginning of Persian rule. It reveals that the entrepreneurial activities of this family focused primarily on land management on behalf of the Eanna temple at Uruk, the Ebabbar temple at Larsa, and the royal estates. Other documents from Larsa not belonging to the archive of Itti-Šamaš-balāṭu do not form a coherent body of texts.

4. Texts from Nippur

Eleven documents were drafted at Nippur or in neighboring communities (8, 16, 19, 28, 29, 34, 36, 37, 38, 61, and 80). All but one of them (no. 29) belong to the archive of one Bēl-ēṭir-Šamaš, son of Aplâ. One fragment of unknown provenience probably also belongs to it (no. 29a). In his survey of Neo- and Late Babylonian texts from Nippur (722/21–317/16 B.C.), R. Zadok identified, among the 1,281 nonliterary texts found there (including the published as well as the

13. A survey of indices of personal names in publications of Late Babylonian texts indicates that this ancestral name is so far attested only at Borsippa in the Neo-Babylonian period. See Joannès, *Archives de Borsippa*, 378, where several attestations are listed.

14. See the edition of this text in P.-A. Beaulieu, "Prébendiers d'Uruk à Larsa," *RA* 87 (1993) 144.

15. See P.-A. Beaulieu, "Neo-Babylonian Larsa: A Preliminary Study," *Or*NS 60 (1991) 60–74, including transliterations and translations of texts nos. 7 and 55; as well as Paul H. Wright, *The City of Larsa in the Neo-Babylonian and Achaemenid Periods: A Study of Urban and Intercity Relations in Antiquity* (Ph.D. Dissertation, Hebrew Union College, Cincinnati, April 1994), who studies the texts preserved at Andrews University.

unpublished ones known to him), no fewer than 17 different private archives.[16] Most of these archives are made up of fewer than a dozen documents, while the Murašû archive alone includes the vast majority of archival documents found on the site. The archive of Bēl-ēṭir-Šamaš was not known and so far it is represented only in the holdings of the Yale Babylonian Collection. During the cataloguing of the Collection, an additional 18 tablets from this archive were identified by the author, most of them dated to the reign of Cyrus. With a total of 29 documents, the archive of Bēl-ēṭir-Šamaš is one of the largest Neo-Babylonian private archives from Nippur.[17] The commercial and financial activities of Bēl-ēṭir-Šamaš were quite varied: sales of slaves, sales of animals, *ḫarrānu* commercial partnership agreements, and leases of land for cultivation are represented in the archive, while the majority of documents are promissory notes on silver.

5. Texts from Other Sites

The 13 remaining tablets come from the following sites: Babylon (4, 7, 101, and 155), Sippar (22, 23, and 96), Marad (46 and 54), Kish (no. 57), Dilbat (no. 3), Elammu (no. 25), and Ṣidunu (no. 32).[18] Of special interest is text 101, drafted at Babylon, now in the possession of the Harvard Semitic Museum. The text records a trial and judgment before the royal court of justice at Babylon, a category of legal documents of which only a handful of examples has survived.[19] The parties involved in the dispute are one Nergal-rēṣū'a, the slave of one Iddin-Marduk, and a boatman named Amurru-natan. The latter was accused of having embezzled part of a load of dates, which he was bound by written agreement to carry to Babylon on behalf of Nergal-rēṣū'a, who was acting as agent for his master. The judges decided the case in favor of Nergal-rēṣū'a, and Amurru-natan was ordered to make reimbursement for the missing cargo of dates. The text belongs to the archive of the Nūr-Sîn family of Babylon. Iddin-Marduk was the head of that family during most of the sixth century, and his slave, Nergal-rēṣū'a, appears in many transactions of the archive, carrying on business on behalf of his master.[20] Another noteworthy aspect of the documents is the well-preserved seal impressions on the edges. As revealed by the captions, the seals belonged to the judges who attended the trial. Their names are also listed on the reverse of the tablet.

16. R. Zadok, "Archives from Nippur in the First Millennium B.C.," in *Cuneiform Archives and Libraries*, XXXème RAI, Leiden, 1983 (Leiden: Publications de l'Institut Historique-Archéologique Néerlandais de Stamboul LVII, 1986) 278–88.

17. A list of the texts belonging to the archive is found in P.-A. Beaulieu, *Late Babylonian Texts in the Nies Babylonian Collection* (CBCY I; CDL Press: Bethesda, Md., 1994), 89.

18. This is possibly a namesake of Sidon located in Babylonia rather than the Phoenician city itself. For a parallel case with Tyre, see F. Joannès, "La localisation de Ṣurru à l'époque néo-babylonienne," *Sémitica* 32 (1982) 35–43, and "Trois textes de Ṣurru à l'époque néo-babylonienne," *RA* 81 (1987) 147–58.

19. See, for instance, Strassmaier, *Nbn* 13, 356, 495, 720, 1113, 1128; TCL 12, 86, and 122; *RA* 12 (1915) 6; *TBER* pls. 58–59 (= AO 18897 + 18898) and pls. 60–61 (= AO 19536).

20. See the reconstruction of the archive by L.B. Shiff, *The Nūr-Sîn Archive: Private Entrepreneurship in Babylon (603–507 B.C.)* (Ph.D. dissertation, University of Pennsylvania, 1987). See also the more recent and more complete study by C. Wunsch, *Die Urkunden des babylonischen Geschäftsmannes Iddin-Marduk* (Groningen, 1993), esp. pp. 43–45 on Nergal-rēṣū'a. On Nergal-rēṣū'a see also M.A. Dandamaev, *Slavery in Babylonia*, 365–71.

Catalogue [21]

TEXT	MUSEUM NUMBER	MEASUREMENTS IN mm	DATE	DESCRIPTION
1	YBC 16216	103×64×29	14.09.13	Deed of exchange of land for bronze,[22] tin, and blue-colored wool
2	NCBT 1203	99×61×26	08?.09.22	Sale of orchard
3	MLC 1195	80×55×28	10?.xx.xx	Sale of arable land
4	YBC 11670	115×80×31	14.13.25	Sale of arable land and orchard in Babylon
5	NBC 8395	74×49×24	15.01.25	Sale of arable land and orchard in the district of Borsippa (Joannès, *Archives de Borsippa*, 350–51, T, 82, Tr)
6	NBC 4585	55×68×19	00.04.25	Sale of slaves
7	YBC 7378	66×40×22	01.07.30	Gift of slave with malediction formula (Beaulieu, *OrNS* 60 [1991] 68–69, T, Tr)
8	NBC 6226	39×53×18	10?.02.25?	Sale of slave
9	NCBT 1252	33×43×14	xx.06.09	Sale of an ox
10	NBC 8345	35×43×15	11.04.28	Lease of house (Joannès, *Archives de Borsippa*, 341, T, 93–94, Tr)
11	NBC 6183	40×56×18	17.04.29	Lease of boat to the Eanna
12	NCBT 1139	41×56×18	17.06.xx	Lease of boat to the Eanna
13	NCBT 1086	33×45×16	01.08.18	Promissory note to repay a sum of silver to the Eanna

21. The texts are arranged according to type of transaction, generally following the organizing principle adopted in D.B. Weisberg, *Texts from the Time of Nebuchadnezzar* (YOS 17). Some of the texts published here have been discussed in previous publications. In these cases, reference to those publications is provided in the DESCRIPTION section. Abbreviations used in this catalogue are: C = copy, T = transliteration, Tr = translation, PN = personal name, PNs = personal names. The date of each text is given in the following order: Year, Month, Day. The month intercalary Ulūlu is indicated by 6A, intercalary Addaru by 13.

22. The logogram UD.KA.BAR (= *siparru*) may denote *bronze, unworked bronze*, or *copper* in this period; see J.A. Brinkman, "Textual Evidence for Bronze in Babylonia in the Early Iron Age, 1000–539 BC," in *Bronze-Working Centres of Western Asia c.1000–539 B.C.*, ed. by J. Curtis (London and New York, 1988), 135–68. Although it is not always clear which material was meant, I have translated UD.KA.BAR as *bronze* throughout this catalogue.

TEXT	MUSEUM NUMBER	MEASUREMENTS IN mm	DATE	DESCRIPTION
14	NCBT 1148	35×52×18	02.11.05	Promissory note to repay a sum of silver to the Eanna
15	NCBT 513	38×47×17	06.09.10	Promissory note to repay a sum of silver
16	NBC 6200	32×41×17	06.09.20	Promissory note to repay a sum of silver, the remainder of a debt
17	NBC 6219	49×64×24	15.01.20	Promissory note to pay a sum of silver, a woman's dowry
18	NBC 6214	35×43×17	[x]4.09.13	Promissory note to repay a sum of silver
19	NBC 6192	39×32×20	xx.xx.25	Promissory note to repay a sum of silver
20	NCBT 531	45×55×22	xx.xx.14?	Promissory note to repay a sum of silver
21	NBC 8407	49×59×25	⌜1⌝.06.11	Promissory note to repay a sum of silver (Joannès, *Archives de Borsippa*, 354, T, 106, Tr)
22	NBC 6120	39×47×17	10.11.06	Loan of silver with pledge of real estate
23	NBC 6113	40×52×18	11.11.28	Loan of silver with pledge of slave and penalty clause
24	NBC 4593	48×62×21	12.12.13	Loan of silver with pledge
25	NBC 6196	37×45×18	08.08.01	Loan of silver at 33⅓% interest
26	YBC 11591	37×46×19	10.6A.[x]8	Loan of silver with interest
27	YBC 9048	41×53×20	15.06.04	Loan of silver with interest
28	NBC 6174	41×52×22	16.12.11	Loan of silver with interest
29	NBC 4755	25×44×18	07.01.02	Loan of silver
29a	NBC 4755A	10×42×15	xx.xx.xx	Legal document of uncertain nature
30	NBC 4501	35×51×17	01.10.24?	Promissory note to deliver a quantity of barley to the Eanna
31	NCBT 1265	32×41×15	02.04.09	Promissory note to pay a quantity of barley
32	NBC 6232	35×47×20	09.12.21	Promissory note to pay a quantity of barley
33	NCBT 623	40×49×18	09.12.27	Promissory note to pay a quantity of barley, the remainder of a debt
34	NBC 6233	42×52×19	10.11.10	Promissory note to deliver barley to royal storehouse
35	NCBT 554	39×47×17	12.11.23	Promissory note to pay a quantity of barley, the remainder of a debt
36	NBC 6186	37×49×20	14.01.13	Promissory note to repay a debt of dates with barley
37	NBC 6171	39×50×17	15.xx.16	Promissory note to repay a quantity of barley

TEXT	MUSEUM NUMBER	MEASUREMENTS IN mm	DATE	DESCRIPTION
38	NBC 6119	38×53×19	15.12.26?	Promissory note to repay a quantity of barley
39	NCBT 523	41×54×20	10?.02?.12	Promissory note to repay a quantity of barley
40	NCBT 533	43×49×17	10?.01.12?	Promissory note to repay a quantity of barley
41	NCBT 1072	44×51×20	xx.xx.xx	Promissory note to repay a quantity of barley
42	YBC 11308	36×45×18	xx.xx.[x]6	Promissory note to repay a quantity of barley, with pledge and guarantor
43	NBC 8328	34×44×20	12.12.10	Loan of barley with pledge, free of interest (Joannès, *Archives de Borsippa*, 334, T)
44	NCBT 549	42×58×20	10.6A.25	Promissory note to repay a quantity of barley
45	MLC 381	31×41×17	[x]4.xx.xx	Promissory note to repay a quantity of dates (Joannès, *Archives de Borsippa*, 330, T)
46	YBC 11269	34×42×18	11.03.05	Promissory note to repay a quantity of dates
47	NBC 8330	38×45×18	17.05.06	Promissory note to repay a quantity of dates (Joannès, *Archives de Borsippa*, 335, T)
48	YBC 8288	34×45×18	03.05.23	Promissory note to repay a quantity of sesame[23]
49	NCBT 580	36×46×19	05.06.29	Promissory note to repay a quantity of sesame (Beaulieu, *RA* 87 [1993] 144, T, Tr)
50	NBC 8347	38×47×15	13.04.18	Promissory note to deliver quantity of sesame (Joannès, *Archives de Borsippa*, 341–42, T)
51	NCBT 537	42×56×17	12.09.20?	Promissory note to repay in silver a debt of barley to the Eanna
52	NCBT 1286	47×67×21	14.03.04	Promissory note to repay a sum of silver to the Eanna
53	YBC 7397	33×44×18	01.08.10	Receipt of partial payment of a debt of barley
54	YBC 11535	38×52×20	05.08.24	Settlement of debts
55	NCBT 547	34×49×17	09.01.07	Receipt of dates by Ebabbar of Larsa as payment of tithe (Beaulieu, *Or*NS 60 [1991] 72, T, Tr)

23. I have translated the logogram ŠE.GIŠ.Ì (= *šamaššamū*) as *sesame* throughout this work. There has been a long debate as to whether ŠE.GIŠ.Ì denotes *sesame* or *flax*, but a consensus has now emerged that *sesame* is the only likely possibility. The arguments are summarized in *CAD* Š/1 s.v. *šamaššamū*, and several discussions of the problem have appeared in *Bulletin for Sumerian Agriculture* II (Cambridge, 1985). Latest discussion by M.A. Powell, "Epistemology and Sumerian Agriculture: The Strange Case of Sesame and Linseed," in P. Michalowski et al., eds., *Velles Paraules. Ancient Near Eastern Studies in Honor of Miguel Civil on the Occasion of his Sixty-Fifth Birthday* (Aula Orientalis Vol. IX/1–2; Barcelona, 1991), 155–64. I have translated the logogram Ì.GIŠ as *sesame oil*, although it may denote any kind of oil.

TEXT	MUSEUM NUMBER	MEASUREMENTS IN mm	DATE	DESCRIPTION
56	NCBT 1114	34×45×16	10.10.16	Receipt of silver in the Eanna as repayment of debt
57	NBC 6193	30×39×16	12.02.27	Receipt of silver as payment for rent of house
58	NBC 8324	32×42×16	14.09.xx	Receipt of silver (Joannès, *Archives de Borsippa*, 333, T)
59	YBC 6856	40×49×20	15.04.30	Receipt of barley as repayment of debt
60	NBC 8357	38×46×16	15.08.05	Receipt of dates as payment (Joannès, *Archives de Borsippa*, 342, T)
61	NBC 6179	32×49×14	16.01.30	Record of repayment of a quantity of dates
62	NBC 6216	39×45×20	xx.05.07?	Contract to raise sheep drafted as a promissory note in silver (Joannès, *Archives de Borsippa*, 331–32, T, 40, Tr)
63	YBC 7369	40×52×20	04.xx.06	Transfer of a debt of barley
64	YBC 11608	38×49×16	13.05.02	Personal guarantee
65	YBC 3755	46×63×20	xx.13.xx	Personal guarantee
66	NCBT 866	47×60×18	xx.xx.12	Personal guarantee
67	YBC 3847	51×68×21	05.10.05	*Ḫarrānu* joint venture agreement
68	NCBT 955	33×48×16	xx.xx.19	Contract to perform the work of fuller
69	YBC 3520	48×65×20	⌜09?⌝.07.03	Contract to cultivate land
70	YBC 7385	45×53×16	17.07.02?	Contract to cultivate land
71	YBC 7562	49×65×21	12.04.10	Contract to perform agricultural work, dialogue document
72	MLC 347	38×53×20	⌜08.04.27⌝	Contract to cultivate land (Joannès, *Archives de Borsippa*, 329–30, T)
73	NCBT 1091	34×44×15	10.6A.26	Contract to mold and deliver bricks
74	NBC 4529	27×34×16	15.02.28	Contract to weave a quantity of wool
75	YBC 4048	55×40×20	01.xx.xx	List of estimated yields (*imittu*) of barley fields
76	NCBT 538	43×61×22	05.06.27	Promissory note to deliver estimated yield (*imittu*) of date grove
77	NBC 8336	28×40×13	07.05.23	Promissory note to deliver estimated yield (*imittu*) of date grove (Joannès, *Archives de Borsippa*, 336, T, 40, Tr)
78	NCBT 621	40×55×18	07.xx.15	Promissory note to deliver estimated yield (*imittu*) of date grove

TEXT	MUSEUM NUMBER	MEASUREMENTS IN mm	DATE	DESCRIPTION
79	NBC 8338	34×38×16	15.06.23	Promissory note to deliver estimated yield (*imittu*) of date grove (Joannès, *Archives de Borsippa*, 337, T)
80	NBC 8377	36×49×20	16.01.04	Promissory note to deliver estimated yield (*imittu*) of barley field
81	YBC 11265	35×46×16	xx.06.11	Promissory note to deliver estimated yield (*imittu*) of date grove
82	YBC 11577	31×56×21	xx.xx.xx	Promissory note to deliver estimated yield (*imittu*) of date grove
83	NCBT 1285	44×64×19	04.05.01	Receipt of estimated yield (*imittu*) of date grove in the Eanna
84	NCBT 924	27×37×15	05.09.03	Receipt of estimated yield (*imittu*) of date grove
85	YBC 7046	52×41×20	00.xx.22	Promissory note to deliver estimated yield (*imittu*) of barley field
86	NCBT 1014	36×54×21	01.xx.18	Promissory note to deliver estimated yield (*imittu*) of barley field to the Eanna
87	YBC 4055	43×53×20	02.12.12	Promissory note to deliver quantity of barley, remainder of estimated yield (*imittu*) of field
88	MLC 1664	44×52×21	08.09.25	Promissory note to deliver dates (Joannès, *Archives de Borsippa*, 331, T)
89	NBC 8341	32×41×17	10?.08.20	Payment of arrears of estimated yield (*imittu*) of date grove (Joannès, *Archives de Borsippa*, 339, T)
90	NCBT 1050	52×73×21	01.10.26	Deposition before witnesses concerning theft of sheep
91	YBC 4140	54×73×22	02.xx.xx	Report of court decision concerning status of temple slaves
92	NBC 11487	56×74×22	13.10.22	Record of deposition concerning date of written document
93	NBC 4594	46×64×24	15.12.10	Deposition before witnesses
94	NCBT 535	43×57×18	17.05.[x]5	Deposition before witnesses concerning shipments of barley to Babylon as offerings for Ištar (Beaulieu, YNER 10, 221–22, T, Tr)
95	NBC 4790	42×58×18	xx.01.27	Fragmentary record of a deposition
96	NBC 6128	35×54×22	⌜03?⌝.03.21	Quitclaim
97	YBC 11270	35×46×15	04.08.03	Indictment to convict man when someone testifies against him

TEXT	MUSEUM NUMBER	MEASUREMENTS IN mm	DATE	DESCRIPTION
98	NBC 4515	35×48×16	08.02.26	Indictment for penalty to be imposed if witness or accuser testifies against PN
99	NCBT 997	49×61×20	10?.12.08	Promissory note to settle the arrears of a debt
100	YBC 3706	40×55×17	01.11.08	Settlement of dispute over ownership of house (duplicate of YOS 6, 18)
101	HSM 890.4.8	106×66×27	10.12.04	Record of decision made by the royal court at Babylon
102	NBC 8364	37×47×20	07.03.20	Work contract (Joannès, *Archives de Borsippa,* 344–45, T, 143, Tr)
103	NCBT 21	59×30×16	Undated	Letter from Belshazzar to Nabû-šar-uṣur concerning weighing of gold
104	NCBT 42	56×29×15	Undated	Letter from Belshazzar to Nabû-šar-uṣur concerning cultic matters
105	YBC 11441	60×29×16	Undated	Letter to Nabû-šar-uṣur concerning Šum-ukīn and crown prince
106	YBC 11303	24×31×13	04.09.13	Letter order to allot beer to PN
107	YBC 11304	24×32×14	08.04.26	Letter order to give rations to workmen
108	NCBT 1112	25×34×14	10.12.06	Letter order to allot beer to PN
109	NCBT 493	29×41×15	12.05.02	Letter order to allot rations of barley
110	NBC 11488	43×61×20	15.03.04	Injunction to not read excerpt tablets to temple slaves (Beaulieu, *ZA* 82 [1992] 99–101, C, T, Tr)
111	NBC 4937	70×44×20	01.10.05	List of workmen employed to carry dates
112	NBC 4935	64×44×19	02.11.18	List of runaway temple slaves brought back by PN
113	NBC 4592	48×63×18	01.02.18	Promissory note to keep watch over portion of the Eanna domain, with oath
114	YBC 3509	43×72×21	xx.xx.xx	Assignment of PNs to temple watch
115	NBC 4855	177×98×35	xx.xx.xx	List of workmen assigned to the watch of the Eanna temple
116	NCBT 985	42×56×18	14.05.18	Consecration of a man by his family to the Lady-of-Uruk
117	NCBT 1102	32×21×13	09.10.04	List of cattle at the disposal of PN
118	NCBT 614	38×24×14	09.10.07	List of cattle at the disposal of PNs
119	NBC 8389	39×23×11	xx.xx.xx	List of sheep and goats at the disposal of PN
120	NCBT 1269	27×38×13	05.02.02	Receipt of dead cow by PN

TEXT	MUSEUM NUMBER	MEASUREMENTS IN mm	DATE	DESCRIPTION
121	NCBT 1186	45×27×14	06.11?.22	Receipt of dead cattle by PN
122	NBC 4751	62×41×19	14.03.14	Receipt of sheep and goats by PN
123	NBC 4548	40×25×16	09.04.06	List of sheep and goats at the disposal of PN
124	NCBT 1253	31×21×12	10.05.17	List of sheep and goats at the disposal of PN
125	NCBT 1290	87×50×19	11.12.04	List of sheep and goats at the disposal of PN
126	NBC 4535	31×44×17	04.02.15	Record of sheep taken away for silver
127	NCBT 1088	29×43×14	08.10.24	Record of sheep taken away by PN
128	NCBT 1262	29×40×16	⸢04?⸣.xx.26	Memorandum concerning sheep sent to Šamaš
129	NBC 4834	82×51×22	⸢04?⸣.03.07	List of sheep and goats
130	NBC 4703	31×43×15	04.12.07	Memorandum concerning carcasses of sheep and goats
131	YBC 7423	84×58×22	15.12.25	Record of oxen and sheep taken to the Ebabbar
132	NBC 4588	43×58×21	11.02.16	Receipt of dates by PN, partly as payment
133	NBC 4936	71×44×18	01.06.13	Allotment of dates as rations and *maššartu*
134	NCBT 599	73×109×26	01.xx.xx	Monthly allotment of Dilmun dates to bakers as *maššartu*
135	NBC 4907	92×61×23	02.06.11	Allotment of dates to temple slaves and workmen as rations
136	NBC 4772	39×55×18	03.⸢08⸣.02	Allotment of Dilmun dates to PN for one month
137	YBC 10473	64×42×21	⸢04⸣.xx.01	Account of monthly allotments of dates to bakers as *maššartu*
138	NCBT 1216	58×81×23	xx.06.xx	Monthly allotment of Dilmun dates to bakers as *maššartu*
139	NCBT 1275	23×38×11	04.12.24	Withdrawal of Dilmun dates by PN
140	NCBT 624	57×40×19	05.⸢09⸣.25	Account concerning dates
141	NCBT 1267	31×46×16	03.⸢07?⸣.09	Memorandum concerning dates
142	NCBT 492	33×48×15	04.02.12	Transaction in dates as rations
143	NCBT 697	48×65×22	04.06.11	Transactions in dates as rations
144	NBC 4646	30×45×15	04.12.01	List of PNs with quantities of dates
145	NBC 4500	38×52×17	16.11.18	Account of dates, the monthly rations of PNs
146	NCBT 1144	42×57×18	10.12.20	Transactions in dates as rations
147	NCBT 1266	26×37×14	11.03.16	Memorandum concerning dates as rations

TEXT	MUSEUM NUMBER	MEASUREMENTS IN mm	DATE	DESCRIPTION
148	NBC 4736	38×52×17	⌜04?⌝.xx.xx	Record of various transactions in dates
149	NCBT 619	34×45×16	⌜06.13.18⌝	Transaction in dates
150	NBC 4591	66×45×21	xx.xx.xx	List of PNs with quantities of dates
151	NBC 4522	27×36×14	01.04.13	Receipt of barley as *maššartu*
152	NBC 4811	69×46×20	⌜02⌝.12.11	Receipt of barley for various purposes
153	NBC 6221	26×38×17	10.6A.06	Receipt of barley by PN as rations (Joannès, *Archives de Borsippa*, 332, T)
154	NCBT 617	31×41×16	10.07.10	Receipt of barley by PN
155	YBC 11306	33×47×17	03.06.xx	Barley at the disposal of PN
156	NBC 4830	50×65×19	01.xx.19	Allotment of barley to bakers as *maššartu* for one month
157	NCBT 1228	41×55×18	07.11.21	Withdrawal of barley by PN as rations for PNs
158	NCBT 1108	25×32×13	09.09.15	Withdrawal of barley by PN as rations
159	NBC 8329	28×37×14	17.03.21	Transaction in barley (Joannès, *Archives de Borsippa*, 334–35, T)
160	NBC 4749	79×55×24	⌜01⌝.13.xx.	List of quantities of barley, mostly rations for PNs
161	NBC 4720	39×51×15	04.10.15	Record of transactions in barley, mostly withdrawals
162	NCBT 1260	31×43×16	06.xx.[x]8	Transaction in barley
163	YBC 7565	27×37×16	08.01.13	Transaction in barley as rations
164	NBC 4511	42×52×21	08.08.01	List of names with quantities of barley
165	NBC 8381	29×38×16	04.12.21	Withdrawal of emmer as *maššartu*
166	NBC 6222	27×38×15	09.02.03	Withdrawal of emmer by PN for offerings
167	NCBT 1101	25×37×13	03.10.18	Memorandum concerning emmer
168	NCBT 1250	28×38×15	04.03.24	Memorandum concerning emmer
169	NCBT 1087	35×48×18	04.10.04	Receipt of sesame by PNs
170	NCBT 1092	32×43×18	05.09.13	Receipt of sesame by PN
171	NCBT 1273	25×41×16	01.02.01	Allotment of sesame to oil pressers
172	NBC 4537	36×50×17	01.09.16	Record of various transactions in sesame
173	NCBT 2329	25×33×14	04.07.18	Receipt of beer by PN for the carpenters
174	NCBT 1276	23×29×14	04.09.30	Receipt of beer by PN for the temple slaves
175	NBC 4542	22×29×14	05.07.12	Receipt of beer by PN for the door carpenters
176	NCBT 484	24×31×12	10.04.14	Receipt of beer by PN

TEXT	MUSEUM NUMBER	MEASUREMENTS IN mm	DATE	DESCRIPTION
177	NCBT 469	22×32×11	10.06.11	Receipt of beer by PN for a team of workmen
178	NCBT 2331	23×30×12	10.06.22	Receipt of beer by PN for the scribes
179	NCBT 1264	21×29×11	10.6A.01	Receipt of beer by PN for a sick man
180	YBC 9038	24×37×14	10.6A.02	Receipt of a beer jug by PN
181	NCBT 1274	24×32×14	10.6A.⌜28?⌝	Receipt of beer by PN for the temple slaves
182	NCBT 1104	22×28×12	10.07.20	Receipt of beer by PN for a sick temple slave
183	NCBT 1261	22×28×12	10.10.13	Receipt of beer by PN for a door carpenter
184	NCBT 485	23×30×13	10.10.30	Receipt of beer by PN
185	NCBT 1268	23×31×13	10.11.05	Receipt of beer by PN for the jewelers and goldsmiths
186	NCBT 430	23×31×12	11.03.20	Receipt of beer by PN for the carpenters
187	NBC 4551	27×35×14	11.03.29	Receipt of beer by PN for a team of workmen
188	NCBT 1007	34×43×17	02.11.24	Withdrawal of salt by PN for offerings
189	NCBT 1201	32×44×15	03.01.28	Withdrawal of salt by PN for the king's rations
190	NCBT 2328	35×45×18	03.06.26	Withdrawal of salt by PNs for offerings
191	NCBT 1278	27×36×14	03.10.23	Withdrawal of salt by PN for offerings
192	NBC 4618	31×44×15	05.03.30	Withdrawal of salt by PNs for offerings
193	NBC 4669	34×48×17	02.11.23	List of quantities of salt for various deities and sanctuaries
194	NBC 4759	39×57×18	00.07.29	Record of various transactions in salt
195	NCBT 1113	27×35×13	02.01.⌜03?⌝	Receipt of oil by PN
196	NCBT 1270	24×31×12	04.11.04	Receipt of sesame oil by PN
197	NCBT 1103	24×33×14	04.11.21	Receipt of sesame oil by PN
198	NCBT 2330	25×34×15	07.10.08	Receipt of sesame oil by PN
199	NCBT 1181	23×31×12	07.11.13	Receipt of beer by PN for the Eanna
200	NCBT 1106	28×37×14	03.11.02	Withdrawal of honey by PN
201	NBC 4526	27×37×16	04.02.25	Withdrawal of honey by PN
202	NCBT 1122	27×35×14	15.12.11	Allotment of cress to PNs
203	NCBT 830	36×50×15	01.08.28	Receipt of barley, wheat, and cress by PN
204	NBC 4695	32×44×15	02.11.06	Withdrawal of honey and butter by PN to make pastries
205	YBC 11462	41×54×16	02.xx.⌜02⌝	Withdrawals of unknown substance by PNs as *maššartu*
206	NCBT 1232	34×48×15	02.08.11	Receipt of silver by PN, the price of a cow

TEXT	MUSEUM NUMBER	MEASUREMENTS IN mm	DATE	DESCRIPTION
207	NBC 4528	29×39×17	02.12.08	Receipt of silver by PN, the price of *a kasû* field
208	NCBT 1248	28×38×15	⌜05?⌝.10.02	Receipt of silver by PN after smelting
209	NCBT 1281	33×46×15	⌜07?⌝.01.28	Receipt of silver by PN, the price of iron
210	NCBT 1107	22×31×13	10.03.18	Receipt of silver by PN for mounting base of alabastron
211	YBC 11493	23×26×12	05.11.29	Silver at the disposal of PN to mold bricks
212	NCBT 1258	26×33×13	08.06.26	Silver at the disposal of PN, a goldsmith, to repair vessel
213	NBC 4856	163×84×28	13.xx.xx	Account of silver transactions in livestock industry from years 1 to 13 of Nabonidus
214	NCBT 880	36×46×17	02.03.11	Allotment of silver to PNs for various purposes
215	NBC 4930	48×70×20	02.06.01	Allotment of silver put at the disposal of PNs
216	NBC 4525	26×37×13	02.10.03	Allotment of silver to PN
217	NCBT 474	28×36×15	03.11.10	Withdrawal of silver by PNs for rations
218	NCBT 949	32×43×16	04.01.28	Receipt and withdrawal of silver for blue-colored wool
219	NBC 6204	31×40×14	04.02.03	Withdrawal of silver by PN, the price of 12 hides
220	NCBT 1259	26×34×13	07.04.29	Withdrawal of silver by PN, for sesame oil
221	NCBT 496	26×35×15	⌜08⌝.02.21	Withdrawal of silver by PN, for sesame
222	NCBT 1131	42×56×18	08.09.02	List of various transactions in silver
223	NCBT 1282	35×50×16	09.12.11	Withdrawal of silver, for dates
224	NCBT 1240	36×51×16	10.06.08	List of various transactions in silver
225	NCBT 1173	29×39×15	02.12.14	Record of quantities of silver taken away for various purposes
226	NCBT 425	30×40×16	03.12.19	Record of silver taken to Babylon for tin
227	NCBT 1280	33×44×16	06.12.27	Record of silver deducted and withdrawn to Babylon
228	NCBT 1097	35×51×18	01.09.⌜12⌝	Withdrawal of silver by PNs for travel provisions
229	NCBT 1046	26×34×14	04.04.11	Memorandum concerning silver as salary for shepherds
230	NBC 4572	37×43×15	04.xx.xx	Allotment of silver to carpenters for rations of barley

TEXT	MUSEUM NUMBER	MEASUREMENTS IN mm	DATE	DESCRIPTION
231	NBC 11499	29×39×16	xx.07.22	Record of silver for hired workmen performing task in the Eanna
232	NCBT 1296	33×47×16	⌜02?⌝.09.13	List of various transactions in silver
233	NBC 4714	31×43×14	02.11.21	List of various transactions in silver
234	NCBT 1229	47×62×18	02.12.12	List of various transactions in silver
235	NCBT 1063	44×62×19	⌜03.06.18⌝	List of various transactions in silver
236	NBC 4854	52×70×21	03.08.23	Record of two transactions in silver
237	NBC 8352	34×45×17	03.12.18	Receipt of silver
238	NBC 4748	39×53×16	11.06.25	Record of silver at the disposal of various PNs for performing tasks
239	YBC 11263	30×40×13	xx.07.xx	Record of silver taken for barley, and of silver allotted to PN
240	NCBT 928	28×40×13	03.03.17	Transaction in silver to make bricks
241	YBC 11657	36×47×15	⌜03.08.10⌝	Memorandum concerning silver and wool
242	NCBT 1075	31×46×17	04.05.09	Transaction in silver, for a house
243	NCBT 1243	25×32×25	⌜08?⌝.13.19	Memorandum concerning silver income from the offering box
244	NCBT 1263	25×33×14	05.11.02	Receipt of gold by goldsmiths to repair sacred jewelry
245	NCBT 1298	21×31×14	07.12.01	Receipt of gold by goldsmiths to repair sacred jewelry and other paraphernalia
246	NBC 4507	34×44×16	03.02.22	Record of gold at the disposal of goldsmiths to repair sacred paraphernalia
247	NCBT 483	24×31×14	06.06.17	Record of gold at the disposal of goldsmiths
248	NBC 11563	38×48×18	08.11.26	Record of gold from various sources at the disposal of goldsmiths
249	NCBT 1256	26×36×13	09.10.25	Record of gold income at the disposal of a goldsmith for smelting
250	NCBT 596	38×51×17	06.08.23	Withdrawal of gold by PNs for silver
251	NBC 6203	22×26×13	06.12.30	Memorandum concerning gold smelting
252	NBC 6187	40×51×19	16.⌜01.02⌝	Receipt of gold or silver by PN
253	NCBT 1249	32×43×17	01.09.06	Withdrawal of silver(?) by PN, the price of dyes
254	NCBT 482	24×32×14	01.06.03	Transaction concerning gold, silver, and *kasû* (Beaulieu, YNER 10, 122, T, Tr)

TEXT	MUSEUM NUMBER	MEASUREMENTS IN mm	DATE	DESCRIPTION
255	NCBT 1283	36×49×18	02.01.28	Account of silver and gold deposited in offering box
256	NBC 4505	32×44×16	04.⌜04⌝.17	Record of various transactions in silver and gold (Beaulieu, YNER 10, 157, T, Tr)
257	NBC 4506	30×42×15	01.11.27	Receipt of bronze by bronze smith
258	NCBT 1179	22×29×14	09.04.21?	Record of bronze at the disposal of PN
259	NBC 4527	28×43×16	03.11.29	Record of various transactions in bronze, silver, and wool
260	NCBT 476	26×31×13	11.05.18	Receipt of iron tools by PN
261	NCBT 475	32×44×16	07?.01.02	Record of iron tools at the disposal of PN
262	NBC 8333	26×34×14	11.01.02	Record of iron tools at the disposal of PN
263	NBC 4689	27×37×17	11.04.01	Memorandum concerning slave put in iron fetters
264	NCBT 1158	47×29×15	08.01.⌜11⌝	List of iron tools with PNs
265	NBC 4533	35×50×16	10.01.30	Receipt of iron spears by PN
266	NCBT 1055	76×44×21	01.⌜07.08⌝	List of sacred vessels taken out of the treasury for religious ceremonies
267	NBC 4580	87×48×22	02.12.06	List of sacred vessels taken out of the treasury for religious ceremonies
268	YBC 8781	33×42×17	10.6A.xx	Memorandum concerning weight of silver container
269	NBC 8332	28×40×17	00.xx.xx	Sacred gold ornaments at the disposal of goldsmiths for cleaning
270	NCBT 2327	61×91×26	14.04.30	Receipt of garments, linen, and colored thread by weavers for clothing of deities
271	YBC 7549	53×71×22	14.xx.15	Receipt of garments, linen, and colored thread by PN for clothing of deities
272	NCBT 1257	28×38×14	11.06.10	Record of linen at the disposal of PN
273	NCBT 1242	39×54×18	03.09.02	List of garments withdrawn
274	NCBT 1149	39×52×21	00.09.11	Record of wool at the disposal of a weaver
275	NCBT 269	27×37×14	03.07.29	Withdrawal of wool to repair sacred garments
276	NCBT 1230	35×51×16	04.03.03	Receipt of sacks by PN
277	NCBT 1239	32×49×17	14.09.⌜28⌝	List of quantities of woolen thread
278	NCBT 1198	27×38×14	16.03.16	Receipt of iron(?) by PNs

TEXT	MUSEUM NUMBER	MEASUREMENTS IN mm	DATE	DESCRIPTION
279	NBC 4568	27×39×15	03.02.03	Record of sacks to carry barley at the disposal of PNs
280	YBC 11277	19×28×11	xx.12.01	Receipt of hides by PN
281	NCBT 1020	38×52×16	03.01.28	Transaction in hides
282	NCBT 1078	38×49×18	04.03.28	Transaction in dyes and silver
283	NBC 4540	35×49×16	01.09.05	Withdrawal and receipt of beeswax by PN
284	YBC 11266	32×44×17	01.⸢11⸣.05	Record of various transactions in silver, wool, bronze, and goats
285	YBC 11542	46×64×18	xx.11.15	Receipt of goats by PN
286	NBC 4900	47×63×19	02.08.21	Record of various transactions in silver and wool
287	NCBT 1089	34×44×15	⸢03?⸣.03.07	Receipt of alum, from Belshazzar, the crown prince, in the Eanna
288	NCBT 1096	35×50×17	03.04.03	Receipt of sheep by PN
289	NCBT 954	36×49×15	03.⸢09⸣.29	Withdrawal of sesame oil, salt, and cress as rations by PN
290	NBC 4670	32×47×16	03.10.03	Record of stones at disposal of PN for sacred jewelry (Beaulieu, *ASJ* 13 [1991] 100, T, Tr)
291	YBC 11260	26×34×15	04.08.16	Allotment of silver, salt, and cress to PN as rations
292	NBC 4673	40×42×20	06.04.15	List of various substances and aromatics
293	NCBT 1009	36×49×16	07.12.08	Withdrawal of silver, sheep, flour, and sesame oil by PN
294	YBC 11267	38×26×16	12.13.21	Account of transactions in sesame oil, wool, ducks, and paint
295	NBC 4578	73×51×22	13.02.10	Record of various transactions in animals, bronze, tin, and barley
296	NCBT 634	99×63×22	15.08.10	Record of various transactions in silver, dead sheep, dates, door hinges, and iron
297	YBC 6931	90×60×23	15.10.16	Record of various transactions in sesame oil, silver, tin, bronze, ducks, oxen, and donkeys
298	MLC 1006	25×33×14	05.11.20	Memorandum concerning *kasû*
299	MLC 985	29×34×15	06.⸢04?⸣.29	Record of transaction in barley and malt
300	MLC 746	33×36×16	12.09.07	Record of administrative transaction
301	MLC 753	29×34×16	13.09.13	Record of transaction in barley and malt
302	MLC 536	31×35×17	13.12.11	Record of transaction in barley and malt

TEXT	MUSEUM NUMBER	MEASUREMENTS IN mm	DATE	DESCRIPTION
303	MLC 754	34×36×16	⸢14.08.12⸣	Record of transaction in barley and malt
304	MLC 732	29×33×17	14.09.⸢14?⸣	Record of transaction in barley
305	MLC 734	28×30×15	15.02.21?	Record of transaction in barley and malt
306	MLC 762	23×30×14	17.02.15	Record of transaction in barley and malt
307	MLC 1011	26×34×17	⸢17.06.28⸣	Record of transaction in barley
308	YBC 11578	36×57×17	05.03.28	(too badly preserved to assess)
309	NCBT 467	32×41×16	⸢07.07.09⸣	(too badly preserved to assess)
310	NBC 4202	75×50×21	01.13.18	Account of sesame oil at the disposal of oil pressers
311	YBC 3463	42×50×19	09.03.22	Lease of donkey
312	YBC 7560	34×45×17	⸢10⸣.11.01	Promissory note to repay quantity of barley
313	RBC 739	29×42×16	11.08.10	Transaction concerning a house

Catalogue of Seal Impressions

Text 1

LeE Seal 1 (owner: Kurbanni-Marduk, *šatammu* of Eanna):
Worshiper raising his hand to lunar crescent.
Caption: NA_4 KIŠIB ^{I}*kur-ban-ni-*^{d}AMAR.UD ^{lú}ŠÀ.TAM É.AN.NA

LeE Seal 2 (owner: Madānu-aḫḫē-iddin, overseer of the brewers):
Bearded winged genius.
Caption: NA_4 KIŠIB ^{I}DI.KUD-PAP.ME-MU ^{lú}UGULA SIRAŠ.MEŠ

LeE Seal 3 (owner: Lābâši-Marduk, overseer of the bakers):
Bearded hero holding a beast by the head, preparing to smite it.
Caption: NA_4 KIŠIB ^{I}*la-ba-ši-*^{d}AMAR.UD ^{lú}UGULA MUḪALDIM.MEŠ

RE Seal 4 (owner: Ili-rīmanni, *bēl piqitti* of Eanna):
Bearded worshiper raising his hand to divine symbols standing on an altar, with lunar crescent in upper field.
Inscription: $^{[d]}$PA PAP ZI (= *Nabû uṣur napišti* "O Nabû, preserve my existence").
Caption: NA_4 KIŠIB ^{I}DINGIR-*ri-man-ni* ^{lú}EN *pi-qit-tu*$_4$ É.AN.NA

RE Seal 5 (owner: Innin-šum-uṣur, overseer of the meat carvers):
Worshiper raising his hand to divine symbols standing on an altar, with lunar crescent and star in upper field.
Caption: NA_4 KIŠIB ^{Id}*in-nin*-MU-ÙRI ^{lú}UGULA GÍR.LÁ.MEŠ
The worshiper depicted on the seal wears a dagger, which seems appropriate considering the title of the seal owner.

Text 29

LeE Seal
Eight-pointed star.

Text 46

Rev Faint traces of seal, not reproduced.

Text 101

LeE Seal 1 (owner: Nergal-ušallim, judge):

Two bearded heroes on either side of a kneeling man, each holding his hair and preparing to smite him.

Caption: NA$_4$ KIŠIB ^{Id}U.GUR-GI ^{lú}DI.KUD

LeE Seal 2 (owner: Nabû-aḫḫē-iddin, judge):

Standing worshiper type (not reproduced, only top of head of bald worshiper is visible).

Caption: NA$_4$ KIŠIB ^{Id}NÀ-ŠEŠ.MEŠ-MU [^{lú}D]I.KUD

LeE Seal 3 (owner: Nabû-šum-ukīn, judge):

Standing worshiper raising his hand (impression partly lost).

Caption: NA$_4$ KIŠIB ^{Id}NA-⸢MU⸣-GI.NA ^{lú}D[I].KUD

RE Seal 4 (owner: Bēl-aḫḫē-iddin, judge):

Torso of hero in profile holding beast by the hind legs with his hand.

Caption: NA$_4$ KIŠIB ^{Id}EN-ŠEŠ.MEŠ-MU ^{lú}DI.KUD

RE Seal 5 (owner: Bēl-ēṭir, judge):

Bearded worshiper raising his hand to two divine symbols; remains of an inscription.

Caption: NA$_4$ [KIŠIB] ^{Id}EN-KA[R-*ir*] ^{lú}DI.KUD

Seals 4 and 5 were wider than the edge of the tablet, so only about ½ to ⅔ of each design was impressed on the clay.

Text 115

Rev Seal 1

Bearded worshiper before divine symbols standing on altar; remains of an inscription.

Rev Seal 2

Bearded worshiper raising his hand to divine symbols, lunar crescent in upper field.

Rev Seal 3

Bearded worshiper raising his hand to divine symbols, lunar crescent in upper field.

Text 155

UE Faint traces of seal (not copied).

Text 252

Rev Old Babylonian Seal:

Two lions attacking an animal, with a winged lion attacking a kneeling man from behind.

Discussed by B. Buchanan, *Early Near Eastern Seals in the Yale Babylonian Collection* (New Haven/London, 1981), no. 978x.

Indices

PERSONAL NAMES

In the following index the personal names are arranged in alphabetical order, with each name being taken as a unit. Thus the name *Iddinâ* precedes *Iddin-Amurru* and *Iddin-Bēl*, while *Ea-taqbi-līšir* is listed after *Eanna-zēr-iddin*. The relationships between individuals are abbreviated as follows: <f. of> = father of; <g.f. of> = grandfather of; <g.s. of> = grandson of; <desc. of> = descendant of; <anc. of> = ancestor of. The relationship expressed in Neo-Babylonian texts by <PN$_1$ A(=*apil*) PN$_2$> usually means "PN$_1$ descendant of PN$_2$," but the expression was also often employed in administrative texts as an abbreviation for <PN$_1$ A-*šú šá* (=*apilšu ša*) PN$_2$> "PN$_1$ son of PN$_2$," leading to some confusion for the modern interpreter. In the present index <PN$_1$ A PN$_2$> has been consistently rendered as "PN$_1$ descendant of PN$_2$," except in a few cases where the evidence is overwhelmingly in favor of interpreting <A> as <A-*šú šá*>. As a result, many names are provided with two entries, in which probably the same individual is listed separately as both son and descendant of the same man: e.g., under *Arad-Bēl*, where a man by that name occurs as (7) son of *Ṣillâ* in text 206:3 and as (11) descendant of *Ṣillâ* in text 213:85, while *Ṣillâ* in these two texts is probably the same person. Accordingly there are two separate entries under *Ṣillâ*, listing him as both father and ancestor of *Arad-Bēl*.

The problems posed by the transcription of Neo-Babylonian personal names are considerable. One major impediment is the pervasive use of logograms, sometimes with several possible readings, leading to a certain ambiguity in the interpretation of many names. To take an extreme example, the name written MU-A can be read in four different ways, depending on the interpretation of MU as being either the verb *nadānu* "to give" or the substantive *šumu* "name," and of A either as a logogram for *aplu* "son, heir" or as the phonetic complement /a/. So MU-A may be read as *Nādin-apli*, *Šumâ*, *Iddinâ*, or *Nādnâ*, the latter being a hypocoristic form of *Nādin-apli*, itself a short form of a theophoric name of the type <DN-*nādin-apli*>. Such cases of possible confusion are pointed out in footnotes, with alternative transcriptions of the ambiguous name listed independently.

An even more considerable problem is the complex interplay between graphemics and phonemics in the first millennium. By the Neo-Babylonian period the cuneiform script had become ill-adapted to the rendering of a dialect that had undergone substantial phonological mutations since the classical stage of the language, in Old Babylonian times. The discrepancies between the spoken dialect of first-millennium Babylonia and modern transliterations of Late Babylonian texts are evident when one compares the latter with contemporary Greek and

Aramaic transcriptions of Akkadian words and personal names. In the present index no attempt has been made to phonemicize the names accurately, largely because the phonemics of Late Babylonian are still too poorly understood to do so without creating even more confusion. Therefore the names are listed with an idealized transcription, based on a standard grammatical reading and transliteration of each element. Divine names are read conventionally, for example, Ninurta rather than the probable Late Babylonian pronunciation /*enošta/, Ningal rather than the more probable Nikkal, Enlil instead of Illil. The only concession to the principle of phonetic transcription concerns the direct object of the verb, with coalescence of the final vowel with the vocalic prefix of the verb (e.g., *Nabû-zēr-ibni* rather than *Nabû-zēru-ibni*). When the verb has an initial consonant, however, the direct object is provided with the Neo-Babylonian accusative ending /u/ (e.g., *Gula-šumu-līšir* and *Nabû-zēru-līšir* rather than *Gula-šum-līšir* and *Nabû-zēr-līšir*). Finally, hypocoristic names of the Ca-a type, which end with an additional grapheme <a> (e.g., *Šu-ma-a*, *Kal-ba-a*), have consistently been transcribed with a final /â/. The question as to whether the additional <a> denotes an ending /aya/ or /ayu/, a final diphthong /ay/, or a contracted diphthong /â/ remains open.

Aḫiya'u (ŠEŠ-*ia-ú*)[24]
1. anc. of *Nādin* and *Aplâ* 95:3

Aḫulapia (*a-ḫu-lap-ia*)
1. son of *Bēl-šum-iškun*, desc. of ^{d}x-*aplu-uṣur* 95:9

Aḫulap-Ištar (*a-ḫu-lap-*^{d}INNIN)
1. f. of *Gimillu* 81:13
2. f. of *Gimillu*, desc. of *Ḫunzû* 78:15

Aḫu-lūmur (ŠEŠ-IGI; ŠEŠ-*lu-mur*)
1. *ša rēši* 152:9; 266:39; 273:6
2. son of *Abdiya* 32:3
3. f. of *Kî-Nabû* 44:3

Akkuddanu (*ak-ku-ud-da-nu*)
1. ^{h}*ṣābu* ^{h}*agru* 111:30

^{f}*Al*-x-x-x-*mil-ki*
1. a slave 23:5

Am-[...]
1. 150:18

Amēl-Ea (LÚ-^{d}BE)
1. anc. of *Bēl-uballiṭ* and *Ea-iddin* 95:6
2. anc. of *Ina-Esagil-zēri* and *Ša-pī-Bēl* 91:6; 92:6
3. anc. of *Mušēzib-Marduk* and ^{d}[...] 132:10
4. anc. of *Mušēzib-Marduk* and *Bēl-uballiṭ* 98:16

Amēl-Nabû (LÚ-^{d}NÀ)
1. f. of *Arad-Innin* 155:5
2. f. of *Šamaš-ana-bītišu* 65:2
3. anc. of *Bēl-aḫḫē-iqīša* 282:4
4. anc. of *Bēl-zēr-ibni* 49:13
5. anc. of *Innin-šum-uṣur* 162:3

Amēl-Nanaya (LÚ-^{d}*na-na-a*)
1. f. of *Nabû-aḫḫē-ušallim* 256:3
2. f. of *Ṣillâ* 83:5
3. f. of *Ubār* 115:9

Ammâ (*am-ma-a*)
1. f. of *Amurru-natan* 101:6

Amurru-iddin (^{d}KUR.GAL-MU)[25]
1. desc. of *Nabû-aḫ-ēreš* 117:10

Amurru-natan (^{d}KUR.GAL-*na-tan*)
1. ^{h}*malaḫḫu*, son of *Ammâ* 101:5,13,21,22,29,33

Amurru-sākû(?) (^{d}KUR.GAL-*sa*$_{16}$-*ku-ú*)
1. f. of *Ištar-zēr-ibni* 91:9

Amurru-šar-uṣur (^{d}KUR.GAL-LUGAL-ÙRI)
1. 283:2

Amurru-zēr-ibni (^{d}KUR.GAL-NUMUN-DÙ)
1. f. of *Kalbâ* 57:5
2. anc. of *Iddin-Amurru* 286:7

Ana-bītišu (*a-na*-É-*šú*)
1. 125:10
2. ^{h}*nagār dalāti* 213:38; 230:4
3. ^{h}*rē'û* 90:17

^{f}*Andiya* (^{f}*an-di-iá*)
1. 89:3
2. 153:6,11

Anu-[...] (^{d}*a-nu*-[...])
1. son of *Innin-šum-uṣur* 105:20

Anu-aḫ-iddin (^{d}60-ŠEŠ-MU; ^{d}*a-nu*-ŠEŠ-MU; ^{d}*a-nu-um*-ŠEŠ-MU)
1. 294:3
2. son of *Gimillu*, desc. of *Kurî* 83:17
3. son of *Nabû-gāmil*, ? of ^{f}*A-pa-su*-x-x 24:3,4
4. f. of *Nergal-tēšî-ēṭir* 24:14
5. anc. of *Nūrea* 213:70

Anu-bēl-uṣur (^{d}*a-num*-EN-ÙRI)
1. 297:4

Anu-erība (^{d}*a-nu*-SU)
1. 310:6

Anu-ikṣur (^{d}*a-nu-um-ik-ṣur*)
1. 150:8
2. ^{h}*agru* 297:1

Anu-mukīn-apli (^{d}*a-nu*-DU-A)
1. ^{h}[*ṭupšarru*], son of [...], desc. of *Gimil-Nanaya* 86:4'

Anu-šar-uṣur (^{d}*a-nu*-LUGAL-ÙRI)
1. anc. of *Rīm*[*ūt*] 115:16

Anu-šum-ibni (^{d}*a-num*-MU-DÙ)
1. son of *Nergal-tēšî-ēṭir* 59:3

24. Possibly same as preceding, and to be transcribed **Ahiyaw*, a common West Semitic name.
25. The divine name ^{d}KUR.GAL can also be read Enlil in the Neo-Babylonian period.

Anu-zēr-[...] (^{d}*a-nu*-NUMUN-[...])
1. ^{h}*nagār dalāti*, desc. of *Ibni-Ištar* 115:23

^{f}*A-pa-su*-x-x
1. ? of *Anu-aḫ-iddin* 24:4

Aplâ (A-*a*; *ap-la-a*)
1. son of *Gula-zēr-ibni*, desc. of *Isinayu* 92:3
2. son of *Iqīšâ* 25:2
3. ^{h}*ṭupšarru*, son of *Nabû-ēṭir* 87:12
4. f. of [...], desc. of *Aḫḫē*-[...] 312:15
5. f. of [...]-*Bēl* 85:12
6. f. of *Arad-Bēl*, desc. of ^{h}*nappāḫu* 23:17
7. f. of *Ardiya* 52:3
8. f. of *Bēlessunu* 27:2
9. f. of *Bēl-ēṭir-Šamaš* 8:3; 16:10; 19:4; 28:4; 34:4; 37:2; 38:4; 61:4; 80:4
10. f. of *Gimillu*, desc. of *Šumāti* 100:4,12
11. f. of *Iddin-Bēl* 311:3
12. f. of *Innin-ina-tēšî-ēṭir*, desc. of *Kurî* 100:19
13. f. of *Innin-zēr-ušabši*, desc. of *Sîn-lēqi-unninni* 66:19
14. f. of *Nabû-ēṭir* 288:6
15. f. of *Nādin*, desc. of *Aḫiya'u* 95:3
16. f. of *Ṣillâ* 311:15
17. f. of *Šamaš-zēru-lišir* 27:13; 70:17
18. anc. of *Bāniya* 231:5; 238:9
19. anc. of *Innin-zēr-ušabši* 219:8
20. anc. of *Nabû*-[...] 213:52
21. anc. of *Nabû-ēṭir* 134:12; 136:5; 137:7; 138:5; 148:4; 151:3; 156:6; 213:66
22. anc. of *Nādin* 134:6; 138:19; 156:13; 213:54
23. anc. of *Šulâ* 144:6

Aqara (*a-qar-a*)
1. 225:4
2. ^{h}*atû* 133:22
3. f. of *Šamaš-ibni* 90:6

Arad-Bānītu (ÌR-^{d}DÙ-*tu*$_4$)
1. f. of *Arad-Mullišu* 22:3

Arad-Bēl? (ÌR-^{d}EN?)
1. 301:1

Arad-Bēl (ÌR-^{d}EN)
1. 95:15
2. 307:5
3. ^{h}*ṭupšarru*, son of *Aplâ*, desc. of ^{h}*nappāḫu* 23:17
4. son of *Lugal-Marada-ibni* 46:12
5. son of *Marduk-nāṣir*, desc. of *Ilūtu-bani* 21:14
6. son of *Mušēzib*-^{d}[...], desc. of *Nūr-Papsukkal* 21:12
7. son of *Ṣillâ* 206:3
8. son of *Šamaš-iddin*, desc. of ^{h}*rē'i alpi* 7:19
9. son of *Šamaš-zēr*-[...], desc. of ^{h}*rē'i alpi* 41:2
10. desc. of *Kidin-Nanaya* 302:7
11. desc. of *Ṣillâ* 213:85
12. ^{h}*išpar birmu*, desc. of ^{f}*zakītu* 115:4
13. f. of *Lābâši-Marduk*, desc. of *Egibi* 1:36; 110:11
14. f. of *Nabû-ēṭir-napšāti*, desc. of *Egibi* 66:18; 95:1; 99:22
15. f. of *Nabû-mukīn-apli*, desc. of *Kurû* 6:7
16. f. of *Rīmūt*, desc. of *Dābibi* 48:12
17. anc. of *Nabû-ēṭir-napšāti* 138:20,28

Arad-Gula (ÌR-^{d}*gu-la*; ÌR-^{d}ME.ME)
1. 278:3
2. 313:3
3. f. of *Innin-tabni-uṣur*, desc. of *Gimil-Nanaya* 76:14

Arad-Innin (ÌR-^{d}*in-nin*; ÌR-^{d}*innin-na*)
1. 75:5
2. 135:6
3. 213:20,54,62,80
4. 248:2
5. son of *Amēl-Nabû* 155:5
6. son of *Bēl-iddin*, desc. of *Kurî* 91:7; 92:4
7. ^{h}*ṭupšarru*, son of *Ibni-Ištar*, desc. of *Gimil-Nanaya* 15:13
8. desc. of *Ibni-Ištar* 297:16
9. ^{h}*nuḫatimmu*, desc. of *Ibni-Ištar* 137:12; 138:6,26
10. desc. of *Nabû-na'id* 281:7; 284:7
11. f. of *Nabû-bēlšunu* 84:13
12. f. of *Nabû-bēlšunu*, desc. of *Kurî* 132:19
13. f. of *Zēriya* 232:11
14. anc. of *Ardiya* 213:31

1. anc. of *Marduk-nāṣir* and *Marduk-šum-iddin* 4:9

^{h}*asû* (^{lú}A.ZU; ^{lú}*a-su-ú*)
1. anc. of *Marduk-šum-ibni* and *Bēl-iddin* 6:11
2. anc. of *Šamaš-zēr-ibni* and *Nabû-šum-uṣur* 6:1

^{h}*ašlāku* (^{lú}AZALAG)
1. anc. of *Eanna-līp-uṣur* and *Ibni-Ištar* 1:41; 52:15
2. anc. of *Nabû-gāmil* and *Ṭābiya* 62:14
3. anc. of *Šumâ* and *Ibni-Ištar* 66:21

Aššur (*aš-šur*; *aš-šur*^{ki})[26]
1. anc. of [... ŠE]Š.MEŠ and *Bēl-aḫ-ušabši* 6:21
2. anc. of ^{f}*Ṭābatu* and *Nādin* 3:10

Aššur-bāni-apli (AN.ŠÁR-DÙ-IBILA)
1. (king of Assyria) 92:17

Aššur-ēreš (AN.ŠÁR-KAM)
1. f. of *Nabû-mukīn-apli*, desc. of ^{h}*rē'i alpi* 53:16

Aššur-uballiṭ (AN.ŠÁR-TIN-*iṭ*)
1. f. of *Ša-pī-kalbi* 116:3

Atkal-ana-Bēl (*at-kal-a-na*-^{d}EN)
1. 213:5

^{h}*atkuppu* (^{lú}AD.KID)
1. anc. of *Marduk-šum-ibni* and *Nabû-ēṭir* 313:2
2. anc. of *Nabû-ittannu* and *Bunnanu* 77:5

^{h}*atû* (^{lú}Ì.DU$_8$)
1. anc. of *Ardiya* and *Silim-Bēl* 94:18
2. anc. of *Ina-ṣilli-Urdimmu* and *Nabû-bāni-aḫi* 65:2

Ayaḫu (*a-a-ḫu*)
1. son of *Bānītu-ēreš* 48:4
2. f. of *Nabû-nādin-aḫi* 84:2

Ayigašu (*a-a-ga-šú*; *a-a-i-ga-a-šú*)
1. *ša rēš šarri*/^{h}*ša muḫḫi quppu* 66:14; 126:2

Ba[...]
1. 150:17

Bābilayu (TIN.TIR^{ki}-*a-a*)
1. son of *Ḫa*[...] 90:7

Babūtu (*ba-bu-tu*; *ba-bu-tu*$_4$)
1. anc. of *Kiribtu* and *Nādin* 66:16
2. anc. of *Nabû-mušētiq-ūdi* and *Marduk-šum-ibni* 6:13

Baḫû (*ba-ḫu-ú*)
1. 213:36
2. son of *Nabû*-[...]-*uballiṭ* 213:37

^{h}*bā'iru* (^{lú}ŠU.KU$_6$)
1. anc. of *Bēl-ibni* and *Bulluṭ* 2:44; 91:5; 92:8
2. anc. of *Bēl-uballiṭ* and *Iqīša* 39:14
3. anc. of *Kiribtu-Marduk* and *Šum-ukīn* 18:4
4. anc. of *Kunâ* and [...] 91:4
5. anc. of *Nabû-bāni-aḫi* and *Zēriya* 3:34
6. anc. of *Nabû-mukīn-apli* and *Kabtiya* 4:13'

Balāssu (TIN-*su*; *ba-laṭ-su*)
1. son of *Arad-Nanaya*, desc. of *Kurî* 95:8
2. ^{h}*ṭupšarru*, son of *Šamaš-šum-uṣur*, desc. of ^{h}*šangû Šamaš* 55:12
3. ^{h}*ṭupšarru*, son of *Šāpik-zēri*, desc. of ^{h}*rab-banî* 63:17
4. ^{h}*ṣāḫit ginê*, desc. of *Arad-Nanaya* 171:3
5. f. of *Nabû-ēṭir-napšāte*, desc. of *Būṣâ* 26:9
6. f. of *Nabû-iddin*, desc. of ^{h}*rē'i sisi* 45:11
7. f. of *Nabû-mušētiq-ūdi* 215:3
8. f. of *Nabû-mušētiq-ūdi*, desc. of *Damiqu* 2:15,22
9. f. of *Ṣillâ*, desc. of *Nabû-ēṭir* 113:15
10. f. of *Šumâ*, desc. of ^{h}*šangû parakki* 37:11
11. anc. of *Marduk-šum-ibni* 266:34
12. anc. of *Marduk-šumu-līšir* 296:6

Balāṭu (TIN; TIN-*ṭu*; *ba-la-ṭu*)
1. 38:2
2. 61:3,8
3. 75:9
4. 80:3

26. The alternative reading of this name is *Ēdu-ēṭir*, but the presence of the determinative KI in text 3:10 indicates that the name should, at least in some cases, be read *Aššur*.

5. 193:1
6. ^{h}*kāṣir* 157:5
7. son of *Bēl-iqīša*, desc. of *Nūr-Papsukkal* 62:3,10
8. son of *Iqīšâ*, desc. of ^{h}*ṣāḫit-ginê* 23:15
9. ^{h}*ṭupšarru*, son of *Mušēzib-Bēl* 81:15;83:19
10. son of *Nabû-šum-uṣur* 87:5
11. ^{h}*ṭupšarru*/^{h}*ṭupšar Eanna*, son of *Sîn-ibni*, desc. of ^{h}*rē'i alpi* 1:46; 51:16; 93:20; 110:13; 114:12'
12. son of *Zākir*, desc. of *Kidin-Marduk* 92:9
13. ^{h}x, desc. of *Arad-Innin* 172:6
14. desc. of *Arad-Nabû* 286:8
15. desc. of *Ibni-Ištar* 150:6
16. desc. of *Innin-šum-ibni* 235:16
17. desc. of *Innin-šum-uṣur* 213:30
18. desc. of *Nabû-*[...] 190:3
19. ^{h}*nuḫatimmu*, desc. of *Nabû-bēlšunu* 138:8
20. desc. of *Nabû-ušallim* 192:3; 213:31
21. desc. of *Sîn-ibni* 266:36
22. ^{h}*nuḫatimmu*, desc. of *Šumâ* 137:13; 138:21
23. f. of *Ibnâ* 71:3
24. f. of *Nādin* 92:13
25. f. of *Nādin*, desc. of *Maštuk* 23:2
26. f. of *Nūrea*, desc. of *Iddin-Papsukkal* 65:19
27. anc. of *Bēl-iddin* and *Mušallim-Marduk* 2:39
28. anc. of *Kalbâ* 157:4
29. anc. of *Lābâši-Marduk* and *Nabû-aḫḫē-bulliṭ* 2:38
30. anc. of *Marduk-šum-iddin* and *Nabû-aḫḫē-uballiṭ* 92:1
31. anc. of *Mušallim-Marduk* and *Zēriya* 2:35
32. anc. of *Nabû-bāni-aḫi* and *Kabtiya* 95:5
33. anc. of *Nabû-bēlšunu* 134:9, 136:2; 138:14; 152:8
34. anc. of *Ṣillâ* and *Nabû-kāṣir* 88:13

Bālti-il (*bal-ti-ìl*)

1. 272:3
2. 284:4

Bānītu-ēreš (^{d}DÙ-tu_4-KAM)

1. f. of *Ayaḫu* 48:4
2. f. of *Gurâ* 48:11

^{f}*Bānītu-râmat* ($^{f\,d}$DÙ-tu_4-*ra-mat*)

1. a slave, mother of ^{f}*Gāmiltu* 91:15,17,23,26

Bāniya (DÙ-*ia*; DÙ-*iá*; *ba-ni-ia*; *ba-ni-iá*)

1. 159:8,12
2. 188:4
3. 192:7
4. 213:32,57
5. ^{h}*nuḫatimmu* 156:12
6. son of *Innin-šum-uṣur*, desc. of *Gimil-Nanaya* 132:14
7. son of [*Itti-Nabû*]-*gūzu* 37:8
8. son of *Nabû-nāṣir* 20:15
9. son of *Nabû-nāṣir*, desc. of *Nabû-*[...]-*ilī* 66:3
10. son of *Nabû-nāṣir-apli* 91:18,31
11. ^{h}*ṭupšarru*, son? of *Nabû-šum-iddin* 40:13
12. son of *Šamaš-šumu-līšir*, desc. of ^{h}*rab-banî* 20:16
13. desc. of [...] 135:28
14. desc. of *Aplâ* 231:5; 238:9
15. desc. of *Nabû-balāssu-iqbi* 152:11; 266:37
16. desc. of *Nabû-nāṣir* 213:13
17. desc. of *Nūr-Papsukkal* 300:9
18. desc. of *Šamaš-dannu* 240:2
19. desc.? of *Šumâ* 213:25
20. f. of *Sîn-ibni* 266:36
21. f. of *Sîn-kēšir*, desc. of ^{h}*nappāḫu* 17:11

Banna? (*ba*?-*an-na*)

1. anc. of *Imbiya* and *Nabû-mušētiq-ūdi* 15:11

Barik-il (*ba-ri-ik-ki-ìl*)

1. son of *Bēl-ašbâ* 28:14

Basiya (*ba-si-ia*; *ba-si-iá*; *ba-as-si-ia*)

1. anc. of *Bēlšunu* and *Zēriya* 59:11
2. anc. of *Kalbâ* and *Iqīša* 24:2; 82:2'
3. anc. of *Silim-Bēl* and *Bēl-zēri* 6:18; 85:11
4. anc. of *Šamaš-mukīn-apli* and *Bēlšunu* 18:11
5. anc. of *Šum-ukīn* and *Bēl-zēri* 76:3; 78:4; 81:4; 82:1'; 83:3; 85:3; 86:4; 87:5

6. anc. of *Zēr*-[...] and *Nabû-zēru-līšir* 43:14

Batâ (*ba-ta-a*)

1. f. of *Nabû-išdi* 36:12

^{f}*Ba'u*-x ($^{f\,d}$KÁ-x)

1. 29:5

Ba'u-ēreš ($^{[d]}$*ba-ú*-APIN-*e*[*š*]; ^{d}KÁ-KAM)

1. f. of [...], desc. of ^{h}*šangû Enamtila* 91:3
2. f. of *Šamaš*-[...] 40:10

Bazuzu (*ba-zu-zu*)

1. a slave 293:5
2. son of *Ibni-Ištar*, brother of *Šamaš-bāni-aḫi* 166:3
3. son of *Ibni-Ištar*, desc. of *Gimil-Nanaya* 94:2
4. ^{h}*nuḫatimmu*, desc. of *Ibni-Ištar* 156:10
5. desc. of *Nādin* 115:27
6. f. of *Līšir* 4:5,22

Bēl-[...] (^{d}EN-[...])

1. f. of *Nabû-šum-iškun*, desc. of *Irani* 3:33
2. anc. of *Tarību* 135:8

Bēl-[...]*ir* (^{d}EN-[...]-*ir*)

1. ^{h}*dayānu*, desc. of *Sîn-tabni* 101:40 + seal caption on R.E.

Bēl-aḫḫē-[...] (^{d}EN-ŠEŠ.MEŠ.[...])

1. 41:13

Bēl-aḫḫē-erība (^{d}EN-ŠEŠ.MEŠ-SU; ^{d}EN-PAP.ME-SU)

1. 58:5
2. ^{h}*rab būli* 242:4
3. son of *Nabû-bēlšunu*, desc. of *Kurî* 98:12
4. f. of *Marduk-zēr-ibni* 63:14
5. f. of *Nabû-šum-uṣur* 42:5
6. anc. of *Nanaya-iddin* 150:5
7. anc. of *Nergal-nāṣir* 122:13

Bēl-aḫḫē-iddin (^{d}EN-ŠEŠ.MEŠ-MU; ^{d}EN-ŠEŠ.ME-MU; ^{d}EN-ŠEŠ.MEŠ-SUM.NA)

1. 4:18'
2. son of *Marduk-šarrani*, desc. of *Adad*-x-x 2:9
3. son of *Marduk-zēr-ibni*, desc. of *Nūr-Sîn* 3:31
4. ^{h}*dayānu*, desc. of *Nūr-Sîn* 101:39 + seal caption on R.E.
5. f. of *Kid*[*in* ...], desc. of *Nūru* 252:12

Bēl-aḫḫē-iqīša (^{d}EN-ŠEŠ.MEŠ-BA-*šá*; ^{d}EN-ŠEŠ.ME-BA-*šá*; ^{d}EN-PAP.ME-BA-*šá*)

1. 217:4
2. 302:8
3. 305:5
4. ^{h}*mār šipri* 300:10; 303:8
5. son of *Silim-Bēl* 54:12
6. desc. of *Amēl-Nabû* 282:4
7. f. of [...] 12:17
8. f. of *Nabû-ittannu*, desc. of *Arrab* 47:16
9. f. of *Nabû-šumu-līšir* 9:7
10. f. of *Nādin*, desc. of *Egibi* 1:42; 11:15; 51:19; 52:16; 65:17; 93:19; 95:2; 99:25; 114:15'
11. anc. of *Nādin* 213:43; 234:15

Bēl-aḫ-iddin (^{d}EN-ŠEŠ-MU)

1. f. of *Ardiya*, desc. of ^{h}*rē'i* 25:4
2. anc. of *Madānu-šar-uṣur* 119:10

Bēl-aḫ-ušabši (^{d}EN-ŠEŠ-GÁL-*ši*; ^{d}EN-ŠEŠ-TIL)

1. son of *Sîn-bani* 42:17
2. son of *Ša-pī-Bēl*, desc. of [...] 95:10
3. f. of [... ŠE]Š.MEŠ, desc. of *Aššur* 6:21
4. f. of *Nabû-bēlšunu*, desc. of *Imbu-īniya* 10:13

Bēl-āli (EN-URU)

1. ^{h}*mār šipri* 61:2

Bēl-aplu-iddin (^{d}EN-*ap-lu*-SUM.NA)

1. son of *Nabû-mukīn-apli*, desc. of *Rīmūt-Ea* 4:12'

Bēl-aplu-uṣur (^{d}EN-A-ÙRI)

1. anc. of *Nabû-bāni-zēri* and *Bēlšunu* 2:36
2. anc. of *Nabû-ēṭir-napšāti* and *Bēl-iqīša* 98:15

Bēl-ašbâ (^{d}EN-*áš-ba-a'*)

1. f. of *Barik-il* 28:15

Bēl-ēreš (^{d}EN-KAM)

1. 115:30
2. son of *Nabû-kāṣir* 46:10
3. son of *Nergal-ibni*, desc. of ^{h}*šangû Adad* 83:16
4. anc. of *Innin-kibsu-abi-uṣur* 213:89
5. anc. of *Nabû-ušallim* 194:2

Bēl-erība (^{d}EN-SU)
1. son of *Nādin*, desc. of *Nūr-Marduk* 233:3

^{f}*Bēlessunu* (^{f}*be-let-su-nu*)
1. daughter of *Aplâ* 27:1,10

Bēl-ēṭir (^{d}EN-SUR)
1. 205:6
2. son of *Nabû-aḫ-iddin*, desc. of *Maštuk* 17:12
3. son of *Šagib-il* 91:11
4. son of *Zērūtu* 37:3
5. f. of *Nā*[*din*?] 36:4
6. f. of *Šamaš*-[...], desc. of ^{h}*rē'i alpi* 41:17
7. f. of *Šamaš-erība*, desc. of *Šamaš-bāri* 48:2; 49:14
8. anc. of *Bēl-kāṣir* and *Ṣillâ* 110:4

Bēl-ēṭir-[...] (^{d}EN-SUR-[...])
1. son of [...]-*Marduk*, desc. of *Irani* 32:13

Bēl-ēṭir-Nabû (EN-KAR-^{d}NÀ)
1. 133:6
2. 161:6
3. 239:10
4. a slave 252:2

Bēl-ēṭir-Šamaš (^{d}EN-KAR-^{d}UTU; EN-KAR-^{d}UTU; ^{d}EN-SUR-^{d}UTU; EN-*e-ṭir*-^{d}UTU; EN-*e-ṭè-ru*-^{d}UTU)
1. 29:3'
2. a slave 7:7
3. son of *Aplâ* 8:3; 16:10; 19:3; 28:3,7,11; 34:4; 36:5; 37:1; 38:3; 61:4,9,11; 80:4
4. son of *Zāriqu-ēreš*, desc. of x 34:2; 36:2

Bēl-ibni (^{d}EN-DÙ; ^{d}EN-*ib-ni*)
1. 133:14
2. ^{h}*kutimmu* 244:4; 245:6; 246:10; 247:3
3. ^{h}*ṭupšarru*, son of *Bulluṭ*, desc. of ^{h}*bā'iru* 2:43; 91:5; 92:8
4. desc. of *Nādin* 143:2
5. anc. of *Innin-zēr-ušabši* 208:3

Bēl-iddin (^{d}EN-MU)
1. ^{h}*išparu* 270:16
2. son of *Mušallim-Marduk*, desc. of *Balāṭu* 2:39
3. son of *Nādin*, desc. of *Maštuk* 17:4; 18:5; 252:4
4. ^{h}*nappāḫ siparri*, son of *Šumâ* 115:20
5. desc. of *Ilu-gabir* 123:14
6. f. of *Arad-Innin*, desc. of *Kurî* 91:7; 92:4
7. f. of *Marduk-šum-ibni*, desc. of ^{h}*asû* 6:11

Bēl-īpuš (^{d}EN-DÙ-*uš*)
1. f. of [...] 31:8
2. f. of *Nabû-mukīn-apli*, desc. of *Kurî* 82:4'
3. f. of *Nabû-tabni-uṣur*, desc. of *Sîn-tabni* 100:14
4. f. of *Šum-ukīn* 69:3

Bēl-iqīša (^{d}EN-BA-*šá*)
1. 159:10
2. ^{h}*ṭupšarru*, desc. of *Sîn-tabni* 101:42
3. f. of *Balāṭu*, desc. of *Nūr-Papsukkal* 62:4
4. f. of *Nabû-ēṭir-napšāti*, desc. of *Bēl-aplu-uṣur* 98:14
5. anc. of [*Nabû*]-*ēṭir-napšāti* 234:6

Bēl-kāṣir (^{d}EN-KÁD; ^{d}EN-*ka-ṣir*)
1. son of [...]-*zēr-ušabši* 50:8
2. son of *Marduk*, desc. of *Kidin-Marduk* 92:7
3. son of *Ṣillâ*, desc. of *Bēl-ēṭir* 110:3

Bēl-kēšir (^{d}EN-*ke-šìr*)
1. ^{h}*ṭupšarru*, son of *Nabû-šum-ibni*, desc. of ^{h}*gallābu* 88:14

Bēl-lē'i (^{d}EN-DA)
1. f. of *Nabû-mušētiq-ūdi*, desc. of *Ili-bani* 5:33
2. f. of *Šamaš-erība* 15:4

Bēl-nādin-apli (^{d}EN-*na-din*-A; ^{d}EN-*na-din*-IBILA; ^{d}EN-*na-din-ap-lu*; ^{d}EN-SUM-A)
1. 284:2
2. son of *Nergal-ušallim*, desc. of *Ile''i-Marduk* 4:5
3. son of *Zēr-Bābili*, desc. of *Ile''i-Marduk* 91:4
4. desc. of *Zēr-Bābili* 223:3

Bēl-na'id (^{d}EN-I)
1. f. of *Nabû-aḫḫē-ušallim*, desc. of *Iddin-Papsukkal* 49:2

Bēl-rēṣū'a (^{d}EN-*re-ṣu-ú*-[*a*])
1. *ša rēš šarri* 55:8

Bēl-[rīmanni] (^{d}E[N-*ri-man-ni*])
1. f. of *Itti-enši-Nabû*, desc. of *Egibi* 55:10

Bēl-suppê-muḫur (^{d}EN-*su-pe-e-mu-ḫur*)
1. 213:56

Bēl-šar-uṣur (^{d}EN-LUGAL-ÙRI)
1. *mār šarri* 103:1 (no title); 104:1 (no title); 287:4

Bēl-šum-iškun (^{d}EN-MU-GAR-*un*)
1. son of *Nabû-gāmil* 259:3
2. f. of *Aḫulapia*, desc. of ^{d}x-*aplu-uṣur* 95:9
3. f. of *Šumâ*, desc. of ^{h}*šangû bīt Bābili* 46:2

Bēl-šum-uṣur (^{d}EN-MU-ÙRI)
1. 105:1

Bēlšunu (^{d}EN-*šú-nu*; EN-*šú-nu*)
1. 133:9
2. 202:3
3. son of *Zēriya* 15:4
4. ^{h}*ṭupšarru*, son of *Zēriya*, desc. of *Basiya* 59:10
5. desc. of *Lābâši*-[...] 293:9
6. ^{h}*nuḫatimmu*, desc. of *Nabû-aḫḫē-iddin* 134:10; 138:4; 205:4
7. f. of *Nabû-bāni-zēri*, desc. of *Bēl-aplu-uṣur* 2:36
8. f. of *Nabû-zēru-līšir*, desc. of *Kurî* 92:5
9. f. of *Šamaš-mukīn-apli*, desc. of *Basiya* 18:11

Bēl?-uballiṭ (^{d}EN?-TIN-*iṭ*)
1. 284:18

Bēl-uballiṭ? (^{d}EN-TIN?-*iṭ?*)
1. f. of [...]-*šunu* 34:10

Bēl-uballiṭ (^{d}EN-TIN-*iṭ*; ^{d}EN-*ú-bal-liṭ*)
1. 295:3'
2. 310:12
3. son of *Ea-iddin*, desc. of *Amēl-Ea* 95:6
4. son of *Iqīša*, desc. of ^{h}*bā'iru* 39:13
5. son of *Nabû-balāssu-iqbi* 223:4
6. son of *Šum-ukīn* 191:4
7. son of *Zēriya* 99:5
8. son of *Zēriya*, desc. of *Egibi* 15:11
9. desc. of [...] 213:68
10. desc. of *Ea-iddin* 133:14; 136:3
11. ^{h}*nuḫatimmu*, desc. of *Nabû-kēšir* 134:7; 138:24
12. f. of *Itti-Nabû-balāṭu*, desc. of *Dābibi* 18:14
13. f. of *Murašû*, desc. of *Eppeš-ilī* 93:18
14. f. of *Mušēzib-Marduk*, desc. of *Amēl-Ea* 98:16
15. anc. of *Mušēzib-Marduk* 213:21

Bēl-ukīn (^{d}EN-DU)
1. f. of *Nādin*, desc. of *Sîn-lēqi-unninni* 67:4,14

Bēl-upaḫḫir (^{d}EN-NIGIN-*ir*)
1. f. of *Ibni-Ištar* 260:4
2. anc. of *Ibni-Ištar* 115:10; 265:6

Bēl-ušallim (^{d}EN-GI; ^{d}EN-*ú-šal-lim*)
1. ^{h}*ṭupšarru*, desc. of *Ea-eppeš-ilī* 4:16'
2. son of *Šamaš-unammir*, desc. of *Miṣirayu* 96:11

Bēl-zēr-[...] (^{d}EN-NUMUN-[...])
1. 300:11

Bēl-zēri (EN-NUMUN)
1. f. of *Silim-Bēl*, desc. of *Basiya* 6:17; 85:11
2. f. of *Šum-ukīn*, desc. of *Basiya* 76:3; 78:3; 81:3; 82:1'; 83:3; 85:3; 86:4; 87:4

Bēl-zēr-ibni (^{d}EN-NUMUN-DÙ)
1. desc. of *Amēl-Nabû* 49:12

Bēl-zēr-ukīn (^{d}EN-NUMUN-DU)
1. f. of *Nabû-kāṣir*, desc. of *Ḫuṣābu* 102:16

Bibe[a] (*bi-bé-*[*e-a*])
1. f. of *Nanaya-iddin* 90:13

Bulluṭ (*bul-luṭ*; *bul-lu-ṭu*)
1. f. of *Bēl-ibni*, desc. of ^{h}*bā'iru* 2:43; 91:5; 92:8
2. f. of *Ezida-aplu-iqīša*, desc. of *Šigû'a* 2:11

Bulṭâ (*bul-ṭa-a*)
1. anc. of *Nabû-kēšir* 266:35

Bunnanu (*bu-un-na-nu*)
1. f. of *Nabû-ittannu*, desc. of ^{h}*atkuppu* 77:4

Būṣâ (*bu-ṣa-a*)
1. anc. of *Nabû-ēṭir-napšāti* and *Balāssu* 26:10

Būṣu (*bu-ú-ṣu*)

1. anc. of *Taqīš-Gula* and *Iddin-Marduk* 46:16

^{h}*da*-x-x (^{lú}*da*-x-x)
1. anc. of *Nabû-šum-ibni* and *Nabû-šum-iddin* 8:11

Dābibi (*da-bi-bi*)
1. anc. of x-x-*a* and *Iddinunu* 18:13
2. anc. of *Itti-Nabû-balāṭu* and *Bēl-uballiṭ* 18:14
3. anc. of *Lūṣi-ana-nūri* and *Nabû-aḫḫē-uballiṭ* 64:16
4. anc. of *Nabû-mukīn-apli* and *Nādin* 1:40
5. anc. of *Nabû-mukīn-zēri* and *Nādin* 11:11; 12:12
6. anc. of *Rīmūt* and *Arad-Bēl* 48:13
7. anc. of *Silim-Bēl* and *Kudurru* 48:10

Dādiya (*da-di-ia*; *da-di-iá*)
1. 42:3
2. 89:3

Damiq (*da-mi-iq*; *da-mi-qu*)
1. anc. of *Itti-Nabû-balāṭu* and *Innin*-x-*ibni* 2:42
2. anc. of *Nabû-mušētiq-ūdi* and *Balāssu* 2:15,23

Dannê (*dan-né-e*)
1. anc. of *Pir'u* and x-x-A 46:3

Dannea (*dan-né-e-a*)
1. anc. of *Tabnea* and *Zērūtu* 54:5

Dannu-^{d}[...] (*dan-nu*-^{d}[...])
1. ^{h}*ṭupšarru* 71:17

Dannu-Nergal (*dan-nu*-^{d}U.GUR)
1. f. of *Lābâši* 35:12

Dannu-rigiššu (*da-a-nu-ri-gi-iš-šú*)
1. anc. of *Ištar-nādin-apli* and *Kidinnu* 6:15

Dummuq (*du-um-muq*)
1. 135:7
2. f. of *Gimillu*, desc. of ^{h}*rab-banî* 293:4

Dūr-apli (BÀD-A)
1. ^{h}*bēl piqitti* 301:9; 302:9

E-x
1. f. of *Silim-Bēl*, desc. of *Kidin-Sîn* 29:3"

É-[...]
1. son of *Nādin* 84:9

Ea-eppeš-ilī (^{d}*é-a*-DÙ-*eš*-DINGIR)
1. anc. of [*Bē*]*l-ušallim* 4:16'

Ea-iddin (^{d}BE-MU)
1. f. of *Bēl-uballiṭ*, desc. of *Amēl-Ea* 95:6
2. anc. of *Bel-uballiṭ* 133:14; 136:3

Ea-ilūtu-bani (^{d}BE-DINGIR-*ta*-DÙ; ^{d}BE-[*i-l*]*u-tú*-DÙ), mostly attested in the short form *Ilūtu-bani* (DINGIR-*ta*-DÙ)
1. anc. of ^{d}x-*šūzibanni* and *Zēr-Bābili* 45:3
2. anc. of *Arad-Bēl* and *Marduk-nāṣir* 21:15
3. anc. of *Gimillu* and *Nabû-šum-iddin* 98:12
4. anc. of *Itti-Nabû-balāṭu* and *Nabû-mušētiq-ūdi* 5:30
5. anc. of *Mušēzib-Bēl* and *Zēr-Bābili* 5:8; 10:12; 50:2; 102:2,15
6. anc. of *Nabû-bēl-šumāti* and *Rīmūt* 58:10
7. anc. of *Nabû-ēreš* and *Zēr-Bābili* 21:14; 62:3; 77:3
8. anc. of *Nabû-nādin-aḫi* and *Šulâ* 5:35; 60:12
9. anc. of *Nabû-šum-ibni* and *Nādin* 79:6
10. anc. of *Rīmūt-Gula* and *Ṣullê-Marduk* 77:11
11. anc. of *Šumâ* and *Nabû-mukīn-zēri* 79:14
12. anc. of *Zēr-Bābili* and *Nabû-šum-iškun* 21:4

Ea-kāṣir (^{d}BE-*ka-ṣir*)
1. f. of *Lāqīp* 11:4

Eanna-bāni-aḫi (*é-an-na*-DÙ-ŠEŠ)
1. son of *Nanaya-iddin* 87:11

Eanna-ibni (*é-an-na*-DÙ)
1. 266:18
2. anc. of *Nanaya-iddin* 111:17

Eanna-iddin (*é-an-na*-MU)
1. son of *Nādin* 132:13

Eanna-līp-uṣur (^{d}*é-an-na-lip*-ÙRI; *é-an-na-lip*-ÙRI; *é-an-na-li-pi*-ÙRI)
1. 140:8
2. 239:3

1. 302:1
2. 306:4
3. 307:3
4. desc. of x-x-x 303:7
5. desc. of *Nūr*-^{d}[...] 300:8
6. f. of *Šamaš-zēr-iddin* 53:6
7. f. of *Šamaš-zēr-ušabši* 49:3
8. anc. of ^{d}[...]-*zēr-ibni* 133:11

Etel-pī (*e-tel-pi*)
1. son of *Kudurru*, desc. of ^{h}*šangû Ninurta* 83:15

Etušgina-ibni (É.TUŠ.GI.NA-DÙ)
1. f. of *Niqūdu*, desc. of *Šamaš*-BA[...] 99:2

Ezida-aplu-iqīša (*é-zi-da*-A-BA-*šá*; *é-zi-da*-A-BA-*šá*)
1. son of *Bulluṭ*, desc. of *Šigû'a*, f. of *Mušēzib-Marduk* 2:10,12,15,20,47

Ezida-šar-uṣur (*é-zi-da*-LUGAL-ÙRI)
1. son of *Nabû*-x 46:13

Gabâ (*ga-ba-a'*)
1. f. of *Ṭāb-Uruk* 87:10

Gabbi-ilī-šar-uṣur (*gab-bi*-DINGIR.MEŠ-LUGAL-ÙRI; *gab-bi*-DINGIR.ME-LUGAL-ÙRI)
1. ^{h}*qīpu ša Eanna* 99:19; 225:7; 234:10

Gaḫal (*ga-ḫal*)
1. anc. of *Nūrea* 232:9

^{h}*gallābu* (^{lú}ŠU.I)
1. anc. of *Bēl-kēšir* and *Nabû-šum-ibni* 88:15
2. anc. of *Libluṭ* and *Nabû-šum-ibni* 26:12

^{f}*Gāmiltu* (^{f}*ga-mil-tu*$_{4}$)
1. a slave, daughter of ^{f}*Bānītu-râmat* 91:18,30,34

GAR-[...]
1. anc. of *Puzur-Nabû* 135:10

GI-[...]
1. desc. of *Arad-Nabû* 213:86

Gimillu (ŠU; *gi-mil-lu*)
1. 162:4
2. 196:2
3. 215:21
4. 310:15
5. ^{h}U.MUG 157:6
6. son of ^{d}[...]-*zēru-līšir*? 25:9
7. son of *Aḫulap-Ištar* 81:13
8. son of *Aḫulap-Ištar*, desc. of *Ḫunzû* 78:15
9. son of *Aplâ*, desc. of *Šumāti* 100:4,9,12
10. son of *Ardâ* 216:3
11. son of *Dummuq*, desc. of ^{h}*rab-banî* 293:3
12. son of *Innin-zēr-iddin* 94:20
13. son of *Marduk-zēr-ibni* 35:13
14. son of *Nabû-šum-iddin*, desc. of *Ea-ilūtu-bani* 98:11
15. son of *Nabû-zēr-iqīša*, desc. of *Adad-rabi* 74:10
16. son of *Nanaya-aḫ-iddin* 132:18
17. son of *Qīštiya*, desc. of *Rīmānu* 83:12
18. son of *Zēriya*, desc. of *Šigû'a* 113:13
19. ^{h}*širku*, brother of *Nanaya-iddin*, desc. of ^{f}*Šarruk*? 112:5
20. desc. of [...] 235:2
21. desc. of *Ardâ* 172:3; 215:3; 224:3; 286:5
22. desc. of *Nergal*-[...] 293:6
23. desc. of *Šakin-šumi* 197:2
24. desc. of *Zēriya* 152:7
25. f. of [...] 51:5
26. f. of *Anu-aḫ-iddin*, desc. of *Kurî* 83:18
27. f. of *Madānu-aḫḫē-iddin*, desc. of *Šigû'a* 1:34; 20:14; 65:16; 66:17; 97:12; 99:21; 114:9'
28. f. of *Marduk*?[...], desc. of *Ši*[...] 64:13
29. f. of *Nanaya-iddin* 198:5; 199:3
30. f. of *Nūrea*, desc. of ^{h}*išparu* 74:4
31. anc. of *Madānu-aḫḫē-iddin* 138:22; 213:6; 234:17
32. anc. of *Nabû-bēlšunu* 138:3
33. anc. of *Nādin* 138:12
34. anc. of *Nanaya-iddin* 213:39
35. anc. of *Nergal-nāṣir* 158:4; 213:44; 266:36

Gimil-Nanaya (ŠU-^{d}*na-na-a*)
1. anc. of *Anu-mukīn-apli* and [...] 86:5'
2. anc. of *Arad-Innin* and *Ibni-Ištar* 15:14
3. anc. of *Bāniya* and *Innin-šum-uṣur* 132:15
4. anc. of *Bazuzu* and *Ibni-Ištar* 94:3
5. anc. of *Ibni-Ištar* and *Šulâ* 91:37

6. anc. of *Innin-šum-uṣur* and *Nabû-ušabši* 132:12
7. anc. of *Innin-tabni-uṣur* and *Arad-Gula* 76:14
8. anc. of *Innin-zēr-ušabši* and *Nanaya-īpuš* 56:6'
9. anc. of *Marduk-šum-iddin* and *Nabû-balāssu-iqbi* 91:1
10. anc. of *Nabû-ēṭir* and *Mušallim-Marduk* 30:8

Gimil-Ninurta (*gi-mil-lu-*^{d}MAŠ)
1. f. of *Enlil-tabni-uṣur* 38:12

Gimil-Šamaš (ŠU-^{d}UTU)
1. son of *Nabû-lē'i*, desc. of *Sîn-lēqi-unninni* 2:40

Gula-šumu-līšir (^{d}ME.ME-MU-GIŠ)
1. anc. of *Arad-Šamaš* and *Šamaš-zēr-iddin* 55:11

Gula-zēr-ibni (^{d}*gu-la*-NUMUN-DÙ)
1. f. of *Aplâ*, desc. of *Isinayu* 92:3
2. f. of *Nabû-uṣuršu* 76:6

Gurâ (*gu-ra-a'*)
1. son of *Bānītu-ēreš* 48:11

Gūzanu (*gu-za-nu*)
1. 148:6
2. 150:10
3. ^{h}*atû* 160:1
4. ^{h}*ṣābu*, ^{h}*musaḫḫiru* 111:20
5. s. of [...]*-za-a-nu-ēreš* 12:4
6. son of *Mušēzib-Bēl* 20:6
7. desc. of *Nabû-bāni-aḫi* 213:68

Ḫa-[...]
1. f. of *Bābilayu* 90:8

Ḫakberu (*ḫa-ak-be-ru*)
1. ^{h}*nuḫatimmu* 156:17

Ḫan[...] (*ḫa-a*[*n*...])
1. f. of *Tabnea* 90:1

Ḫananu (*ḫa-na-na*)
1. f. of *Adad-laḫatu* 22:4

Ḫanbu (*ḫa-an-bu*; *ḫa-an-bi*)
1. anc. of *Nabû-šum-imbi* and *Taqīš-Gula* 100:23
2. anc. of *Šamaš-zēr-ibni* and *Nanaya-iddin* 1:28; 99:24

Ḫanṭušu (*ḫa-an-ṭu-šú*)
1. f. of *Nabû-aḫḫē-ušallim* 49:11

Ḫarmaṣu (*ḫar-ma-ṣu*)
1. f. of *Lāqīp* 237:3
2. anc. of *Nabû-aḫ-iddin* 160:2
3. anc. of *Nanaya-iddin* 266:33

Ḫašdâ (*ḫaš-da-a*)
1. 164:3
2. son of ^{d}[...] 9:1,10,19
3. son of *Nabû-mukīn-apli* 28:13
4. ^{h}*nappāḫ parzilli*, desc. of *Mannu-akî-Arba'ilu* 115:12,13; 265:3; 296:8

Ḫašdānu (*ḫaš-da-a-nu*)
1. 215:15

Ḫašdayu (*ḫaš-da-a-a*; *ḫaš-šá-da-a-a*)
1. 248:6
2. son of *Sîn-zēr-ušabši* 250:7

Ḫašdiya (*ḫaš-di-ia*; *ḫaš-di-iá*)
1. 75:15
2. f. of *Nusku-šar-u*[*ṣur*] 9:13
3. anc.? of [...] 115:15

^{f}*Ḫiptâ* (^{f}*ḫi-ip-ta-a*)
1. daughter of *Nādin*, desc. of ^{h}*itinnu* 10:3,5,9

Ḫumḫum-iddin (^{d}*ḫum-ḫum*-MU)
1. 202:2

Ḫunzû (*ḫu-un-zu-ú*)
1. anc. of [...]MU and *Šamaš-iddin* 12:16
2. anc. of [...]TIN and *Kudurru* 6:22
3. anc. of *Gimillu* and *Aḫulap-Ištar* 78:16
4. anc. of *Nūrea* and *Nergal-iddin* 24:13
5. anc. of *Ṭābiya* and *Nabû-nādin-šumi* 1:10; 2:7; 83:15

Ḫuṣāb (*ḫu-ṣab*)
1. anc. of *Nabû-kāṣir* and *Bēl-zēr-ukīn* 102:17
2. anc. of *Šum-ukīn* 21:5

Ibnâ (DU-*a*; *ib-na-a*)
1. *ša muḫḫi sūti ša Šerua*, son of *Balāṭu* 71:2,6

2. son of *Nabû-aḫḫē-ušallim* 125:16
3. son of *Nabû-aḫḫē-ušallim*, desc. of ^{h}*šangû parakki* 12:14
4. son of *Nanaya-aḫ-iddin* 49:5
5. f. of *Zēriya*, desc. of *Egibi* 51:12; 64:4; 65:5,13; 114:3'
6. anc. of *Nabû-balāssu-iqbi* 213:20; 234:18
7. anc. of *Zēriya* 201:5

Ibni-Ezida (DÙ-*é-zi-da*)

1. desc. of ^{f}*zakītu* 115:30

Ibni-Ištar (DÙ-^{d}INNIN; DÙ-^{d}15; DÙ-^{d}*iš-tar*; *ib-n*[*i*-^{d}INNIN])

1. 164:13
2. 218:5
3. 228:5
4. 284:5
5. ^{h}[...] 164:6
6. ^{h}[...] 295:2'
7. ^{h}*ašlāku* 275:7
8. ^{h}*nappāḫ parzilli* 286:11
9. ^{h}*nappāḫ siparri* 257:3
10. ^{h}*ṣābu* 111:23,37
11. son of *Bēl-upaḫḫir* 260:3
12. ^{h}*ṭupšarru*, son of *Innin-šum-uṣur* 35:14
13. son of *Nergal-īpuš*, desc. of *Kurî* 100:18
14. son of *Nergal-šum-ibni*, desc. of *Kurî* 113:15
15. ^{h}*ṭupšarru*, son of *Šulâ*, desc. of *Gimil-Nanaya* 91:36
16. son of *Šum-ukīn*, desc. of *Ekur-zākir* 12:15
17. desc. of *Bēl-upaḫḫir* 265:6
18. ^{h}*nappāḫ parzilli*, desc. of *Bēl-upaḫḫir* 115:10,11
19. desc. of *Nergal-uballiṭ* 213:75
20. desc. of *Šum-ukīn* 129:10a,12
21. f. of [...]MU 6:24
22. f. of *Arad-Innin*, desc. of *Gimil-Nanaya* 15:13
23. f. of *Bazuzu*, desc. of *Gimil-Nanaya* 94:3
24. f. of *Bazuzu* and *Šamaš-bāni-aḫi* 166:4
25. f. of *Eanna-līp-uṣur*, desc. of ^{h}*ašlāku* 1:41; 52:15
26. f. of *Šumâ*, desc. of [...] 95:22
27. f. of *Šumâ*, desc. of ^{h}*ašlāku* 66:21
28. anc. of *Anu-zēr-*[...] 115:23
29. anc. of *Arad-Innin* 137:12; 138:6,26; 297:16
30. anc. of *Balāṭu* 150:6
31. anc. of *Bazuzu* 156:10
32. anc. of *Šumâ* 152:5

Iddin-[...] (SUM.NA-[...])

1. 295:13

Iddinâ (SUM.NA-*a*)[27]

1. 310:12

Iddin-aḫu (see *Nādin-aḫi*)

Iddin-Amurru (MU-^{d}KUR.GAL)[28]

1. desc. of *Amurru-zēr-ibni* 286:7

Iddin-Bēl (MU-^{d}EN)

1. son of *Aplâ* 311:2,5,9,13

Iddin-Enlil (see *Iddin-Amurru*)

Iddin-Marduk (MU-^{d}AMAR.UD)

1. 101:1,3,9,27,34
2. f. of *Taqīš-Gula*, desc. of *Būṣu* 46:15

Iddin-Nabû (SUM.NA-^{d}NÀ; MU-^{d}NÀ)

1. 18:5
2. 89:4,7
3. 94:14
4. son of *Manna-dāmu* 113:1,3
5. f. of *Innin-šum-uṣur*, desc. of *Kidin-Marduk* 1:48; 52:13; 65:18; 95:7; 114:10'
6. anc. of *Innin-šum-uṣur* 213:11

Iddin-Papsukkal (MU-^{d}*pap-sukkal*; SUM.NA-^{d}*pap-sukkal*)

1. anc. of *Nabû-aḫḫē-ušallim* and *Bēl-na'id* 49:2
2. anc. of *Nabû-mukīn-apli* and *Zēr-Bābili* 62:16

27. Read possibly also *Nādnâ* (SUM-*na-a*) or *Nādin-apli* (SUM.NA-A), since the frozen form SUM.NA can apparently represent any form of the verb *nadānu*.

28. Read possibly *Iddin-Enlil*.

1. f. of *Ištar-aḫ-iddin* 233:8
2. f. of *Nanaya-karābi* 93:12; 279:4

Ina-ṣilli-Nergal (*ina*-GISSU-^{d}U.GUR)
1. anc. of *Šamaš-aḫ-iddin* 115:6

Ina-ṣilli-Urdimmu (*ina*-GISSU-^{d}UR.IDIM)[29]
1. ^{h}*agru* 297:2
2. son of *Nabû-bāni-aḫi*, desc. of ^{h}*atû* 65:1

Ina-ṣilli-Zababa (*ina*-GISSU-^{d}*za-ba*$_4$-*ba*$_4$)
1. son of *Esagil-mukīn-apli*, desc. of ^{h}*paḫḫāru*? 29:2

Ina-tēšî-ēṭir (*ina*-SÙḪ-SUR)
1. 151:5
2. ^{h}*širku* 182:2
3. son of *Nanaya-aḫ-iddin* 63:5
4. son of *Nanaya-iddin* 42:16
5. f. of *Nabû-aḫḫē-iddin*, desc. of *Nabû-bullissu* 10:14
6. anc. of *Lāqīp* 213:49
7. anc. of *Nabû-zēr-ušabši* 134:8; 284:12
8. anc. of *Nergal*-x-x 213:23
9. anc. of *Nergal-šum-iddin* 138:11; 156:14

Innin-[...] (^{d}*in-ni*[*n*...]; ^{d}*innin-na*-[...]; ^{d}*in-nin-na*-[...])
1. 164:8
2. ^{h}*gallābu* 213:78
3. son of ^{d}*Na*[...] 164:1
4. desc. of *Zērūtu* 235:23

Innin-x-*ibni* (^{d}*innin-na*-x-DÙ)
1. f. of *Itti-Nabû-balāṭu*, desc. of *Damiq* 2:42

Innin-[...]-*iddin* (^{d}*in-nin*-[...]-MU)
1. 281:4

Innin-x-*uṣur* (^{d}*in-nin*-x-ÙRI)
1. anc. of *Madi-il* 288:7

Innin-aḫḫē-iddin (^{d}*in-nin*-ŠEŠ.ME-MU)
1. desc. of *Lūmur-dumqi-Ištar* 263:4

Innin-ina-tēšî-ēṭir (^{d}*in-nin-ina*-SÙḪ-SUR)
1. son of *Aplâ*, desc. of *Kurî* 100:19

Innin-kibsu-abi-uṣur (^{d}*in-nin-kib-si*-AD-ÙRI)
1. desc. of *Bēl-ēreš* 213:89

Innin-kibsu-šarri-uṣur (^{d}*in-nin-kib-su*-LUGAL-ÙRI)
1. 235:14

^{f}*Innin-šarrat* (^{d}*in-nin-šar-rat*)
1. daughter of *Kidinnu*, spouse of *Nabû-šum-uṣur* 6:2

Innin-šar-uṣur (^{d}*in-nin*-LUGAL-ÙRI)
1. 120:3
2. son of *Nergal-ušallim* 13:8; 121:12

Innin-šum-ibni (^{d}*in-nin*-MU-DÙ; [^{d}*innin*]-*na*-MU-DÙ)
1. desc. of *Nabû-bēlšunu* 225:11
2. anc. of [...]-*ēṭir* 115:16
3. anc. of *Balāṭu* 235:16

[*Inn*]*in-šum-iddin* ([^{d}*in-n*]*in*-MU-MU)
1. ^{h}*gallābu* 213:87

Innin-šum-iškun (^{d}*in-nin*-MU-GAR-*un*)
1. 52:7
2. desc. of *Nergal-ibni* 213:82

Innin-šum-uṣur (^{d}*in-nin*-MU-ÙRI; ^{d}*in-nin*-MU-PAP; ^{d}*innin-na*-MU-PAP; ^{d}*innin-na*-MU-ÙRI; ^{d}*in-nin-ni*-MU-ÙRI)
1. 136:6
2. 263:2
3. ^{h}*šāpir ṭābiḫē*, son of *Iddin-Nabû*, desc. of *Kidin-Marduk* 1:38 + seal caption on R.E.; 52:13; 65:18; 95:7; 114:10'
4. son of *Nabû-ušabši*, desc. of *Gimil-Nanaya* 132:11
5. ^{h}*ṭupšarru*, son of *Nergal-ušēzib*, desc. of *Kidin-Marduk* 24:16; 76:17; 94:19
6. son of *Ṭāb-Uruk* 74:2,9
7. ^{h}*nuḫatimmu*, desc. of A-x-[...] 137:8
8. desc. of *Amēl-Nabû* 162:3
9. desc. of *Ardâ* 213:73
10. desc. of *Iddin-Nabû* 213:11
11. desc. of *Mār-Bēl-dannu* 213:79
12. desc. of *Nanaya-aḫ-iddin* 133:12
13. desc. of *Nanaya-ēres* 207:4
14. ^{h}*išpar birmu*, desc. of *Ṭāb-Uruk* 115:3,4
15. f. of [...], desc. of *Ekur-zākir* 6:23
16. f. of *Anu*-[...] 105:21,26
17. f. of *Bāniya*, desc. of *Gimil-Nanaya* 132:14

29. On this name see P.-A. Beaulieu, "Lion-Man: *uridimmu* or *urdimmu*?" *N.A.B.U* 1990/21.

18. f. of *Ibni-Ištar* 35:15
19. f. of *Šum-uṣur* 115:6
20. anc. of *Balāṭu* 213:30
21. anc. of *Šamaš-zēr-iqīša* 297:12

Innin-tabni-uṣur (^{d}*in-nin-tab-ni*-ÙRI)
1. 286:2
2. son of *Arad-Gula*, desc. of *Gimil-Nanaya* 76:13

Innin-zēr-[...] (^{d}*in-nin*-NUMUN-[...]; ^{d}*innin-na*-NUMUN-[...])
1. 152:3
2. 264:7

Innin-zēr-ibni (^{d}*in-nin*-NUMUN-DÙ)
1. 214:12
2. desc. of *Arad-Innin* 213:8
3. ^{h}*širku*, desc. of *Nergal-uballiṭ* 112:7

Innin-zēr-iddin (^{d}*in-nin*-NUMUN-MU)
1. desc. of *Zērūtu* 265:12; 280:2
2. f. of *Gimillu* 94:20

Innin-zēr-iqīša (^{d}*in-nin*-NUMUN-BA-*šá*)
1. 213:83
2. son of *Nabû-aḫḫē-ušallim*, desc. of ^{h}*šangû Ninurta* 15:1

Innin-zēr-ušabši (^{d}*in-nin*-NUMUN-GÁL-*ši*; ^{d}*in-nin*-NUMUN-TIL)
1. 83:11
2. 140:7
3. 190:6
4. 215:9
5. 238:2
6. ^{h}*nagār dalāti* 230:3
7. ^{h}*nāru* 286:4
8. son of ^{d}[...] 235:5
9. son of *Aplâ*, desc. of *Sîn-lēqi-unninni* 66:19
10. ^{h}*išpar birmu*, son of *Nanaya-iddin*, brother of *Nanaya-aḫ-iddin* 115:5,7
11. ^{h}*ṭupšarru*, son of *Nanaya-īpuš*, desc. of *Gimil-Nanaya* 56:5'
12. desc. of *Aplâ* 219:7
13. ^{h}*nappāḫu*, desc. of *Bēl-ibni* 208:2
14. ^{h}*širku*, son of ^{f}*Šeṭua*, g.s. of *Šamaš-erība* 112:11
15. f. of *Ištar-mukīn-*[...] 66:2
16. anc. of *Rīmūt* 160:9

Ipriya (*ip-ri-ia*)
1. son of x[...] 96:3

Iqbâ (*iq-ba-*[*a*])
1. 150:19

Iqīša (BA-*šá*)
1. f. of *Bēl-uballiṭ*, desc. of ^{h}*bā'iru* 39:13
2. f. of *Kalbâ*, desc. of *Basiya* 24:2; 78:4; 81:4; 82:2'

Iqīša-[...] (BA-*šá*-[...])
1. anc. of *Kalbâ* 209:3

Iqīšâ? (BA?-*šá-a*)
1. f. of *Mušēzib-*[...] 40:12

Iqīšâ (BA-*šá-a*)
1. son of *Arad-Nabû*, desc. of *Ilšu-abušu* 5:6
2. son of *Šum-ukīn*, desc. of ^{h}*nappāḫu* 60:8
3. f. of *Aplâ* 25:3
4. f. of *Balāṭu*, desc. of ^{h}*ṣāḫit ginê* 23:16
5. f. of *Nādin-aḫi*, desc. of *Isinayu* 4:15'

Irani (*ir-a-ni*)
1. anc. of *Bēl-ēṭir-*[...] and [...]-*Marduk* 32:14
2. anc. of *Nabû-šum-iškun* and *Bēl-*[...] 3:33
3. anc. of *Nabû-šum-ukīn* 101:38

Isinayu (^{lú}PA.ŠE^{ki}; *i-sin-na-a-a*)
1. f. of *Nabû-balāssu-iqbi* 29:5
2. anc. of *Aplâ* and *Gula-zēr-ibni* 92:3
3. anc. of *Nādin-aḫi* and *Iqīšâ* 4:15'

Iṣṣur (*iṣ-ṣur*)
1. 150:13

^{h}*išparu* (^{lú}UŠ.BAR)
1. anc. of *Kudurranu* and *Nabû-balāssu-iqbi* 42:14
2. anc. of *Nabû-ittannu* and *Murašû* 77:13
3. anc. of *Nūrea* and *Gimillu* 74:5

^{f}*Iššar-dannat* (^{f}*iš-šar-dan-na-at*)
1. ^{f}*zakītu*, anc. of *Nabû-aḫḫē-uballiṭ* 112:9

Ištar-[...] (^{d}*Innin-*[...]; ^{d}15-[...])
1. 135:9
2. 235:8
3. son of *Šamaš-uballiṭ* 56:2

Ištar-aḫ-[...] (^{d}INNIN-ŠEŠ-[...])
1. 284:22

3. son of *Nādin-aḫi* 44:19
4. f. of *Šamaš-šar-uṣur* 28:16
5. anc. of *Nabû-bēlšunu* and *Mušēzib-Nabû* 10:17

Kudurru (NÍG.DU)
1. f. of [...]TIN, desc. of *Ḫunzû* 6:22
2. f. of *Etel-pī*, desc. of ^{h}*šangû Ninurta* 83:15
3. f. of *Nabû-ušallim*, desc. of ^{h}*rē'i ginê* 56:3'
4. f. of *Silim-Bēl*, desc. of *Dābibi* 48:10
5. f. of *Šūzubu* 288:2
6. f. of *Šūzubu*, desc. of ^{h}*rē'i ginê* 11:13; 52:14; 114:14'
7. anc. of *Lābâši* 263:7
8. anc. of *Marduk-šāpik-zēri* 172:2
9. anc. of *Nādin-aḫi* 160:7

Kulbību (*kul-bi-bi*)
1. 205:5
2. 273:7
3. ^{h}*rab bīt kīli* 157:3

Kunâ (*ku-na-a*)
1. son of [...], desc. of ^{h}*bā'iru* 91:3

KUR-[...]
1. anc. of *Šamaš-šum-ukīn* and [...]MU 94:17

Kurb[anni? ...] (*kur-b[an?-...]*)
1. 235:26

Kurbanni-Marduk (*kur-ban-ni-*^{d}AMAR.UD)
1. 42:11
2. ^{h}*šatammu Eanna*, son of *Zēriya*, desc. of *Sîn-damāqu* 1:30 + seal caption on Le.E; 52:10; 92:14; 93:2; 110:1; 116:5

Kurî (*ku-ri-i*; *kur-i*)
1. anc. of *Arad-Innin* and *Bēl-iddin* 91:7; 92:4
2. anc. of *Anu-aḫ-iddin* and *Gimillu* 83:18
3. anc. of *Balāssu* and *Arad-Nanaya* 95:8
4. anc. of *Bēl-aḫḫē-erība* and *Nabû-bēlšunu* 98:13
5. anc. of *Ibni-Ištar* and *Nergal-īpuš* 100:18
6. anc. of *Ibni-Ištar* and *Nergal-šum-ibni* 113:16
7. anc. of *Innin-ina-tēšî-ēṭir* and *Aplâ* 100:19
8. anc. of *Nabû-bēlšunu* and *Arad-Innin* 132:20
9. anc. of *Nabû-mukīn-apli* and *Bēl-īpuš* 82:4'
10. anc. of *Nabû-zēru-līšir* and *Bēlšunu* 92:5
11. anc. of *Rīmūt* and *Marduk-šum-ibni* 76:17
12. anc. of *Rīmūt* and *Nabû-šumu-līšir* 1:14
13. anc. of *Sîn-erība* and *Šamaš-zēru-līšir* 74:14

Kurû (*ku-ru-ú*)
1. anc. of *Nabû-mukīn-apli* and *Arad-Bēl* 6:7

Kūtayu (GÚ.DU$_{8}$^{ki}*-a-a*)
1. son of *Aḫiyāma* 36:12

Lābâši (*la-ba-ši*; *la-ba-a-ši*; *la-a-ba-ši*)
1. 112:16
2. ^{h}*nappāḫ siparri* 115:21
3. son of *Dannu-Nergal* 35:12
4. son of *Nabû-aḫ-iddin* 116:3
5. desc. of *Kudurru* 263:6
6. f. of *Itti-Šamaš-balāṭu* 7:2; 44:2; 55:4; 63:10; 69:1
7. f. of *Šamaš-zēr-iddin* 7:24; 39:15; 59:9
8. f. of [...] 41:9

Lābâši-[...] (*la-ba-[ši-...]*)
1. anc. of *Bēlšunu* 293:9

Lābâši-Marduk (*la-a-ba-ši-*^{d}AMAR.UD; *la-ba-ši-*^{d}AMAR.UD; *la-ba-a-ši-*^{d}ŠÚ)
1. ^{h}*šāpir nuḫatimmē*, son of *Arad-Bēl*, desc. of *Egibi* 1:36 + seal caption on Le.E.; 110:11
2. son of *Nabû-aḫḫē-bulliṭ*, desc. of *Balāṭu* 2:38

Lāqīp (*la-qip*; *la-qí-pu*; *la-qí-pi*)
1. ^{h}*malaḫḫu* 287:5
2. son of *Ea-kāṣir* 11:4
3. son of *Ḫarmaṣu* 237:2
4. desc. of *Ina-tēšî-ēṭir* 213:48

Libluṭ (*lib-luṭ*; *lib-lu-ṭu*)
1. 256:4
2. 273:4
3. ^{h}*aškāpu* 115:25
4. *ša rēš šarri ša muḫḫi quppi* 91:2
5. son of ^{d}x[...] 29:4'

6. ^{h}*ṣābu*, son of *Ištar-šum-ēreš* 111:21
7. son of *Nabû-šum-ibni*, desc. of ^{h}*gallābu* 26:11
8. son of *Nabû-šum-ukīn* 68:1,8
9. ^{h}*nappāḫ parzilli*, desc. of ^{f}*zakītu* 115:12

Libūr (*li-bu-ru*)
1. 213:50
2. anc. of *Nabû-zēr?-ukīn* 284:13

Līšir (*li-šìr*; *li-ši-ru*; *li-šir*$_{x}$[BÀD])
1. 193:9
2. son of *Bazuzu* 4:4,22
3. son of *Nādin* 65:3
4. f. of *Ninurta-erība* 16:9
5. anc. of *Sūqayu* 80:10

Lū-attū'a (*lu-ú-at-tu-ú-a*)
1. ^{h}*ṣābu*, ^{h}*agru* 111:32

Lugal-Marada-ibni (^{d}LUGAL-AMAR.DA-DÙ)
1. f. of *Arad-Bēl* 46:13

Lūmur-dumqi-Ištar (*lu-mur-dum-qí-*^{d}15; *lu-mur-dum-qí-*^{d}INNIN)
1. ^{h}*ṣābu*, ^{h}*ummânu*, ^{h}*mušallimānu* 111:11
2. anc. of *Innin-aḫḫē-iddin* 263:5

Lūṣi-an[*a-nūri*...] (È-*a-n*[*a*-ZÁLAG...])
1. 114:1'

Lūṣi-ana-nūri (*lu-uṣ-ana*-ZÁLAG; *lu*-È-*ana*-ZÁLAG; È-*ana*-ZÁLAG)
1. 285:5
2. ^{h}*ṭupšarru*, son of *Nabû-aḫḫē-uballiṭ*, desc. of *Dābibi* 64:15
3. son of *Zēriya* 82:4'
4. desc. of *Šamaš-šum-ukīn* 130:3

Lūṣi-ana-nūri-Marduk (*lu-ṣi-a-na*-ZÁLAG-^{d}AMAR.UD; *lu*-È-*a-na*-ZÁLAG-^{d}AMAR.UD; *lu*-È-*ana*-ZÁLAG-^{d}AMAR.UD; È-*a-na*-ZÁLAG-^{d}ŠÚ)
1. f. of *Nādin* and *Širiktu*, desc. of *Ili-bani* 5:10,14; 43:5; 45:5; 47:4; 60:2; 72:2; 79:4; 88:2

Madānu-aḫḫē-iddin (^{d}DI.KUD-ŠEŠ.MEŠ-MU; ^{d}DI.KUD-ŠEŠ.ME-MU; ^{d}DI.KUD-PAP.ME-MU)
1. 235:19
2. ^{h}*nuḫatimmu*, desc. of *Gimillu* 137:11; 138:22; 213:6; 234:17,18
3. ^{h}*šāpir sirâšē*, son of *Gimillu*, desc. of *Šigû'a* 1:34 + seal caption on Le.E.; 20:13; 65:15; 66:16; 97:11; 99:20; 114:8'

Madānu-aḫ-iddin (^{d}DI.KUD-ŠEŠ-MU)
1. 157:9
2. 266:34

Madānu-ēreš (^{d}DI.KUD-KAM)
1. 133:24; 148:2; 173:5; 174:5; 175:3; 176:4; 177:6; 178:3; 179:3; 180:2; 181:3; 182:4; 183:3; 184:2; 185:4; 186:4; 187:6
2. 213:54,81

Madānu-šar-uṣur (^{d}DI.KUD-LUGAL-ÙRI)
1. *ša rēši ša muḫḫi* ^{h}*qašti? eššēti* 94:6
2. desc. of *Bēl-aḫ-iddin* 119:9

Madi-il (*ma-di-il*)
1. 141:2
2. desc. of *Innin*-x-*uṣur* 288:7

^{h}*maḫḫû* (^{lú}GUB.BA)
1. anc. of *Ištar-aḫ-iddin* and *Rīmūt-Bēl* 100:8,10
2. anc. of *Šamaš-šum-ukīn*, *Nabû-zēr-ukīn*, and *Marduk-ēṭir* 100:1,7

Man-[...]
1. 281:6

^{h}*mandidu* (^{lú}*man-di-dí*)
1. anc. of *Ardiya* and *Šamaš-šum-ukīn* 11:14
2. anc. of *Šamaš-šum-ukīn* and *Šulâ* 73:4
3. anc. of *Šulâ* and *Nergal-ušallim* 100:4

Manna-dāmu (*man-na-da-mu-ú*)
1. f. of *Iddin-Nabû* 113:1

Mannu-akî-Arba'il (*man-na-a-ki-i-ar-ba-i-lu*; *man-na-a-ki-i-ar-ba-'i-il*)
1. 142:4
2. anc. of [*Ḫašdâ*] 115:12

Mannu-gīrû (*man-nu-gi-ru*)
1. anc. of *Nabû-šum-iddin* and *Rīmūt-Gula* 72:4

Mār-Bēl-dannu (^{d}DUMU-^{d}EN-*da-a-nu*; DUMU-^{d}EN-*da-a-nu*)
1. anc. of [...]-*šum-uṣur* 134:3'
2. anc. of *Innin-šum-uṣur* 213:59,79

30. This name can also be read *Kīnâ* (DU-*a*).

3. son of ^{d}x-x-x, desc. of ^{d}x-x-x 2:37
4. son of ^{d}[...], desc. of *Amēl-Ea* 132:9
5. ^{h}*ṭupšarru*, son of *Bēl-uballiṭ*, desc. of *Amēl-Ea* 98:15
6. son of *Ezida-aplu-iqīša*, desc. of *Šigû'a* 2:11,16,20,48
7. desc. of *Bēl-uballiṭ* 213:21
8. desc. of *Kabtiya* 136:4; 139:3

Mušēzib-Nabû (*mu-še-zib*-^{d}NÀ)
1. son of *Adad-iddin* 44:14
2. f. of *Nabû-bēlšunu*, desc. of *Kudurranu* 10:16

Mušu-natan (*mu-ú-šú-na-tan*)
1. f. of *Marduk-zēr-ibni* 91:10

Na-[...]
1. son of ^{d}x-*šum-iddin*, desc. of ^{h}*rē'i sisi* 72:12
2. son of *Nabû-šum-iškun* 19:7
3. ^{h}*ṭupšarru*, desc. of *Egibi* 20:18

^{d}*Na*-[...]
1. f. of *Innin*-[...] and *Erībšu* 164:2

Nabû-[...] (^{d}NÀ-[...])
1. 26:2
2. 135:27
3. 148:3
4. 213:76
5. 284:23
6. 302:2
7. 307:2
8. ^{h}*ṭupšarru*, son of *Marduk-erība* 42:19
9. son of *Šamaš-ušēzib* 86:1'
10. desc. of *Aplâ* 213:52
11. f. of *Ezida-šar-uṣur* 46:14
12. f. of *Rīmūt* 296:12
13. anc. of *Balāṭu* 190:3
14. anc. of *Rīmūt-Bēl* 134:3

Nabû-[...]-*ilī* (^{d}NÀ-[...]-DINGIR.MEŠ)
1. anc. of *Bāniya* and *Nabû-nāṣir* 66:3

Nabû-[...]-*ni* (^{d}NÀ-[...]-*ni*)
1. a slave 33:2

Nabû-[...]-*uballiṭ* (^{d}NÀ-[...]-TIN)
1. f. of *Baḫû* 213:37

Nabû-aḫ-[...] (^{d}NÀ-ŠEŠ-[...])
1. 19:2
2. f. of *Nabû-bāni-zēri*, desc. of *Sîn-šar-ilī* 313:2'

Nabû-aḫ-ēreš (^{d}NÀ-ŠEŠ-KAM)
1. son of *Nabû-dīn-epuš* 51:7
2. f. of *Ardu-eššu* 22:15
3. anc. of *Amurru-iddin* 117:11

Nabû-aḫḫē-[...] (^{d}NÀ-ŠEŠ.MEŠ-[...]; ^{d}NÀ-ŠEŠ.ME-[...])
1. 237:7
2. 310:16
3. f. of [...] 96:2
4. anc. of *Šamaš-uballiṭ* 235:18

Nabû-aḫḫē-bulliṭ (^{d}NÀ-ŠEŠ.MEŠ-*bul-liṭ*)
(see also *Nabû-aḫḫē-uballiṭ*)
1. 75:13
2. son of *Marduk-zēr*-[...], desc. of *Arkât-ili-damqā* 43:12
3. son of *Nabû-aḫḫē-iddin*, desc. of *Miṣirayu* 47:2,7
4. ^{h}*ṭupšarru ša Eanna*, son of *Ša-Nabû-šû* 91:2
5. f. of *Lābâši-Marduk*, desc. of *Balāṭu* 2:38

Nabû-aḫḫē-erība (^{d}NÀ-ŠEŠ.MEŠ-SU)
1. 70:5,11,14

Nabû-aḫḫē-iddin (^{d}NÀ-ŠEŠ.MEŠ-MU; ^{d}NÀ-PAP.ME-MU)
1. ^{h}*dayānu*, desc. of *Egibi* 101:37 + seal captions on L.E.
2. son of *Ina-tēšî-ēṭir*, desc. of *Nabû-bullissu* 10:14
3. f. of [...], desc. of [...] 72:14
4. f. of *Kīnâ* 215:7
5. f. of *Nabû-aḫḫē-bulliṭ*, desc. of *Miṣirayu* 47:3
6. f. of *Zēriya* 87:9
7. anc. of *Bēlšunu* 134:10; 138:4; 205:4

Nabû-aḫḫē-uballiṭ (^{d}NÀ-ŠEŠ.MEŠ-TIN-*iṭ*; ^{d}NÀ-ŠEŠ.MEŠ-TIN; ^{d}NÀ-ŠEŠ.ME-TIN; ^{d}NÀ-PAP.ME-TIN-*iṭ*; ^{d}NÀ-PAP.ME-TIN)
(see also *Nabû-aḫḫē-bulliṭ*)
1. 190:10

2. son of *Nanaya-ēreš* 68:13
3. ^{h}*širku*, desc. of ^{f}*Iššar-dannat* 112:8
4. f. of *Lūṣi-ana-nūri*, desc. of *Dābibi* 64:16
5. f. of *Marduk-šum-iddin*, desc. of *Balāṭu* 92:1
6. f. of *Nabû-ušallim* 228:5
7. f. of *Padâ*, desc. of ^{h}*šangû* ^{d}[...] 88:5
8. anc. of *Nādin* 266:32

Nabû-aḫḫē-ušallim (^{d}NÀ-ŠEŠ.MEŠ-GI; ^{d}NÀ-ŠEŠ.ME-GI; ^{d}NÀ-PAP.ME-GI)
1. ^{h}*ḫāṣib qanâti* 147:3
2. son of *Amēl-Nanaya* 256:2
3. son of *Bēl-na'id*, desc. of *Iddin-Papsukkal* 49:1
4. son of *Ḫanṭušu* 49:10
5. son of *Nabû-šum-ukīn*, desc. of ^{h}*šangû Ninurta* 91:8
6. son of *Nergal-uballiṭ* 214:3
7. desc. of ^{h}*šangû Ninurta* 1:11,16
8. desc. of *Šu*-x-x 97:7
9. f. of *Ibnâ* 125:17
10. f. of *Ibnâ*, desc. of ^{h}*šangû parakki* 12:14
11. f. of *Innin-zēr-iqīša*, desc. of ^{h}*šangû Ninurta* 15:2

Nabû-aḫ-iddin (^{d}NÀ-ŠEŠ-MU)
1. 115:23
2. 205:5
3. ^{h}*mār šipri* 170:3
4. ^{h}*sepīru* 133:8
5. *ša rēš šarri bēl piqitti Eanna* 11:11; 12:12
6. desc. of *Ḫarmaṣu* 160:2
7. f. of *Bēl-ēṭir*, desc. of *Maštuk* 17:12
8. f. of *Eanna-šum-*[...] 34:12
9. f. of *Ištar-šum-ēreš* 64:3
10. f. of *Lābâši* 116:4,7
11. f. of *Nabû-balāssu-iqbi* 68:14
12. f. of *Rīmūt* 50:3
13. f. of *Ubārya* 40:5

Nabû-aḫ-uballiṭ (^{d}NÀ-ŠEŠ-TIN-*iṭ*)
1. 145:8

Nabû-aḫ-uṣur (^{d}NÀ-ŠEŠ-ÙRI; ^{d}NÀ-ŠEŠ-PAP)
1. son of *Nabû-šūzibanni* 44:17
2. son of *Nabû-utēr* 28:2,9; 32:2

Nabû-alsi-ul-abâš (^{d}NÀ-*al-si-ul-ba-áš*)
1. a slave 102:4,6,9,12

Nabû?-aplu-iddin (^{d}NÀ?-[IBI]LA-SUM.NA)
1. ^{h}*ṭupšarru*, son of *Nabû-balāssu-iqbi*, desc. of ^{h}x 26:13

Nabû-aplu-iddin (^{d}NÀ-A-MU; ^{d}NÀ-ENDURU-MU; ^{d}NÀ-IBILA-MU; ^{d}NÀ-IBILA-SUM.NA)
1. 18:4
2. son of *Nabû-šum-iškun*, desc. of ^{h}*paḫāru* 5:4
3. son of *Zēr-ukīn* 31:9
4. ^{h}*rab-banî ša Bēlti ša Uruk*, desc. of *Nabû-nādin-šumi* 97:5
5. ^{h}*nuḫatimmu*, desc. of *Nabû-uballiṭ* 134:5
6. ^{h}*ṭupšarru*, desc. of ^{h}*paḫāru* 89:12
7. f. of *Arad-Nabû*, desc. of ^{h}*nappāḫu* 79:15
8. son of *Nabû-šum-iddin*, desc. of *Esagil-mansum* 60:5

Nabû-aplu-uṣur (^{d}NÀ-A-ÙRI; ^{d}NÀ-DIL-ÙRI)
1. anc. of *Ilu-dannu-aḫḫēšu-ibni* 115:14
2. anc. of *Rīmūt* and [...] 57:11

Nabû-balāssu-iqbi (^{d}NÀ-TIN-*su*-E; ^{d}NÀ-TIN-*su-iq-bi*)
1. 93:15
2. 165:5
3. 213:15,54,62
4. son of *Adad-ibni* 63:15
5. son of *Isinayu* 29:4
6. son of *Nabû-aḫ-iddin* 68:14
7. desc. of <...> 234:6
8. desc. of *Ibnâ* 213:19; 234:18
9. f. of *Aḫ-*[...] 40:11
10. f. of *Bēl-uballiṭ* 223:4
11. f. of *Kudurranu*, desc. of ^{h}*išparu* 42:14
12. f. of *Marduk-šum-iddin*, desc. of *Gimil-Nanaya* 91:1
13. f. of *Nabû?-aplu-iddin*, desc. of ^{h}x 26:14
14. f. of *Nabû-bāni-aḫi*, desc. of *Sîn-lēqi-unninni* 13:12;97:15
15. f. of *Nabû-nādin-šumi* 13:5; 14:3
16. f. of *Pir'u*, desc. of *Eppeš-ilī* 234:14
17. f. of *Rēḫu-Nabû*, desc. of ^{h}*nagāru* 5:31
18. f. of *Šamaš-šum-iddin* 13:10; 167:5

19. anc. of *Bāniya* 152:11; 266:37
20. anc. of *Marduk-šum-iddin* 134:4'
21. anc. of *Nabû-bāni-aḫi* 138:9

Nabû-bāni-[...] (^{d}NÀ-DÙ-x-x-x)
1. 306:2

Nabû-bāni-aḫi (^{d}NÀ-DÙ-ŠEŠ)
1. 19:11
2. 144:4
3. 165:4
4. 213:65
5. ^{h}*nuḫatimmu* 134:15
6. son of *Kabtiya*, desc. of *Balāṭu* 95:5
7. ^{h}*ṭupšarru*, son of *Nabû-balāssu-iqbi*, desc. of *Sîn-lēqi-unninni* 13:11; 97:15
8. ^{h}*ṭupšarru*, son of *Nabû-būnu-šūtur*, desc. of *Rīšū'a* 21:16
9. son of *Nabû-rīmanni*, desc. of *ša* ^{h}*ṭābātišu* 35:3
10. son of *Zēriya*, desc. of ^{h}*bā'iru* 3:34
11. ^{h}*nuḫatimmu*, desc. of *Nabû-balāssu-iqbi* 138:9
12. ^{h}*nuḫatimmu*, desc. of *Šamaš-zēr-iqīša* 156:7
13. ^{h}*ṣāḫit-ginê*, desc. of *Šamaš-zēr-iqīša* 171:4
14. ^{h}*nuḫatimmu*, desc. of *Šulâ* 138:10
15. f. of *Ina-ṣilli-Urdimmu*, desc. of ^{h}*atû* 65:1
16. f. of *Mūrānu*, desc. of *Ekur-zākir* 1:45; 51:17; 110:12; 114:13'
17. f. of *Nūr-Sîn*, desc. of *Nūr-Sîn* 64:14
18. anc. of *Gūzanu* 213:68

Nabû-bāni-zēri (^{d}NÀ-DÙ-NUMUN)
1. son of *Bēlšunu*, desc. of *Bēl-aplu-uṣur* 2:36
2. son of *Nabû-aḫ-*[...], desc. of *Sîn-šar-ilī* 313:2'

Nabû-bēl-šumāti (^{d}NÀ-EN-MU.MEŠ; ^{d}NÀ-EN-MU.ME)
1. son of *Rīmūt*, desc. of *Ilūtu-bani* 58:8
2. son of *Zēr-Bābili*, desc. of *Sîn-tabni* 100:16
3. f. of *Nabû-tāriṣ* 98:5
4. anc. of *Nabû-tāriṣ* 143:6

Nabû-bēlšunu (^{d}NÀ-EN-*šú-nu*)
1. 213:64
2. ^{h}*nagāru* 213:84
3. ^{h}*nuḫatimmu* 137:10; 138:24; 156:11,15
4. son of *Arad-Innin* 84:13
5. ^{h}*ṭupšarru*, son of *Arad-Innin*, desc. of *Kurî* 132:19
6. son of *Bēl-aḫ-ušabši*, desc. of *Imbu-īniya* 10:12
7. ^{h}*ṭupšarru*, son of *Mušēzib-Nabû*, desc. of *Kudurranu* 10:16
8. son of *Nabû-kāṣir*, desc. of ^{h}*šangû bīt Bābili* 46:11
9. son of *Nabû-šum-ukīn* 64:1,7
10. ^{h}*ṭupšarru*, son of *Nādin* 54:19
11. son of *Nergal-dannu* 9:6,20
12. ^{h}*ṭupšarru*, son of *Šamaš-aplu-uṣur*, desc. of ^{h}*šangû Enamtila* 22:16
13. desc. of *Balāṭu* 136:2; 152:8
14. ^{h}*nuḫatimmu*, desc. of *Balāṭu* 134:9; 138:14
15. ^{h}*nuḫatimmu*, desc. of *Gimillu* 138:3
16. f. of *Bēl-aḫḫē-erība*, desc. of *Kurî* 98:13
17. anc. of *Balāṭu* 138:8
18. anc. of *Innin-šum-ibni* 225:11

Nabû-bullissu (^{d}NÀ-<*bul*>-*liṭ-su*)
1. anc. of *Nabû-aḫḫē-iddin* and *Ina-tēšî-ēṭir* 10:15

Nabû-būnu-šūtur (^{d}NÀ-*bu-un-šu-tur*)
1. f. of *Nabû-bāni-aḫi*, desc. of *Rīšū'a* 21:16

Nabû-dannu (or *-mudammiq*) (^{d}NÀ-KAL)
1. 135:6
2. f. of *Nabû-uballiṭ*, desc. of x-x-x-x 25:5

Nabû-dayānu (^{d}NÀ-*da-a-a-nu*)
1. 211:6

Nabû-dīn-epuš (^{d}NÀ-DI.KUD-DÙ-*uš*)
1. f. of *Nabû-aḫ-ēreš* 51:7

Nabû-ēreš (^{d}NÀ-APIN-*eš*; ^{d}NÀ-KAM)
1. son of *Zēr-Bābili*, desc. of *Ea-ilūtu-bani* 21:13; 62:2,8,10; 77:2,7

Nabû-ēṭir (^{d}NÀ-KAR-*ir*; ^{d}NÀ-SUR)
1. 144:2,3
2. 194:3
3. 213:35,56,61
4. 239:10
5. son of *Aplâ* 288:5

6. son of *Mušallim-Marduk*, desc. of *Gimil-Nanaya* 30:7
7. desc. of *Aplâ* 136:5; 148:4; 151:3; 213:66
8. ^{h}*nuḫatimmu*, desc. of *Aplâ* 134:12; 137:7; 156:6
9. f. of *Aplâ* 87:12
10. f. of *Marduk-šum-ibni*, desc. of ^{h}*atkuppu* 313:2
11. f. of *Nabû-kēšir* 4:19
12. f. of *Ṣillâ*, desc. of [...] 3:36
13. anc. of [...] and *Nanaya-aḫ-iddin* 296:4
14. anc. of *Ṣillâ* and *Balāssu* 113:15

Nabû-ēṭir-[...] (^{d}NÀ-SUR-[...])
1. ^{h}*nuḫatimmu* 156:19,20

Nabû-ēṭir-napšāti (^{d}NÀ-KAR-ZI.MEŠ; ^{d}NÀ-SUR-ZI.MEŠ; ^{d}NÀ-SUR-ZI.ME; ^{d}NÀ-SUR-ZI)
1. 248:2
2. ^{h}*nuḫatimmu* 138:30; 156:16
3. son of *Arad-Bēl*, desc. of *Egibi* 66:18; 95:1; 99:22
4. son of *Balāssu*, desc. of *Būṣâ* 26:9
5. son of *Bēl-iqīša*, desc. of *Bēl-aplu-uṣur* 98:14
6. son of *Nabû-kāṣir*, desc. of *Arkât-ili-damqā* 21:2,6,8,19
7. son of *Nabû-šum-ukīn*, desc. of ^{h}*rab-banî* 100:26
8. ^{h}*nuḫatimmu*, desc. of *Arad-Bēl* 138:20,28
9. desc. of *Bēl-iqīša* 234:5
10. f. of *Mušallim-Marduk*, desc. of *Šigû'a* 1:8,23

Nabû-gāmil (^{d}NÀ-*ga-mil*)
1. son of *Ṭābiya*, desc. of ^{h}*ašlāku* 62:13
2. f. of *Anu-aḫ-iddin* 24:3
3. f. of *Bēl-šum-iškun* 259:4

*Nabû-ḫi-ri-*x (^{d}PA-*ḫi-ri-*x)
1. son of *Riḫamâ* 67:10

Nabû-iddin (^{d}NÀ-MU; ^{d}NÀ-SUM.NA)
1. 153:12
2. son of *Balāṭu*, desc. of ^{h}*rē'i sisi* 45:10
3. son of MU[...] 40:6
4. f. of *Ili-bani* 90:1
5. f. of *Nabû-mukīn-apli*, desc. of ^{h}*nappāḫu* 79:12

Nabû-ikṣur (^{d}NÀ-*ik-ṣur*)
1. son of *Nergal-šum-ibni* 226:2
2. f. of *Rīmūt-Bēl* 52:8

Nabû-īpuš (^{d}NÀ-DÙ-*uš*)
1. anc. of *Ištar-šum-ēreš* and *Ina-ṣilli-Eanna* 118:12; 297:15

Nabû-išdi (^{d}NÀ-*iš-di*)[31]
1. son of *Batâ* 36:11

Nabû-ittannu (^{d}NÀ-*it-tan-na*; ^{d}NÀ-*it-tan-ni*)
1. son of *Bēl-aḫḫē-iqīša*, desc. of *Arrab* 47:15
2. son of *Bunnanu*, desc. of ^{h}*atkuppu* 77:4
3. son of *Murašû*, desc. of ^{h}*išparu* 77:12

Nabû-kāṣir (^{d}NÀ-KÁD; ^{d}NÀ-*ka-ṣir*)
1. 153:12
2. 299:10
3. son of *Bēl-zēr-ukīn*, desc. of *Ḫuṣāb* 102:16
4. son of *Itti-Šamaš-balāṭu*, desc. of *Nabunnayu* 102:17
5. f. of *Aḫ-iddin* 84:4; 132:15
6. f. of *Bēl-ēreš* 46:10
7. f. of *Nabû-bēlšunu*, desc. of ^{h}*šangû bīt Bābili* 46:11
8. f. of *Nabû-ēṭir-napšāti*, desc. of *Arkât-ili-damqā* 21:2
9. f. of *Nādin* 58:2
10. f. of *Ṣillâ*, desc. of *Balāṭu* 88:12

Nabû-kēšir (^{d}NÀ-*ke-šìr*)
1. ^{h}*nappāḫ parzilli* 160:5
2. son of *Nabû-ēṭir* 4:19
3. son of *Šum-ukīn* 90:4
4. desc. of *Bulṭâ* 266:35
5. anc. of *Bēl-uballiṭ* 134:7; 138:24

Nabû-kibsu-šarri-[*uṣur*] (^{d}NÀ-*kib-su-*LUGAL-[ÙRI])
1. f. of *Šamaš-uballiṭ* 41:5

Nabû-kudurru-uṣur (^{d}NÀ-NÍG.DU-ÙRI)
1. *šar Bābili* 91:24; 100:5

31. Perhaps to be interpreted as *Nabû-milki* (^{d}NÀ-*mil-ki*!). The sign DI is partly damaged and could also be KI.

Nabû-lē'î (^{d}NÀ-DA)
1. 303:6
2. 305:4
3. 306:5
4. desc. of *Ilšu-abušu* 300:7
5. f. of *Gimil-Šamaš*, desc. of *Sîn-lēqi-unninni* 2:40

Nabû-līp-uṣur (^{d}NÀ-NUNUZ-ÙRI)
1. f. of x-*Marduk*, desc. of ^{h}*nāš patri* 25:13

Nabû-ME?-x (^{d}NÀ-ME?-x)
1. son of *Nabû*-NIM[...]AN[...], desc. of ^{h}*paḫāru* 96:13

Nabû-milki (see *Nabû-išdi*)

Nabû-mīt-uballiṭ (^{d}NÀ-ÚŠ-TIN-*iṭ*)
1. *ša rēši* 288:9
2. son of *Šum-iddin*, desc. of ^{h}*šangû Ištar Bābili* 54:16

Nabû-MU-[...] (^{d}NÀ-MU-[...])
1. 213:50
2. son of [...], desc. of [...]-*Papsukkal* 26:4

Nabû-mudammiq (see *Nabû-dannu*)

Nabû-mukīn-apli (^{d}NÀ-DU-*ap-lu*; ^{d}NÀ-DU-A; ^{d}NÀ-DU-ENDURU; ^{d}NÀ-DU-IBILA)
1. 284:20
2. 310:8
3. son of [...]-*erība* 86:6
4. son of *Arad-Bēl*, desc. of *Kurû* 6:6
5. ^{h}*ṭupšarru*, son of *Aššur-ēreš*, desc. of ^{h}*rē'i alpi* 53:16
6. son of *Bēl-īpuš*, desc. of *Kurî* 82:3',10'
7. son of *Kabtiya*, desc. of ^{h}*bā'iru* 4:13'
8. son of *Nabû-iddin*, desc. of ^{h}*nappāḫu* 79:11
9. ^{h}*ṭupšarru*, son of *Nabû-šumu-līšir*, desc. of *Arkât-ili-damqā* 102:18
10. son of *Nādin*, desc. of *Dābibi* 1:40
11. son of *Nergal-ina-tēšî-ēṭir* 90:3
12. ^{h}*ṭupšarru*, son of *Pir'u*, desc. of *Miṣirayu* 70:18
13. son of *Šamaš-aḫ-iddin*, desc. of *Sîn-karāb-išme* 43:10
14. son of *Zēr-Bābili*, desc. of *Iddin-Papsukkal* 62:15
15. desc. of *Eanna-līp-uṣur* 266:29
16. f. of *Bēl-aplu-iddin*, desc. of *Rīmūt-Ea* 4:12'
17. f. of *Ḫašdâ* 28:14
18. anc. of *Šamaš-zēr-ibni* 115:8

Nabû-mukīn-zēri (^{d}NA-DU-NUMUN)
1. ^{h}*šatammu Eanna*, son of *Nādin*, desc. of *Dābibi* 11:10; 12:11
2. son of [...], desc. of ^{h}*rē'i sisi* 72:11
3. son of *Ṣillâ* 60:10
4. f. of *Šumâ*, desc. of *Ilūtu-bani* 79:13

Nabû-mušētiq-ūdi (^{d}NÀ-*mu-še-tíq-u*$_{4}$-*da*; ^{d}NÀ-*mu-še-ti-iq-u*$_{4}$-*da*; ^{d}NÀ-*mu*-DIB-*u*$_{4}$-*da*; ^{d}NÀ-DIB-*u*$_{4}$-*da*)[32]
1. 84:7
2. 237:5
3. ^{h}*nuḫatimmu* 156:11
4. son of *Balāssu* 215:3
5. son of *Balāssu*, desc. of *Damiq* 2:15,22
6. son of *Bēl-lē'î*, desc. of *Ili-bani* 5:32
7. son of *Marduk-šum-ibni*, desc. of *Babūtu* 6:12
8. son of *Šākin-šumi* 168:2
9. son of *Umāšu* 91:20,32,33
10. desc. of *Šākin-šumi* 133:15; 213:63,77
11. f. of *Imbiya*, desc. of *Bannâ*? 15:10
12. f. of *Itti-Nabû-balāṭu*, desc. of *Ili-bani* 88:4
13. f. of *Itti-Nabû-balāṭu*, desc. of *Ilūtu!-bani* 5:29
14. f. of *Nabû-ušallim*, desc. of *Arkât-ili-damqā* 77:14
15. anc. of *Ištar-aḫ-iddin* 172:10; 290:5
16. anc. of *Nanaya-iddin* 193:5

Nabû?-na-[...] (^{d}NÀ?-*na*-[...])
1. f. of *Šamaš-bāni-aḫi* 155:6

32. On the reading of this name, see R. Caplice, "Akkadian Ud(d)û," in *Studies Presented to A. Leo Oppenheim* (Chicago, 1964), 62–66.

Nabû-nādin-aḫi (^{d}NÀ-*na-din*-ŠEŠ; ^{d}NÀ-SUM.NA-ŠEŠ)
1. son of *Ayaḫu* 84:1
2. ^{h}*ṭupšarru*, son of *Šulâ*, desc. of *Ea-ilūtu-bani* 5:34; 60:11

Nabû-nādin-šumi (^{d}NÀ-*na-din*-MU)
1. 190:8
2. 193:3
3. son of *Nabû-balāssu-iqbi* 13:4
4. ^{h}*šangû ša bīt Nergal*, son of *Nabû-balāssu-iqbi* 14:3,5
5. f. of *Ṭābiya*, desc. of *Ḫunzû* 1:10; 2:7; 83:14
6. anc. of *Nabû-aplu-iddin* 97:5

Nabû-na'id (^{d}NÀ-I; ^{d}NÀ-NÍ.TUK; ^{d}NÀ-*na-'i-id*)
1. *šar Bābili* 101:2; 113:5; *passim* in date formulas
2. f. of *Nergal-ašarīd*, desc. of *Arkât-ili-damqā* 43:3
3. anc. of *Arad-Innin* 281:7; 284:7

Nabû-nāṣir (^{d}NÀ-*na-ṣir*; ^{d}NÀ-PAP)
1. 284:10
2. ^{h}*ṣābu* 111:24
3. son of *Nabû-zēru-līšir* 76:5
4. desc. of *Nādin* 235:7
5. f. of *Bāniya* 20:15
6. f. of *Bāniya*, desc. of *Nabû-*[...]*-ilī* 66:3
7. f. of *Šullum* 31:3
8. anc. of *Bāniya* 213:13
9. anc. of *Nabû-zēru-līšir* 220:4

Nabû-nāṣir-apli (^{d}NÀ-PAP-A)
1. f. of *Bāniya*, brother of *Ina-Esagil-bēlet* 91:19,31

Nabû-natan (^{d}NÀ-*na-tan*)
1. son of *Šarranu* 91:11

Nabû-NIM-[...]-AN-[...] (^{d}NÀ-NIM-[...]-AN-[...])
1. f. of *Nabû*-ME?-x, desc. of ^{h}*paḫāru* 96:13

Nabû-PAP-[...] (^{d}NÀ-PAP-[...])
1. 214:5

Nabû-rīmanni (^{d}NÀ-*ri-man-ni*; ^{d}NÀ-*ri-man*^{an}*-ni*)
1. son of *Nādin* 3:35
2. f. of *Nabû-bāni-aḫi*, desc. of *ša* ^{h}*ṭābātišu* 35:3

Nabû-rēṣū'a (^{d}NÀ-*re-ṣu-ú-a*)
1. ^{h}*mār šipri* 84:6

Nabû-rē'ûšunu (^{d}NÀ-SIPA-*šú-nu*)
1. son of *Nādin*, desc. of *Eppeš-ilī* 3:8,15,23,40

Nabû-silim (^{d}NÀ-*si-lim*)
1. anc. of [...]-A 238:14
2. anc. of *Kalbâ* 115:3

Nabû-ṣābit-qātē (^{d}NÀ-*ṣa-bit*-ŠU.[MIN])
1. ^{h}*rab bīti* 287:7

Nabû-šar-aḫḫēšu (^{d}NÀ-LUGAL-ŠEŠ.MEŠ-*šú*; ^{d}NÀ-LUGAL-ŠEŠ.ME-*šú*)
1. son of *Ea-taqbi-līšir* 12:3
2. anc. of *Šum-uṣur* 297:5

Nabû-šarḫi-ilī (^{d}NÀ-*šar-ḫi*-DINGIR)
1. ^{h}*ikkaru*, son of *Nergal-ina-tēšî-ēṭir* 69:2

Nabû-šar-uṣur (^{d}NÀ-LUGAL-ÙRI)
1. 95:12
2. 205:6
3. 227:2
4. 238:11
5. 239:7
6. 273:2
7. 289:5
8. *ša rēš šarri*/*ša rēš šarri* ^{h}*bēl piqitti Eanna* 20:11; 66:4,6,12; 83:6; 91:12; 99:17; 103:2; 104:2; 105:2; 113:11; 132:7
9. son of *Nanaya-ēreš* 40:1
10. f. of *Saggil-šar-uṣur* 84:3

Nabû-šum-ibni (^{d}NÀ-MU-DÙ)
1. son of *Nabû-šum-iddin*, desc. of ^{h}*da*-x-x 8:10
2. son of *Nādin*, desc. of *Ilūtu-bani* 79:5
3. ^{h}*ṭupšarru*, son of *Rīmūt*, desc. of *Egibi* 69:16
4. f. of *Bēl-kēšir*, desc. of ^{h}*gallābu* 88:14
5. f. of *Libluṭ*, desc. of ^{h}*gallābu* 26:12

Nabû-šum-iddin (^{d}NÀ-MU-MU)
1. son of *Mār-bīti-ušabši*, desc. of ^{h}*nagāru* 76:15
2. son of *Rīmūt-Gula*, desc. of *Mannu-gīrû* 72:3
3. f. of *Bāniya* 40:14

4. f. of *Gimillu*, desc. of *Ea-ilūtu-bani* 98:11
5. f. of *Kidinnu* 53:7
6. f. of *Nabû-aplu-iddin*, desc. of *Esagil-mansum* 60:5
7. f. of *Nabû-šum-ibni*, desc. of h*da*-x-x 8:11
8. f. of *Nādin*, desc. of PA-x 88:13
9. f. of *Nidintu* 44:21

Nabû-šum-imbi (dNÀ-MU-*im-bi*)
1. h*ṭupšarru*, son of *Taqīš-Gula*, desc. of *Ḫanbu* 100:22

Nabû-šum-iškun (dNÀ-MU-GAR-*un*)
1. 300:6
2. 303:4
3. son of *Bēl*-[...], desc. of *Irani* 3:33
4. h*ṭupšarru*, son of *Zēr-u*[*kīn*] 31:10
5. h*ṭupšarru*, desc. of h*rab-banî* 101:41
6. f. of *N*[*a*-...] 19:8
7. f. of *Nabû-aplu-iddin*, desc. of h*paḫāru* 5:4
8. f. of *Zēr-Bābili*, desc. of [*Ilūtu*]-*bani* 21:4

Nabû-šum-ukīn (dNÀ-MU-DU; dNÀ-MU-GI.NA)
1. h*dayānu*, desc. of *Irani* 101:38 + seal caption on Le.E.
2. son of *Šum-uṣur*, desc. of *Ili-bani* 5:12,20
3. f. of *Libluṭ* 68:1
4. f. of *Nabû-aḫḫē-ušallim*, desc. of h*šangû Ninurta* 91:8
5. f. of *Nabû-bēlšunu* 64:2
6. f. of *Nabû-ēṭir-napšāti*, desc. of h*rab-banî* 100:27
7. anc. of *Kidin-Marduk* 213:29

Nabû-šumu-līšir (dNÀ-MU-SI.SÁ; dNÀ-MU-GIŠ)
1. son of *Arad-Nabû*, desc. of *Ša-nāšišu* 252:3
2. son of *Bēl-aḫḫē-iqīša* 9:7,20
3. f. of *Nabû-mukīn-apli*, desc. of *Arkât-ili-damqā* 102:19
4. f. of *Rīmūt*, desc. of *Kurî* 1:14
5. f. of *Sîn-ēreš*, desc. of *Eppeš-ilī* 51:14; 65:14
6. anc. of *Rīmūt* 134:14; 138:13

Nabû?-šum-uṣur? (dNÀ?-MU-ÙRI?)
1. f. of *Ṣillâ* 97:2

Nabû-šum-uṣur (dNÀ-MU-ÙRI; dPA-MU-ÙRI)
1. son? of [...]-*iq* 47:21
2. son of *Bēl-aḫḫē-erība* 42:4
3. son of *Nādin-aḫi*, desc. of *Ili-bani* 60:3
4. f. of *Balāṭu* 87:6
5. f. of *Šamaš-zēr-ibni*, spouse of f*Innin-šarrat*, desc. of h*asû* 6:1

Nabû-šūzibanni (dNÀ-*šu-zib-an-ni*)
1. *ša rēš šarri* 30:6
2. f. of *Nabû-aḫ-uṣur* 44:17

Nabû-tabni-uṣur (dNÀ-*tab-ni*-ÙRI)
1. son of *Bēl-īpuš*, desc. of *Sîn-tabni* 100:14

Nabû-tāriṣ (dNÀ-LAL; dNÀ-*ta-ri-iṣ*)
1. son of *Nabû-bēl-šumāti* 98:4
2. desc. of *Nabû-bēl-šumāti* 143:6

Nabû-te-x-[...] (dNÀ-*te*-x-[...])
1. f. of [...*ṣ*]*ur* 81:12

Nabû-uballiṭ (dNÀ-TIN-*iṭ*)
1. anc. of *Nabû-aplu-iddin* 134:5
2. son of *Nabû-mudammiq/dannu*, desc. of x-x-x-x 25:5

Nabû-ú-da-la-x (dNÀ-*ú-da-la*-x)
1. f. of *Nergal-dannu* 312:7

Nabû-uṣuršu (dNÀ-*ú-ṣur-šú*; dNÀ-ÙRI-*šú*)
1. 159:3
2. h*ṣābu* 111:6
3. son of *Gula-zēr-ibni* 76:6
4. son of *Mušēzib-Bēl*, desc. of *Maštuk* 17:13

Nabû-ušabši (dNÀ-GÁL-*ši*)
1. f. of *Innin-šum-uṣur*, desc. of *Gimil-Nanaya* 132:12

Nabû-ušallim (dNÀ-GI)
1. 157:2
2. son of *Kudurru*, desc. of h*rē'i ginê* 56:3'
3. son of *Nabû-aḫḫē-uballiṭ* 228:4
4. h*ṭupšarru*, son of *Nabû-mušētiq-ūdi*, desc. of *Arkât-ili-damqā* 77:13
5. desc. of *Bēl-ēreš* 194:2
6. f. of *Šum-ukīn*, desc. of h*nappāḫu* 17:10
7. anc. of d[...]-*šá* 241:2
8. anc. of *Balāṭu* 192:4; 213:31

Nabû-utēr (dNÀ-GUR; dNÀ-*ú-ter-ra*; dNÀ-*ú-ter-ru*)
1. son of *Šamaš-zēr-ibni* 53:13
2. f. of *Nabû-aḫ-uṣur* 28:2; 32:2

Nabû-zēr-ibni (^{d}NÀ-NUMUN-DÙ; ^{d}NÀ-NUMUN-*ib-ní*)
1. 301:11
2. 302:11
3. 303:10
4. son of *Kalbâ*, desc. of *Rīmūt-Ea* 4:11'
5. son of [...]-*za-a*, desc. of *Uraš*-AN.AŠ.KUR 3:10

Nabû-zēr-iqīša (^{d}NÀ-NUMUN-BA-*šá*)
1. 281:2
2. f. of *Gimillu*, desc. of *Adad-rabi* 74:11
3. f. of *Rīmūt* 20:5

Nabû-zēr?-ukīn (^{d}NÀ-NUMUN?-DU)
1. desc. of *Libūr* 284:13

Nabû-zēr-ukīn (^{d}NÀ-NUMUN-DU)
1. 310:14
2. son of *Ṣillâ* 78:6
3. f. of *Šameš-bār* 67:2
4. f. of *Šamaš-šum-ukīn*, desc. of ^{h}*maḫḫû*, son of *Marduk-ēṭir* 100:1,7

Nabû-zēru-līšir (^{d}NÀ-NUMUN-GIŠ; ^{d}NÀ-NUMUN-SI.SÁ)
1. ^{h}*ṣābu* 111:37
2. son of *Arad-Marduk* 155:3
3. son of *Bēlšunu*, desc. of *Kurî* 92:5
4. desc. of *Ardiya* 294:5
5. desc. of *Nabû-nāṣir* 220:3
6. f. of *Nabû-nāṣir* 76:5
7. f. of *Zēr*[...], desc. of *Basiya* 43:14

Nabû-zēr-ušabši (^{d}NÀ-NUMUN-GÁL-*ši*)
1. desc. of *Ina-tēšî-ēṭir* 284:12
2. ^{h}*nuḫatimmu*, desc. of [*Ina*]-*tēšî-ēṭir* 134:8
3. f. of *Ina-Esagil-bēlet*, son of *Abi-ilu* 91:14,25

Nabû-zukkanni (^{d}NÀ-*zu-uk-an-ni*)
1. f. of *Ili-iddin* 23:15

Nabunnayu (*na-bu-un-na-a-a*)
1. anc. of *Nabû-kāṣir* and *Itti-Šamaš-balāṭu* 102:18

Nādin? (*na-*[*din?*])
1. son of *Bēl?-ēṭir?* 36:4

Nādin (*na-din*; *na-di-nu*)
1. 71:15
2. 133:16
3. 203:10
4. 213:65
5. ^{h}*ṭupšarru* 266:32
6. ^{h}*ṭupšarru*, son of ^{d}[...], desc. of *Egibi* 66:22
7. son of *Aplâ*, desc. of *Aḫiya'u* 95:3
8. ^{h}*šākin ṭēmi ša Uruk*, son of *Balāṭu* 92:13
9. son of *Balāṭu*, desc. of *Maštuk* 23:1,6,8
10. ^{h}*ṭupšarru*/^{h}*ṭupšarru ša Eanna*, son of *Bēl-aḫḫē-iqīša*, desc. of *Egibi* 1:42; 11:15; 51:18; 52:16; 65:17; 93:19; 95:2; 99:24; 114:15'
11. ^{h}*ṭupšarru*, son of *Bēl-ukīn*, desc. of *Sîn-lēqi-unninni* 67:4,7,13
12. son of *Lūṣi-ana-nūri-Marduk*, brother of *Širiktu*, desc. of *Ili-bani* 5:10,18; 43:4; 45:4; 47:4; 60:2; 72:2; 79:3; 88:1,10
13. son of *Nabû-kāṣir* 58:2
14. son of *Nabû-šum-iddin*, desc. of PA-x 88:13
15. desc. of [...] 135:12
16. desc. of [...] 224:8
17. desc. of *Aplâ* 213:34
18. ^{h}*nuḫatimmu*, desc. of *Aplâ* 134:6; 138:19; 156:13
19. desc. of *Bēl-aḫḫē-iqīša* 213:43; 234:15
20. ^{h}*nuḫatimmu*, desc. of *Gimillu* 138:12
21. desc. of *Nabû-aḫḫē-uballiṭ* 266:32
22. ^{h}*nuḫatimmu*, desc. of *Nabû-erība* 134:4
23. f. of [...]-*zu* 68:15
24. f. of *Bēl-erība*, desc. of *Nūr-Marduk* 233:4
25. f. of *Bēl-iddin* and *Rē'ītu*, desc. of *Maštuk* 17:4,7; 18:6; 252:5
26. f. of *E*[...] 84:10
27. f. of *Eanna-iddin* 132:13
28. f. of ^{f}*Ḫiptâ*, desc. of ^{h}*itinnu* 10:3
29. f. of *Kiribtu* 221:4
30. f. of *Kiribtu*, desc. of *Babūtu* 66:15
31. f. of *Līšir* 65:3
32. f. of *Nabû*-[...]-*šunu*, desc. of *Eppeš-ilī* 3:9
33. f. of *Nabû-bēlšunu* 54:19

34. f. of *Nabû-mukīn-apli*, desc. of *Dābibi* 1:40
35. f. of *Nabû-mukīn-zēri*, desc. of *Dābibi* 11:11; 12:12
36. f. of *Nabû-rīmanni* 3:35
37. f. of *Nabû-šum-ibni*, desc. of *Ilūtu-bani* 79:6
38. f. of *Šamaš-iddin* 70:3
39. f. of ^{f}*Ṭābatu*, desc. of *Aššur* 3:10,17
40. anc. of *Bazuzu* 115:27
41. anc. of *Bēl-ibni* 143:2
42. anc. of *Kiribtu* 213:47
43. anc. of *Nabû-nāṣir* 235:7

Nādin-aḫi (SUM.NA-ŠEŠ)[33]
1. ^{h}*qīpu ša Ebabbar* 55:6
2. son of *Iqīšâ*, desc. of ^{h}*Isinayu* 4:15'
3. desc. of *Kudurru* 160:7
4. f. of *Itti-Šamaš-balāṭu* 24:15
5. f. of *Kudurranu* 44:19
6. f. of *Nabû-šum-uṣur*, desc. of *Ili-bani* 60:4

Nādin-apli (see *Iddinâ* and *Šumâ*)

Nādin-šumi (see *Šum-iddin*)

Nādnâ (*nad-na-a*; see also *Iddinâ* and *Šumâ*)
1. 75:8
2. anc. of *Na'id-Ištar* 115:27

^{h}*nagāru* (^{lú}NAGAR)
1. anc. of *Nabû-šum-iddin* and *Mār-bīti-ušabši* 76:16
2. anc. of *Rēḫu-Nabû* and *Nabû-balāssu-iqbi* 5:32

Na'id-Bēl (I-^{d}EN)
1. f. of [...], ^{h}*dēkû ša* ^{h}*širāku ša Bēlti-ša-Uruk* 93:8

Na'id-Ištar (I-^{d}INNIN; I-^{d}15; I-^{d}*iš-tar*)
1. 73:6
2. son of *Rīmūt* 132:16
3. desc. of *Nādnâ* 115:27

Na'id-Marduk (I-^{d}AMAR.UD)
1. f. of *Rīmūt* 78:14

Nali (*na-li*)
1. anc. of *Marduk-ēṭir* and *Zēriya* 4:25

Nanaya-[...] (^{d}*na-na-a-*[...])
1. 32:4
2. 51:2
3. 266:41
4. ^{h}*ṭupšarru*, son of *Nanaya-*[...] 155:7
5. f. of *Nanaya-*[...] 155:8
6. anc. of *Nergal-šum-ibni* 266:39

Nanaya-aḫ-iddin (^{d}*na-na-a-*ŠEŠ-MU)
1. ^{h}*ṣābu*, ^{h}*musaḫḫiru* 111:18
2. ^{h}*išpar birmu*, son of *Nanaya-iddin*, brother of *Innin-zēr-ušabši* 115:5
3. desc. of *Ištar-rēṣū'a* 115:28
4. ^{h}*mār šipri*, desc. of *Nergal-uballiṭ* 262:3
5. f. of [...], desc. of *Nabû-ēṭir* 296:4
6. f. of *Gimillu* 132:18
7. f. of *Ibnâ* 49:5
8. f. of *Ina-tēšî-ēṭir* 63:5
9. f. of *Nūrea*, desc. of *Sūḫayu* 74:12
10. anc. of *Innin-šum-uṣur* 133:12
11. anc. of *Zēriya* 238:10

^{f}*Nanaya-bēl-bīti* (^{f} ^{d}*na-na-a-*EN-É)
1. daughter of *Nanaya-īpuš*, wife of *Rīmūt-Bēl*, mother of *Ištar-aḫ-iddin* 100:20

Nanaya-ēreš (^{d}*na-na-a-*APIN-*eš*; ^{d}*na-na-a-*KAM)
1. 295:12
2. son? of *Izanapartiana* 71:1
3. f. of [...] 93:7
4. f. of *Nabû-aḫḫē-uballiṭ* 68:13
5. f. of *Nabû-šar-uṣur* 40:2
6. f. of *Sîn-ibni* 90:6,10,15
7. anc. of ^{d}[...] 236:3
8. anc. of *Innin-šum-uṣur* 207:5

Nanaya-ibni (^{d}*na-na-a-*DÙ)
1. f. of x-x-x 56:4'
2. f. of *Arrab* 52:4
3. f. of *Nergal-nāṣir* 30:3; 63:9; 169:3

Nanaya-iddin (^{d}*na-na-a-*MU)
1. 125:2

33. This is preferable to the reading *Iddin(a)-aḫi*. The name is probably a shortened form of various theophoric names of the type <DN-*nādin-aḫi*>.

34. The reading of ˡᵘGÍR.LÁ as a professional name in the Neo-Babylonian period is ʰ*ṭābiḫu*. As an ancestral name, however, it should probably be read ʰ*nāš patri*.

Ninurta-ēṭir (^{d}MAŠ-SUR)
1. son of *Nergal-iddin* 38:8

Ninurta-nādin-šumi ($^{[d]}$MAŠ-*na-din*-MU)
1. desc. of ^{d}x-*aḫḫē-iddin* 80:9

Ninurta-šar-uṣur (^{d}MAŠ-LUGAL-ÙRI)
1. son of *Ekur-zākir* 16:4

Niqūdu (*ni-qu-du*)
1. son of *Etušgina-ibni*, desc. of *Šamaš*-BA-[...] 99:1,4,12,16
2. son of *Rīmūt-Gula*, desc. of *Uraš*-AN.AŠ.KUR 3:5

Nūḫâ (*nu-ḫa-a*)
1. a slave 263:1

Nuḫḫu-Anu (*nu-uḫ-ḫu-*^{d}*a-num*)
1. a slave 102:1,8,10,14

Nuḫ-ḫūd-libbi-ilī (*nu-uḫ-ḫu-ud*-ŠÀ-DINGIR.MEŠ)
1. son of *Kidinnâ* 16:7

Nunua (*nu-nu-a*)
1. 189:3

^{f}*Nūptâ* (^{f}*nu-up-ta-a*)
1. daughter of *Kalbâ*, desc. of *Maštuk* 17:2
2. daughter of *Sîn-ibni* 98:2,6

Nūr-^{d}[...] (ZÁLAG-^{d}[...])
1. anc. of *Etellu* 300:8

Nūrea (ZÁLAG-*e-a*)
1. 256:4
2. ^{h}*agru* 297:1
3. ^{h}*ṣābu* 111:4
4. ^{h}*ṣābu*, ^{h}*ummânu* 111:10
5. son of *Balāṭu*, desc. of *Iddin-Papsukkal* 65:19
6. son of *Gimillu*, desc. of ^{h}*išparu* 74:4
7. son of *Nanaya-aḫ-iddin*, desc. of *Sūḫayu* 74:12
8. son of *Nergal-iddin*, desc. of *Ḫunzû* 24:12
9. desc. of *Anu-aḫ-iddin* 213:70
10. desc. of *Gaḫal* 232:8
11. f. of [...] 84:11

Nūr-Marduk (ZÁLAG-^{d}ŠÚ)
1. anc. of *Bēl-erība* and *Nādin* 233:4

Nūr-Papsukkal (ZÁLAG-^{d}*pap-sukkal*)
1. 307:4
2. anc. of [...]-KI and *Ṣillâ* 26:8
3. anc. of *Arad-Bēl* and *Mušēzib-*^{d}[...] 21:13
4. anc. of *Balāṭu* and *Bēl-iqīša* 62:4
5. anc. of *Bāniya* 300:9

Nūr-Sîn (ZÁLAG-^{d}30)
1. son of *Nabû-bāni-aḫi*, desc. of *Nūr-Sîn* 64:14
2. anc. of *Bēl-aḫḫē-iddin* 101:39
3. anc. of *Bēl-aḫḫē-iddin* and *Marduk-zēr-ibni* 3:32
4. anc. of *Nūr-Sîn* and *Nabû-bāni-aḫi* 64:15

Nūru (*nu-ru*)
1. anc. of *Kid*[...] and *Bēl-aḫḫē-iddin* 252:12

Nusku-šar-ibni (^{d}NUSKU-LUGAL-DÙ)
1. *ša rēš šarri* 4:15,21

Nusku-šar-u[*ṣur*] (^{d}NUSKU-LUGAL-Ù[RI])
1. son of *Ḫašdiya* 9:12

Nusku-šūzibanni (^{d}NUSKU-*šu-zib-an-ni*)
1. son of *Raḫimmâ* 90:2

PA-x
1. anc. of *Nādin* and *Nabû-šum-iddin* 88:13

Padâ (*pa-da-a*)
1. son of *Nabû-aḫḫē-uballiṭ*, desc. of ^{h}*šangû* ^{d}[...] 88:5,11

^{h}*paḫāru* (^{lú}BÁḪAR)
1. anc. of *Ina-ṣilli-Zababa* and *Esagil-mukīn-apli* 29:3
2. anc. of *Nabû-aplu-iddin* 89:13
3. anc. of *Nabû-aplu-iddin* and *Nabû-šum-iškun* 5:5
4. anc. of *Nabû*-ME?-x and *Nabû*-NIM[...]AN[...] 96:14

Pāliḫ (*pa-li-iḫ*)
1. ^{h}*ṣābu* 111:26

Palil-bēl-uṣur: see *Nergal-bēl-uṣur*

Pir'u (*pir-'u*)
1. son of [...], desc. of [...] 69:13
2. son of x-x-A, desc. of *Dannê* 46:3
3. son of *Kīnâ*, desc. of ^{h}x-x 47:13
4. son of *Nabû-balāssu-iqbi*, desc. of *Eppeš-ilī* 234:13
5. son of *Tabnea* 54:6,11

6. f. of *Nabû-mukīn-apli*, desc. of *Miṣirayu* 70:19

Puzur-Nabû (MAN-^{d}NÀ)

1. desc. of GAR[...] 135:10

Qīšat-Gula (NÍG.BA-^{d}*gu-la*)

1. f. of ^{d}x-[...] 70:16

Qīštiya (NĪG.BA-*iá*)

1. f. of *Gimillu*, desc. of *Rīmānu* 83:12

^{h}*rab-banî* (^{lú}GAL-DÙ; ^{lú}GAL-*ba-né-e*)

1. anc. of *Balāssu* and *Šāpik-zēri* 63:18
2. anc. of *Bāniya* and *Šamaš-šumu-līšir* 20:16
3. anc. of *Gimillu* and *Dummuq* 293:4
4. anc. of *Nabû-ēṭir-napšāti* and *Nabû-šum-ukīn* 100:27
5. anc. of *Nabû-šum-iškun* 101:41
6. anc. of *Šamaš*-[...], *Sîn-ili* and *Šāpik-zēri* 39:3

^{h}*rab tarbaṣu* (^{lú}GAL *tar-ba-ṣu*)

1. anc. of *Šamaš-dannu* and *Šāpik-zēri* 59:2

Raḫimmâ (*ra-ḫi-im-ma-a'*)

1. f. of *Nusku-šūzibanni* 90:2

Rēḫu-Nabû (*re-ḫu*-^{d}NÀ)[35]

1. son of *Nabû-balāssu-iqbi*, desc. of ^{h}*nagāru* 5:31

^{h}*rē'i alpi* (^{lú}SIPA GU$_{4}$)

1. anc. of *Arad-Bēl* and *Šamaš-iddin* 7:20
2. anc. of *Arad-Bēl* and *Šamaš-zēr*-[...] 41:3
3. anc. of *Balāṭu* and *Sîn-ibni* 1:46; 51:16; 93:20; 110:13; 114:12'
4. anc. of *Nabû-mukīn-apli* and *Aššur-ēreš* 53:17
5. anc. of *Šamaš*-[...] and *Bēl-ēṭir* 41:17
6. anc. of *Šamaš-šumu-līšir* and *Šākin-šumi* 7:18

^{h}*rē'i ginê* (^{lú}SIPA SA.DU$_{11}$)

1. anc. of *Nabû-ušallim* and *Kudurru* 56:3'
2. anc. of *Šūzubu* and *Kudurru* 11:13; 52:14; 114:14'

^{h}*rē'i sisi* (^{lú}SIPA ANŠE.KUR.RA)

1. anc. of *Na*[...] and ^{d}x-*šum-iddin* 72:13
2. anc. of *Nabû-iddin* and *Balāssu* 45:11
3. anc. of *Nabû-mukīn-zēri* and [...] 72:12

^{f}*rē'ītu* (^{f}*re-'i-i-tu*$_{4}$)

1. daughter of *Nādin* 17:2,6

^{h}*rē'û* (^{lú}SIPA-*ú*)

1. anc. of *Ardiya* and *Bēl aḫ iddin* 25:4

Riḫamâ (*ri-ḫa-ma-a'*)

1. f. of *Nabû-ḫi-ri*-x 67:11

Rīmanni-ilī (*ri-man-ni*-DINGIR.MEŠ)

1. son of ^{d}[...] 8:2

Rīmānu (*ri-ma-nu*)

1. anc. of *Gimillu* and *Qīštiya* 83:13

Rīmūt (*ri-mut*; *ri-mu-tu*)

1. 60:3
2. 96:4
3. 108:3
4. 125:3,9
5. 213:35,64
6. 239:7
7. 289:6
8. ^{h}*gaddāyu* 142:2
9. ^{h}*išparu* 270:16
10. ^{h}*musaḫḫiru* 225:13
11. ^{h}*nuḫatimmu* 137:3'
12. son of [...], desc. of *Nabû-aplu-uṣur* 57:10
13. ^{h}*ṭupšarru*, son of *Arad-Bēl*, desc. of *Dābibi* 48:12
14. son of *Marduk-šum-ibni*, desc. of *Kurî* 76:16
15. son of *Nabû*-[...] 296:12
16. son of *Nabû-aḫ-iddin* 50:3
17. son of *Nabû-šumu-līšir*, desc. of *Kurî* 1:13
18. son of *Nabû-zēr-iqīša* 20:5
19. son of *Na'id-Marduk* 78:14
20. son of *Šum-uṣur*, desc. of *Ili-bani* 89:9
21. ^{h}*širku*, brother of *Nargiya* and *Šamaš-kīnu*, desc. of ^{f}*Tappašri* 112:1
22. ^{h}*pūṣāyu*, desc.? of *Anu-šar-uṣur* 115:16
23. desc. of *Innin-zēr-ušabši* 160:8

35. Possibly an error for *Rīmūt-Nabû*.

24. ^{h}*nuḫatimmu*, desc. of *Nabû-šumu-līšir* 134:14; 138:13
25. desc. of *Nergal-dannu* 234:19
26. f. of *Nabû-bēl-šumāti*, desc. of *Ilūtu-bani* 58:9
27. f. of *Nabû-šum-ibni*, desc. of *Egibi* 69:16
28. f. of *Na'id-Ištar* 132:16
29. anc. of [...]-*šum-ukīn* 80:8
30. anc. of *Taqīš-Gula* 36:14

Rīmūt-Bēl (*ri-mut-*^{d}EN)
1. son of *Nabû-ikṣur* 52:8
2. spouse of ^{f}*Nanaya-bēl-bīti*, f. of *Ištar-aḫ-iddin*, desc. of ^{h}*maḫḫû* 100:8,10,21
3. ^{h}*nuḫatimmu*, desc. of *Nabû-*[...] 134:3

Rīmūt-Ea (*ri-mut-*^{d}*é-a*; *ri-mu-ut-*^{d}*é-a*; *ri-mut-*^{d}BE)
1. 4:29,6'
2. son of [...] 17:8
3. anc. of *Bēl-aplu-iddin* and *Nabû-mukīn-apli* 4:12'
4. anc. of *Nabû-zēr-ibni* and *Kalbâ* 4:11'
5. anc. of *Šamaš-zēr-iqīša* and [*Muš*]*ēzib-Bēl* 6:19

Rīmūt-Gula (*ri-mut-*^{d}*gu-la*; *ri-mut-*^{d}ME.ME)
1. son of *Ṣullê-Marduk*, desc. of *Ilūtu-bani* 77:10
2. f. of *Nabû-šum-iddin*, desc. of *Mannu-gīrû* 72:3
3. f. of *Niqūdu*, desc. of *Uraš*-AN.AŠ.KUR 3:5

Rīmūt-ili (*ri-mut-*DINGIR)
1. son of *Itti-Marduk-balāṭu* 42:18

Rīmūt-Nabû (*ri-mut-*^{d}NÀ) (see also *Rēḫu-Nabû*)
1. son of ^{d}[...], desc. of [...] 45:12

Rīšū'a (SUD-*ú-a*)
1. anc. of *Nabû-bāni-aḫi* and *Nabû-būnu-šūtur* 21:17
2. anc. of *Ṣillâ* 102:5

Saggil-šar-uṣur (*sag-gil-*LUGAL-ÙRI)
1. son of *Nabû-šar-uṣur* 84:3

Silim-Bēl (*si-lim-*^{d}EN)
1. ^{h}*nappāḫu* 135:23
2. son of *Bēl-zēri*, desc. of *Basiya* 6:17; 85:10
3. ^{h}*ṭupšarru*, son of *E*-x, desc. of *Kidin-Sîn* 29:3"
4. son of *Kudurru*, desc. of *Dābibi* 48:9
5. f. of *Ardiya*, desc. of ^{h}*atû* 94:18
6. f. of *Bēl-aḫḫē-iqīša* 54:12
7. f. of *Šamaš-zēr-iddin* 311:16
8. f. of *Šamaš-zēr-ušabši* 85:6,14; 90:19
9. f. of *Ṭābiya* 215:6
10. f. of *Uballissu-Gula*, desc. of ^{h}*šangû parakki* 69:14

Silim-ili (*si-lim-*DINGIR)
1. *ša rēš šarri ša muḫḫi quppi ša šarri* 93:16
2. f. of ^{d}x-x 39:16

Sîn?-x-x (^{d}30?-x-x)
1. son of x-x-*lat-ta-qu* 67:11

Sîn-bani (^{d}30-*ba-ni*)
1. f. of *Bēl-aḫ-ušabši* 42:18

Sîn-damāqu (^{d}30-*da-ma-qu*)
1. anc. of *Kurbanni-Marduk* and *Zēriya* 1:31; 52:11; 92:15; 93:3; 110:2

Sîn-ēreš (^{d}30-KAM)
1. 206:2
2. 266:32
3. son of *Nabû-šumu-līšir*, desc. of *Eppeš-ilī* 51:13; 65:14

Sîn-erība (^{d}30-SU)
1. ^{h}*ṭupšarru*, son of *Šamaš-zēru-līšir*, desc. of *Kurî* 74:13

Sîn-ibni (^{d}30-DÙ)
1. 135:29
2. ^{h}*rē'*[*û*], son of *Nanaya-ēreš* 90:5,10,14
3. son of *Bāniya*, f.? of *Balāṭu* 266:36
4. f. of *Balāṭu*, desc. of ^{h}*rē'i alpi* 1:46; 51:16; 93:20; 110:13; 114:12'
5. f. of ^{f}*Nūptâ* 98:3

Sîn-ili (^{d}30-DINGIR)
1. son of *Šāpik-zēri*, desc. of ^{h}*rab-banî* 39:2

Sîn-karāb-išme (^{d}30-SISKUR-ŠE.GA)
1. anc. of *Nabû-mukīn-apli* and *Šamaš-aḫ-iddin* 43:11

Sîn-kēšir (^{d}30-*ke-šìr*)
1. son of *Bāniya*, desc. of ^{h}*nappāḫu* 17:10

Sîn-lēqi-unninni (^{d}30-TI-ÉR)
1. anc. of *Gimillu-Šamaš* and *Nabû-lēʾi* 2:41
2. anc. of *Innin-zēr-ušabši* and *Aplâ* 66:20
3. anc. of *Nabû-bāni-aḫi* and *Nabû-bālassu-iqbi* 13:12; 97:16
4. anc. of *Nādin* and *Bēl-ukīn* 67:4,14
5. anc. of *Nergal-*[...] and *Šākin-šumi* 91:7
6. anc. of *Nergal-dannu* and *Mukīn-zēri* 67:3
7. anc. of *Šum-iddin* and *Nergal-dannu*? 97:14

Sîn-nādin-aḫi (^{d}30-*na-din*-ŠEŠ)
1. ^{h}*šangû Uri* 254:2

Sîn-nāṣir (^{d}30-PAP)
1. f. of *Nergal-iddin*, desc. of *Arrabtu* 95:4

Sîn-šar-ilī (^{d}30-LUGAL-DINGIR.ME)
1. anc. of *Nabû-bāni-zēri* and *Nabû-aḫ-*[...] 313:3'

Sîn-šum-ušabši (^{d}30-MU-TIL)
1. 82:10'

Sîn-tabni (^{d}30-*tab-ni*)
1. anc. of *Bēl-*[...]*ir* 101:40
2. anc. of *Bēl-iqīša* 101:42
3. anc. of *Nabû-bēl-šumāti* and *Zēr-Bābili* 100:17
4. anc. of *Nabû-tabni-uṣur* and *Bēl-īpuš* 100:15
5. anc. of *Šamaš-erība* and *Nergal-iddin* 91:9; 100:16

Sîn-zēr-ibni (^{d}30-NUMUN-DÙ)
1. ^{h}*ṣābu*, ^{h}*agru* 111:29

Sîn-zēr-ušabši (^{d}30-NUMUN-GÁL-*ši*)
1. f. of *Ḫašdayu* 250:8

Siyatu (*si-a-ti*)
1. anc. of *Marduk-ēreš* and *Šamaš-šum-ukīn* 62:18

Sūḫayu (*su-ḫa-a-a*)
1. anc. of *Marduk-aplu-uṣur* and *Zēriya* 57:13
2. anc. of *Nūrea* and *Nanaya-aḫ-iddin* 74:13

Suppû? (*su-pi*)
1. 135:7

Sūqayu (SILA-*a-a*; *su-qa-a-a*)
1. 150:14
2. 295:7,8
3. ^{h}*nuḫatimmu* 138:31
4. son of *Itti-Šamaš-balāṭu* 27:14
5. desc. of *Līšir* 80:10

Śagib-il (*ta*$_{5}$-*gi-bi-il*)[36]
1. f. of *Bēl-ēṭir* 91:11

Śameš-bār (*ta*$_{5}$-*meš-ba-ar*)[37]
1. son of *Nabû-zēr-ukīn* 67:1,8

^{h}*ṣāḫit-ginê* (^{lú}Ì.SUR-*gi-né-e*; ^{lú}SUR-*gi-né-e*)
1. anc. of x-*ti-ti* and *Kidin-Marduk* 23:13
2. anc. of *Balāṭu* and *Iqīšâ* 23:16
3. anc. of *Mušēzib-Bēl* and *Kīnâ* 54:18

Ṣi-[...]
1. 25:11

Ṣillâ (*ṣil-la-a*)
1. 87:8
2. ^{h}*išparu* 274:3
3. son of *Amēl-Nanaya* 83:5
4. son of *Aplâ* 311:14
5. son of *Balāssu*, desc. of *Nabû-ēṭir* 113:14
6. son of *Nabû-ēṭir*, desc. of [...] 3:36
7. son of *Nabû-kāṣir*, desc. of *Balāṭu* 88:12
8. son of *Nabû*?-*šum-uṣur*? 97:2
9. desc. of *Rīšūʾa* 102:5
10. f. of [...]-KI, desc. of *Nūr-Papsukkal* 26:8
11. f. of *Arad-Bēl* 206:3
12. f. of *Bēl-kāṣir*, desc. of *Bēl-ēṭir* 110:3
13. f. of *Nabû-mukīn-zēri* 60:10
14. f. of *Nabû-zēr-ukīn* 78:7
15. anc. of *Arad-Bēl* 213:85

Ṣullê-Marduk (*ṣu-le-e*-^{d}ŠÚ)
1. f. of *Rīmūt-Gula*, desc. of *Ilūtu-bani* 77:11

36. On this name, see R. Zadok, *On West Semites in Babylonia During the Chaldean and Achaemenian Periods: An Onomastic Study* (Jerusalem, 1977), 109k.

37. On this name, see F.M. Fales, "A Cuneiform Correspondence to Alphabetic Śin in West Semitic Names of the I Millennium B.C.," *Or*NS 47 (1978) 91–98.

^{f}*Ṣullê-tašme* (^{f}*ṣu-le-e-taš-me*)
1. a slave 42:9

Šaddinnu (*šad-din-nu*)
1. 301:2
2. 304:2

Šādidu (*šá-di-dì*)
1. f. of [...]-*balāssu-uṣur* 30:4

^{f}*Šaḫātu* (^{f}*šá-ḫa-tu*$_4$)
1. mother of *Arad-Mullišu* 22:13

Šākin-šumi (GAR-MU)
1. f. of *Nabû-mušētiq-ūdi* 168:3
2. f. of *Nergal*-[...], desc. of *Sîn-lēqi-unninni* 91:7
3. f. of *Šamaš-šumu-līšir*, desc. of ^{h}*rē'i alpi* 7:18
4. anc. of *Ardiya* 295:4'
5. anc. of *Gimillu* 197:3
6. anc. of *Nabû-mušētiq-ūdi* 133:16; 213:63,77

Šamaš-[...] (^{d}UTU-[...])
1. 39:7
2. 39:11
3. 150:11
4. 303:2
5. 304:1
6. son of *Ba'u-ēreš* 40:9
7. ^{h}*ṭupšarru*, son of *Bēl-ēṭir*, desc. of ^{h}*rē'i alpi* 41:16
8. son of *Šamaš-zēru-līšir* 81:14
9. son of *Šāpik-zēri*, desc. of ^{h}*rab-banî* 39:1
10. f. of ^{d}x[...]x-x[...] 78:17

Šamaš-ab-uṣur (^{d}UTU-AD-ÙRI)
1. 217:5

Šamaš-aḫḫē-erība (^{d}UTU-PAP.ME-SU)
1. ^{h}*ṭupšarru*, son of *Šamaš-mukīn-apli* 311:16

Šamaš?-aḫ?-iddin (^{d}UTU?-ŠEŠ?-MU)
1. 41:14

Šamaš-aḫ-iddin (^{d}UTU-ŠEŠ-MU)
1. ^{h}*rab kāri* 132:6
2. *ša rēši* 148:5
3. son of *Nergal-dannu* 56:1; 68:2,5; 73:2,8; 312:9
4. son of *Nergal-ušēzib* 7:21; 44:18
5. ^{h}*ṣābu*, son of *Tattan* 111:5
6. ^{h}*išpar birmu*, desc. of *Ina-ṣilli-Nergal* 115:6
7. f. of *Nabû-mukīn-apli*, desc. of *Sîn-karāb-išme* 43:11
8. f. of *Zēriya* 33:12

Šamaš-ana-bītišu (^{d}UTU-*ana*-É-*šú*)
1. son of *Amēl-Nabû* 65:2

Šamaš-aplu-uṣur (^{d}UTU-DIL-ÙRI; ^{d}UTU-A-PAP)
1. son of *Itti-Šamaš-balāṭu* 33:13
2. f. of *Nabû-bēlšunu*, desc. of ^{h}*šangû Enamtila* 22:16

Šamaš-BA-[...] (^{d}UTU-BA-[...])
1. anc. of *Niqūdu* and *Etušgina-ibni* 99:2

Šamaš-bāni-aḫi (^{d}UTU-DÙ-ŠEŠ)
1. son of *Ibni-Ištar*, brother of *Bazuzu* 166:5
2. son of *Nabû?-na*[...] 155:6
3. son of *Šamaš-zēr-ušabši* 27:4; 70:3,5

Šamaš-bāri (^{d}UTU-*ba-ri*; ^{d}UTU-*a-ba-ri*)
1. anc. of *Šamaš-erība* and *Bēl-ēṭir* 48:3; 49:14
2. anc. of *Šamaš-zēr-iddin* 53:15

Šamaš-dannu (^{d}UTU-KAL; ^{d}UTU-*dan-nu*)
1. 39:10
2. son of *Šāpik-zēri*, desc. of ^{h}*rab tarbaṣu* 59:1
3. anc. of *Bāniya* 240:2

Šamaš-ēreš (^{d}UTU-KAM)
1. desc. of *Ninurta-aḫ*-[...] 80:5

Šamaš-erība (^{d}UTU-SU)
1. 308:1
2. ^{h}*ṣābu* 111:25
3. ^{h}*ṭupšarru*, son of *Bēl-ēṭir*, desc. of *Šamaš-bāri* 48:2; 49:14
4. son of *Bēl-lē'î* 15:3
5. son of *Kî-Nabû* 53:10; 311:1,6,11
6. son of *Nergal-iddin*, desc. of *Sîn-tabni* 91:9; 100:15
7. f. of ^{f}*Šeṭua*, g.f. of *Innin-zēr-ušabši* 112:14
8. anc. of *Šamaš-zēr-ibni* 125:15

Šamaš-ēṭir (^{d}UTU-SUR)
1. ^{h}*išpar birmu*, desc. of ^{f}*zakītu* 115:4

Šamaš-ibni (^{d}UTU-DÙ)
1. ^{h}*naggāru* 286:1

^{f}*Šarruk*? (^{f}*šar-ruk*?)
1. ^{f}*zakītu*, anc. of *Gimillu* and *Nanaya-iddin* 112:5

Ša-^{h}*ṭābātišu* (*šá-*^{lú}MUN.ḪI.A-*šú*)
1. anc. of *Nabû-bāni-aḫi* and *Nabû-rīmanni* 35:4

Šēpē-Bēl-aṣbat (*še-pe-*^{d}EN-*aṣ-bat*)
1. anc. of *Eriš* 115:10

^{f}*Šeṭua* (^{f}*še-ṭu-a*)
1. daughter of *Šamaš-erība*, mother of *Innin-zēr-ušabši* 112:12

Ši-[...]
1. anc. of *Marduk*?[...] and *Gimillu* 64:13

Šigû'a (*ši-gu-ú-a*)
1. anc. of *Ezida-aplu-iqīša* and *Bulluṭ* 2:11,16,28
2. anc. of *Gimillu* and *Zēriya* 113:14
3. anc. of *Madānu-aḫḫē-iddin* and *Gimillu* 1:35; 20:14; 65:16; 66:17; 97:12; 99:21; 114:9'
4. anc. of *Mušallim-Marduk* and *Nabû-ēṭir-napšāti* 1:23
5. anc. of *Mušēzib-Marduk* and *Ezida-aplu-iqīša* 2:12
6. anc. of *Nergal-ušallim* 101:36

Šikkû'a (*šik-ku-ú-a*)
1. 301:5
2. 303:5
3. 304:4
4. desc. of *Ilšu-abušu* 302:5
5. anc. of *Murašû* 89:11

Širiktu (*ši-rik-tu*; *ši-rik-tú*; *ši-ri-ik-*tu_4)
1. ^{h}*kutimmu* 212:7
2. son of *Lūṣi-ana-nūri-Marduk*, brother of *Nādin*, desc. of *Ili-bani* 5:10,14;19

Šu-[...]
1. 285:10
2. anc. of *Nabû-aḫḫē-ušallim* 97:7

Šulâ (*šu-la-a*)
1. 128:1
2. ^{h}*paḫāru* 266:38
3. ^{h}*ṣābu*, ^{h}*musaḫḫiru* 111:14
4. son of *Nergal-ušallim*, desc. of ^{h}*mandidu* 100:3
5. desc. of [...] 296:2
6. desc. of *Aplâ* 144:6
7. ^{h}*nuḫatimmu*, desc. of *Nidintu* 156:8
8. f. of *Ibni-Ištar*, desc. of *Gimil-Nanaya* 91:36
9. f. of *Kalbâ* 24:14
10. f. of *Marduk* 93:2
11. f. of *Nabû-nādin-aḫi*, desc. of *Ea-ilūtu-bani* 5:34; 60:12
12. f. of *Šamaš-šum-ukīn*, desc. of ^{h}*mandidu* 73:4
13. anc. of *Iddinunu* 146:4; 213:41
14. anc. of *Nabû-bāni-aḫi* 138:10

Šullum (*šul-lum*)
1. f. of *Šamaš-mudammiq* 63:15

Šumâ (*šu-ma-a*; MU-*a*)[38]
1. ^{h}*ṭupšarru* 266:33
2. son of *Balāssu*, desc. of ^{h}*šangû parakki* 37:11
3. son of *Bēl-šum-iškun*, desc. of ^{h}*šangû bīt Bābili* 46:2
4. son of *Ibni-Ištar*, desc. of ^{h}*ašlāku* 66:20
5. ^{h}*ṭupšarru*, son of *Ibni-Ištar*, desc. of [...] 95:22
6. son of *Nabû-mukīn-zēri*, desc. of *Ilūtu-bani* 79:13
7. desc. of *Ibni-Ištar* 152:5
8. f. of *Bēl-iddin* 115:20
9. anc. of *Balāṭu* 137:13; 138:21
10. anc.? of *Bāniya* 213:25

Šumāti (MU.MEŠ)
1. anc. of *Gimillu* and *Aplâ* 100:5,13

Šum-ēreš (MU-KAM)
1. 135:7

Šum-iddin (MU-MU)[39]
1. ^{h}*ṣābu*, ^{h}*ummânu* 111:7
2. son of [...] 89:6

38. To be noted is the possibility of reading MU-A as *Nādin-apli* or *Nādnâ* (= MU-*a*).

39. Read possibly *Nādin-šumi* in some cases.

40. Read possibly *Nādin-aḫi* in some cases.

1. 157:1

Tuqnu-eššu (*tuq-qin-eš-šú*)

1. 57:6,7

^{f}*Ṭābatu* (^{f}DU$_{10}$-*ba-tu*$_{4}$)

1. daughter of *Nādin*, desc. of *Aššur* 3:9

^{h}*ṭābiḫu* (see ^{h}*nās patri*)

Ṭābiya (*ṭa-bi-ia*; DÙG.GA-*ia*; DÙG.GA-*iá*)

1. ^{h}*šākin ṭēmi*, son of *Nabû-nādin-šumi*, desc. of *Ḫunzû* 1:10; 2:7; 83:14; 295:2
2. son of *Silim-Bēl* 215:6
3. f. of *Nabû-gāmil*, desc. of ^{h}*ašlāku* 62:14

Ṭāb-šār-Eanna (DÙG.GA-IM-*é-an-na*; DU$_{10}$-IM-*é-an-na*)

1. 200:3
2. 204:5
3. 213:50

Ṭāb-šār-Ištar (DÙG.GA-IM-^{d}INNIN; DÙG.GA-IM-^{d}15)

1. 278:5
2. anc. of *Nanaya-iddin* 294:10

Ṭāb-Uruk (DÙG.GA-UNUG^{ki}; *ṭa-bi*-UNUG^{ki})

1. son of *Gabâ* 87:10
2. f. of *Innin-šum-uṣur* 74:3
3. anc. of *Innin-šum-uṣur* 115:3

Ú-[...]

1. 135:20

Uballissu-Gula (*ú-bal-liṭ-su*-^{d}*gu-la*)

1. son of *Silim-Bēl*, desc. of ^{h}*šangû parakki* 69:14

Ubār (*ú-bar*)

1. ^{h}*ṣābu*, ^{h}*ummânu* 111:8
2. ^{h}*išparu*, son of *Amēl-Nanaya* 115:9
3. son of *Mukīn-zēri* 22:14
4. f. of *Nergal-iddin* 49:4

Ubārya (*ú-bar-ia*; *ú-bar-iá*)

1. 154:5
2. son of *Nabû-aḫ-iddin* 40:5

Umāšu (*u*$_{4}$-*ma-a-šú*)

1. f. of *Nabû-mušētiq-ūdi* 91:20

Uraš-AN.AŠ.KUR (^{d}*uraš*-AN.AŠ.KUR)[41]

1. anc. of *Nabû-zēr-ibni* and [...]-*za-a* 3:11
2. anc. of *Niqūdu* and *Rīmūt-Gula* 3:6

Zababa-šar-uṣur (^{d}*za-ba*$_{4}$-*ba*$_{4}$-LUGAL-ÙRI)

1. an Elamite, desc. of *Iltamamu* 253:3

Zabdâ (*zab-da-a*)

1. f. of *Aḫ-immê* 124:14

Zabdiya (*zab-di-ia*)

1. 214:5

Zākir (*za-kir*)

1. f. of *Balāṭu*, desc. of *Kidin-Marduk* 92:10

^{f}*zakītu* (^{f}*za-ki-tú*)

1. anc. of [...] 115:11
2. anc. of [...]-A-*iddin* 115:13
3. anc. of *Arad-Bēl* 115:4
4. anc. of *Arad-Nabû* 115:11
5. anc. of *Ibni-Ezida* 115:30
6. anc. of *Libluṭ* 115:12
7. anc. of *Šamaš-ēṭir* 115:4

Zāriqu-ēreš (^{d}*za-ri-qu*-KAM)

1. f. of *Bēl-ēṭir-Šamaš*, desc. of x 34:3; 36:3

Zēr-[...] (NUMUN-[...])

1. 213:38
2. ^{h}*ṭupšarru*, son of *Kiribtu* 96:14
3. son of *Nabû-zēru-līšir*, desc. of *Basiya* 43:13

Zēr-Bābili (NUMUN-E^{ki}; NUMUN-TIN.TIR^{ki})

1. son of *Nabû-šum-iškun*, desc. of [*Ilūtu*]-*bani* 21:3,4,11
2. f. of *Bēl-nādin-apli*, desc. of *Ile"i-Marduk* 91:4
3. f. of *Mukīn-apli*, desc. of ^{h}*šangû Adad* 4:14
4. f. of *Mušēzib-Bēl*, desc. of *Ea-ilūtu-bani* 5:8; 10:1; 50:2; 102:2,15; 153:10

41. The element AŠ.KUR should perhaps be read *ina māti* in view of the personal name ^{I}*Ina-māti*, which occurs spelled both ^{I}AŠ.KUR (line 4) and ^{I}*im-ma-a-tu*$_{4}$ in the same document (OIP 97 no. 24), the latter representing an approximate phonetic rendering of the Neo-Babylonian pronunciation of the name: /immat/ < /in-mati/ < /ina-mati/.

GEOGRAPHICAL NAMES[42]

1. Countries, Provinces, and Cities

Ālu [...] *ana pāni ša Bēlti ša Uruk* (URU [...] *ana* IGI *šá* ^{d}GAŠAN *šá* UNUG^{ki}) 86:5'–6'
Ālu ša Arad-^{d}[...][43] (URU *šá* ^{lú}ÌR-^{d}[...]) 19:12
Ālu ša ardāni (URU *šá* ^{lú}⸢ÌR.MEŠ⸣) 34:6
Ālu ša ikkarē (URU *šá* ^{lú}ENGAR.MEŠ) 34:13
Ālu ša Mušēzib-Nabû (URU *šá* ^{I}*mu-še-zib-*^{d}NÀ) 44:21
[*Ālu* ...] *ša Nabû-zēru-līšir* 40:14–15
^{māt}*Ar*[...] (^{kur}*ar-*[...]) 295:15
Ašbat-[...]*-ili* (^{uru}*áš-ba-*tu_4-x-x-DINGIR) 67:15
Bābili (Babylon) (TIN.TIR^{ki}; E^{ki}) 4:3; 17:14; 18:3; 94:3,5,11,15; 95:19; 101:8,20,43; 155:9; 225:12; 226:4; 227:4; 248:3; 284:5; 287:6
Barsip (Borsippa) (*bar-sip*^{ki}; *bar-zip*^{ki}; *bár-síp*^{ki}) 5:3,35; 10:17; 21:17; 26:15; 43:15; 45:9,16; 47:17; 60:13; 62:18; 72:15; 77:15; 79:8,16; 88:15; 89:13; 102:20; 310:10; 313:3'
Bīt-Abda' (^{uru}É ^{I}*ab-da-a'*) 37:13
Bīt-Šama'-il (^{uru}É ^{I}*ša-am-mu-ìl*) 92:11
Bīt-šar-Bābili[44] (^{uru}É-LUGAL-TIN.TIR^{ki}) 95:13
Dilbat (*dil-bat*$^{[ki]}$) 3:38
Dūr-Ugumu (^{uru}BÀD *u-gu-mu*) 90:19
Eber-nāri (*e-ber* ÍD) 52:3; 235:13
Elammu (^{uru}*e-lam-mu*) 25:14
Ḫumē (^{kur}*ḫu-me-e*) 209:2 (cf. ^{lú}*ḫu-ma-a-a* 162:2; 273:4)
Kār-bēl-mātāti (^{uru}*kar-*EN-KUR.KUR) 222:2
Kār-Nanaya (*kar-*^{d}*na-na-a*/^{uru}*kar-*^{d}*na-na-a ši-i-ḫu šá* ^{d}GAŠAN *šá* UNUG^{ki}) 75:21; 94:21–22
Kašappi (^{kur}*ka-šap-pi*) 287:2
Kiš (KIŠ^{ki}) 57:14
Larsa (UD.UNUG^{ki}) 7:27; 27:17; 33:6,16; 39:6,18; 41:18; 48:5,13; 49:6,15; 53:17; 55:13; 59:11; 63:18; 69:17; 70:20; 73:14; 311:17
Lasūtu (^{uru}*la-su-ú-tu*) 31:5
Mar(a)da (AMAR DA^{ki}) 46:6,16; 54:20 (cf. AMAR.DA^{ki}*-a-a* in 54:13)
Maškan-il (^{uru}*maš-kan-*DINGIR [*ši-i-ḫ*]*u šá* ^{d}GAŠAN *šá* UNUG^{ki}) 85:14–15
Niḫlūtu (^{uru}*ni-iḫ-lu-*tu_4) 154:4
Nippur (EN.LÍL^{ki}) 8:13; 16:12; 29:4'; 36:7,15; 38:13; 61:13; 80:6,12
piḫāt Bābili (*pi-ḫat* TIN.TIR^{ki}) 4:3
piḫāt Barsip (*pi-ḫa-ta bár-síp*^{ki}) 5:3
Sippar (*sip-par*^{ki}; ^{uru}*sip-par*$^{[ki]}$) 22:17; 23:18; 96:15
Ṣīdūnu (^{uru}*ṣi-da-nu*) 32:8,14
Šapiya (^{uru}*šá-pi-ia*) 20:4,9
Šarrānu (^{uru}*šar-ra-nu*) 28:17
Šaṭeru (^{uru}*šá-ṭer*) 42:11
Tagarennu (^{uru}*ta-gar-en-na*) 222:2
Udannu[45] (^{uru}*ú-dan-nu*; UBARA^{ki}) 13:2; 290:3
Ur (ŠEŠ.UNUG^{ki}) 254:3
Uruk (UNUG^{ki}) 1:3,47; 2:44; 9:16; 11:16; 15:14; 24:18; 30:10; 35:7,16; 51:20; 52:17; 56:7'; 64:17; 65:21; 74:15; 83:20; 91:37; 92:18; 93:22; 95:17,23; 97:16; 98:17; 99:26; 100:24; 110:14; 113:18; 137:3
Zamē (^{uru}*za-ma-'e-e*) 93:15

2. Fields and Domains

^{tamirtu}*aššurītu* (^{garin}*as-šur-ri-tú*/tu_4) 81:2,16
^{tamirtu}*bīt-bāri* (^{garin}É-^{lú}ḪAL) 75:2
bitqu ša Bēl-ēṭir šīḫu ša Bēlti ša Uruk (*bit-qa* [*šá*] ^{Id}EN-SUR *ši-i-ḫu šá* [^{d}GAŠAN *šá* UNUG^{ki}]) 42:20–21

42. The transcriptions of geographical names are normalized in conformity with RGTC 8.
43. Compare the toponym *Ālu ša Arad-Ea* near Borsippa (RGTC 8 s.v.).
44. On this locality see Beaulieu, *Reign of Nabonidus*, 98–104.
45. On this city see P.-A. Beaulieu, "UBARA(EZENxKASKAL)^{ki} = Udannu," *ASJ* 13 (1991) 97–109; "Kissik, Dūru and Udannu," *OrNS* 61 (1992) 400–24; and W. Horowitz, "Moab and Edom in the Sargon Geography," *IEJ* 43 (1993) 151–56.

eqlu ša Bēlti ša Uruk ša ina muḫḫi nāru bitqu (A.ŠÀ *šá* ^{d}GAŠAN *šá* UNUG^{ki} *šá ina* UGU ÍD *bit-qa*) 76:19
eqlu ša bīt apkalli (A.ŠÀ *šá* É NUN.ME) 77:3
erṣet Eanna (KI-*tì* É.AN.NA) 1:3
^{tamirtu}*Ḫurat-Sūḫayu* (^{garin}*ḫu-ra-du-su-ḫa-a-a*) 5:2
Ḫurizātu ša Taqīš-[...] *šīḫu ša Šerua*[46] (^{uru}*ḫu-ri-za-ti šá* ^{I}*ta-qiš-*^{d}[...] *ši-i-ḫu šá* ^{d}EDIN) 71:18–19
nagû ša Bēlti ša Uruk ša muḫḫi nār šarri (*na-gi-i šá* ^{d}GAŠAN *šá* UNUG^{ki} *šá* UGU ÍD LUGAL) 113:2–3
^{tamirtu}*Naḫal* (^{garin}*na-ḫal*) 78:2
[^{tamirtu}*Naḫal*] *šīḫu ša Bēlti ša Uruk* ([^{garin}*na-ḫal*] *ši-i-ḫu šá* ^{d}GAŠAN *šá* UNUG^{ki}) 78:18–19
qaqqaru ša Bēlti ša Uruk (*qaq-qa-ru šá* ^{d}GAŠAN *šá* UNUG^{ki}) 63:3–4
^{tamirtu}*Qutānu* (^{garin}*qu-ta-*[*nu*]) 72:1
Raqqat-Šamaš (*raq-qat-*^{d}UTU) 214:10
^{tamirtu}*Rāṭu* (^{garin}*ra-a-ṭu*) 86:2
šīḫu ša Bēlti ša Uruk (*ši-i-ḫu šá* ^{d}GAŠAN *šá* UNUG^{ki}) 42:20–21; 78:19; 81:16; 94:21
šīḫu ša Bēlti ša Uruk ša nāru ḫarru ša Nādnâ (*ši-i-ḫi šá* ^{d}GAŠAN *šá* UNUG^{ki} *šá* ÍD *ḫar-ri šá* ^{I}MU-*a*) 84:14–15; 132:20–21
šīḫu ša Bēlti ša Uruk ša ina nār Innin (*ši-i-ḫu ša* ^{d}GAŠAN *ša* UNUG^{ki} *ša ina* ÍD ^{d}*in-nin*) 87:13
šīḫu ša Bīt bāri (*ši-i-ḫi šá* É ^{lú}ḪAL) 75:18
šīḫu ša Kār-Nanaya (*ši-i-ḫi šá kar-*^{d}*na-na-a*) 75:21
šīḫu ša Šerua (*ši-i-ḫu šá* ^{d}EDIN) 71:19
šīḫu ša Uraš (*ši-i-ḫi šá* ^{d}URAŠ) 3:7

3. Rivers, River Banks, and Canals

nār Innin (ÍD ^{d}*in-nin*) 87:13
nār šarri (ÍD LUGAL) 113:3; 140:5; 207:3
nāru bitqu (ÍD *bit-qa*) 76:1,19
nāru eššetu (ÍD *eš-še-ti/tu*$_4$) 2:2,4
nāru ḫarru ša Nādnâ[47] (ÍD *ḫar-ri šá* ^{I}MU-*a*/SUM.NA-*a*/*nad-na-a*) 75:7–8; 84:15; 132:5,21
nāru nēberu (ÍD *né-bé-ri*) 222:14
nāru ša Aḫḫē-šullim (ÍD *ša* ^{I}ŠEŠ.MEŠ-GI) 4:3
Ṣigirtu (^{íd}*ṣi-gir-ti*) 75:8
aḫ Šiliḫtu (GÚ *ši-li-iḫ-tu*$_4$) 38:2
Takkīru (^{íd}*tak-kil*; ^{íd}*tak-ki-ru*) 85:7; 203:5

4. Streets and Gates

abul Enlil (KÁ.GAL ^{d}*en-líl*) 4:3
abul Kanisurra (KÁ.GAL ^{d}*ka-ni-sur-ra*) 242:6
abullāti (KÁ.GAL.MEŠ) 222:14
sūq aḫ nār eššeti (E.SÍR GÚ ÍD *eš-še-tu*$_4$) 2:2
sūqu lā aṣû (E.SÍR *la a-ṣu-ú*) 1:17
sūqu rapsu mūtaq nišē (E.SÍR *rap-šú mu-taq* ^{lú}UN.MEŠ) 1:6
sūqu ša abul Kanisurra (*su-ú-q*[*u*] *šá* KÁ.GAL ^{d}*ka-ni-sur-r*[*a*]) 242:5–6

5. Temples and Parts of Temples

bāb bīt Uṣur-amāssu (KÁ É ^{d}ÙRI-*a-mat-su*) 115:26
bāb Nin-zizli[48] (KÁ ^{d}NIN-TAG.TAG^{li}) 115:18
bīt akīti (É *a-ki-ti/tu*$_4$) 135:25; 198:3; 297:3
bīt Gula (É ^{d}ME.ME) 266:28
bīt ḫilṣi (É *ḫi-il-ṣi/ṣu*) 193:4; 268:2; 284:22; 292:9

46. This word is otherwise attested only at Nuzi (*AHw* and *CAD* s.v. *ḫurizu*), where it designates some kind of building (*CAD* translates "shed for cattle," and *AHw* "palace, mansion").

47. RGTC 8, 355 reads *Ḫarru-ša-Iddinâ*, but the spelling *nad-na-a* indicates a reading *Ḫarru-ša-Nādnâ* in all cases.

48. Probably the same deity as ^{d}NIN-TAG.TAG (= ^{d}nin-zíl-zíl), who is equated with Nanaya in the Emesal god-list MSL 4, p. 9, line 90: [^{d}gašan-zíl-zíl] = ^{d}nin-zíl-zíl = ^{d}*na-na-a*, and also in the late explanatory god-list CT 25, pl. 49, rev. 7: ^{d}nin-zíl-zíl = ^{d}*na-na-a* DUMU.SAL [o o] *šá man-za-as-su šá-qu-u be-lit tak-né-*⸢*e*⸣ [o o] "Nin-zizli = Nanaya, the daughter [o o], whose station is lofty, the mistress of loving care [o o]." The presence of a phonetic complement /l(i)/ in YOS 19, 115:18 ensures the reading of the compound TAG.TAG as zîl-zîl > /zizli/.

DIVINE NAMES

Concordance of Museum Numbers

HSM 890.4.8	101
MLC 347	72
MLC 381	45
MLC 536	302
MLC 732	304
MLC 734	305
MLC 746	300
MLC 753	301
MLC 754	303
MLC 762	306
MLC 985	299
MLC 1006	298
MLC 1011	307
MLC 1195	3
MLC 1664	88
NBC 4202	310
NBC 4500	145
NBC 4501	30
NBC 4505	256
NBC 4506	257
NBC 4507	246
NBC 4511	164
NBC 4515	98
NBC 4522	151
NBC 4525	216
NBC 4526	201
NBC 4527	259
NBC 4528	207
NBC 4529	74
NBC 4533	265
NBC 4535	126
NBC 4537	172
NBC 4540	283
NBC 4542	175
NBC 4548	123
NBC 4551	187
NBC 4568	279
NBC 4572	230
NBC 4578	295
NBC 4580	267
NBC 4585	6
NBC 4588	132
NBC 4591	150
NBC 4592	113
NBC 4593	24
NBC 4594	93
NBC 4618	192
NBC 4646	144
NBC 4669	193
NBC 4670	290
NBC 4673	292
NBC 4689	263
NBC 4695	204
NBC 4703	130
NBC 4714	233
NBC 4720	161
NBC 4736	148
NBC 4748	238
NBC 4749	160
NBC 4751	122
NBC 4755	29
NBC 4755A	29
NBC 4759	194
NBC 4772	136
NBC 4790	95
NBC 4811	152
NBC 4830	156
NBC 4834	129
NBC 4854	236
NBC 4855	115
NBC 4856	213
NBC 4900	286
NBC 4907	135
NBC 4930	215
NBC 4935	112
NBC 4936	133
NBC 4937	111
NBC 6113	23
NBC 6119	38
NBC 6120	22
NBC 6128	96
NBC 6171	37
NBC 6174	28
NBC 6179	61
NBC 6183	11
NBC 6186	36
NBC 6187	252
NBC 6192	19
NBC 6193	57
NBC 6196	25
NBC 6200	16
NBC 6203	251
NBC 6204	219
NBC 6214	18
NBC 6216	62
NBC 6219	17
NBC 6221	153
NBC 6222	166
NBC 6226	8
NBC 6232	32
NBC 6233	34
NBC 8324	58
NBC 8328	43

NBC 8329	159
NBC 8330	47
NBC 8332	269
NBC 8333	262
NBC 8336	77
NBC 8338	79
NBC 8341	89
NBC 8345	10
NBC 8347	50
NBC 8352	237
NBC 8357	60
NBC 8364	102
NBC 8377	80
NBC 8381	165
NBC 8389	119
NBC 8395	5
NBC 8407	21
NBC 11487	92
NBC 11488	110
NBC 11499	231
NBC 11563	248
NCBT 21	103
NCBT 42	104
NCBT 269	275
NCBT 425	226
NCBT 430	186
NCBT 467	309
NCBT 469	177
NCBT 474	217
NCBT 475	261
NCBT 476	260
NCBT 482	254
NCBT 483	247
NCBT 484	176
NCBT 485	184
NCBT 492	142
NCBT 493	109
NCBT 496	221
NCBT 513	15
NCBT 523	39
NCBT 531	20
NCBT 533	40
NCBT 535	94
NCBT 537	51
NCBT 538	76
NCBT 547	55
NCBT 549	44
NCBT 554	35
NCBT 580	49
NCBT 596	250
NCBT 599	134
NCBT 614	118
NCBT 617	154
NCBT 619	149
NCBT 621	78
NCBT 623	33
NCBT 624	140
NCBT 634	296
NCBT 697	143
NCBT 830	203
NCBT 866	66
NCBT 880	214
NCBT 924	84
NCBT 928	240
NCBT 949	218
NCBT 954	289
NCBT 955	68
NCBT 985	116
NCBT 997	99
NCBT 1007	188
NCBT 1009	293
NCBT 1014	86
NCBT 1020	281
NCBT 1046	229
NCBT 1050	90
NCBT 1055	266
NCBT 1063	235
NCBT 1072	41
NCBT 1075	242
NCBT 1078	282
NCBT 1086	13
NCBT 1087	169
NCBT 1088	127
NCBT 1089	287
NCBT 1091	73
NCBT 1092	170
NCBT 1096	288
NCBT 1097	228
NCBT 1101	167
NCBT 1102	117
NCBT 1103	197
NCBT 1104	182
NCBT 1106	200
NCBT 1107	210
NCBT 1108	158
NCBT 1112	108
NCBT 1113	195
NCBT 1114	56
NCBT 1122	202
NCBT 1131	222
NCBT 1139	12
NCBT 1144	146
NCBT 1148	14
NCBT 1149	274
NCBT 1158	264
NCBT 1173	225
NCBT 1179	258
NCBT 1181	199
NCBT 1186	121
NCBT 1198	278
NCBT 1201	189
NCBT 1203	2
NCBT 1216	138
NCBT 1228	157
NCBT 1229	234
NCBT 1230	276
NCBT 1232	206
NCBT 1239	277
NCBT 1240	224
NCBT 1242	273
NCBT 1243	243
NCBT 1248	208
NCBT 1249	253
NCBT 1250	168
NCBT 1252	9
NCBT 1253	124
NCBT 1256	249
NCBT 1257	272
NCBT 1258	212
NCBT 1259	220
NCBT 1260	162
NCBT 1261	183
NCBT 1262	128
NCBT 1263	244
NCBT 1264	179
NCBT 1265	31
NCBT 1266	147
NCBT 1267	141
NCBT 1268	185
NCBT 1269	120

NCBT 1270	196	YBC 3520	69	YBC 11263	239
NCBT 1273	171	YBC 3706	100	YBC 11265	81
NCBT 1274	181	YBC 3755	65	YBC 11266	284
NCBT 1275	139	YBC 3847	67	YBC 11267	294
NCBT 1276	174	YBC 4048	75	YBC 11269	46
NCBT 1278	191	YBC 4055	87	YBC 11270	97
NCBT 1280	227	YBC 4140	91	YBC 11277	280
NCBT 1281	209	YBC 6856	59	YBC 11303	106
NCBT 1282	223	YBC 6931	297	YBC 11304	107
NCBT 1283	255	YBC 7046	85	YBC 11306	155
NCBT 1285	83	YBC 7369	63	YBC 11308	42
NCBT 1286	52	YBC 7378	7	YBC 11441	105
NCBT 1290	125	YBC 7385	70	YBC 11462	205
NCBT 1296	232	YBC 7397	53	YBC 11493	211
NCBT 1298	245	YBC 7423	131	YBC 11535	54
NCBT 2327	270	YBC 7549	271	YBC 11542	285
NCBT 2328	190	YBC 7560	312	YBC 11577	82
NCBT 2329	173	YBC 7562	71	YBC 11578	308
NCBT 2330	198	YBC 7565	163	YBC 11591	26
NCBT 2331	178	YBC 8288	48	YBC 11608	64
		YBC 8781	268	YBC 11657	241
RBC 739	313	YBC 9038	180	YBC 11670	4
		YBC 9048	27	YBC 16216	1
YBC 3463	311	YBC 10473	137		
YBC 3509	114	YBC 11260	291		

Autographed Texts

1

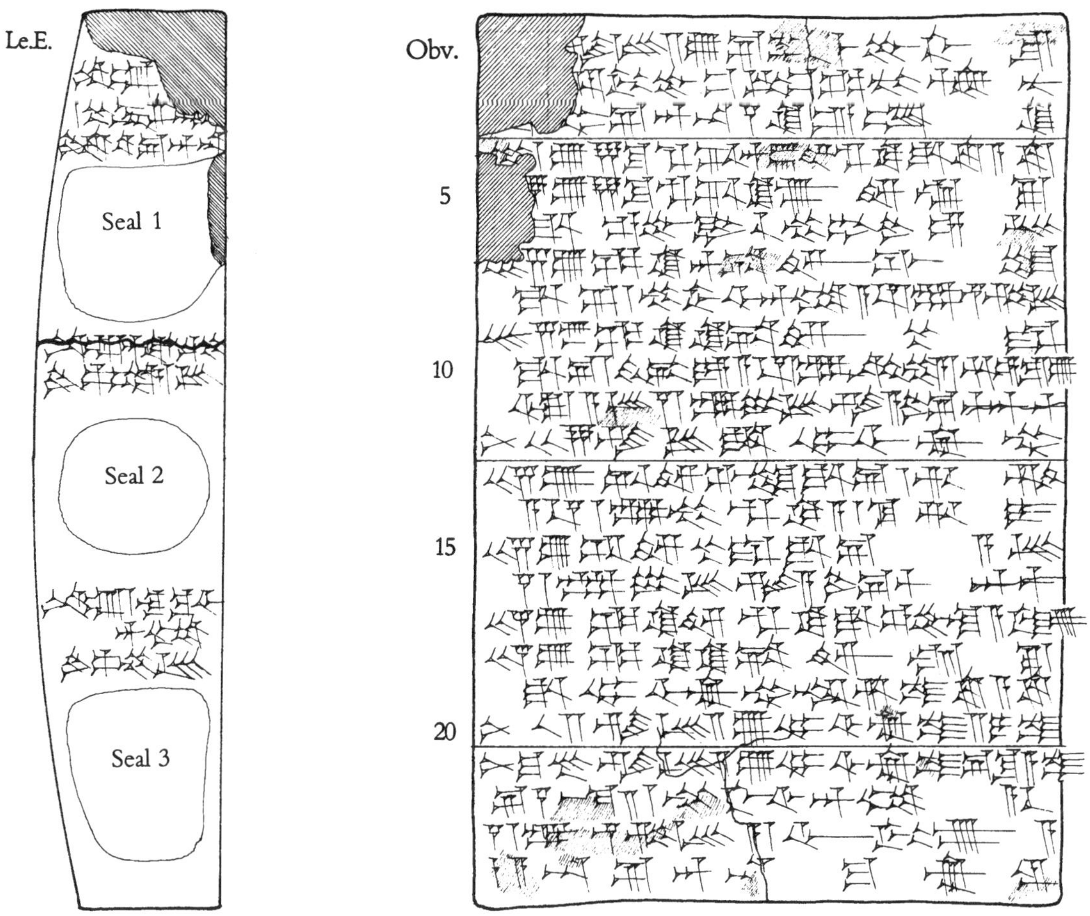

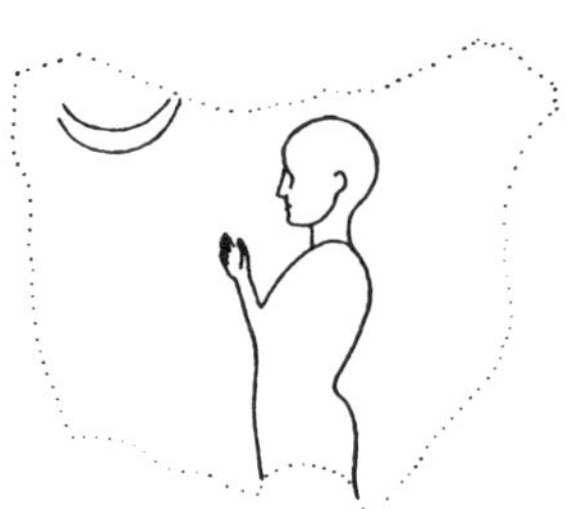
Seal 1

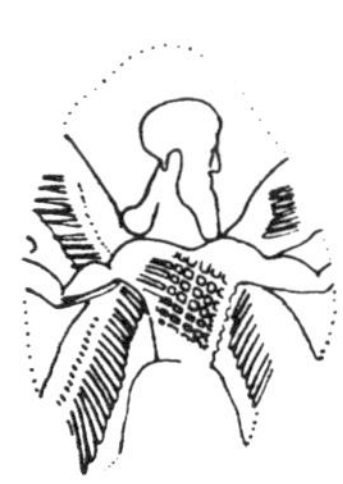
Seal 2

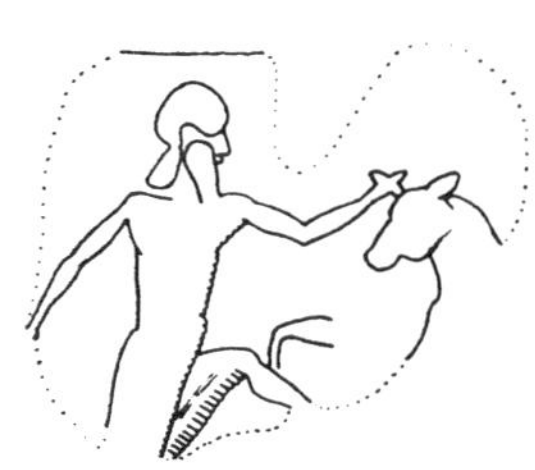
Seal 3

1

Rev.

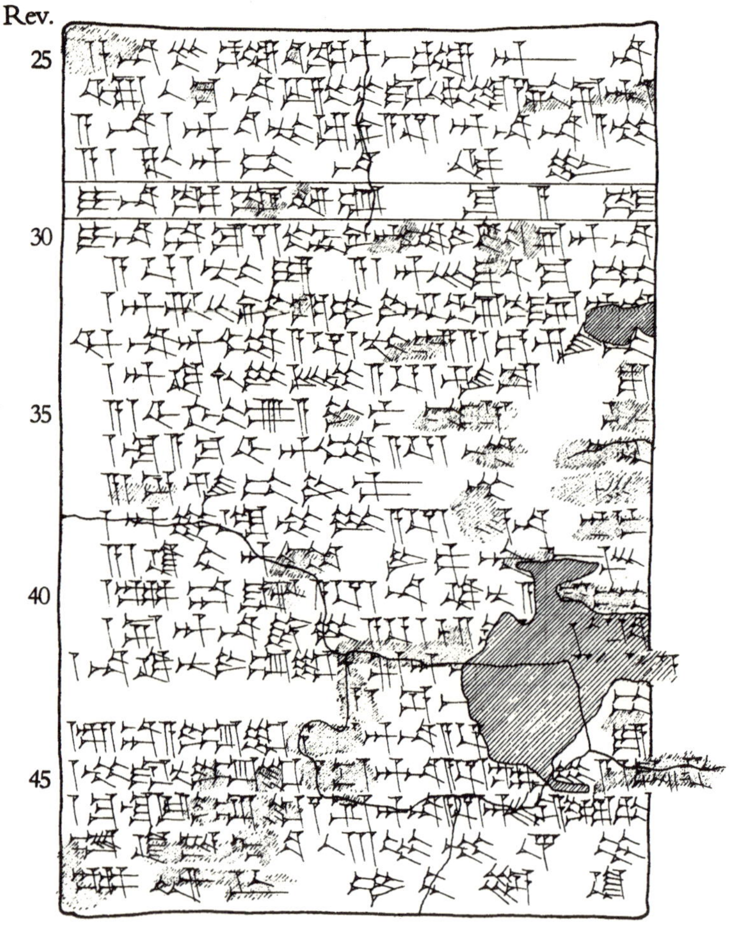

R.E.

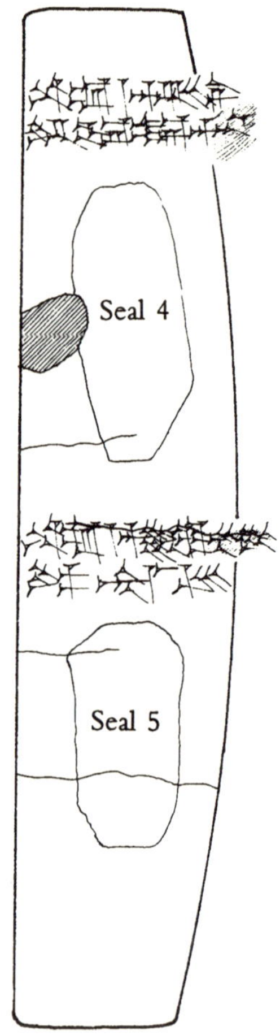

Seal 4

Seal 5

2

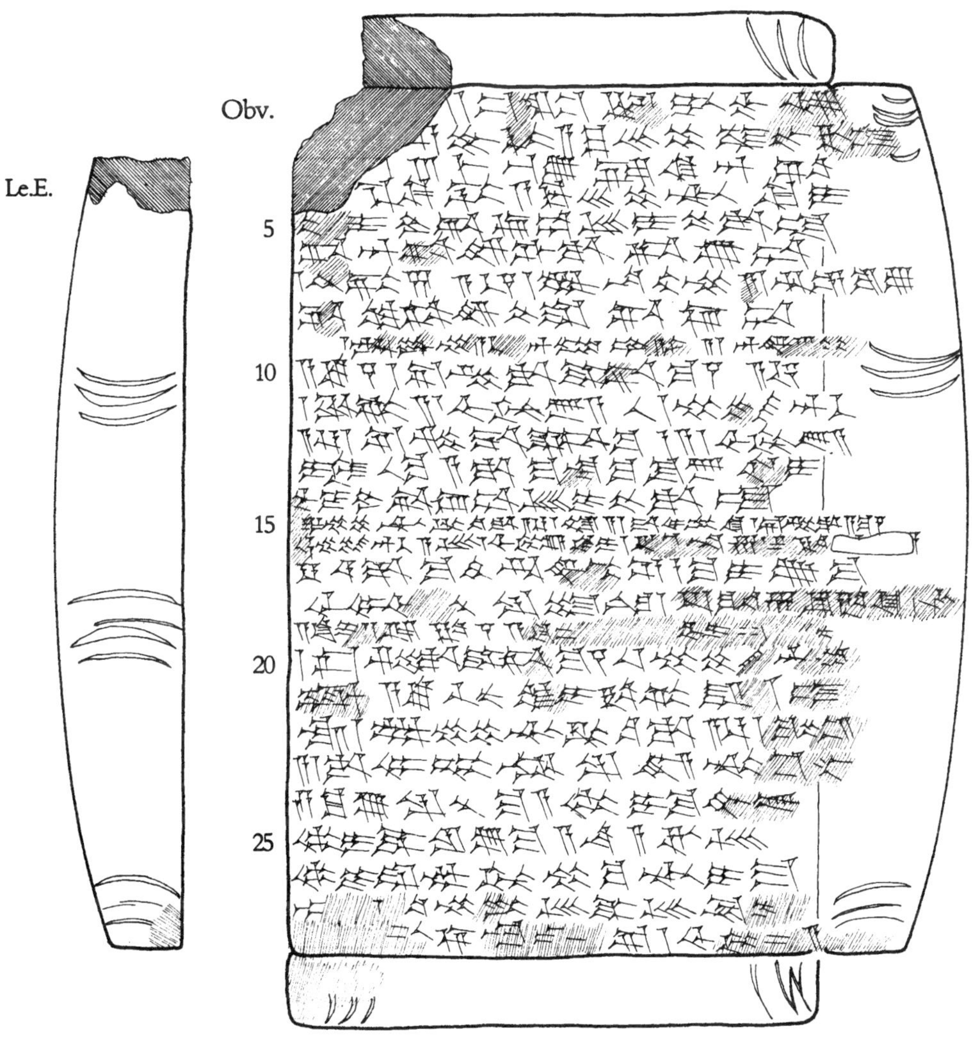

PLATE IV

2

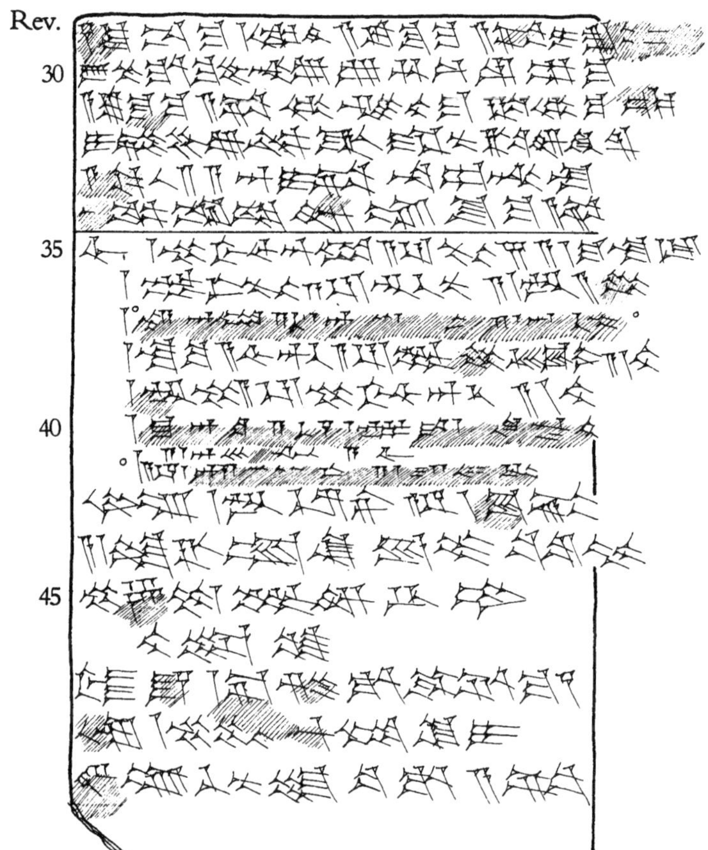

3

Obv.

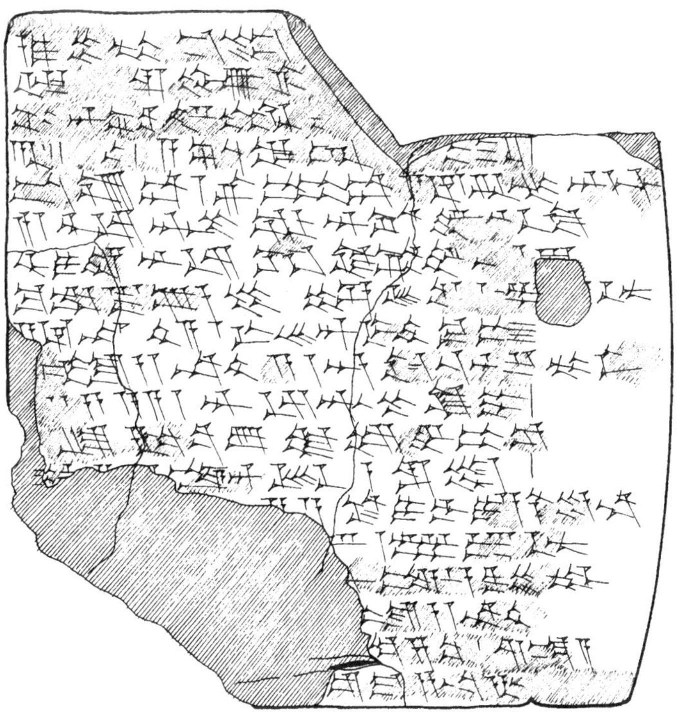

Rev.

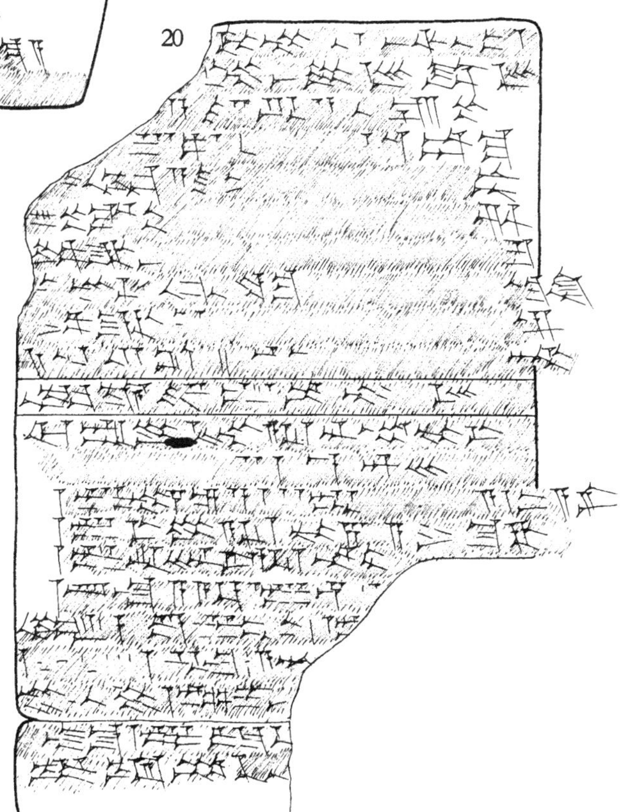

U.E.

4

Obv.

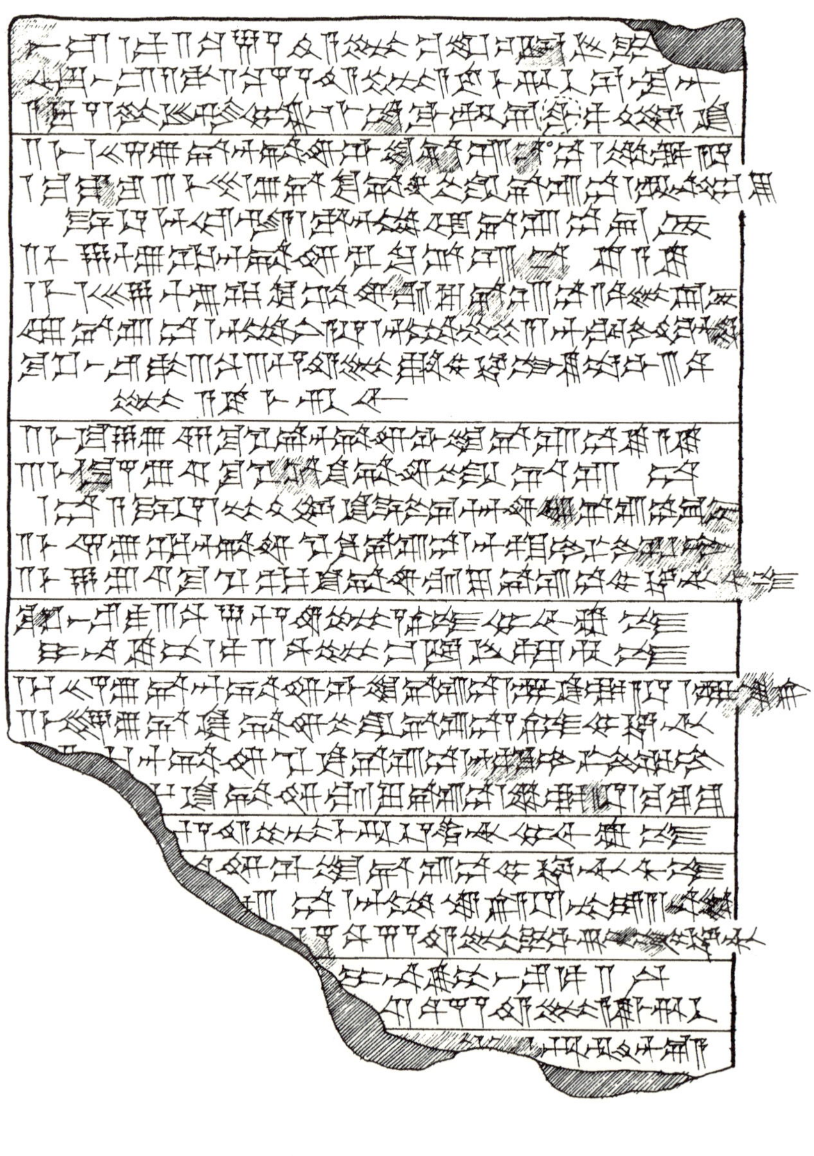

4

Rev.

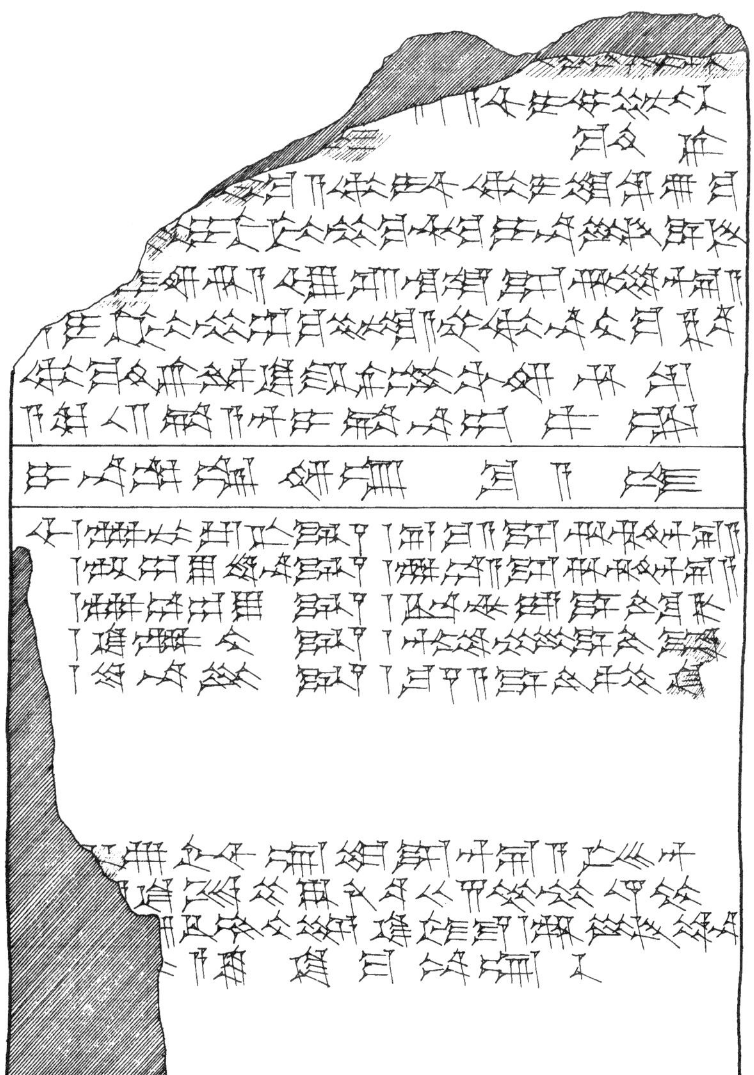

5

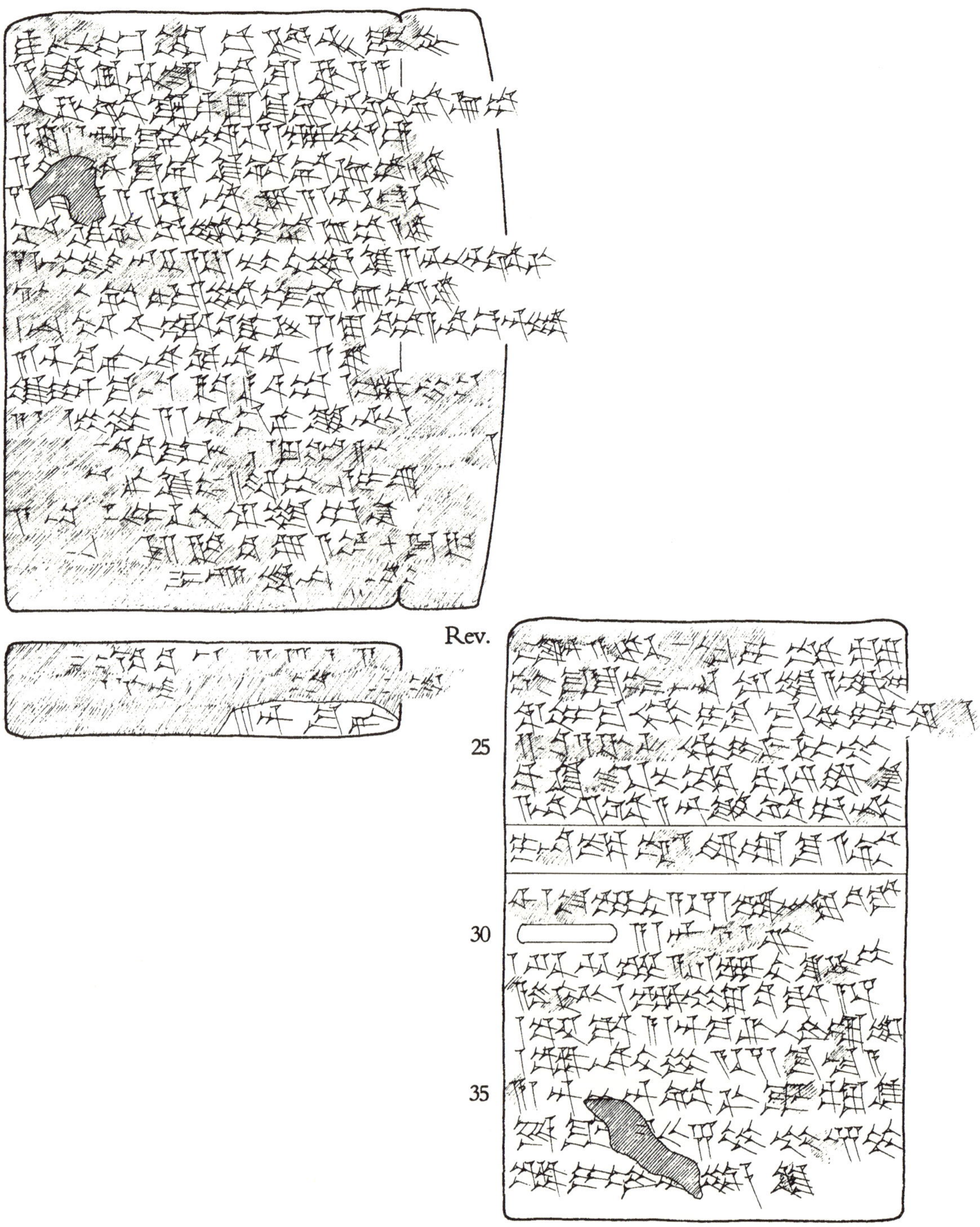

6

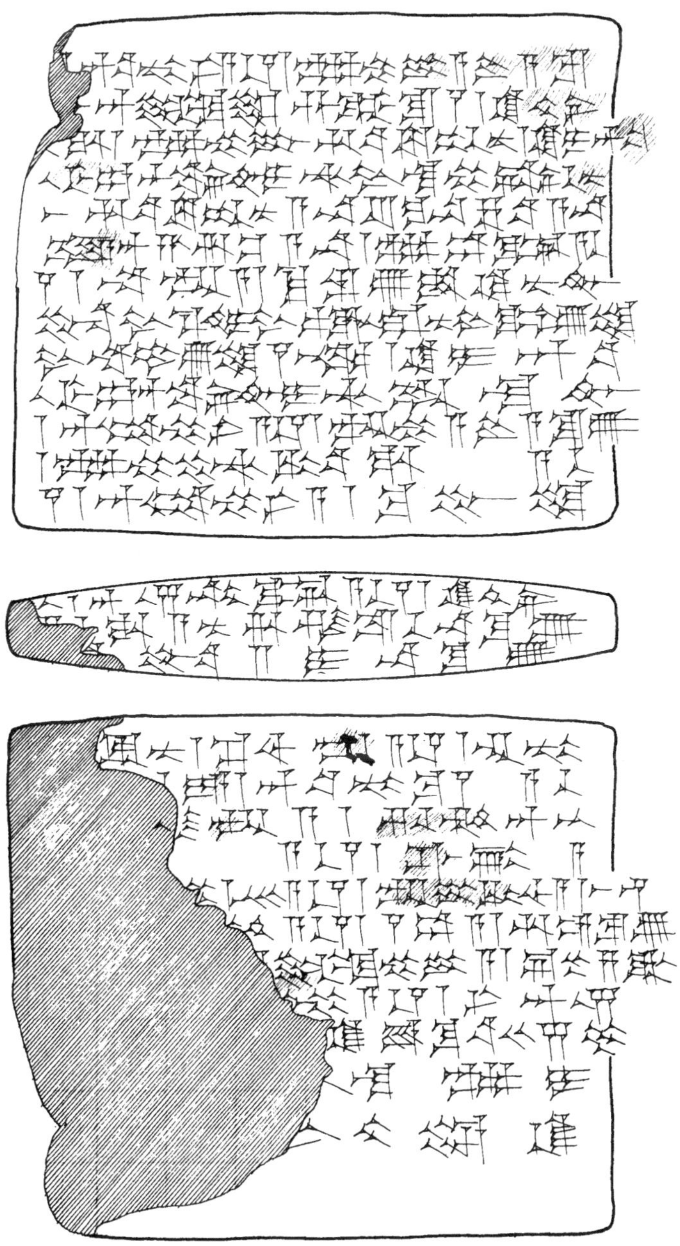

PLATE X

7

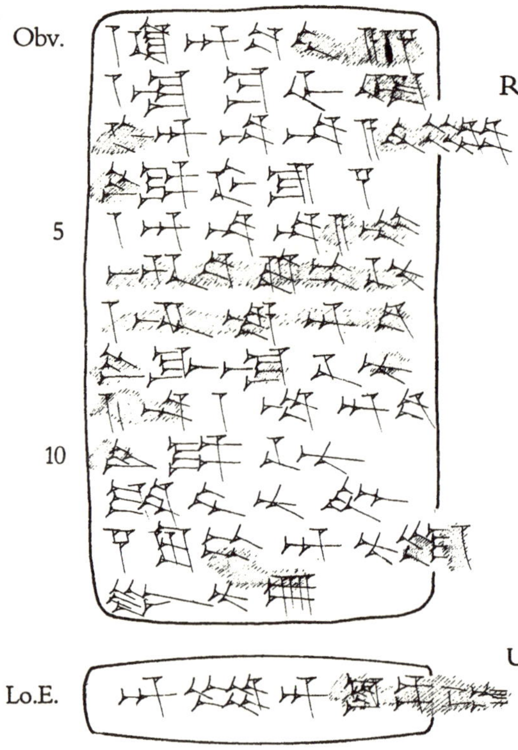

8

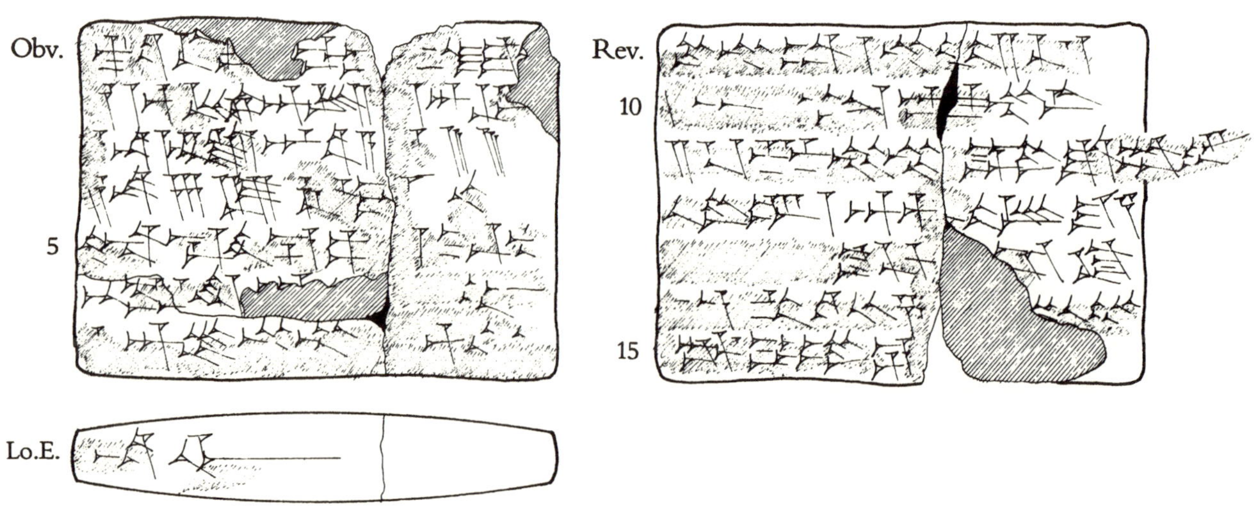

9

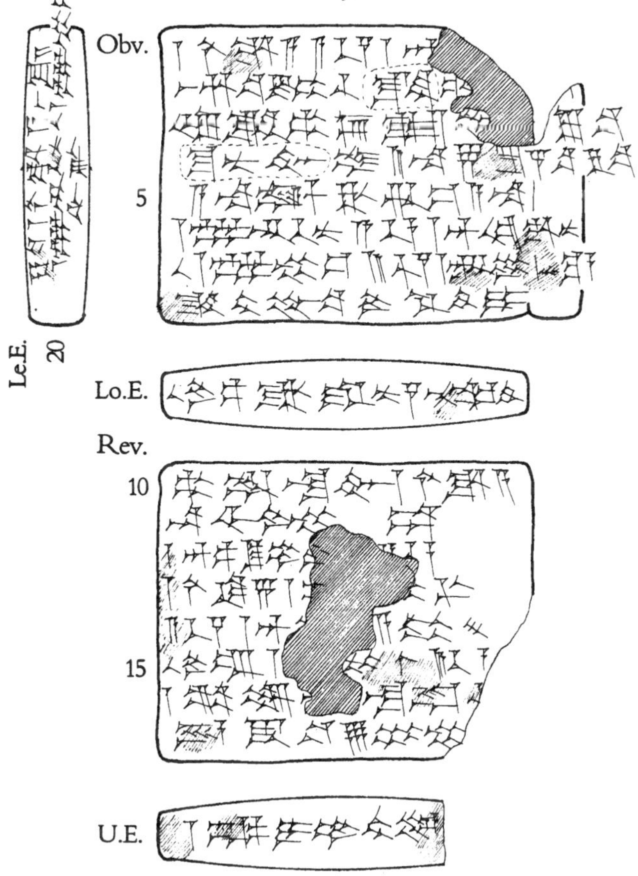

10

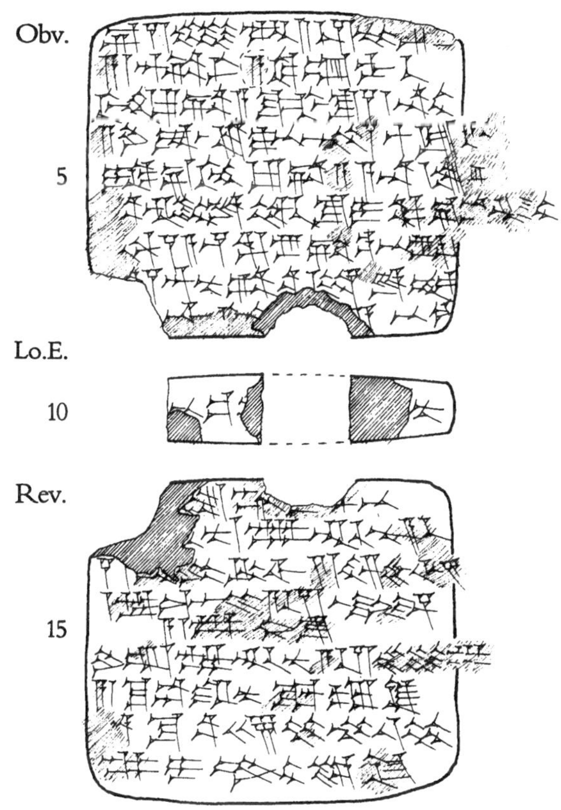

11

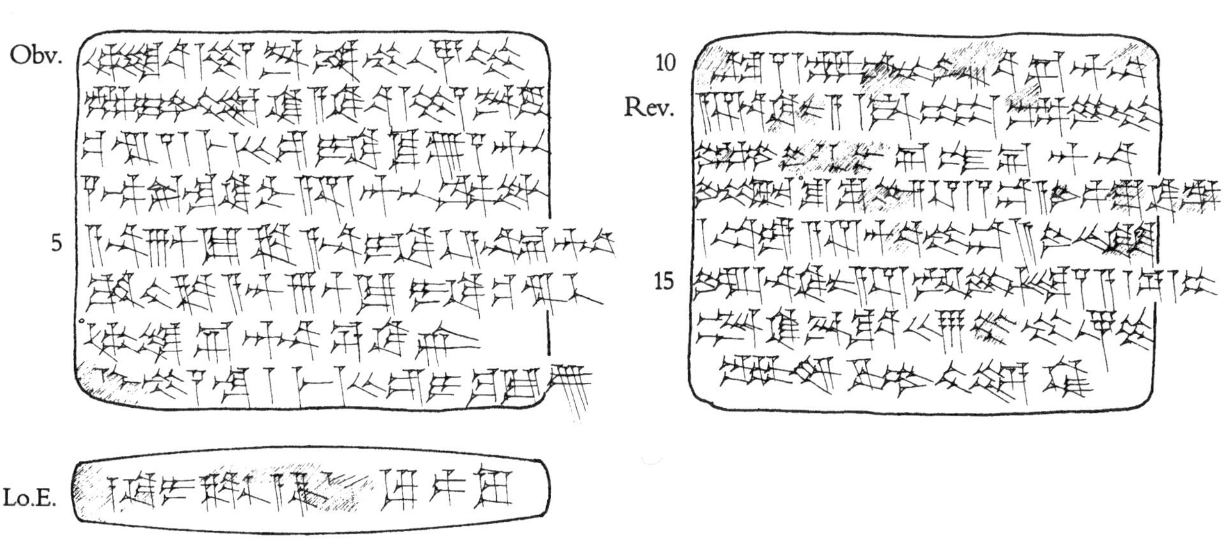

12

Obv.

Lo.E.

Rev.

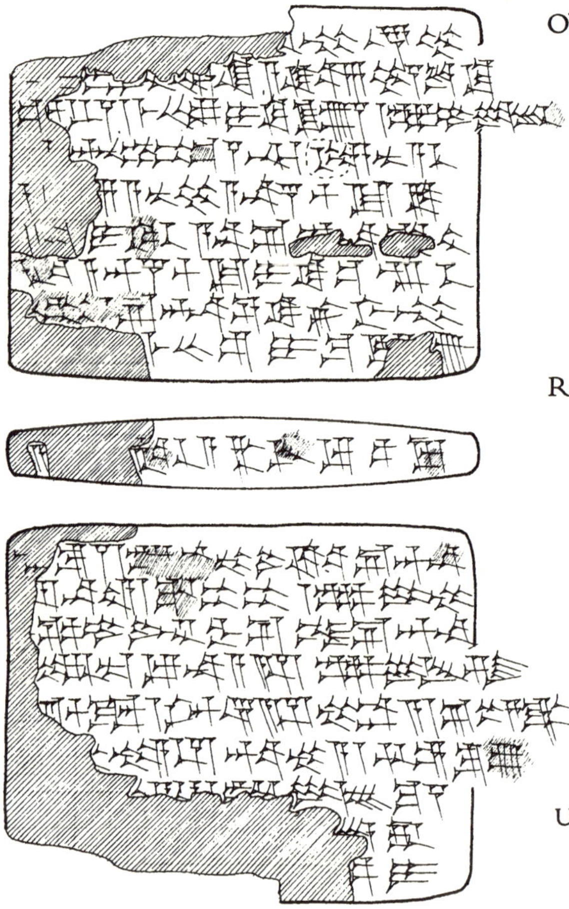

13

Obv.

Rev.

U.E.

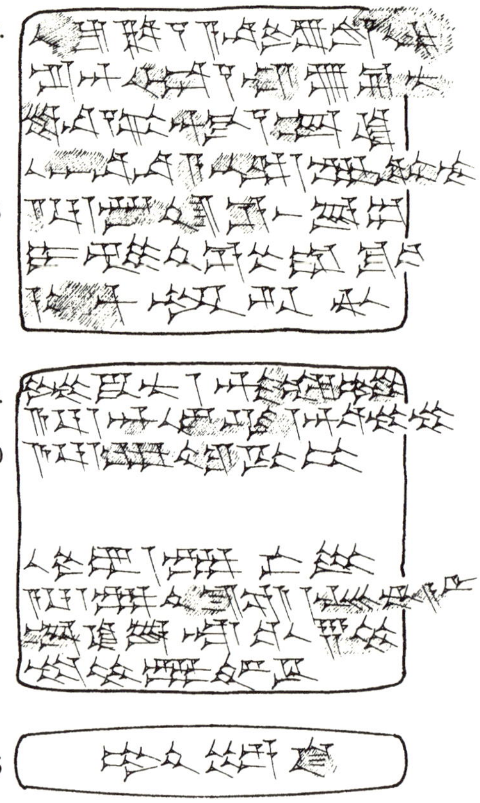

14

Obv.

Rev.

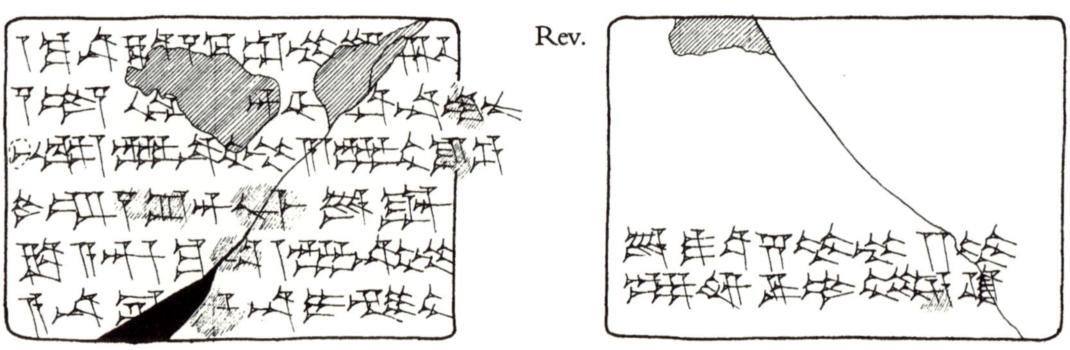

15

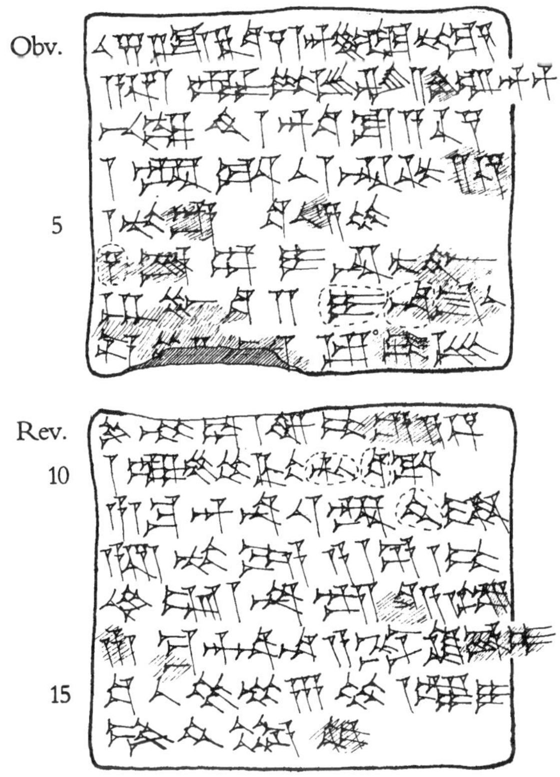

16

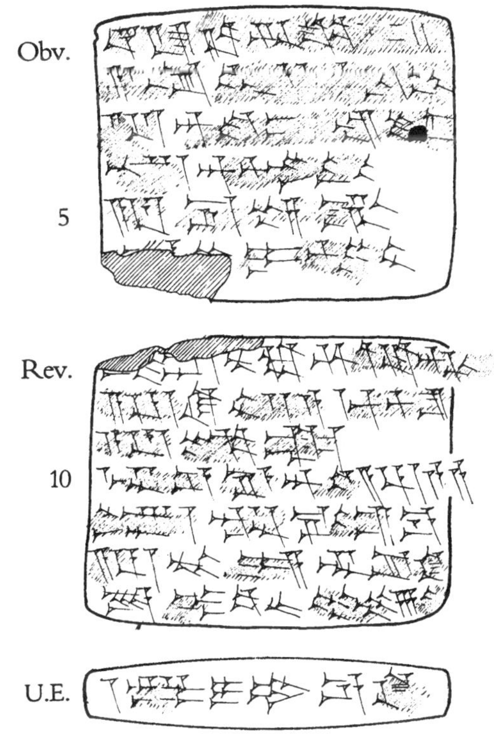

17

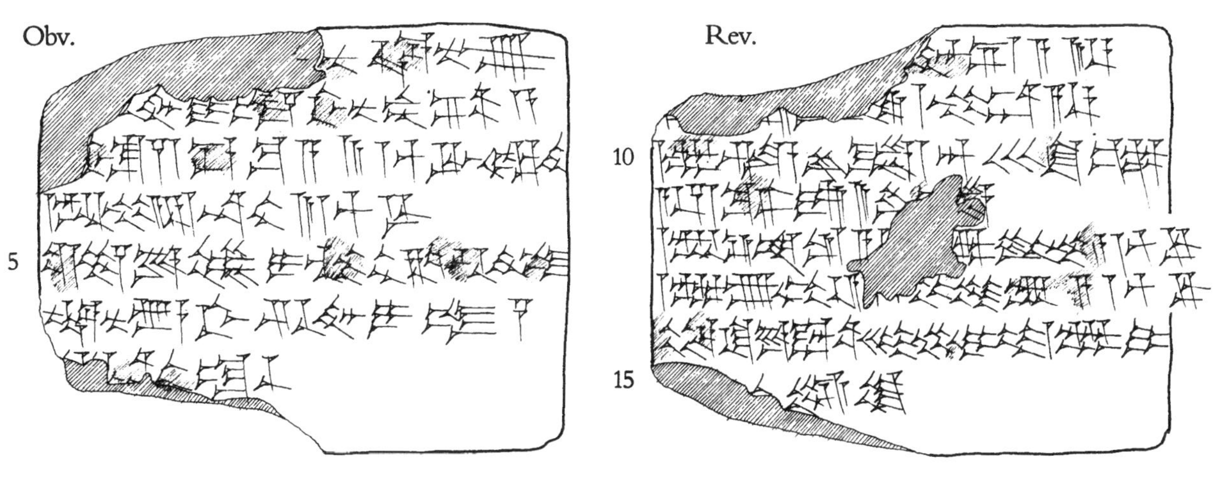

18

Obv.

Lo.E.

Rev.

U.E.

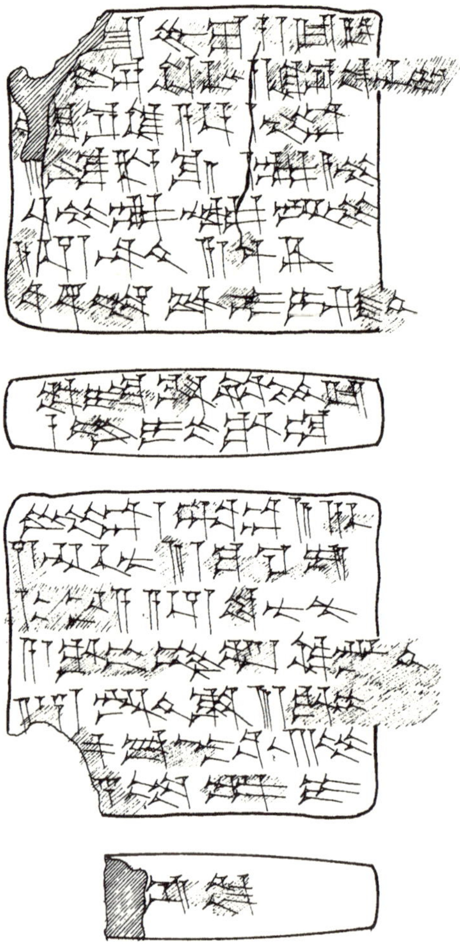

20

Obv.

Lo.E.

Rev.

U.E.

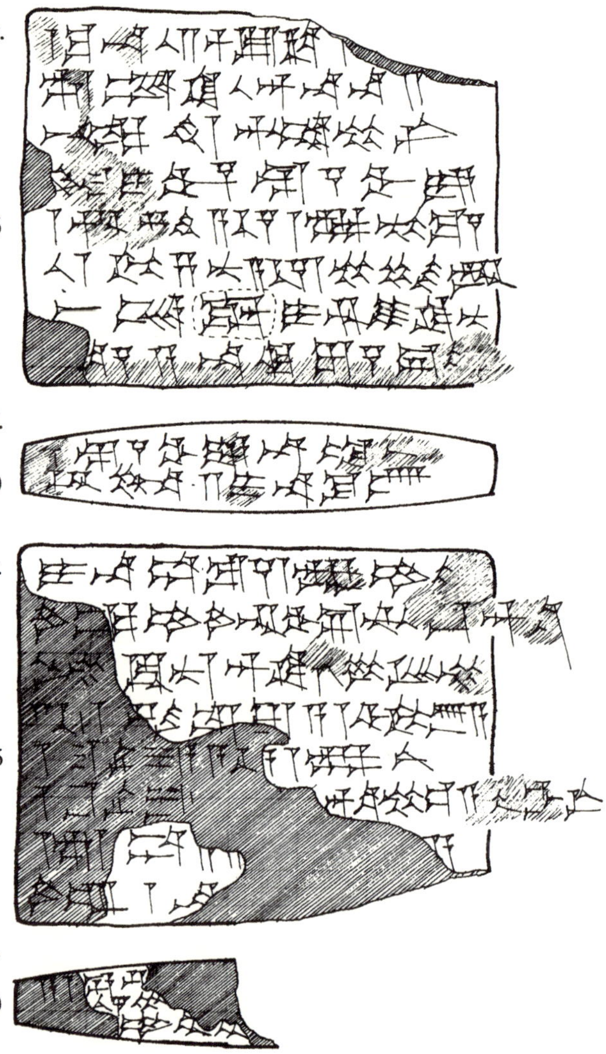

19

Obv.

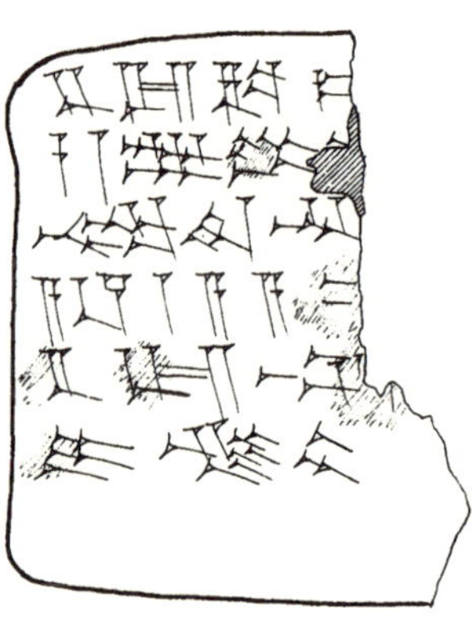

Rev.

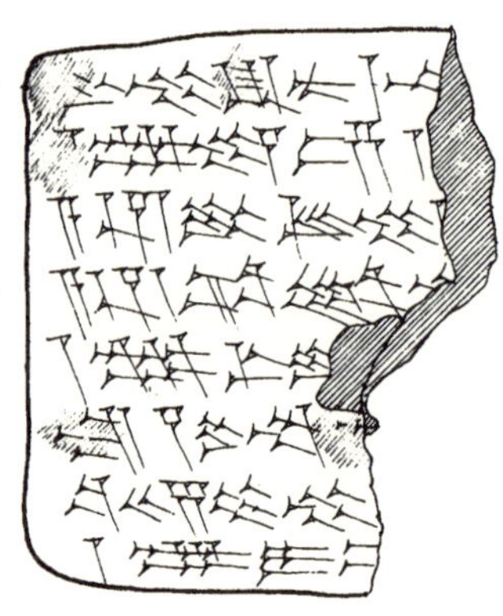

21

Obv.

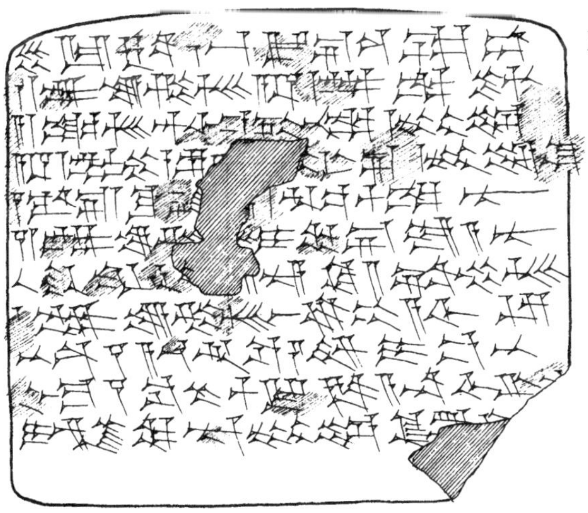

Rev.

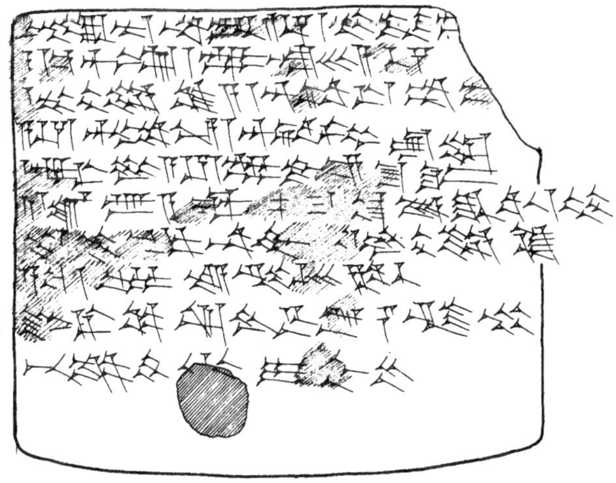

22

Obv.

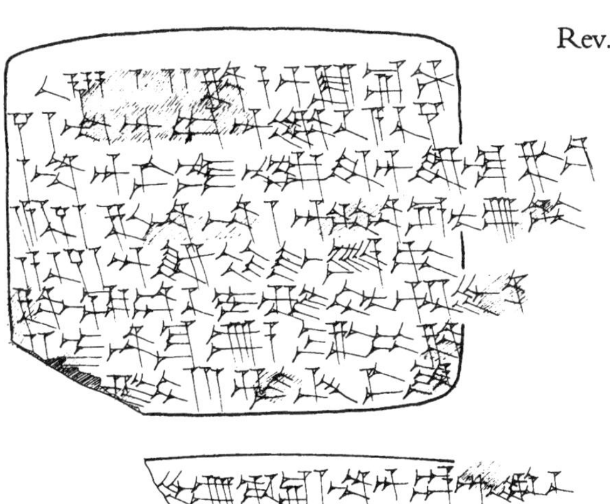

Rev.

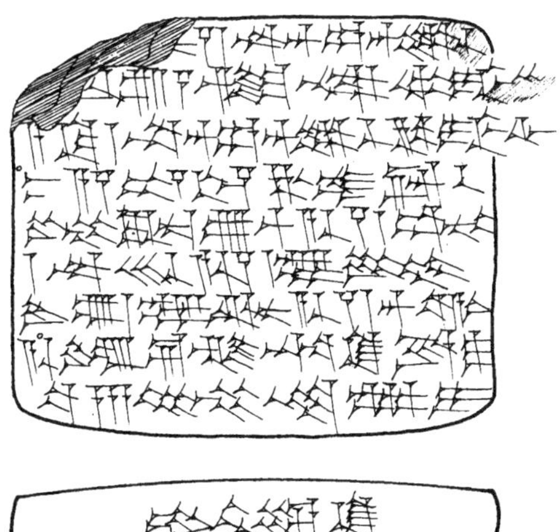

Lo.E.

U.E.

PLATE XVI

23

Obv.

Lo.E.

Rev.

U.E.

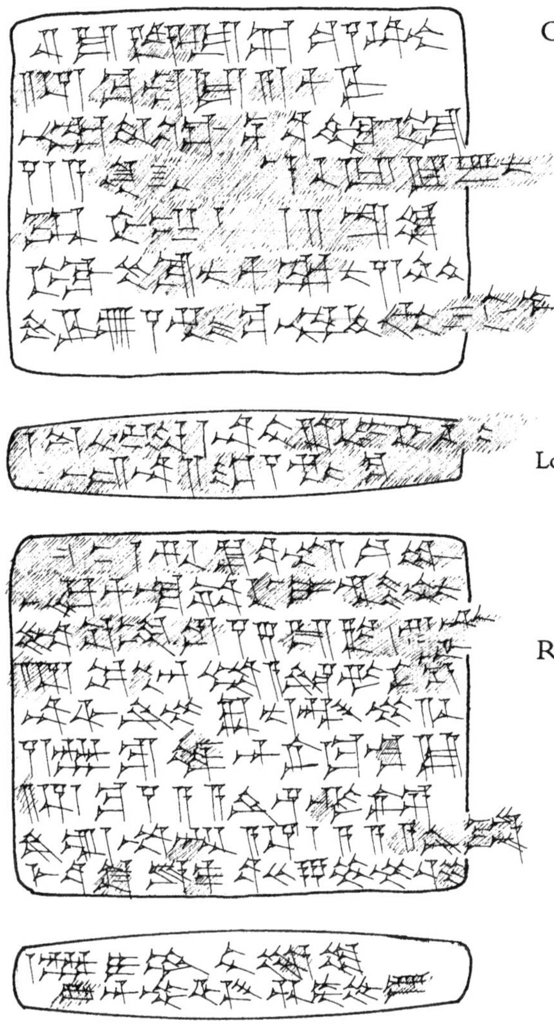

24

Obv.

Lo.E.

Rev.

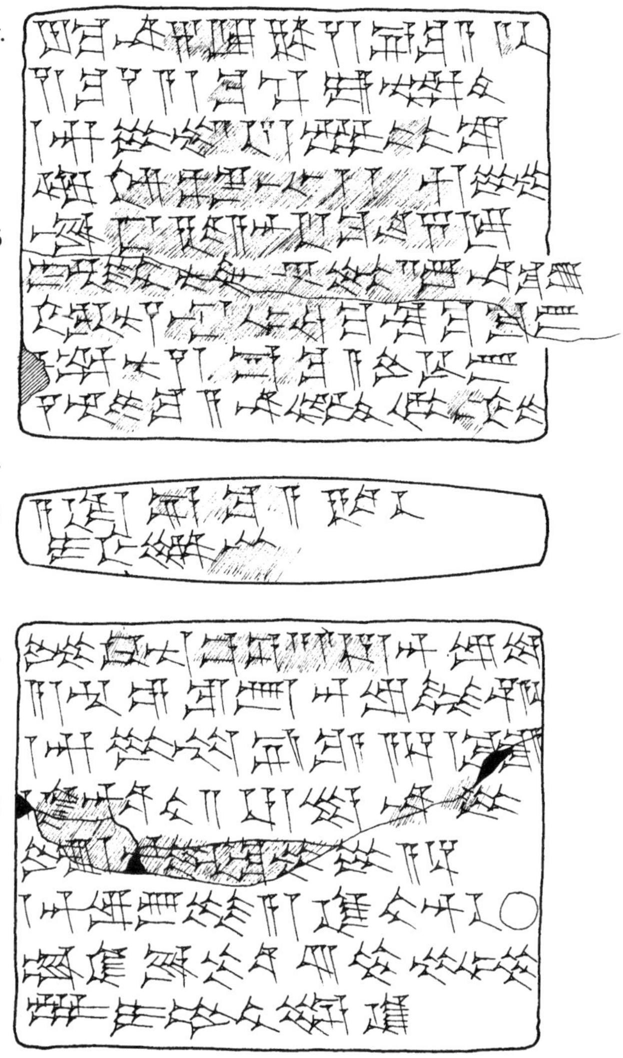

25

Obv.

Rev.

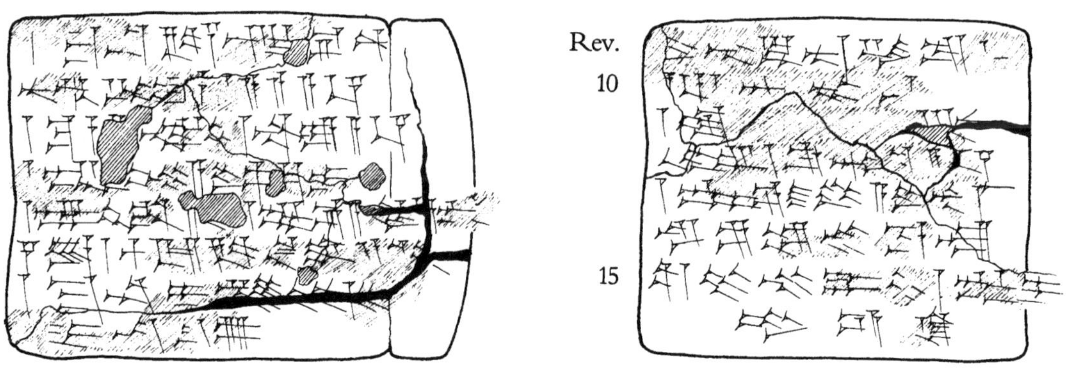

26

Obv.

Rev.

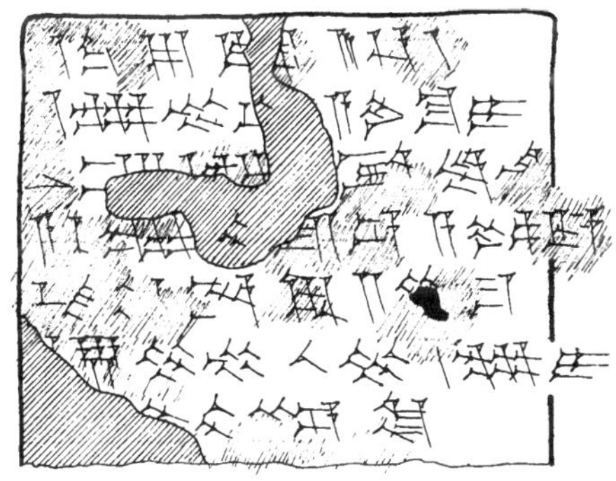

Lo.E.

27

Obv.

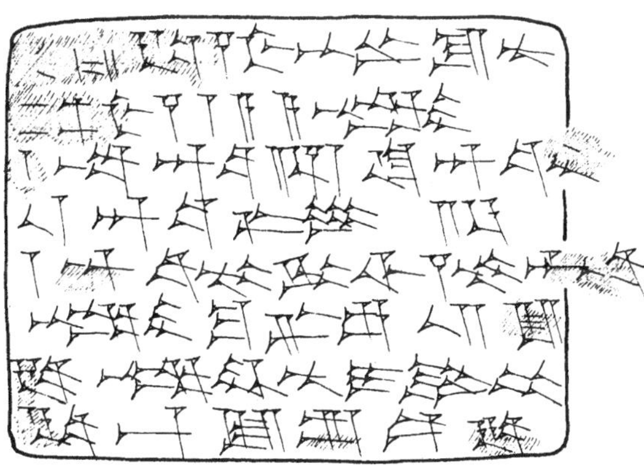

Rev.

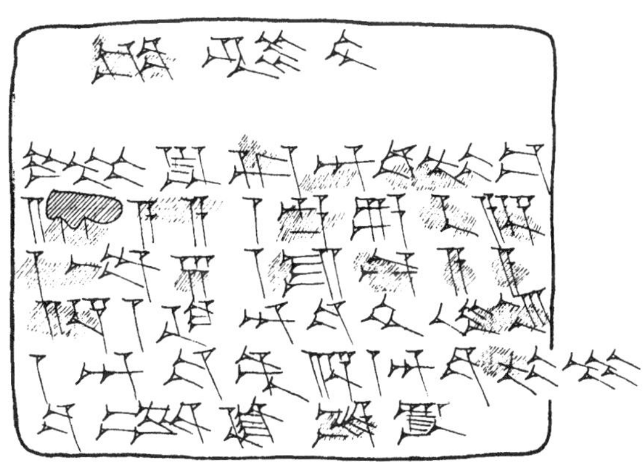

Lo.E.

U.E.

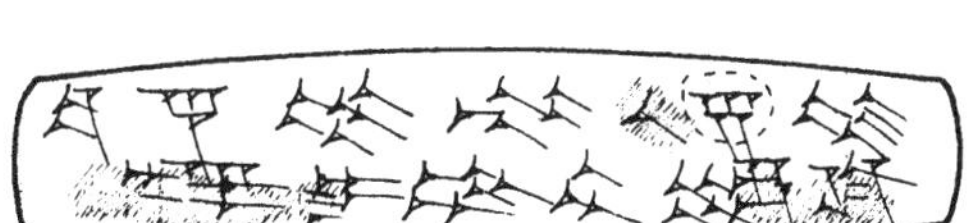

PLATE XVIII

28

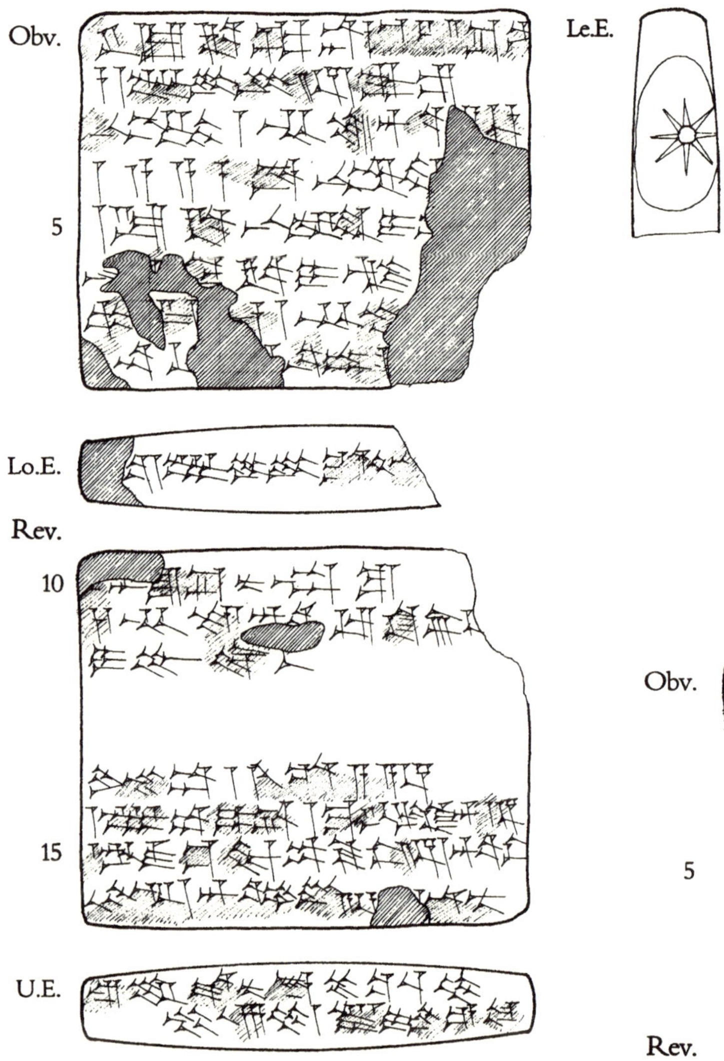

29

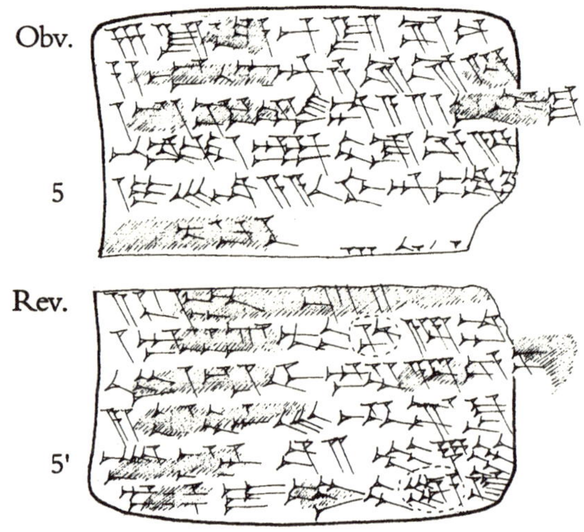

30

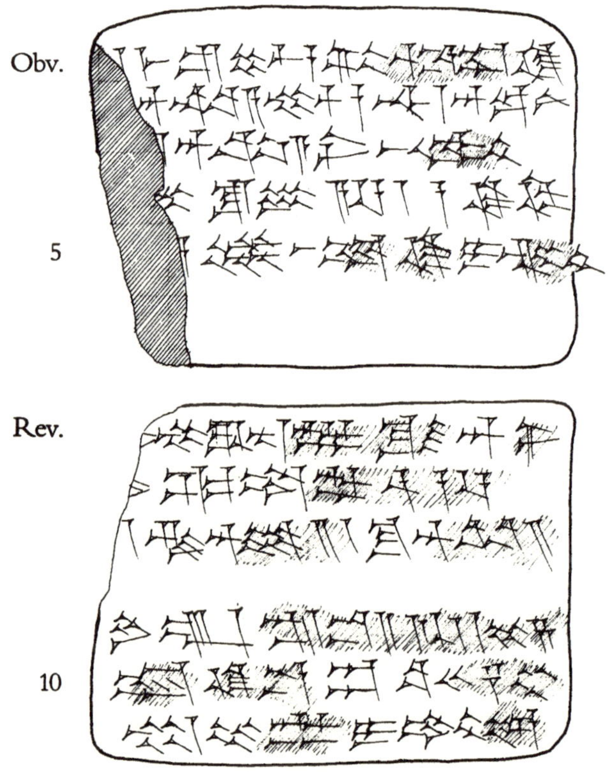

31

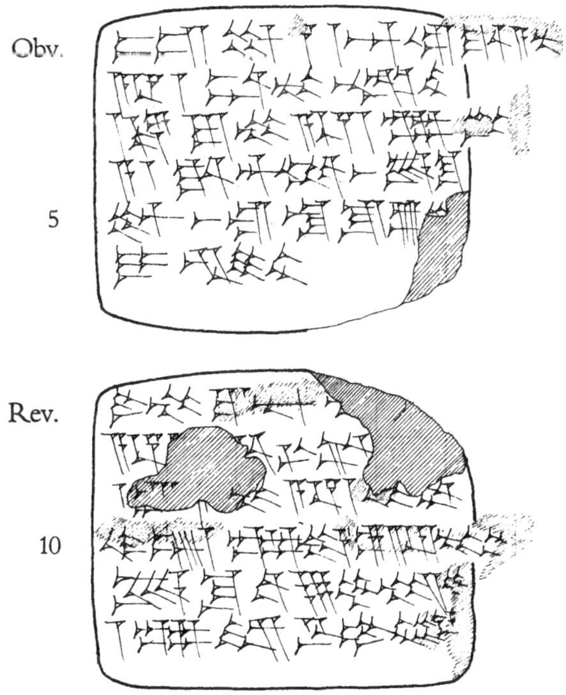

32

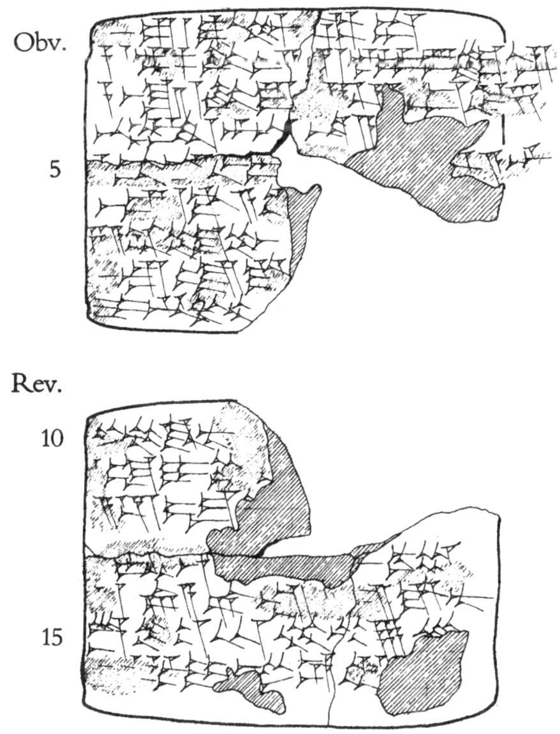

33

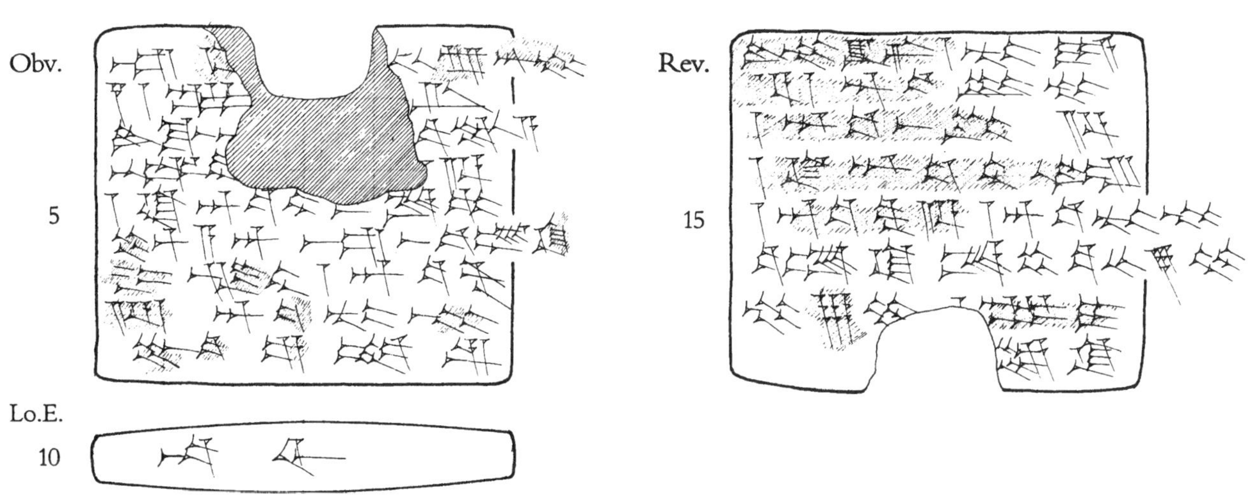

34

Obv.

Lo.E.

Rev.

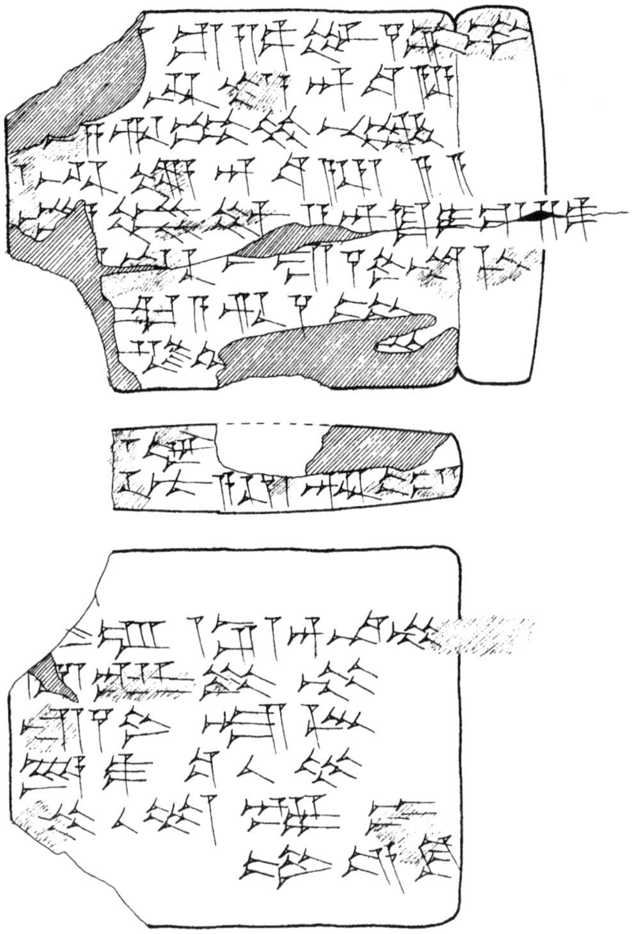

35

Obv.

Lo.E.

Rev.

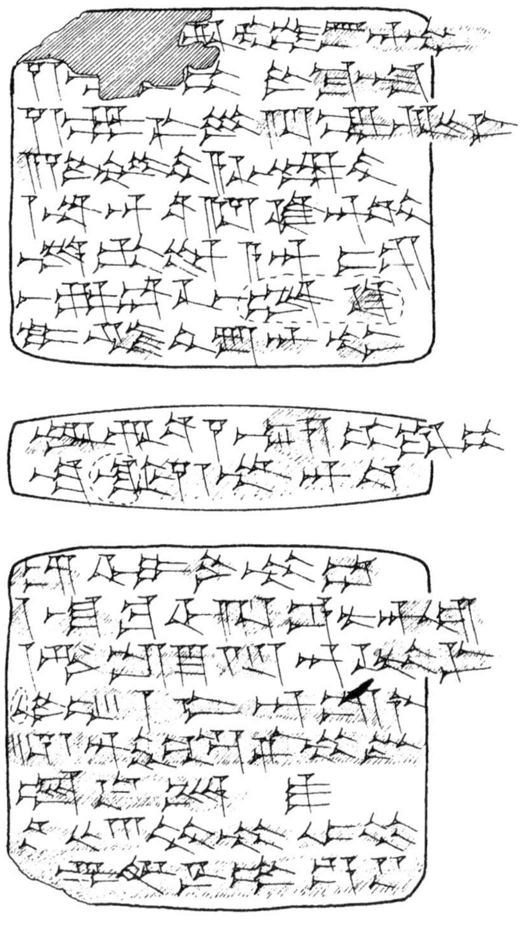

36

Obv.

Lo.E.

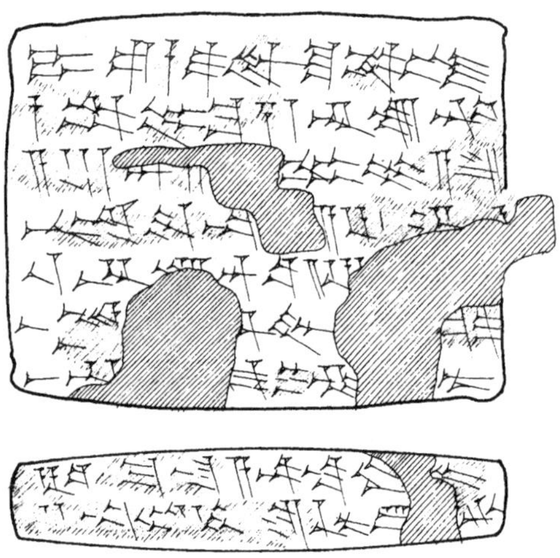

Rev.

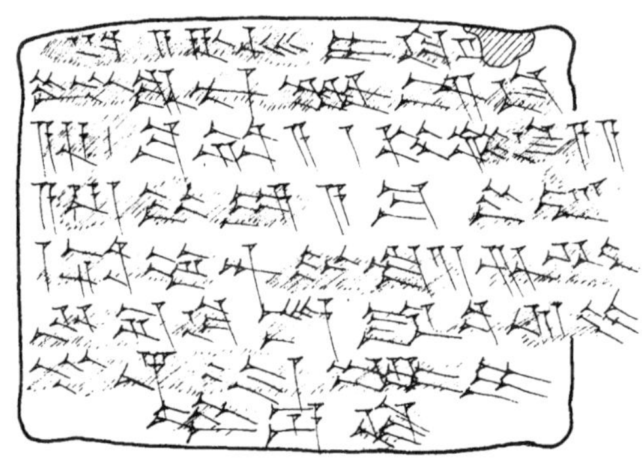

37

Obv.

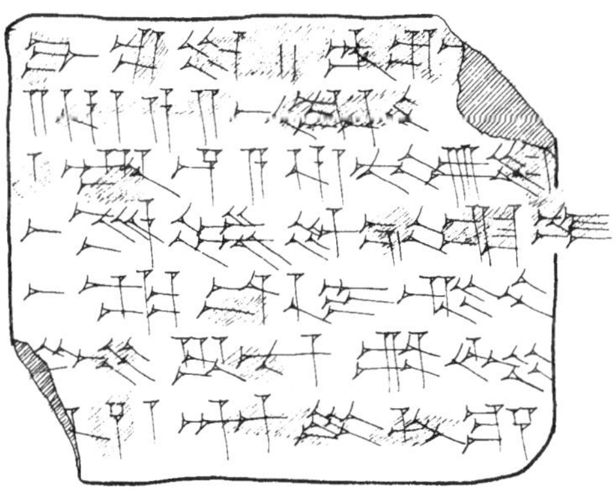

Rev.

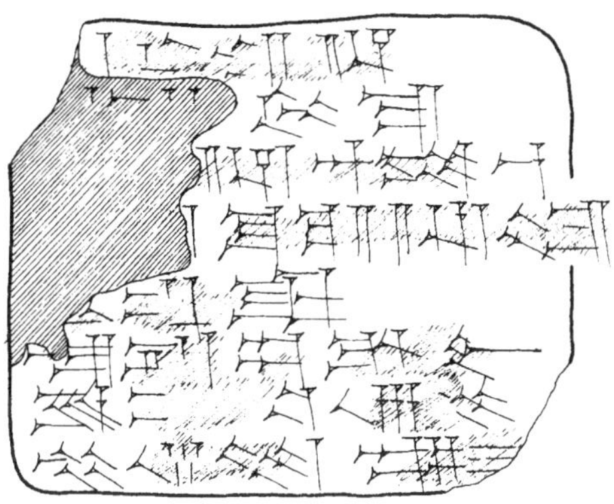

U.E.

38

Obv.

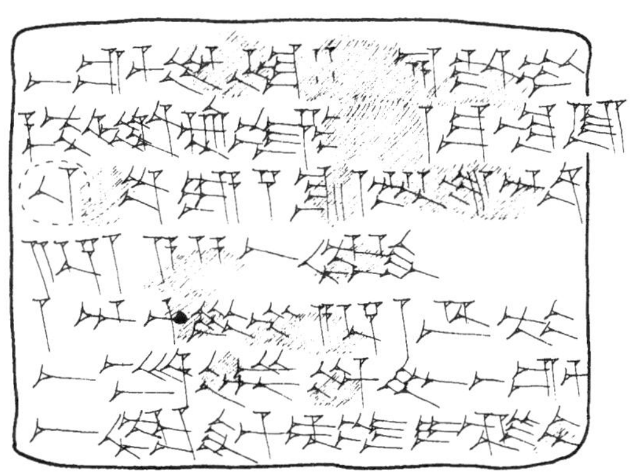

Rev.

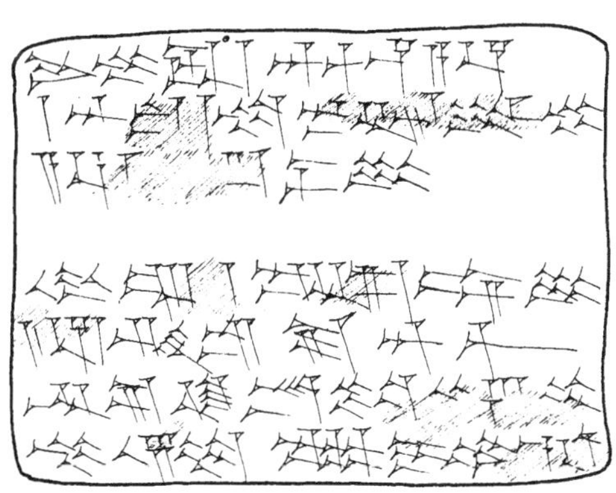

PLATE XXII

39

Le.E.

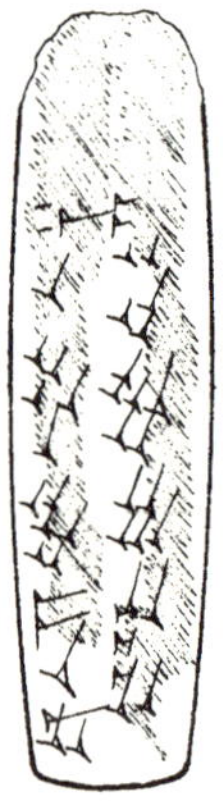

Obv.

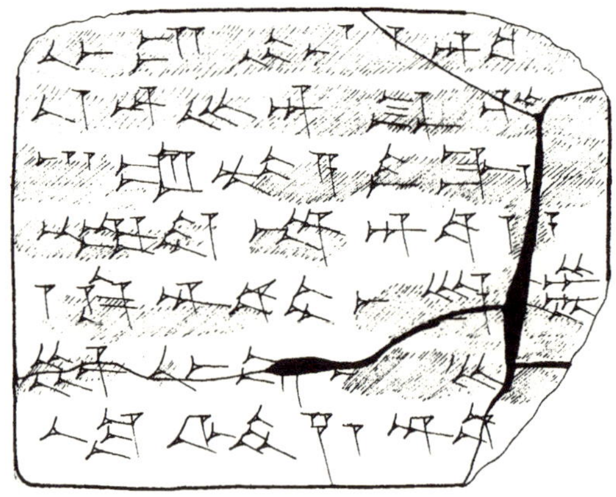

Lo.E.

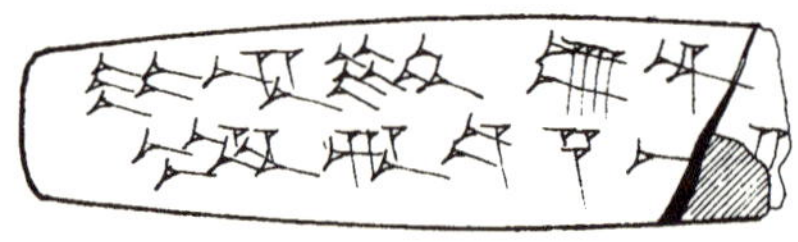

Rev.

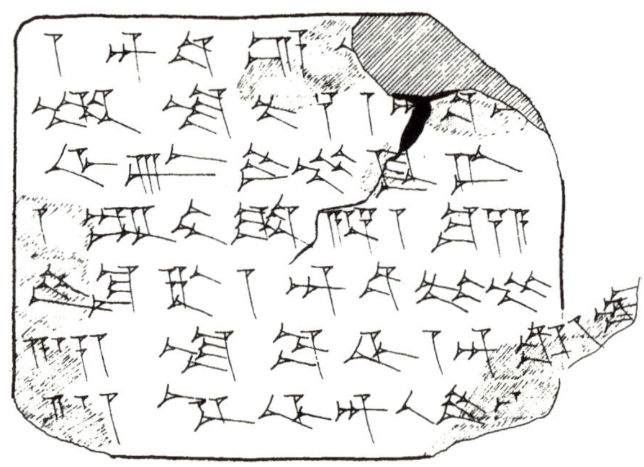

U.E.

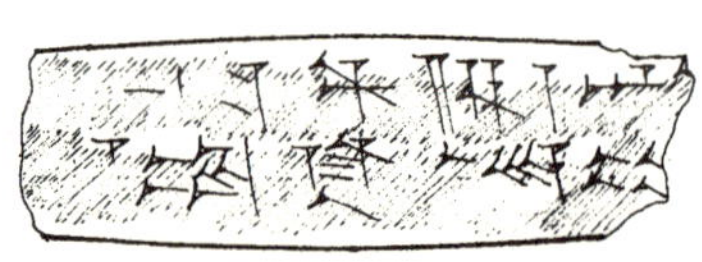

40

Obv.

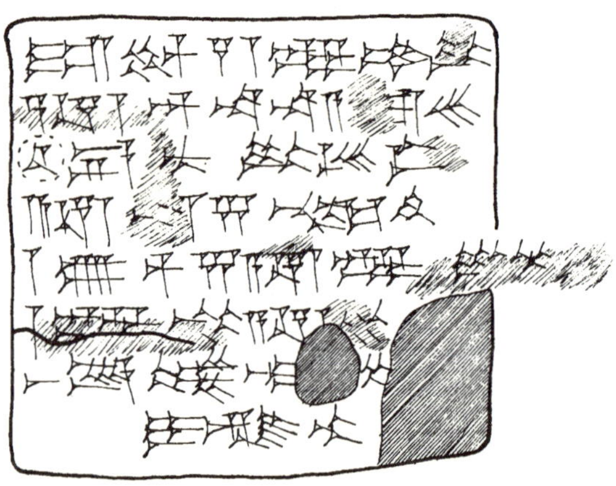

Rev.

U.E.

41

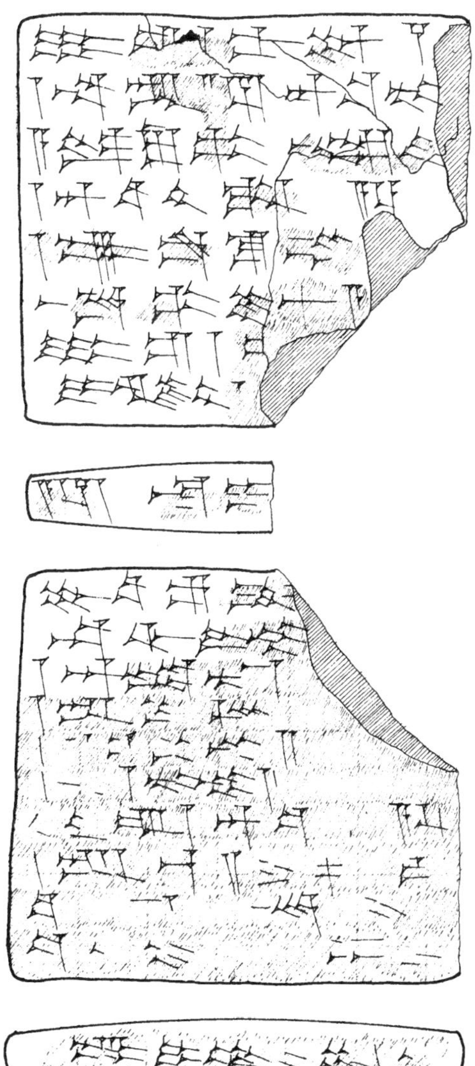

42

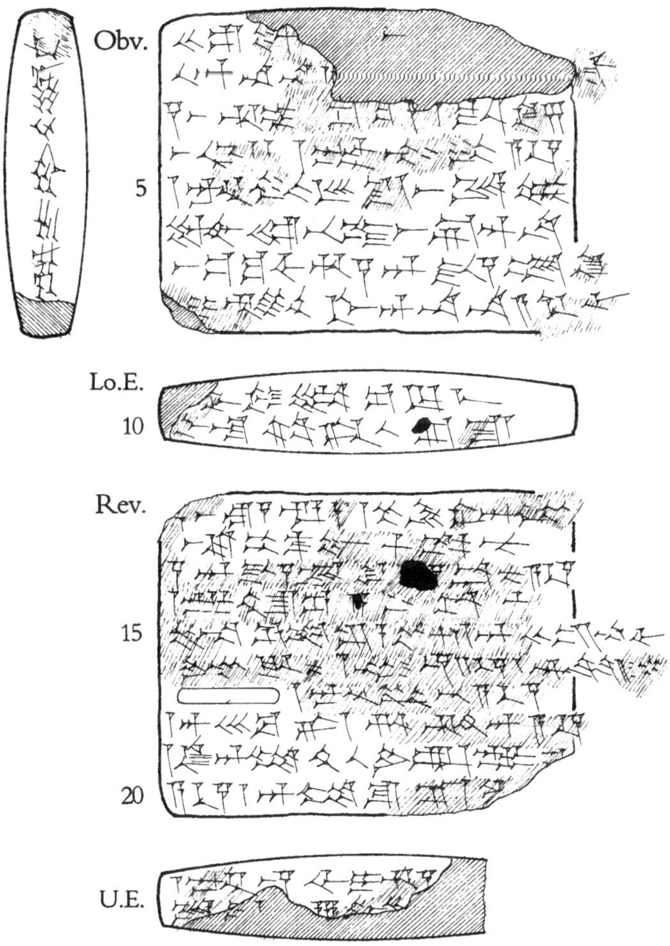

PLATE XXIV

43

Le.E.

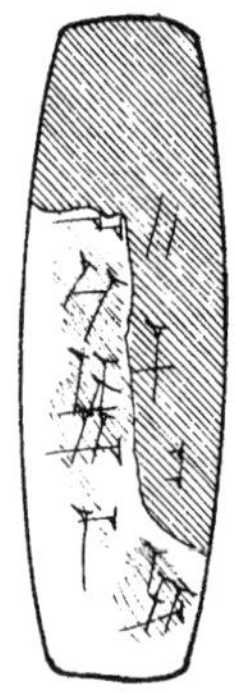

Obv.

Lo.E.

Rev.

U.E.

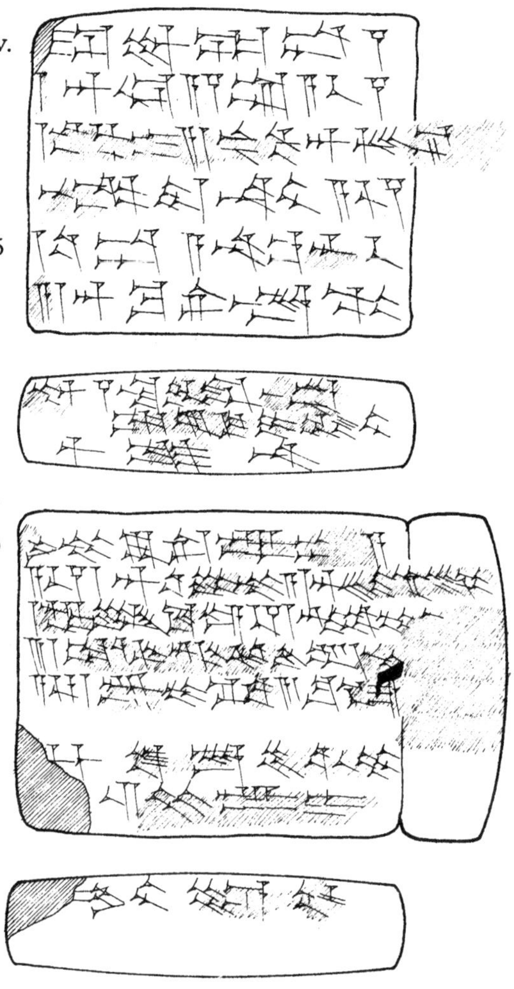

44

Obv.

Lo.E.

Rev.

U.E.

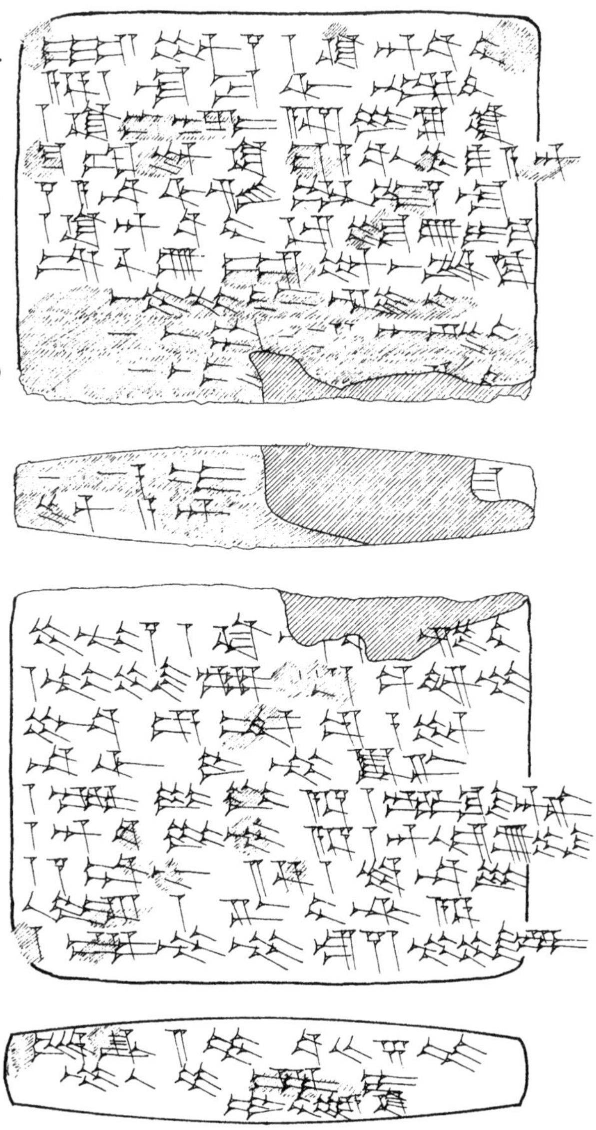

45

Obv.

Rev.

Le.E.

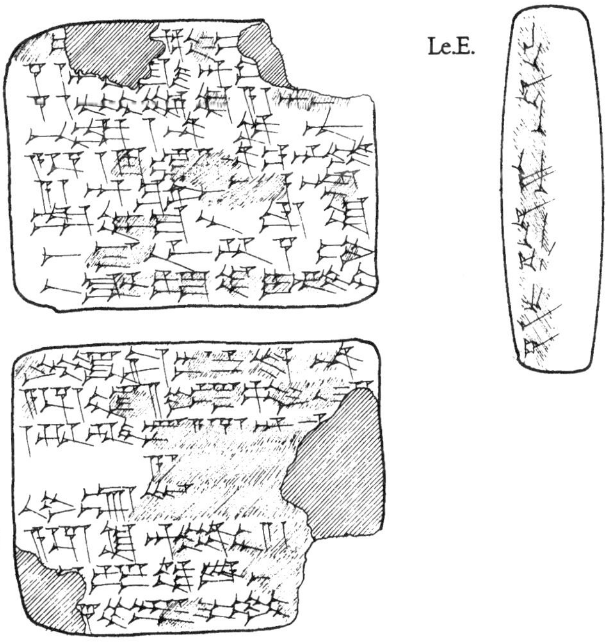

46

Obv.

Lo.E.

Rev.

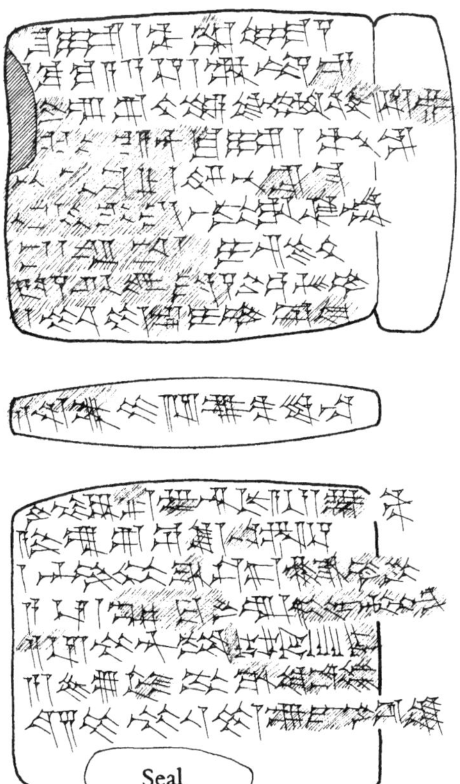

47

Obv.

Lo.E.

Rev.

U.E.

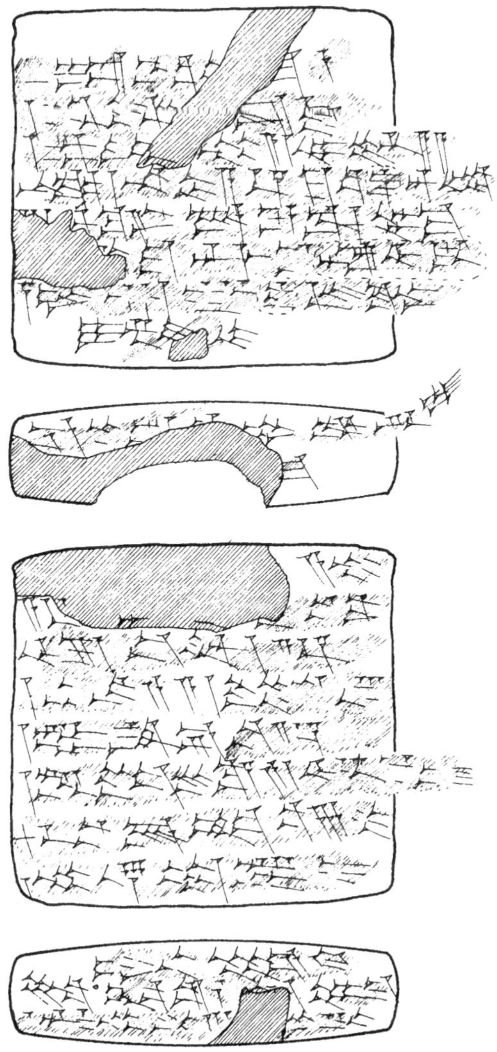

PLATE XXVI

48

Obv.

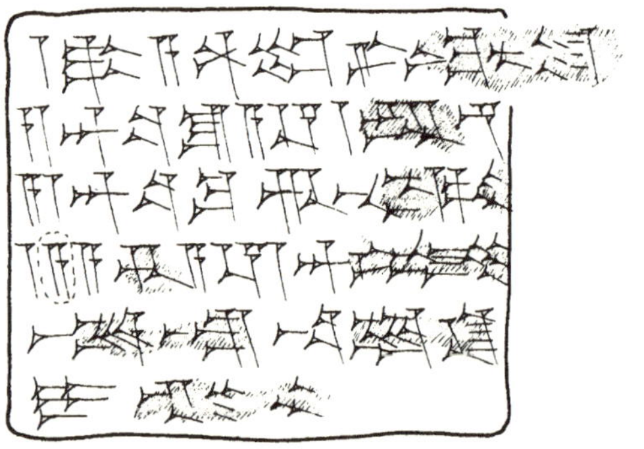

Lo.E.

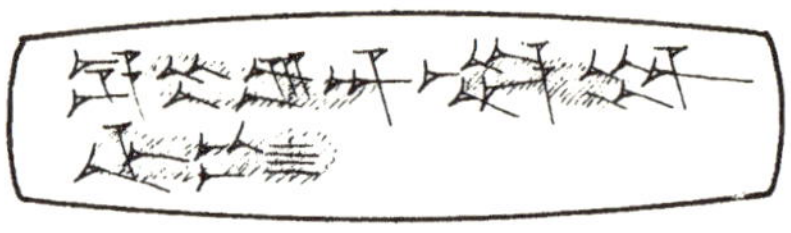

Rev.

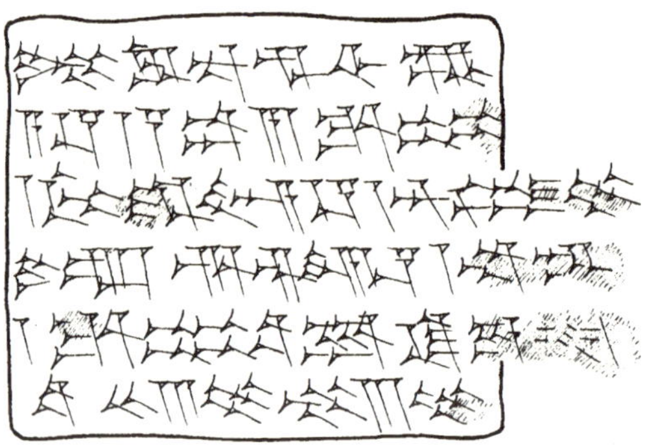

U.E.

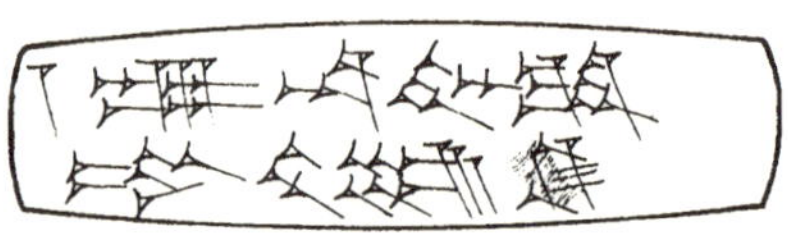

49

Obv.

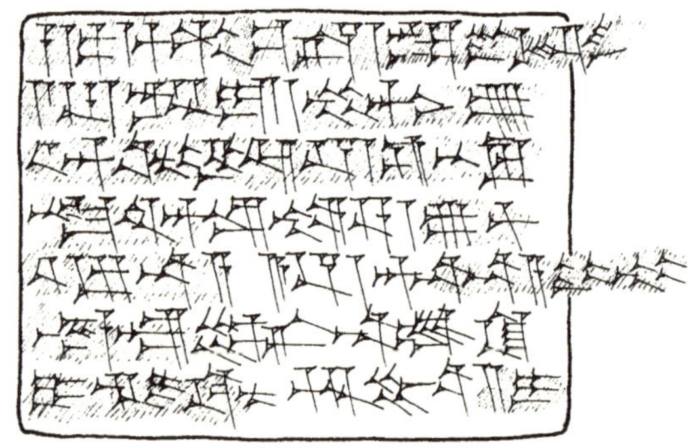

Lo.E.

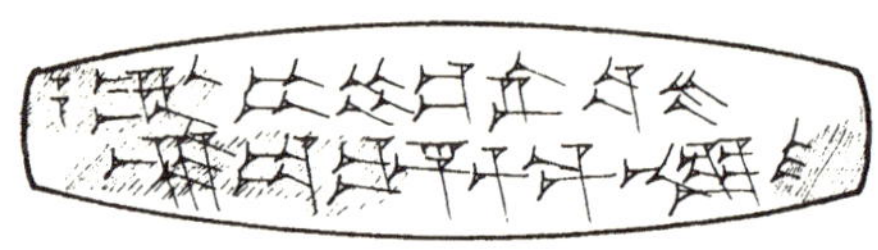

Rev.

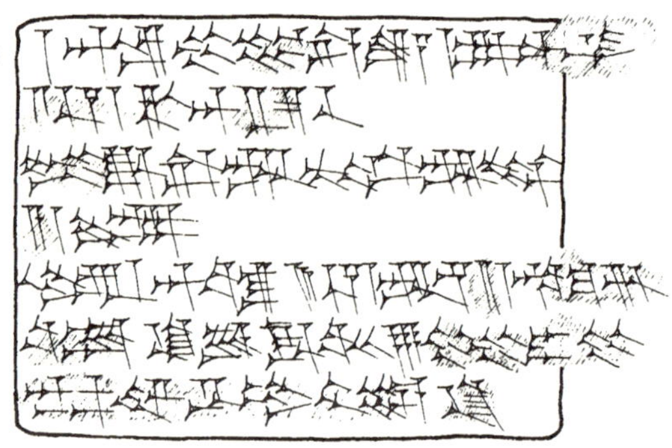

50

Obv.

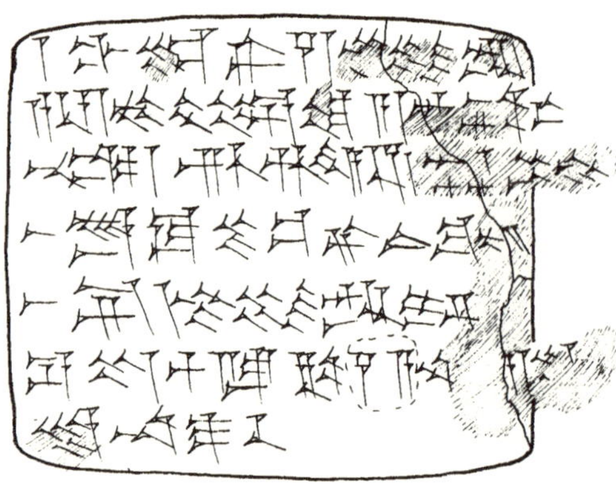

Rev.

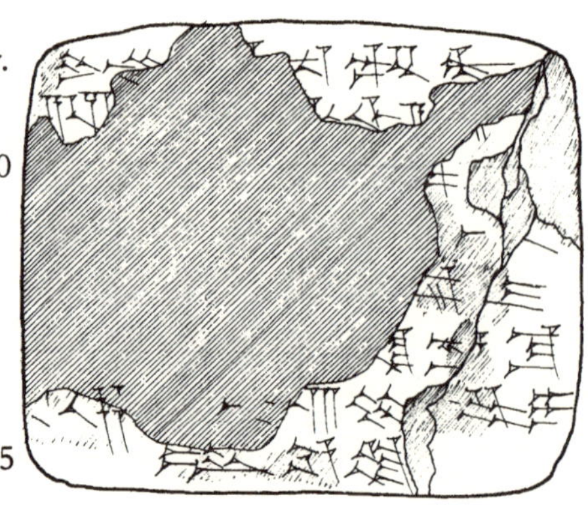

51

Obv.

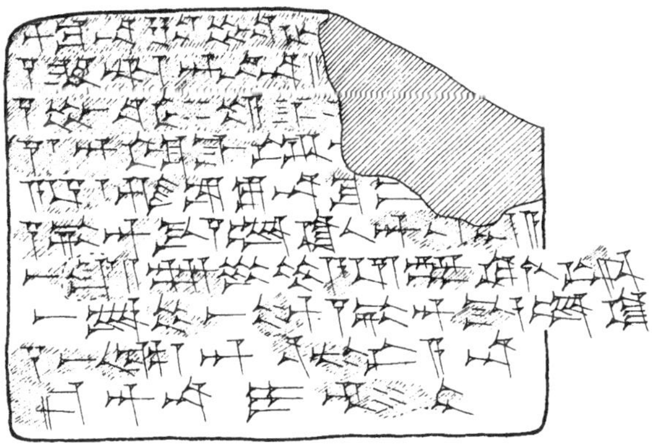

Rev.

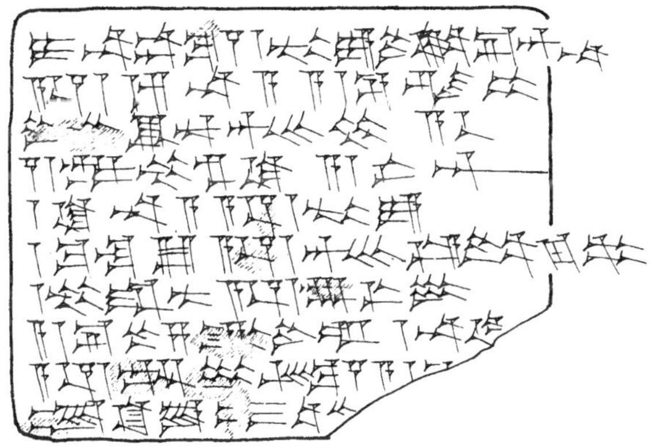

U.E.

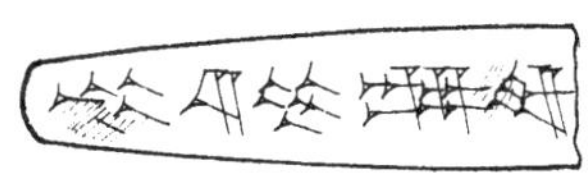

52

Obv.

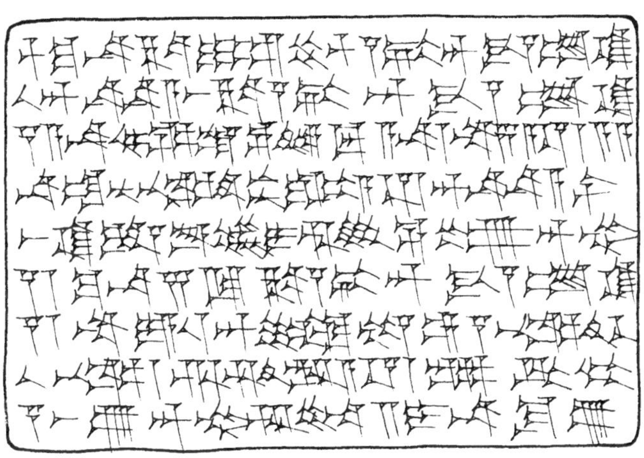

Rev.

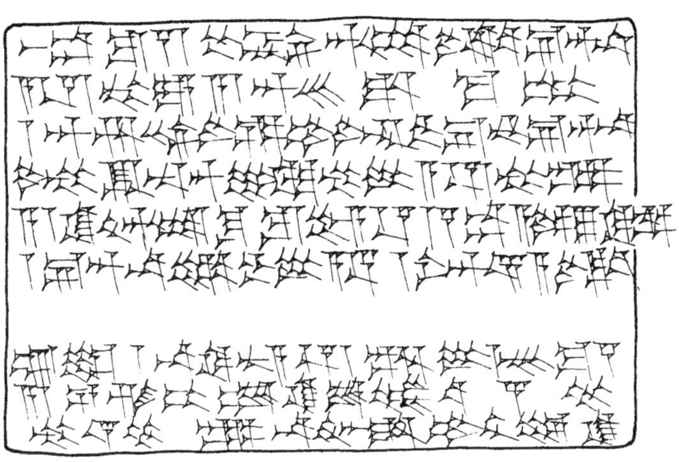

PLATE XXVIII

54

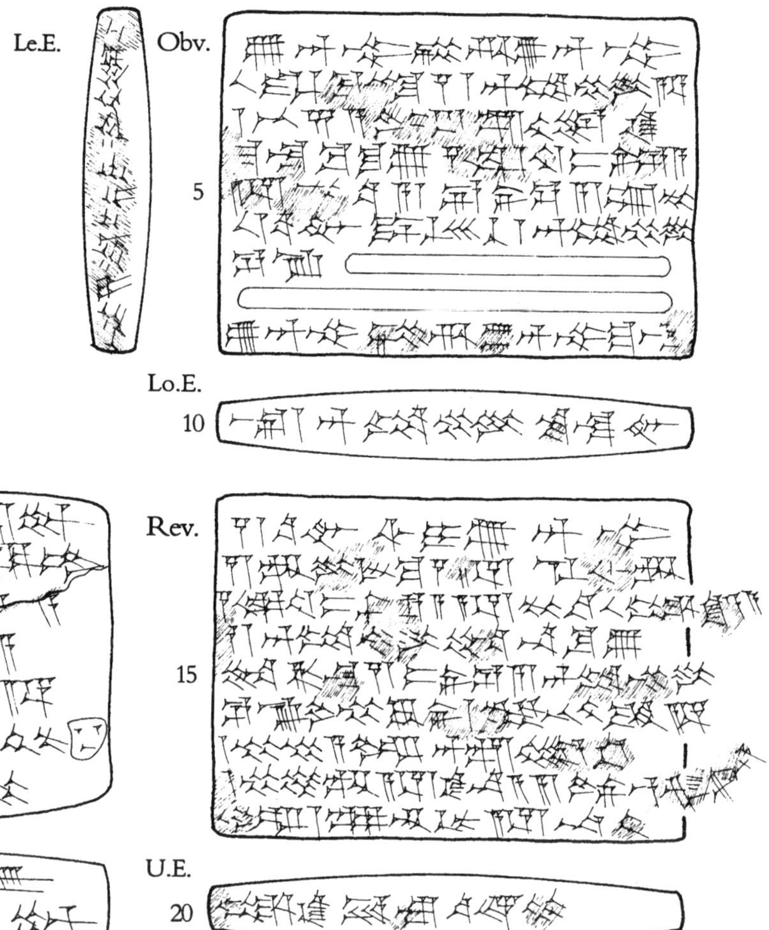

53

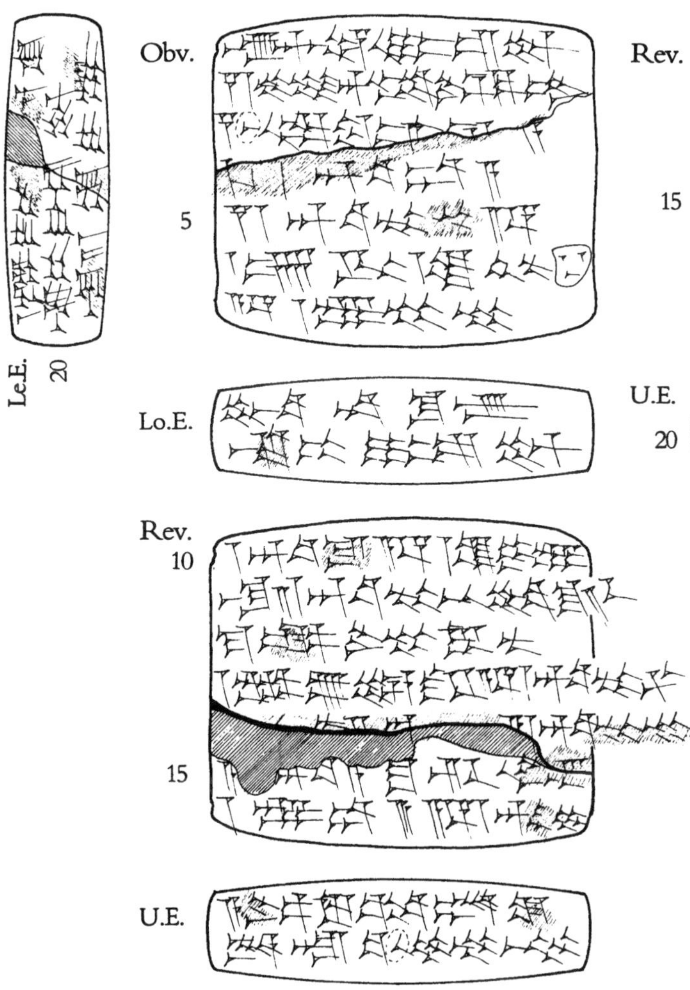

55

Obv.

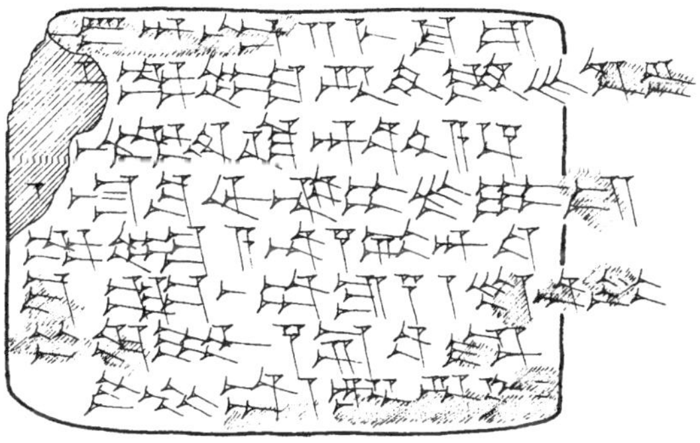

Rev.

56

Obv.

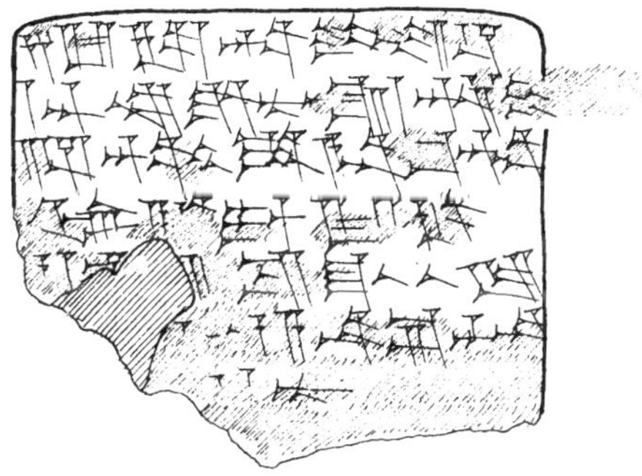

Rev.

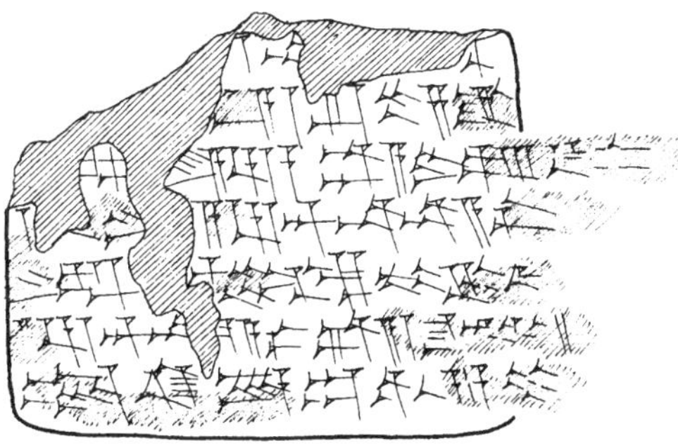

U.E.

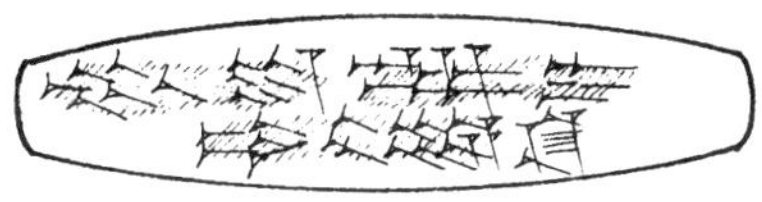

57

Obv.

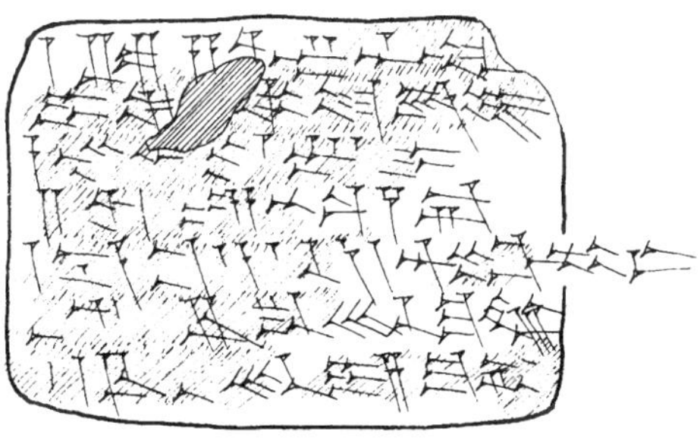

Lo.E.

Rev.

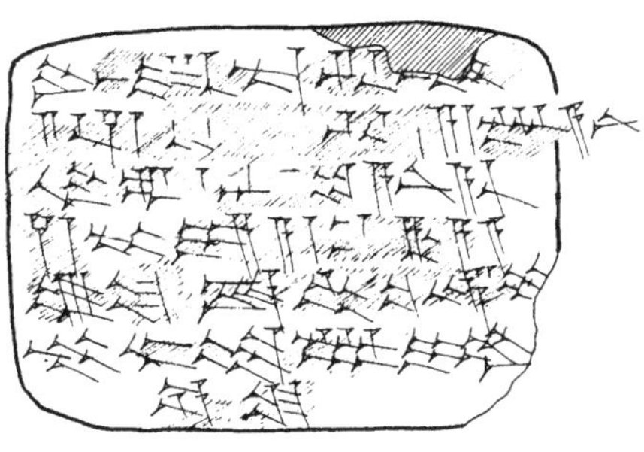

58

Obv.

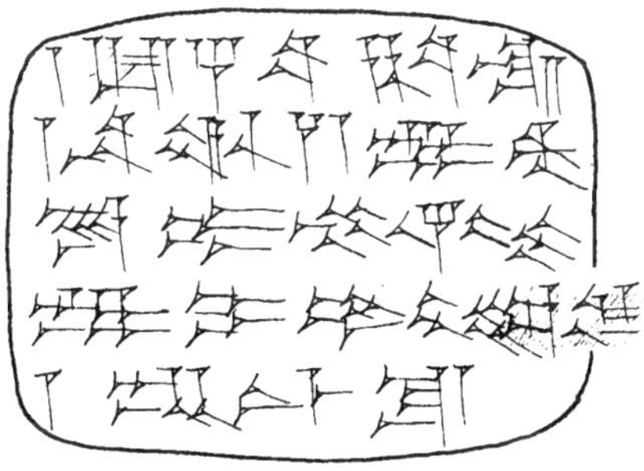

Lo.E.

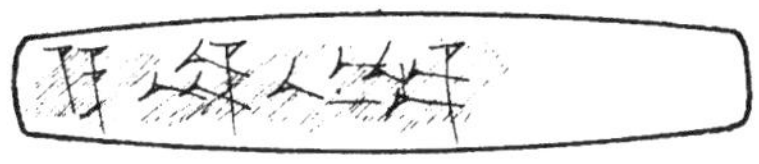

Rev.

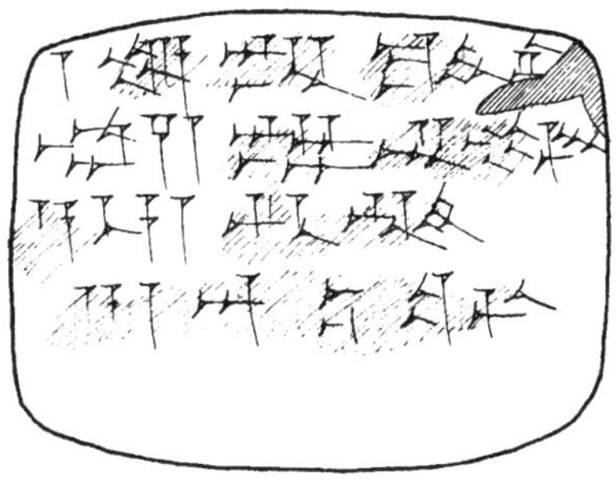

59

Obv.

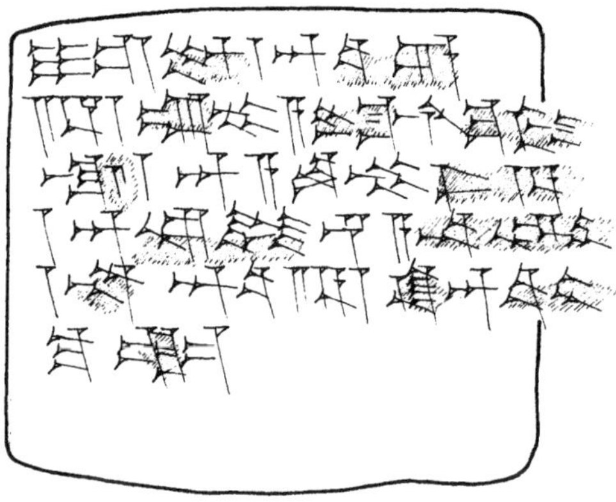

Rev.

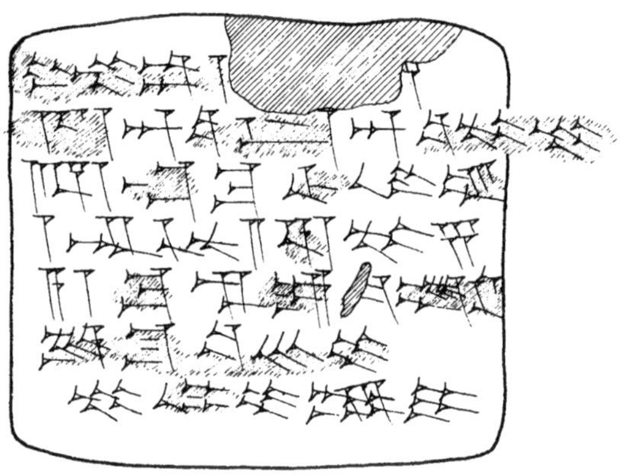

U.E.

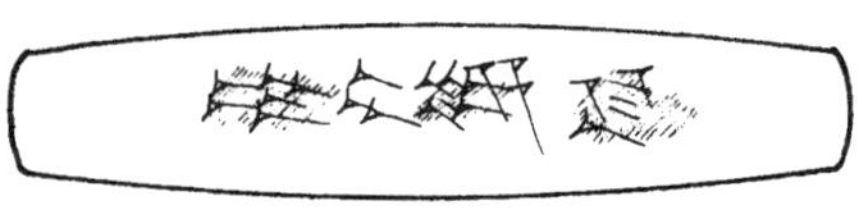

60

Obv.

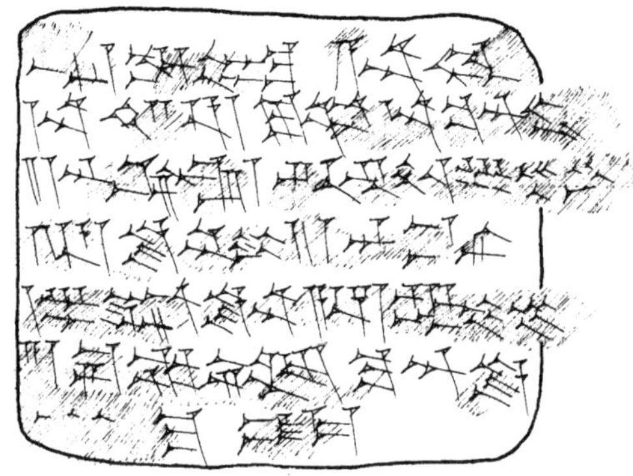

Rev.

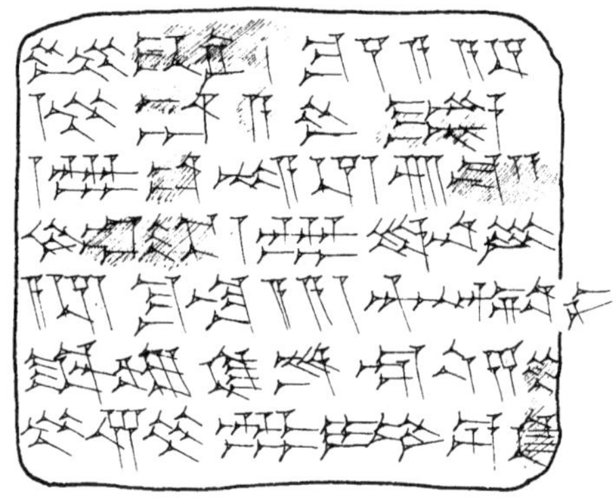

61

Obv.

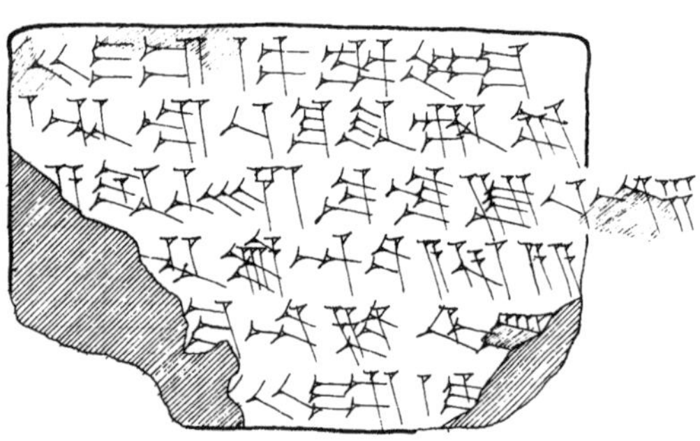

Lo.E.

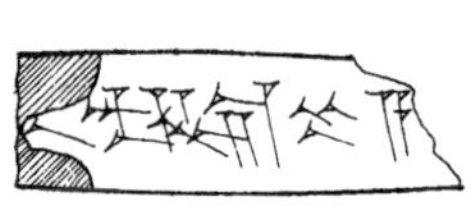

Rev.

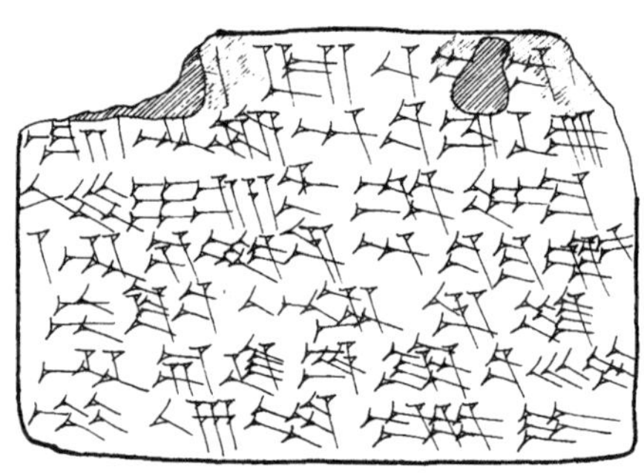

U.E.

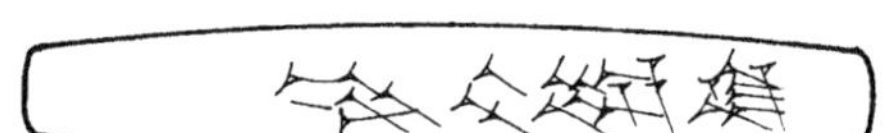

62

Obv.

Lo.E.

Rev.

U.E.

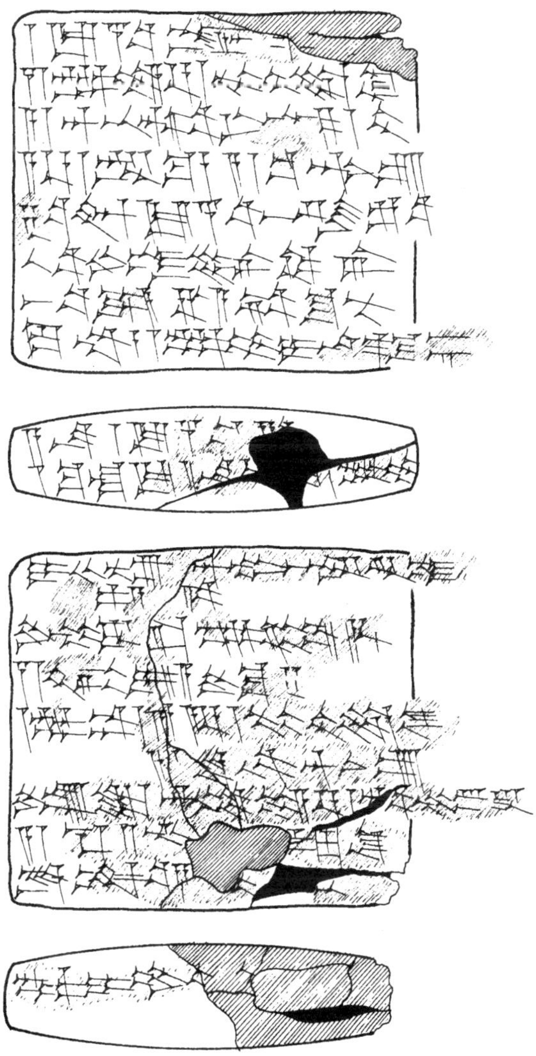

63

Obv.

Lo.E.

Rev.

U.E.

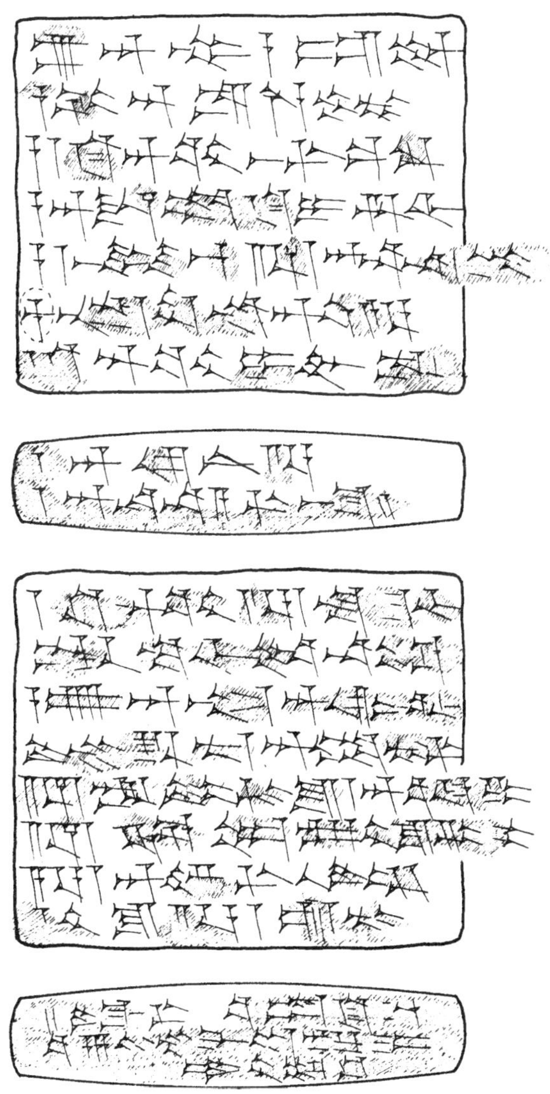

64

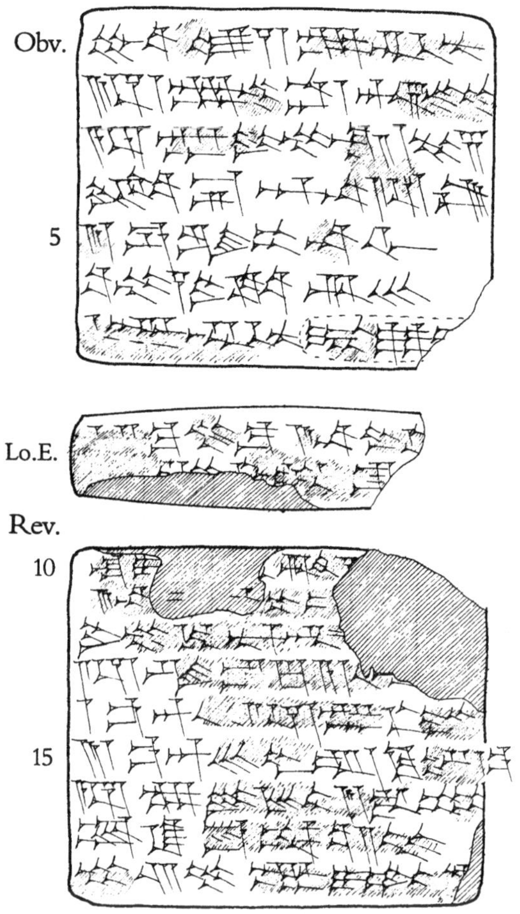

65

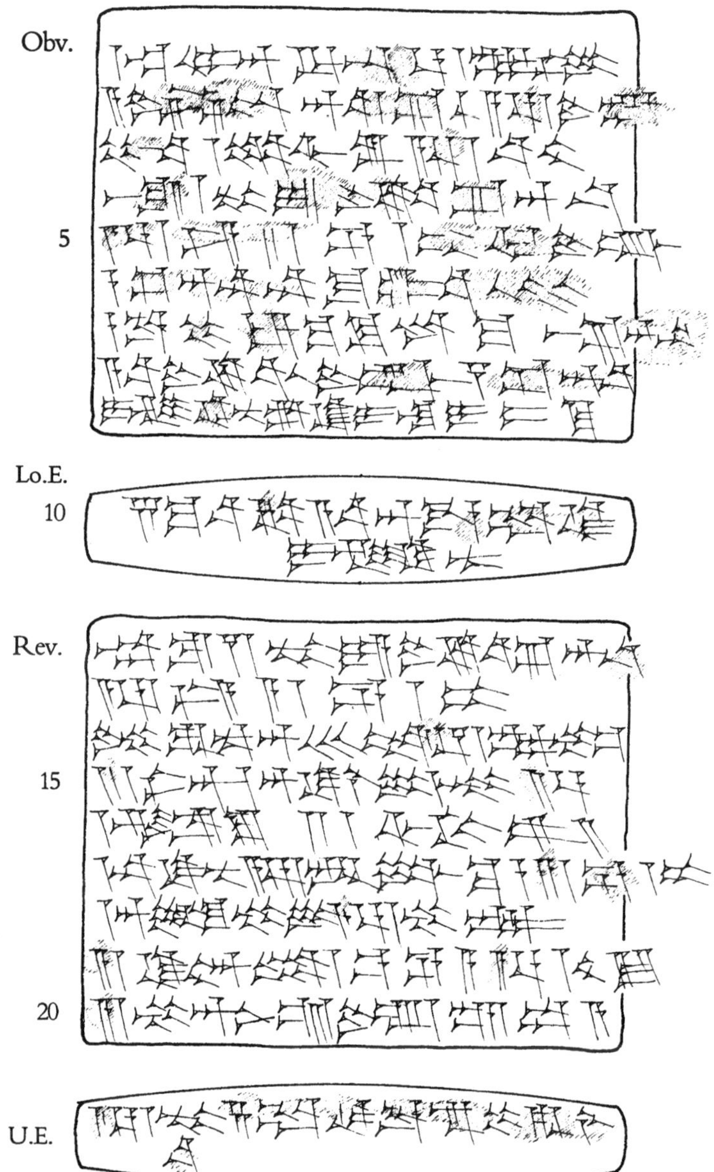

67

Obv.
Rev.
U.E.

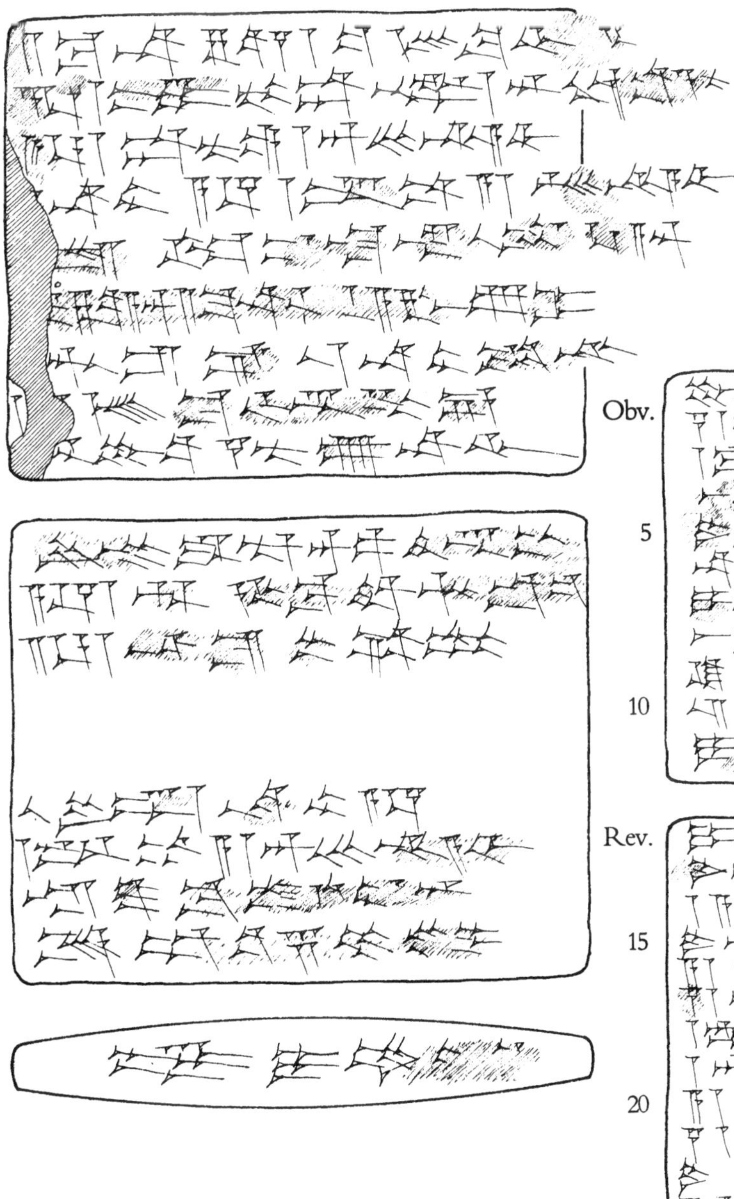

66

Obv.
Rev.
U.E.

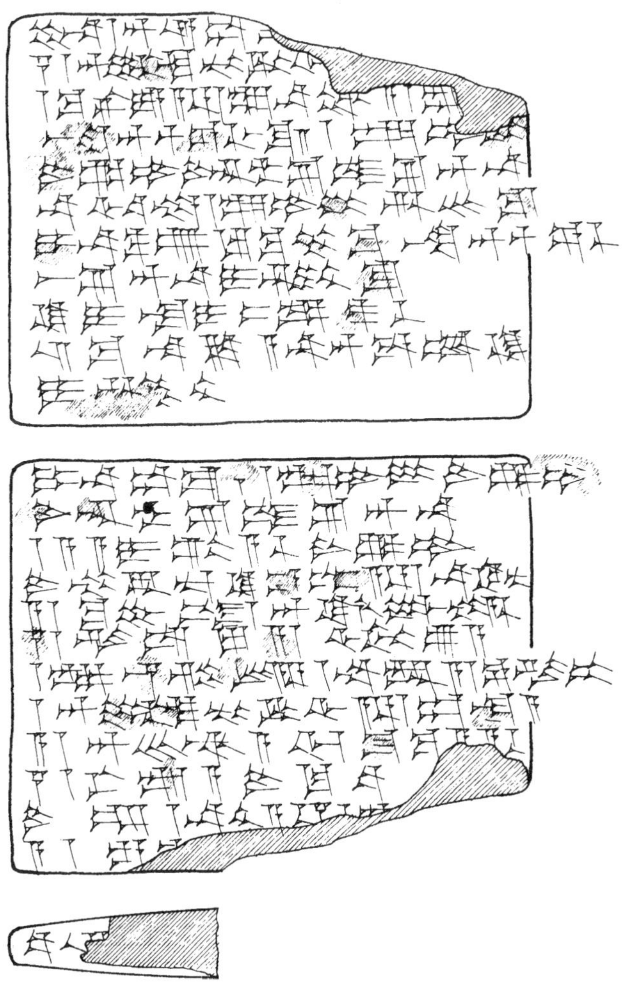

68

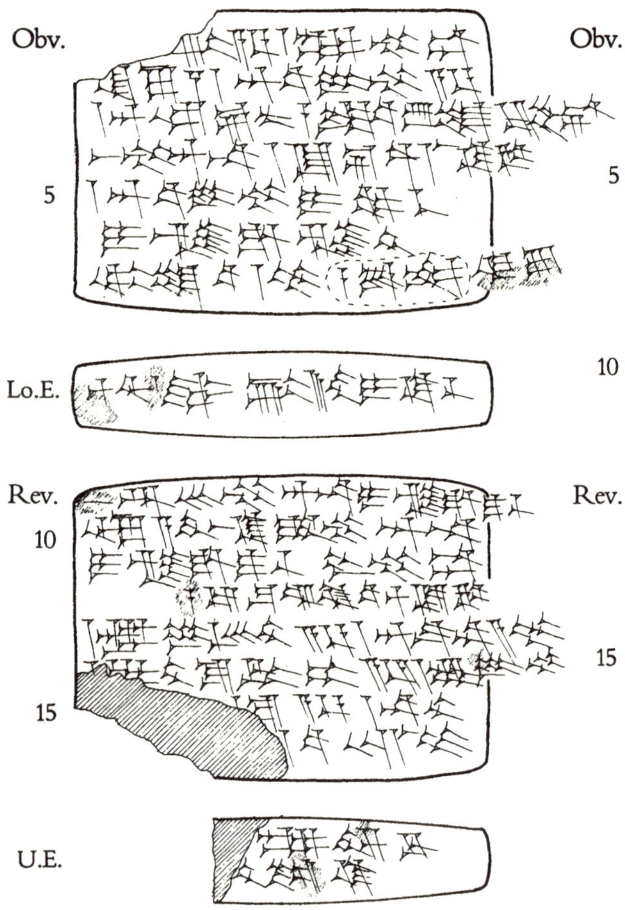

69

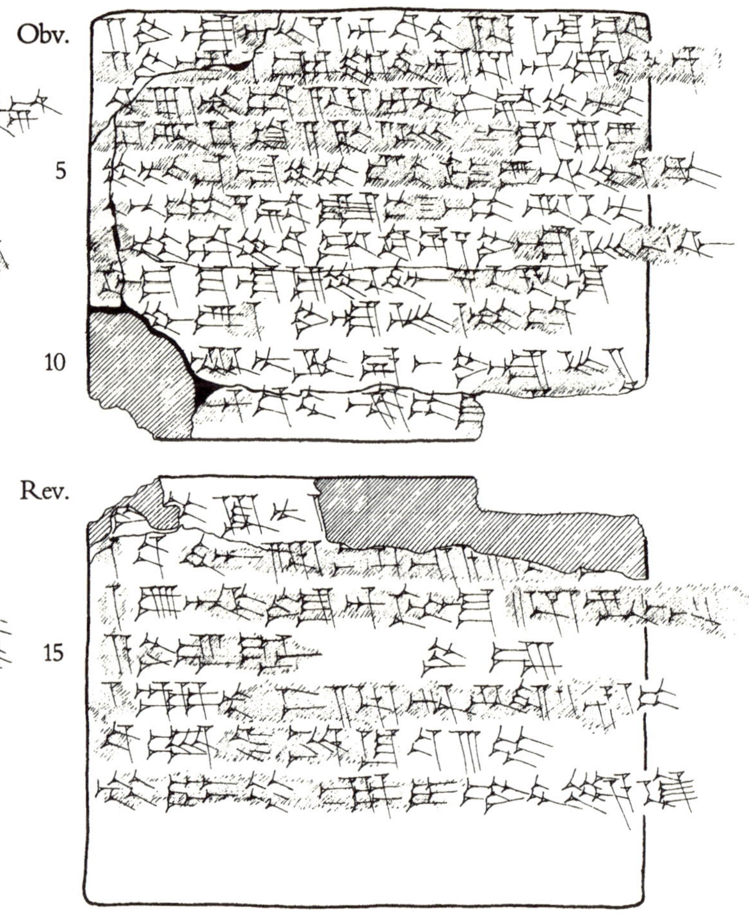

70

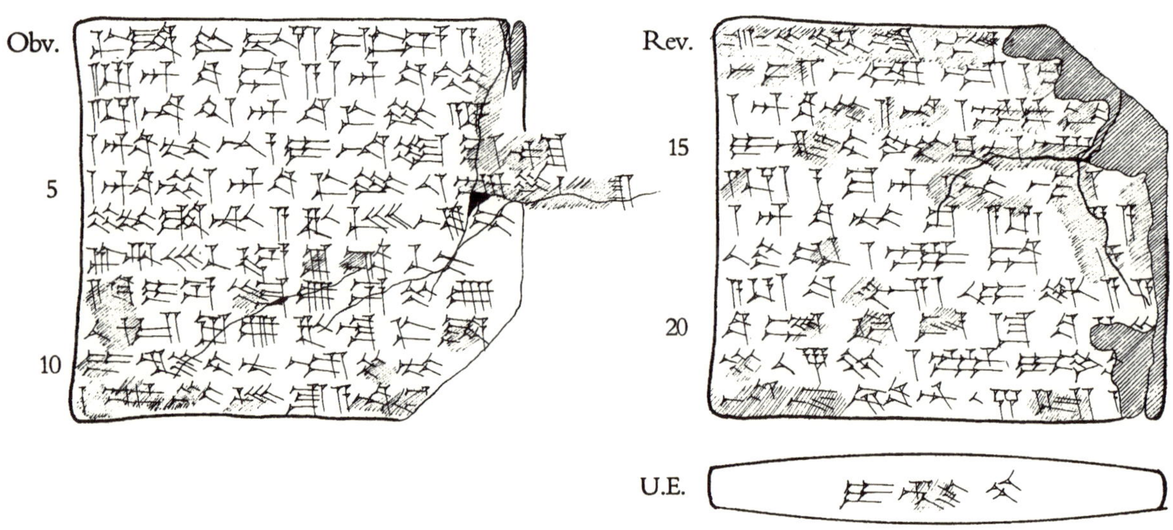

71

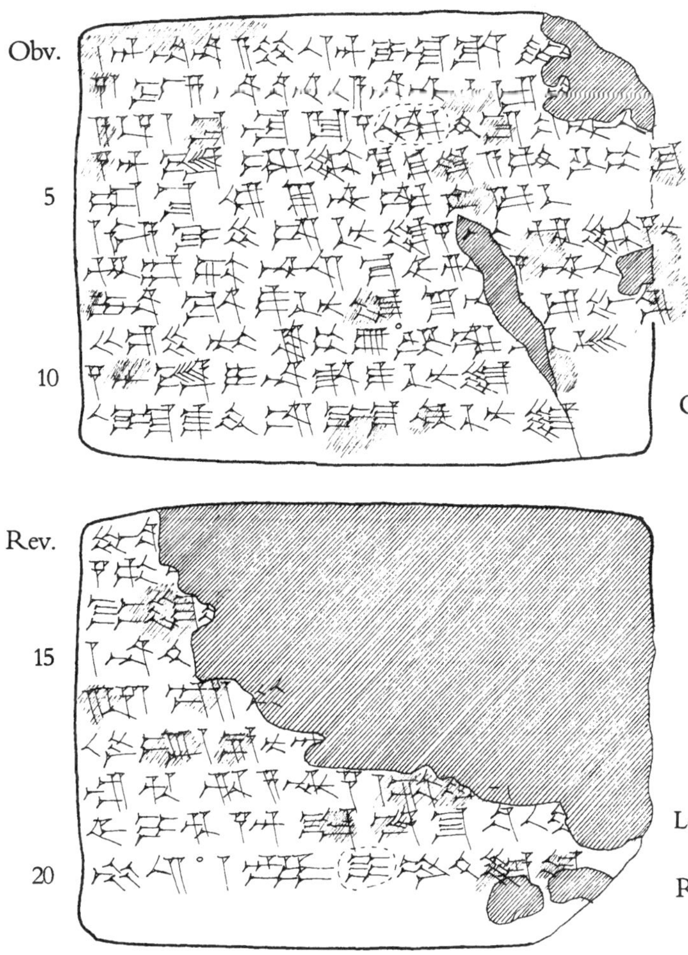

72

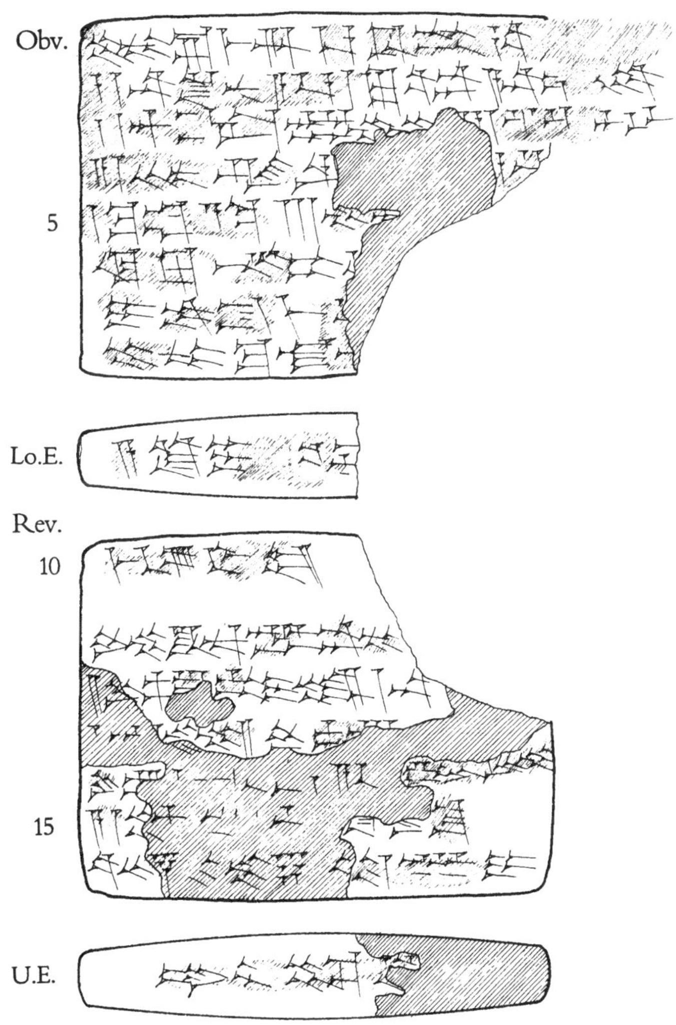

73

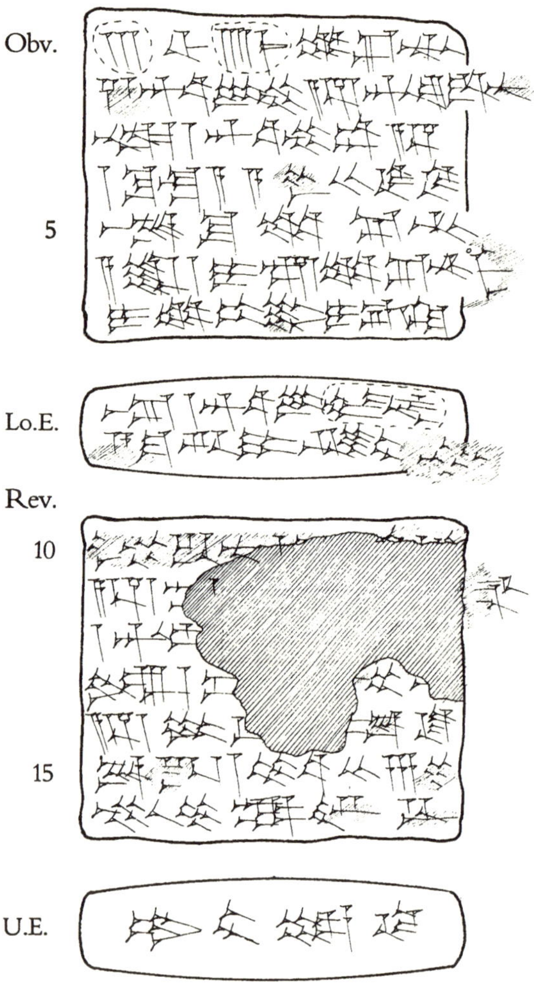

74

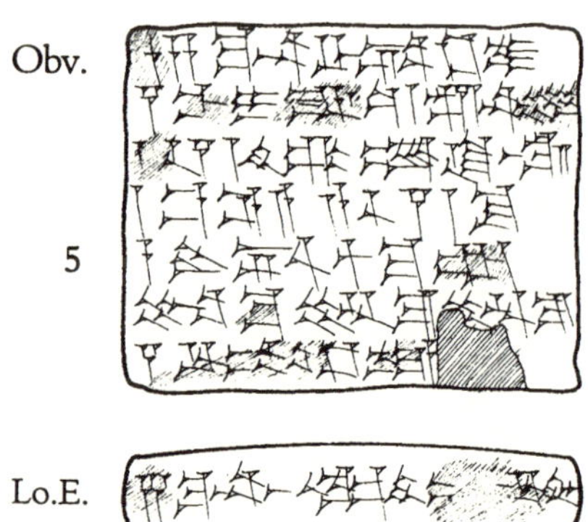

75

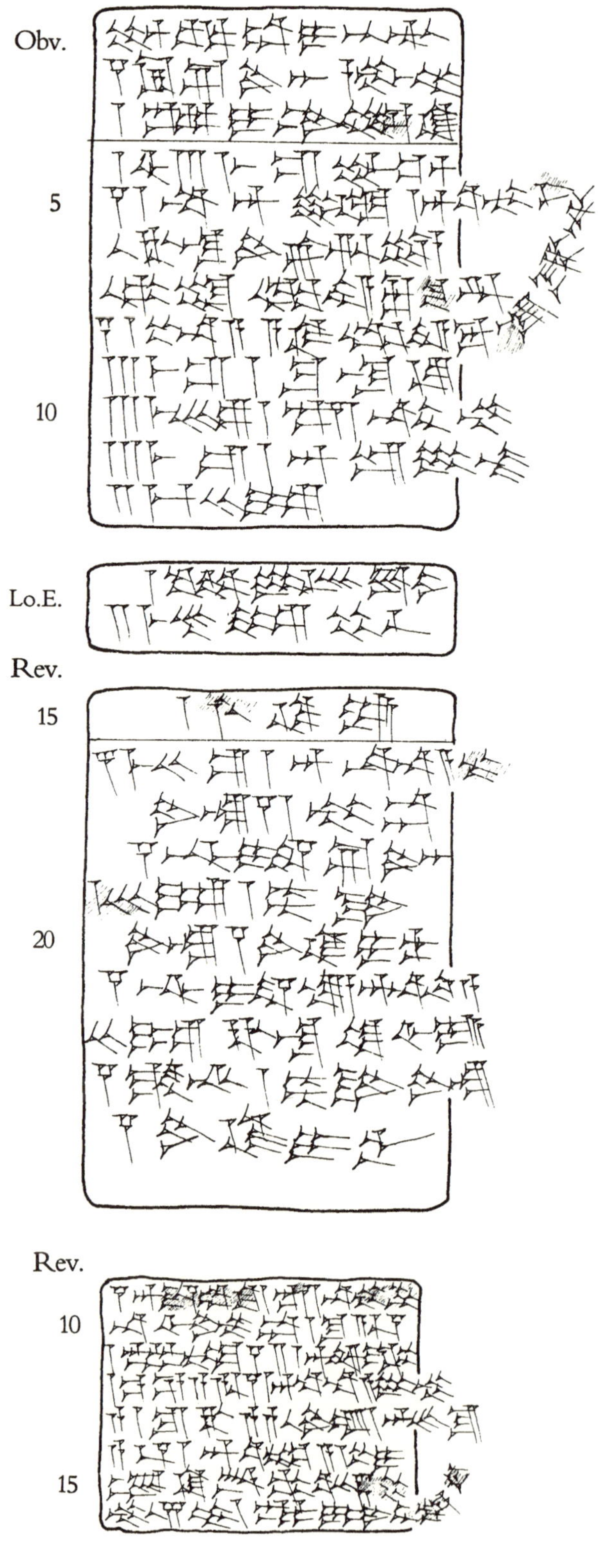

76

Obv.

Lo.E.

Rev.

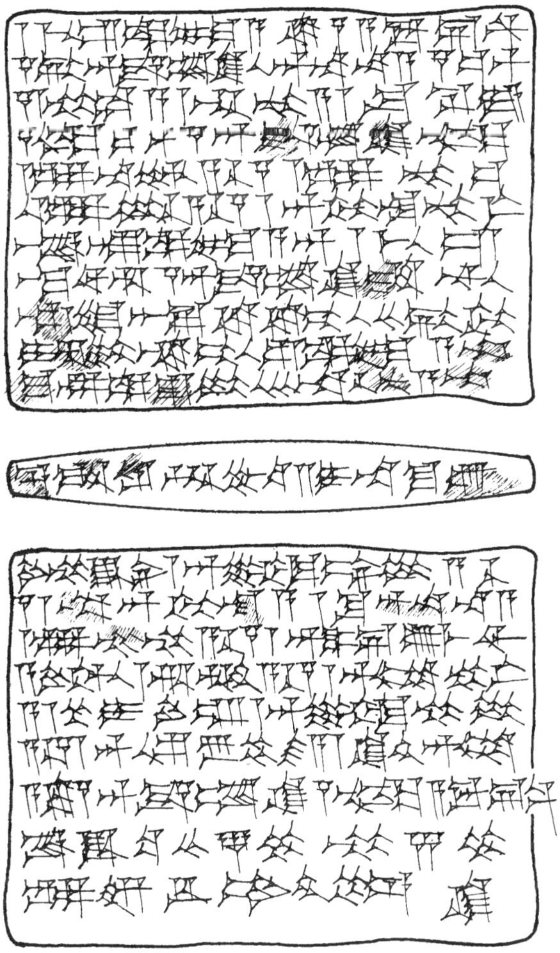

77

Obv.

Lo.E.

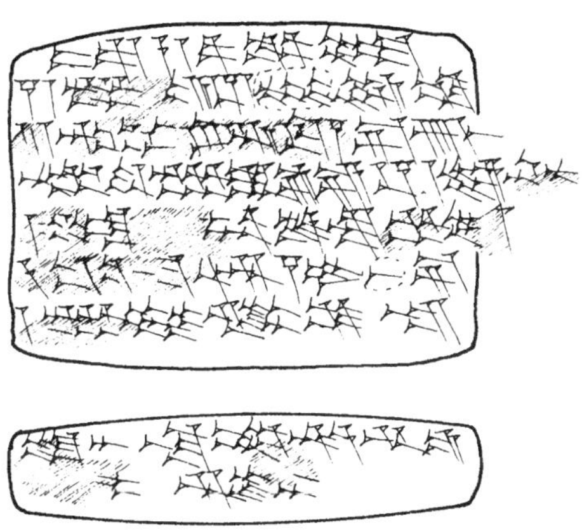

78

Obv.

Lo.E.

Rev.

U.E.

Rev.

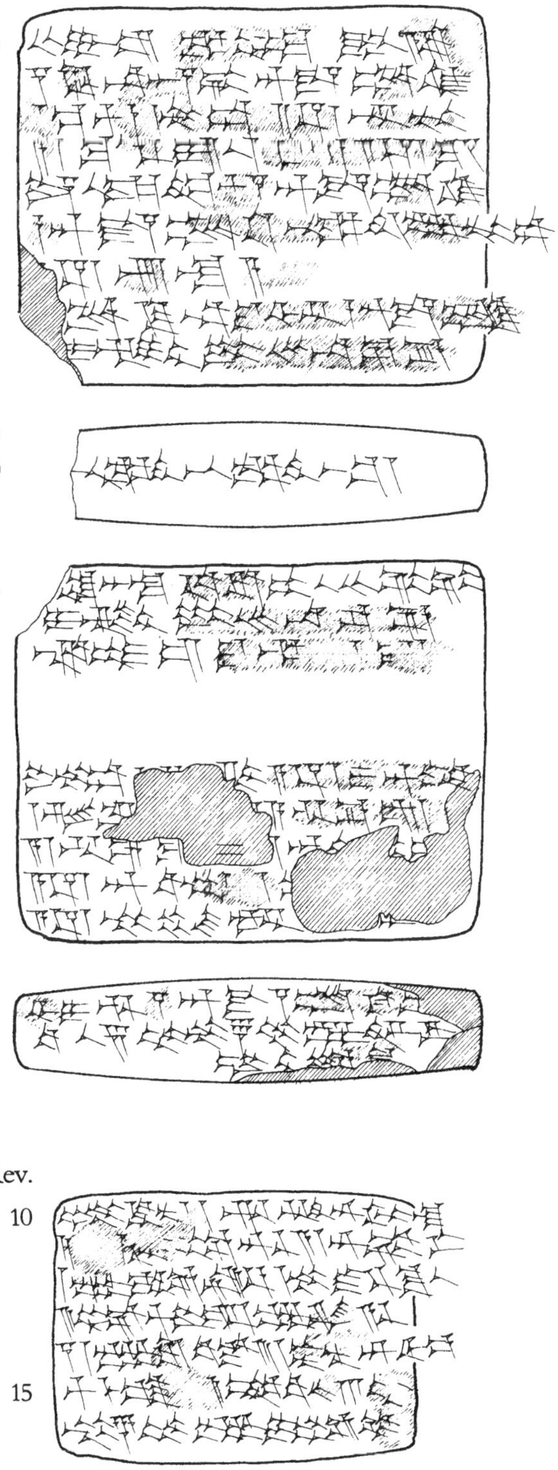

PLATE XXXVIII

79

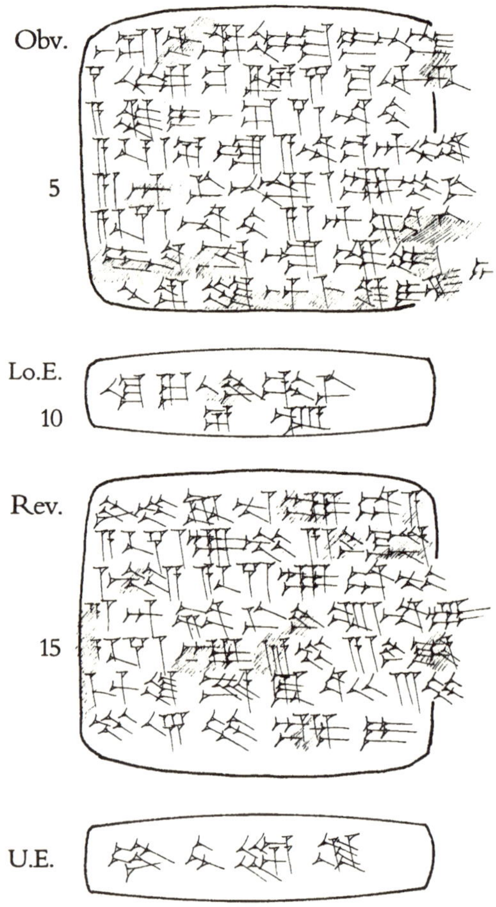

80

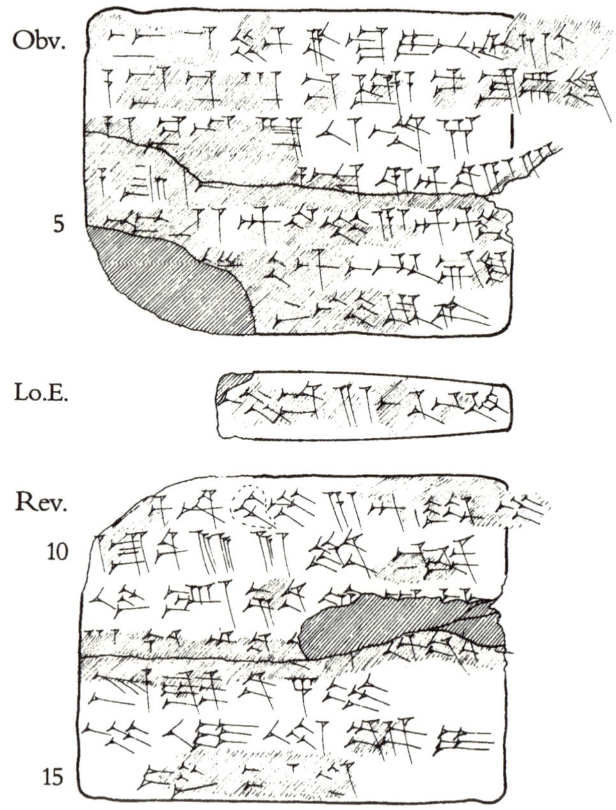

81

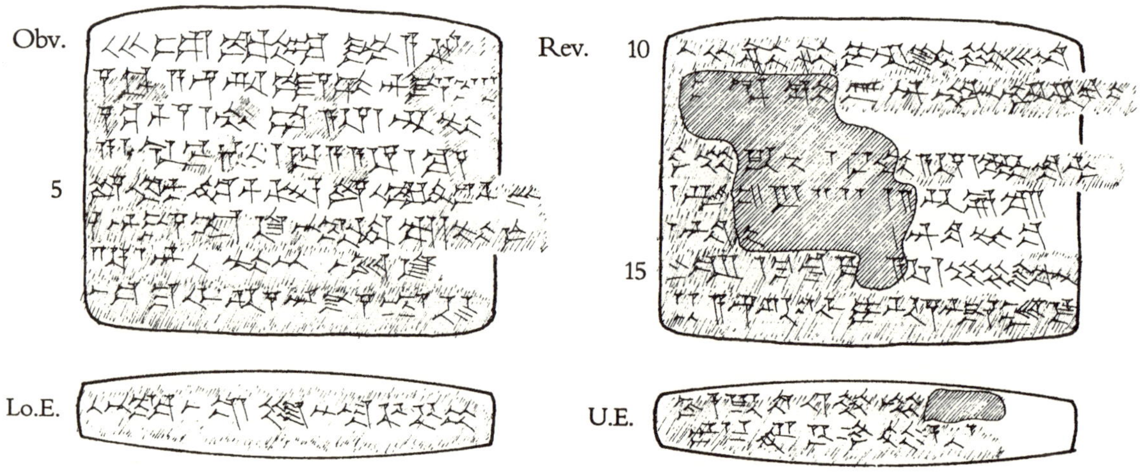

82

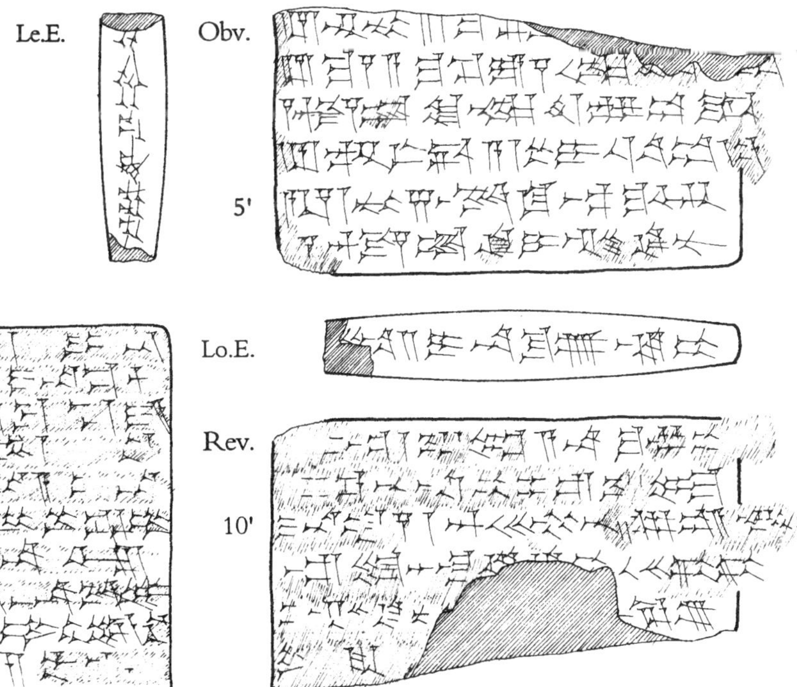

83

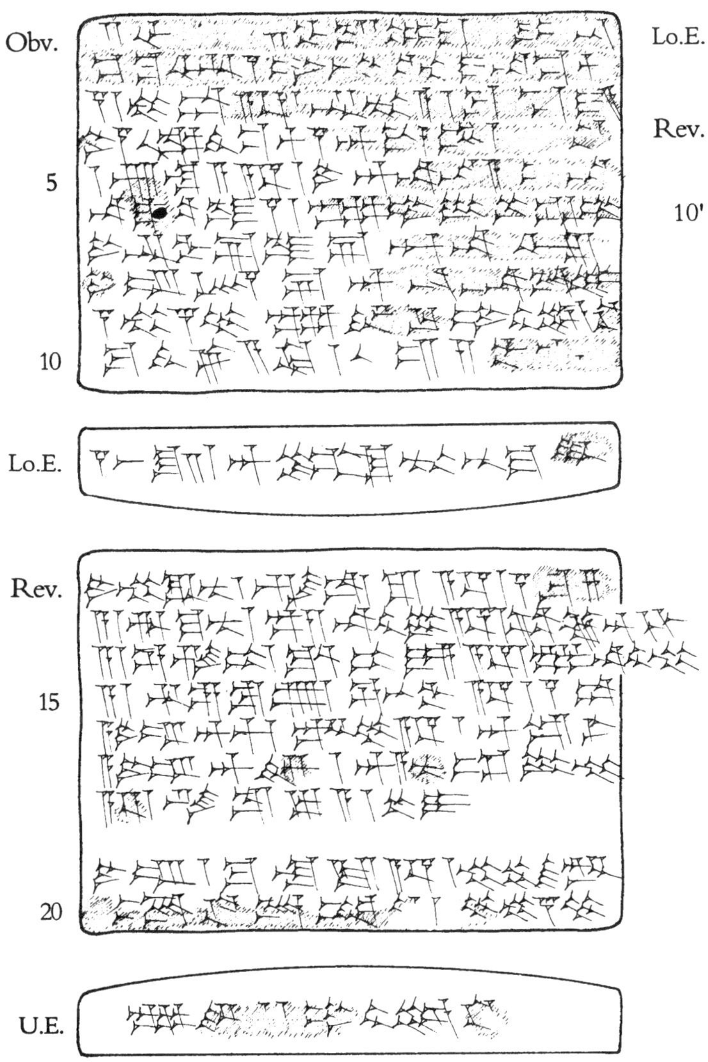

84

Obv.

Lo.E.

Rev.

U.E.

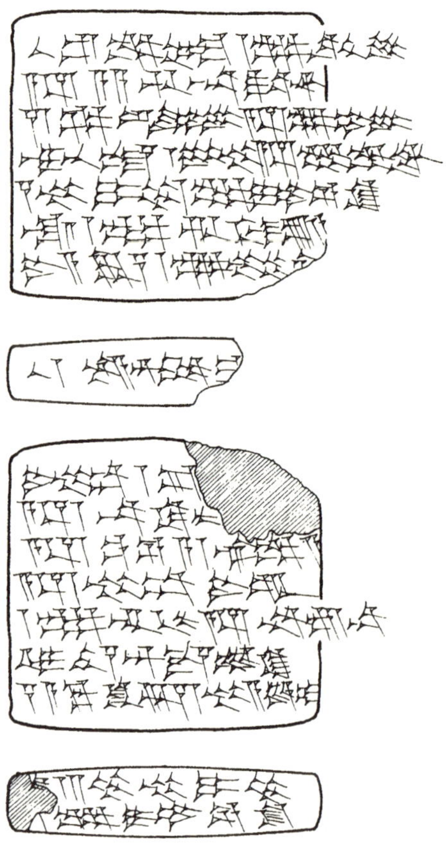

85

Obv.

Rev.

U.E.

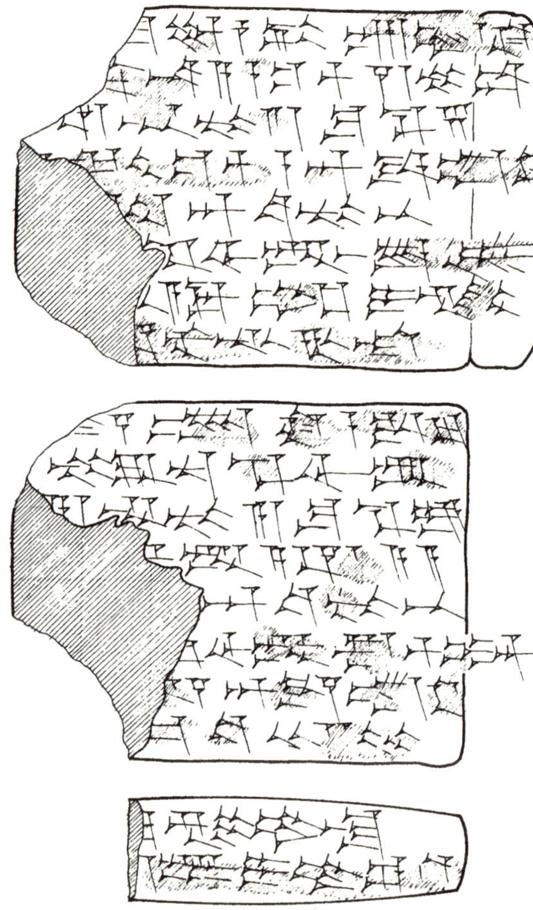

86

Obv.

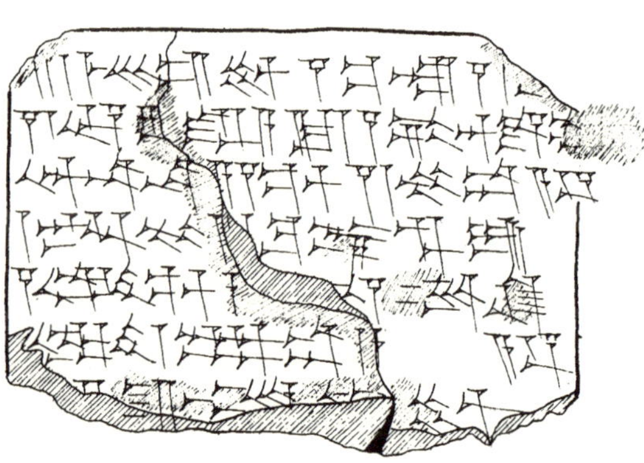

Rev.

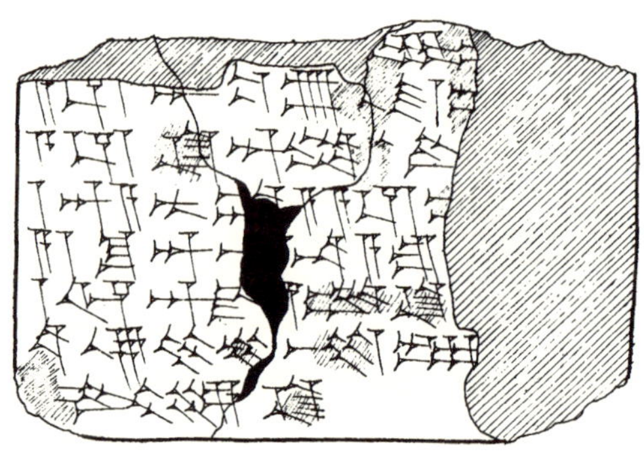

87

Obv.

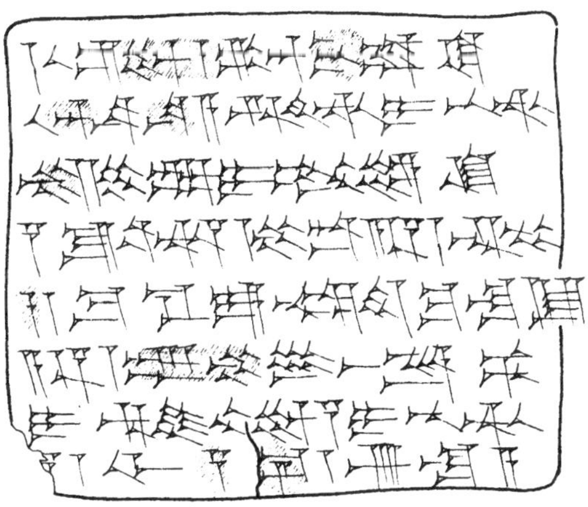

Rev.

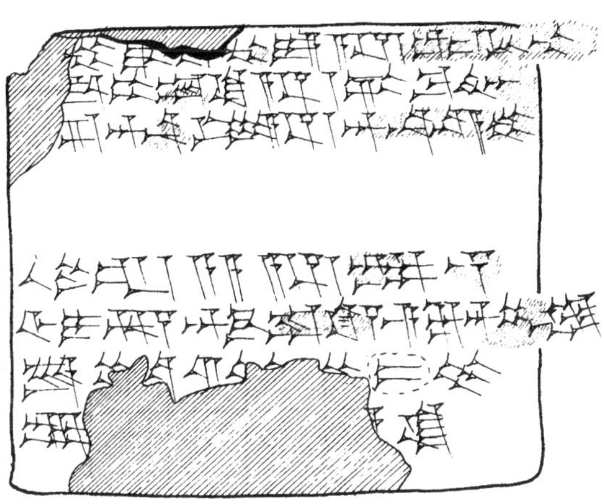

88

Obv.

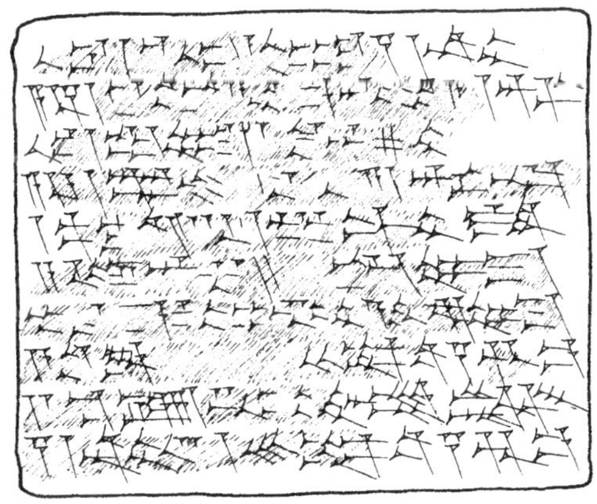

Rev.

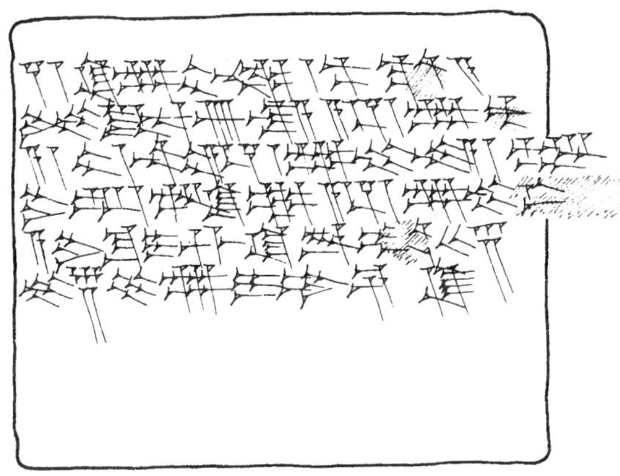

89

Obv.

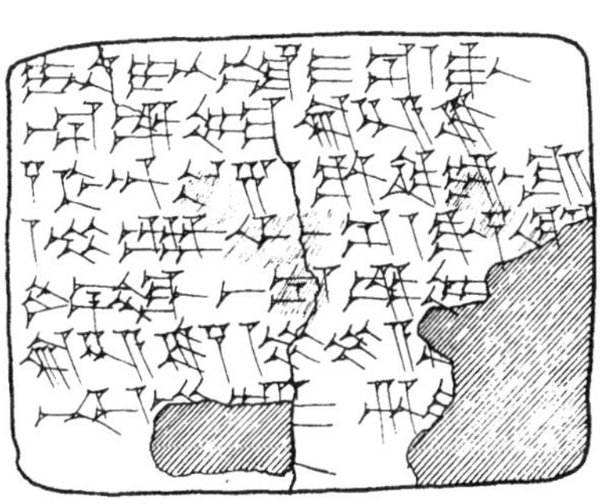

Rev.

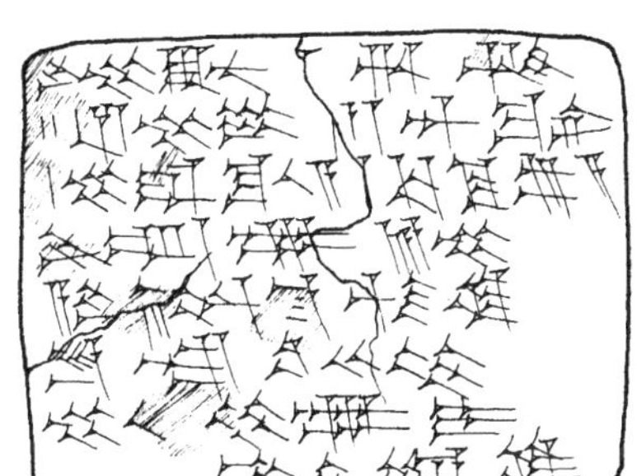

90

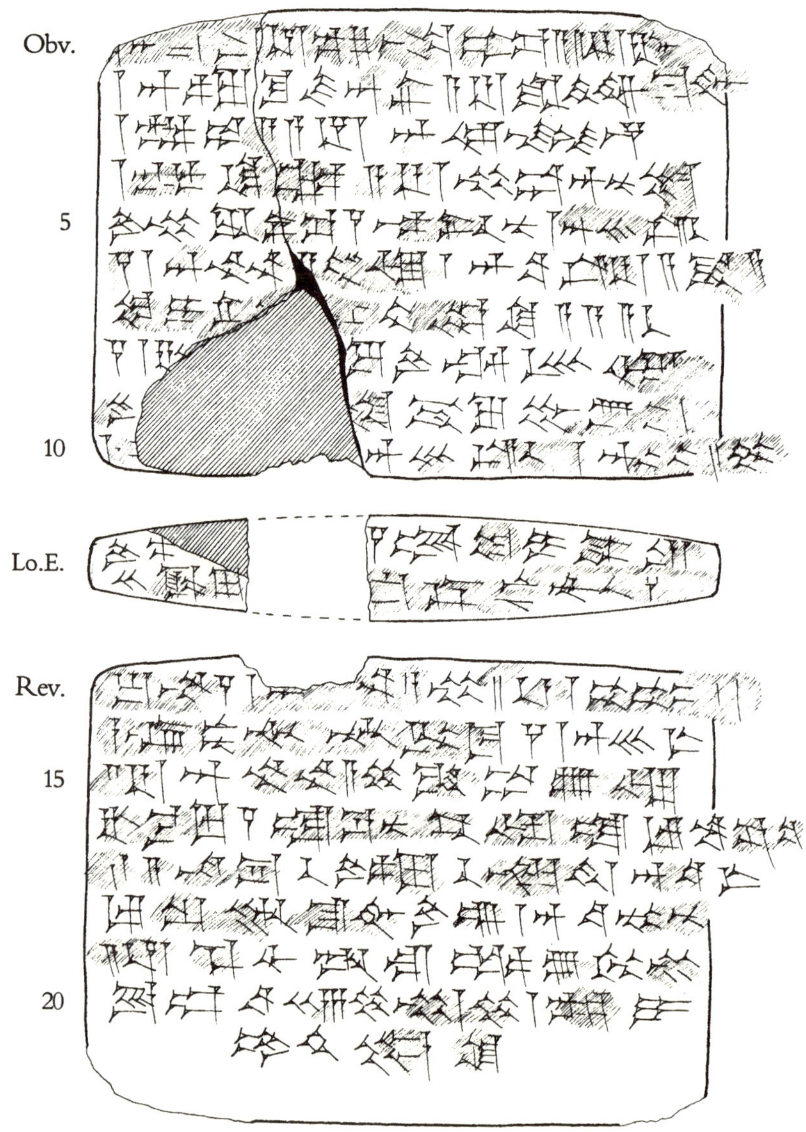

91

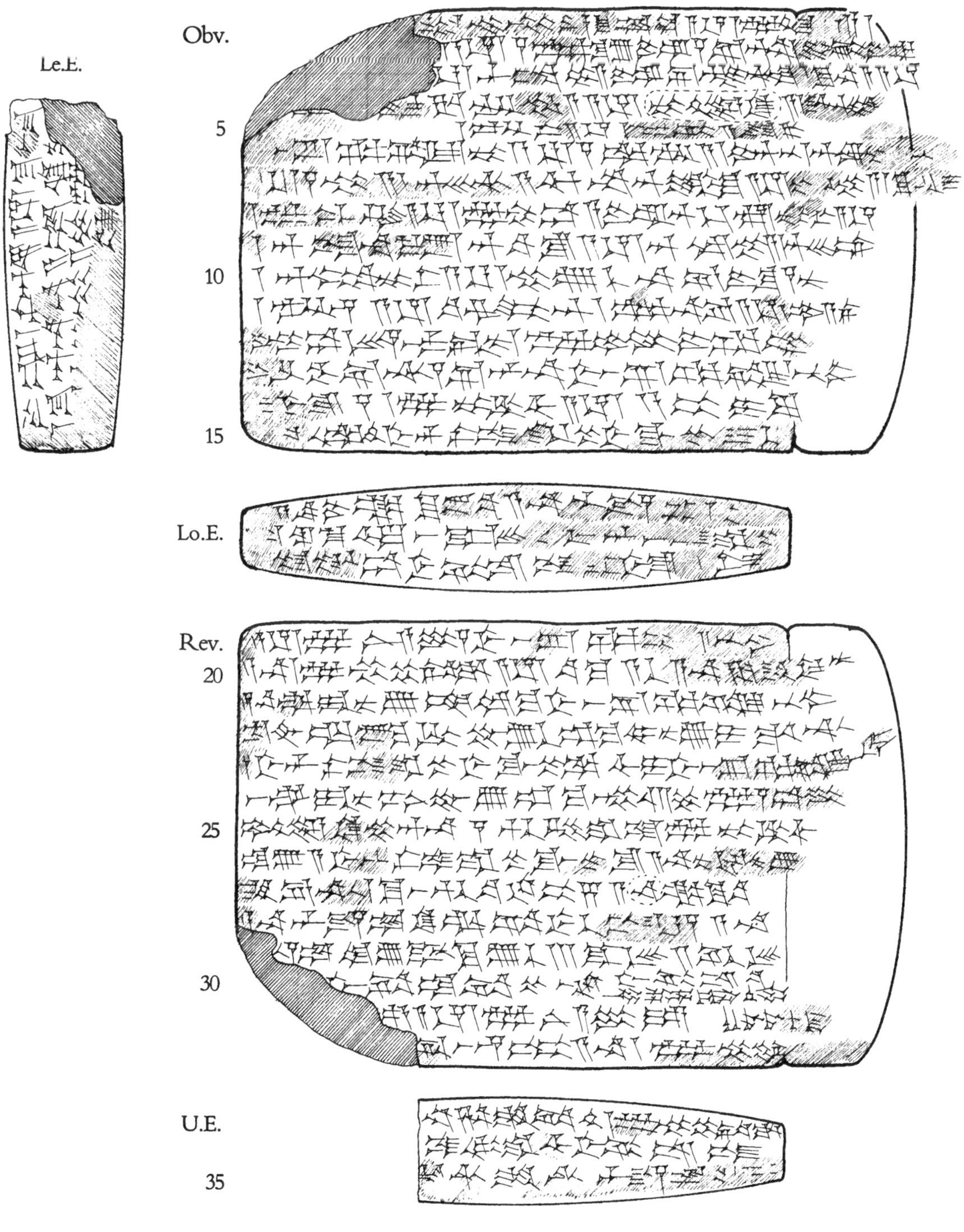

92

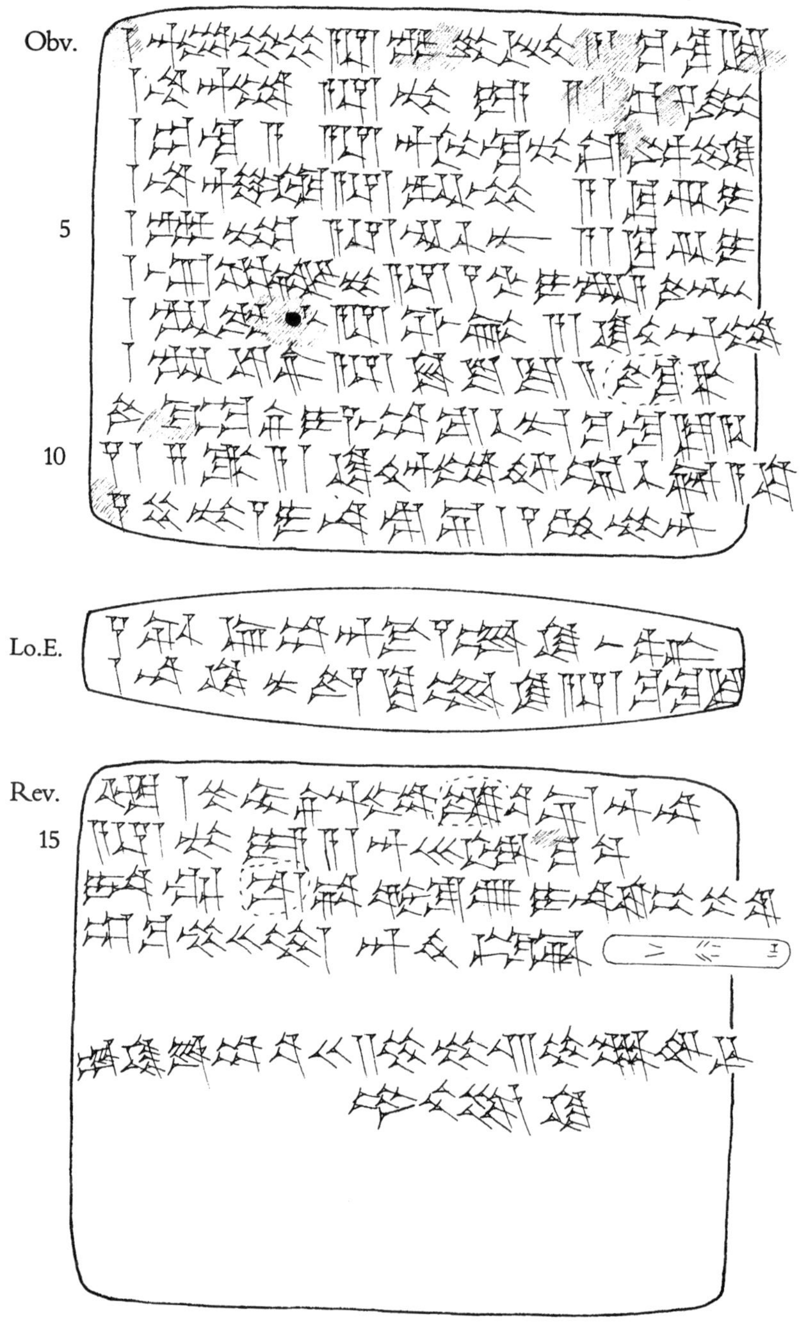

93

Obv.

Lo.E.

Rev.

U.E.

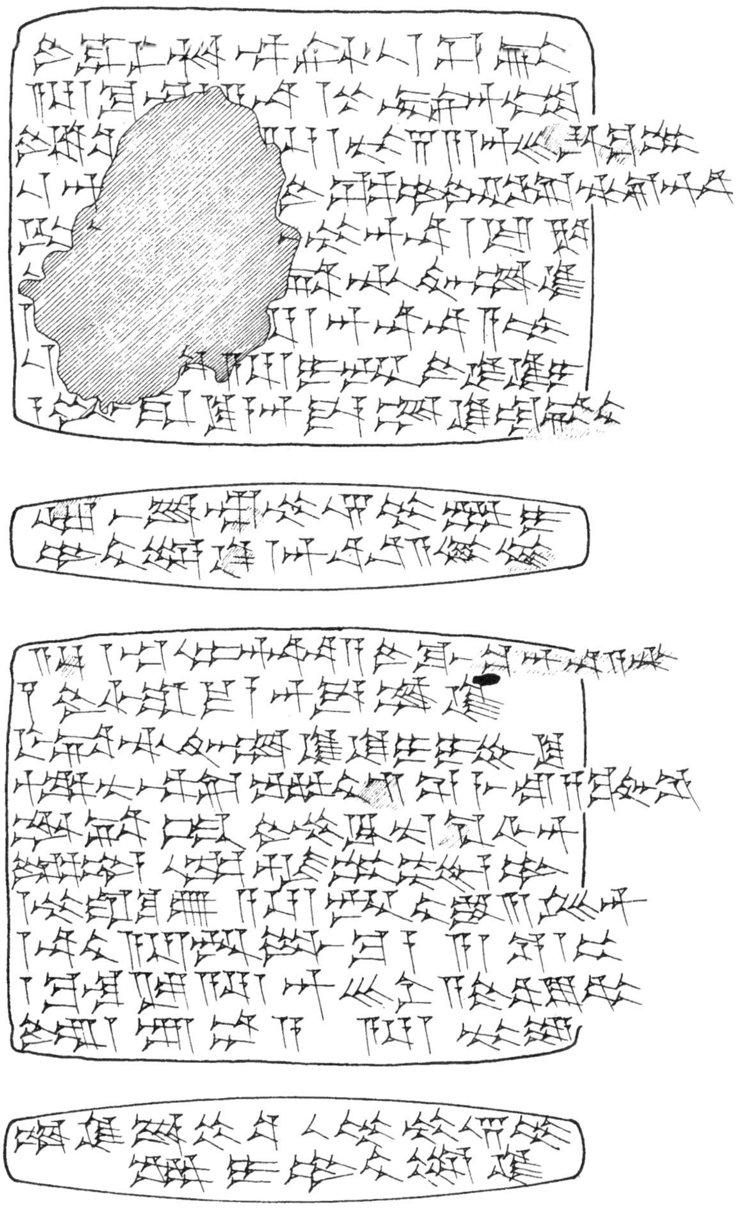

PLATE XLVI

94

Le.E.

Obv.

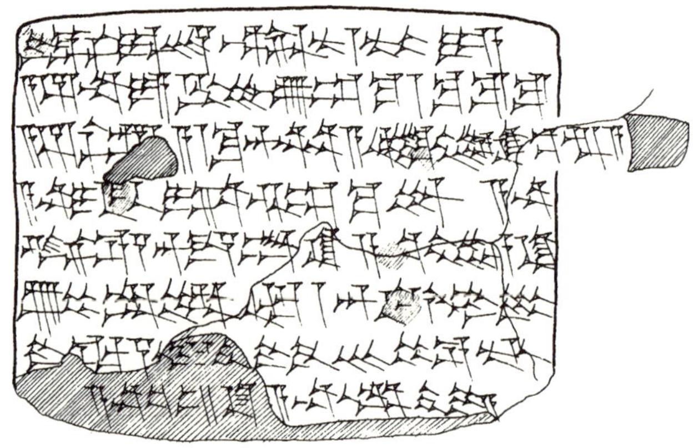

Lo.E.

Rev.

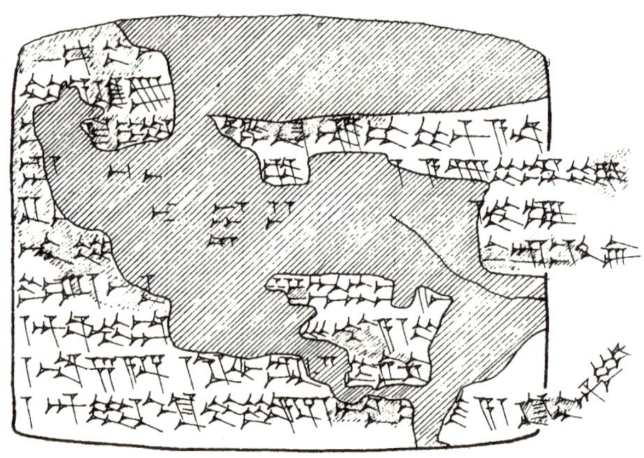

U.E.

95

Obv.

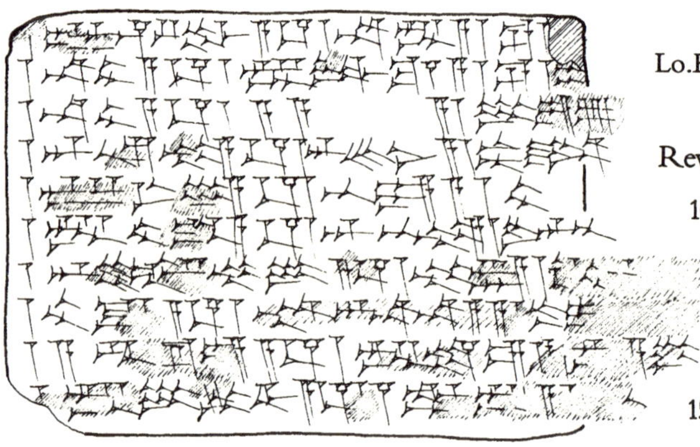

Lo.E.

Rev.

U.E.

96

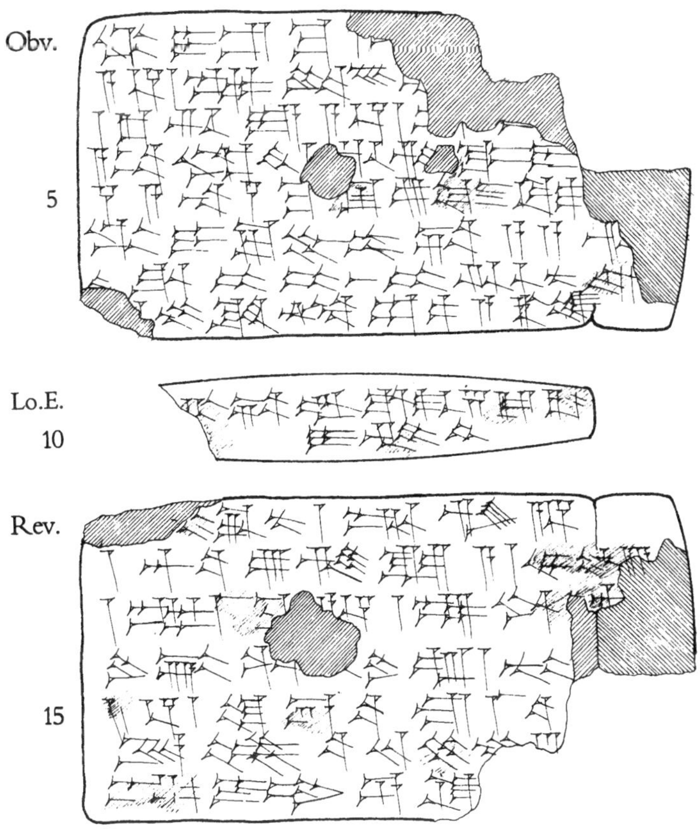

97

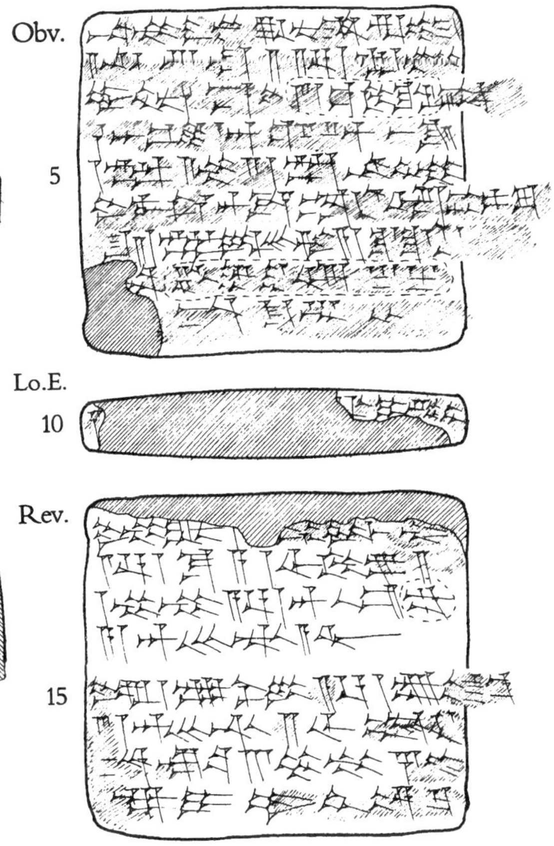

98

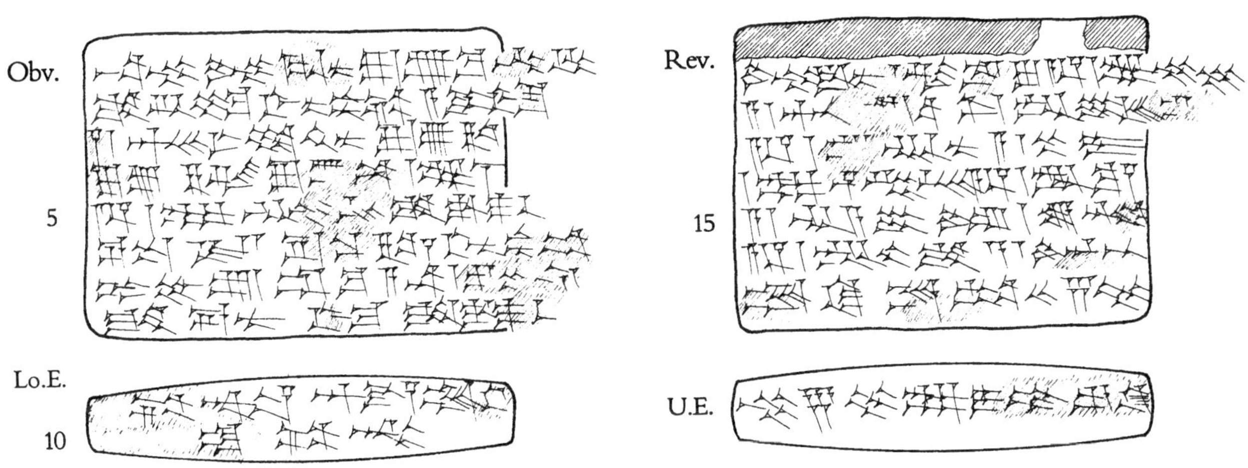

PLATE XLVIII

100

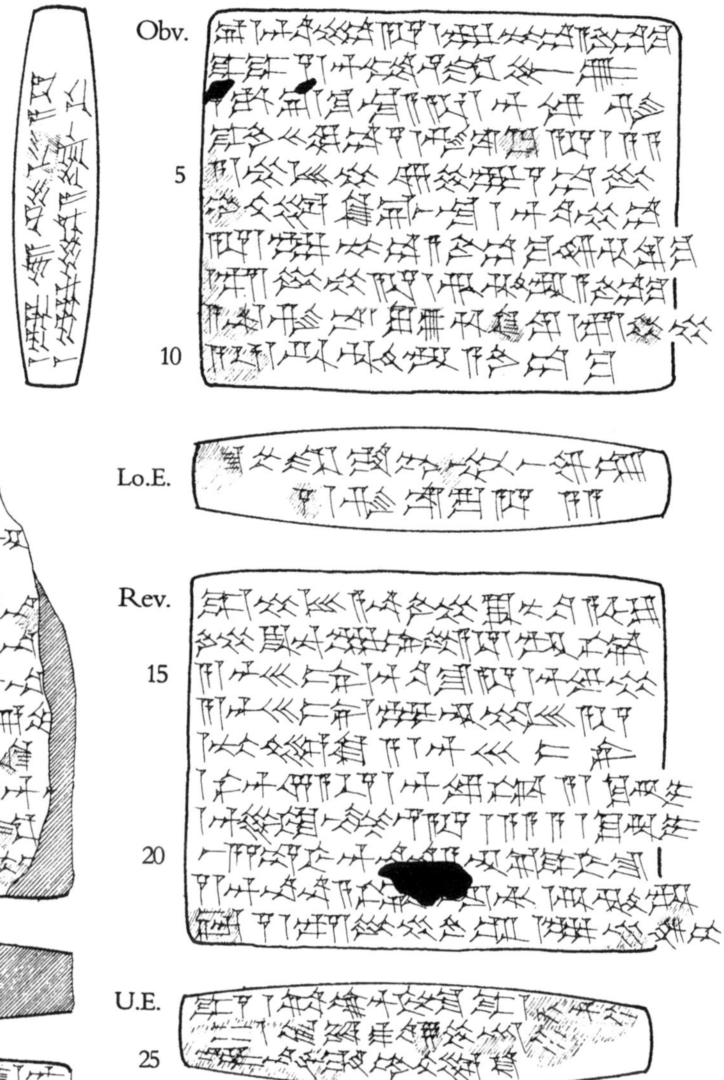

99

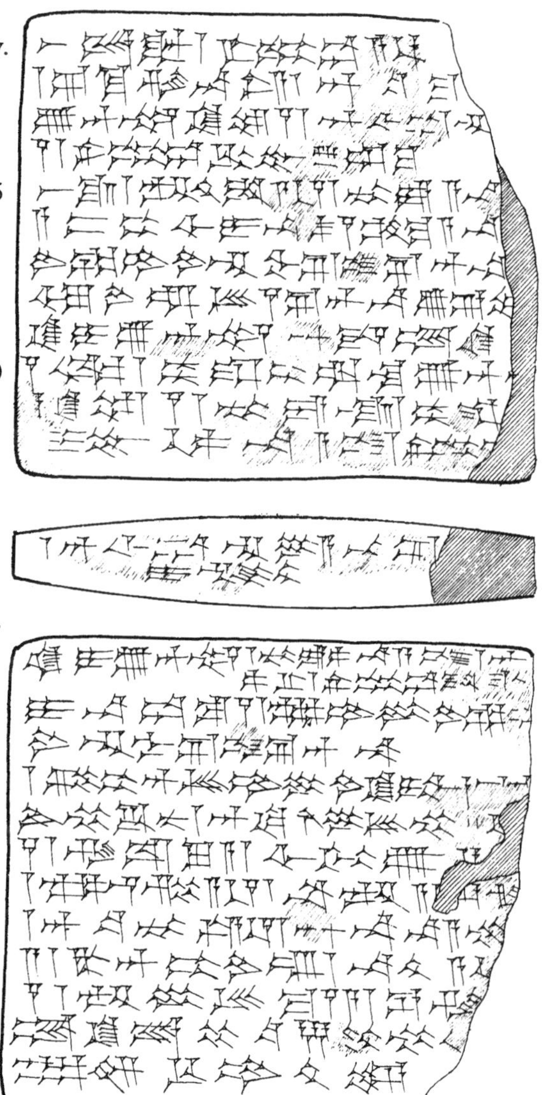

101

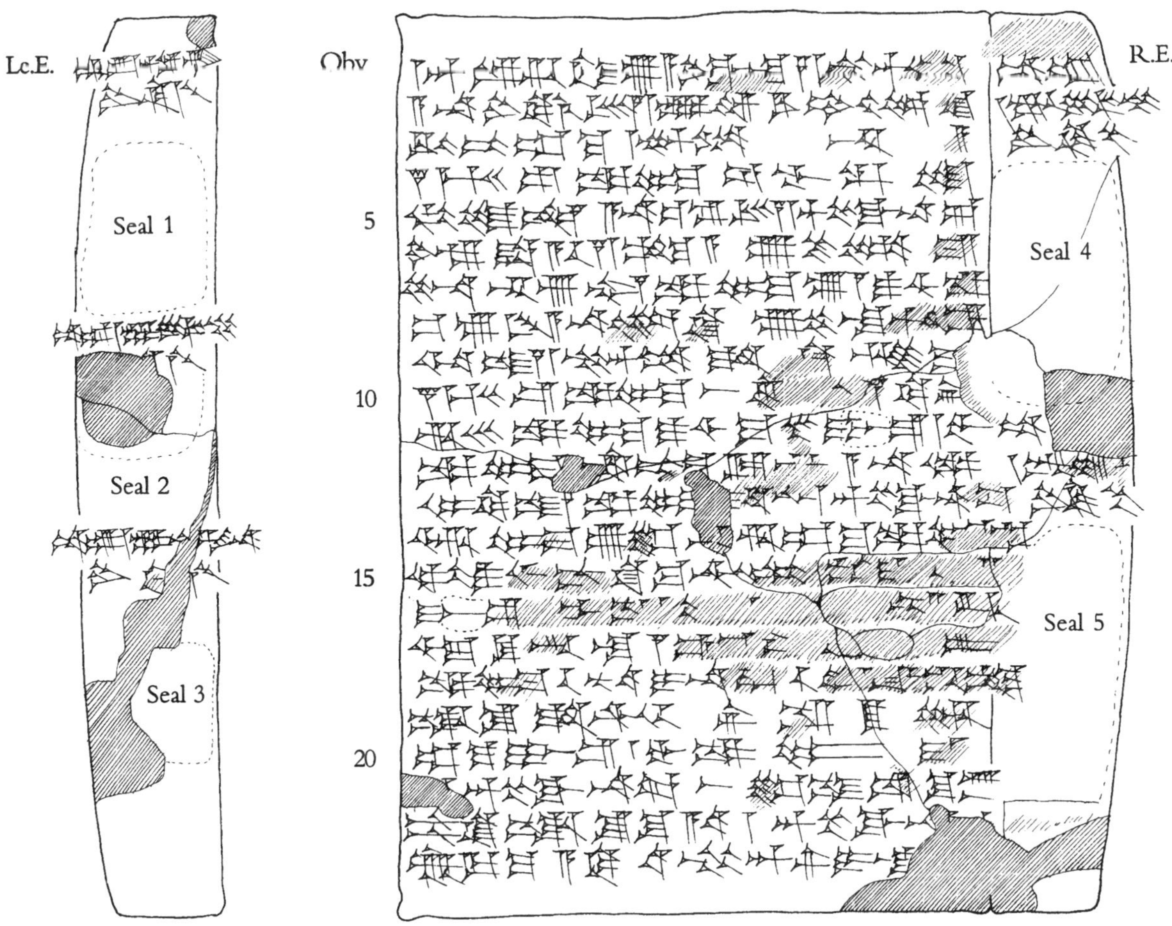

Seal 1

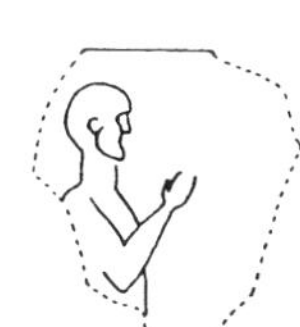

Seal 3

101

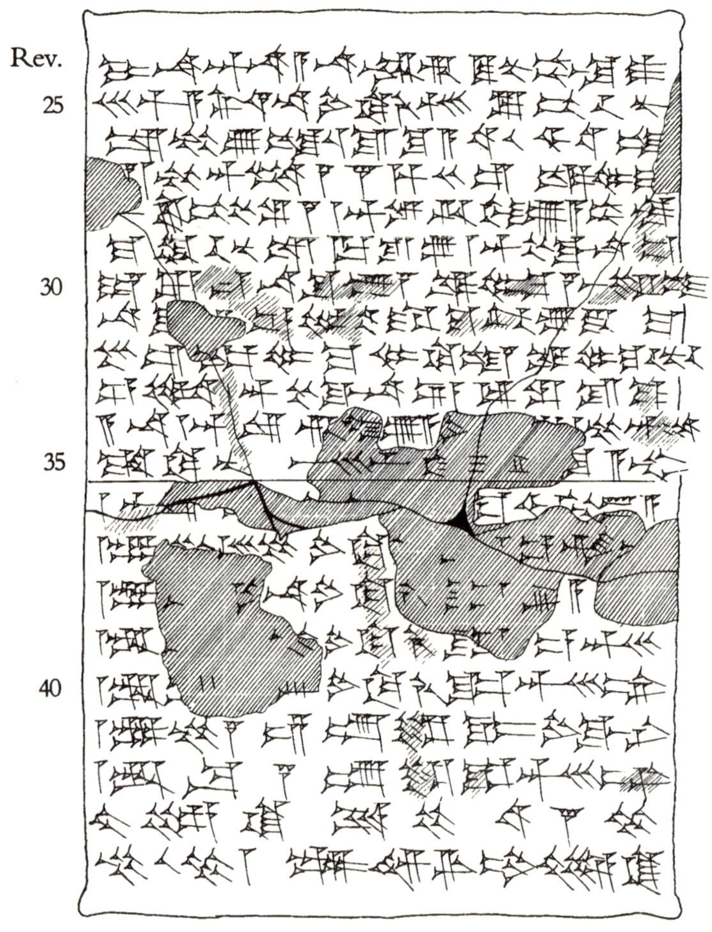

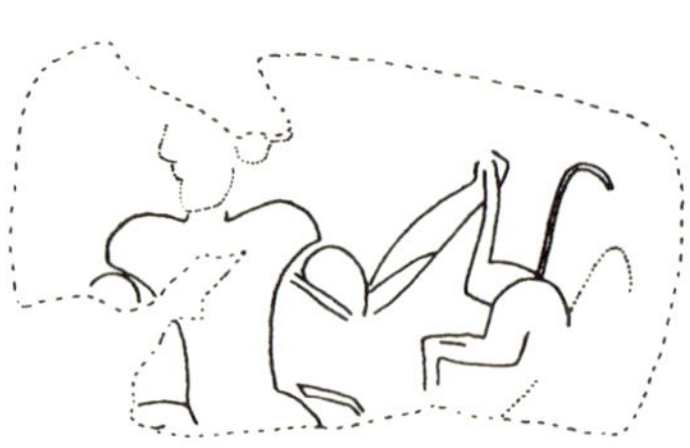

Seal 4

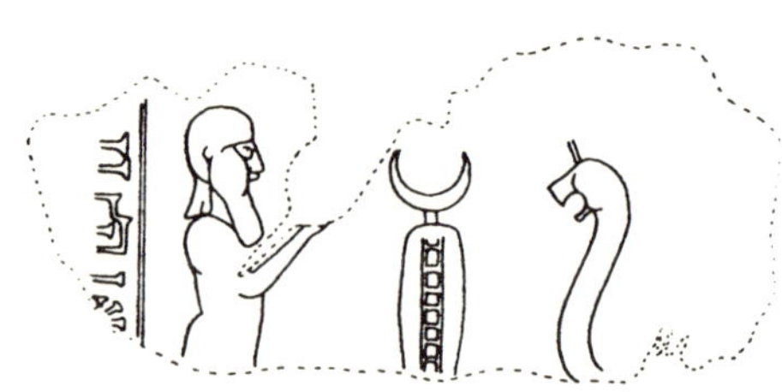

Seal 5

102

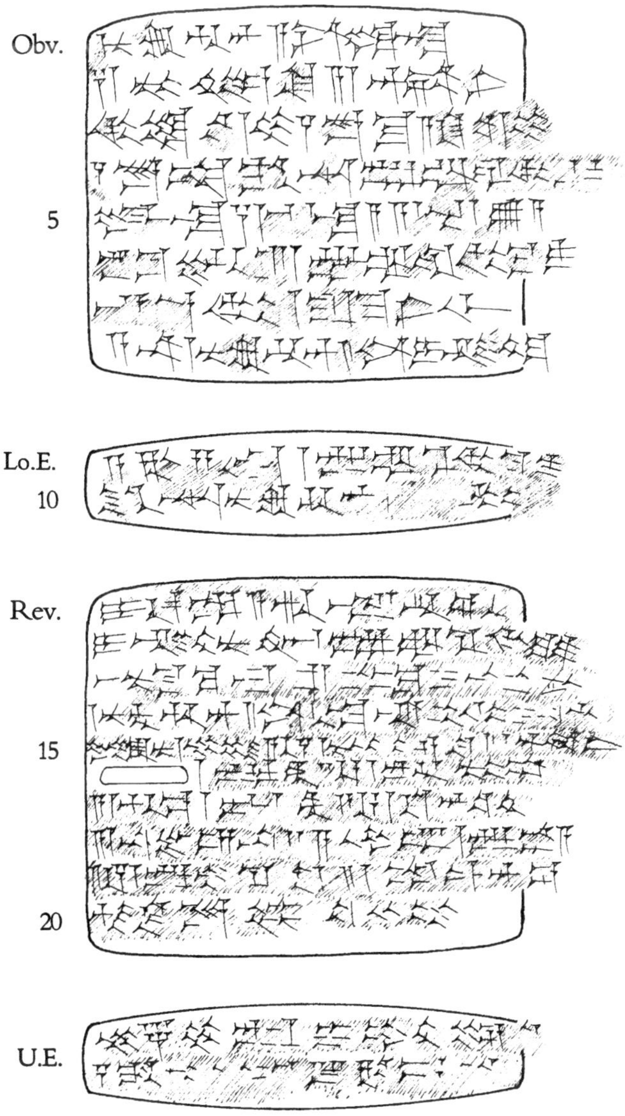

103

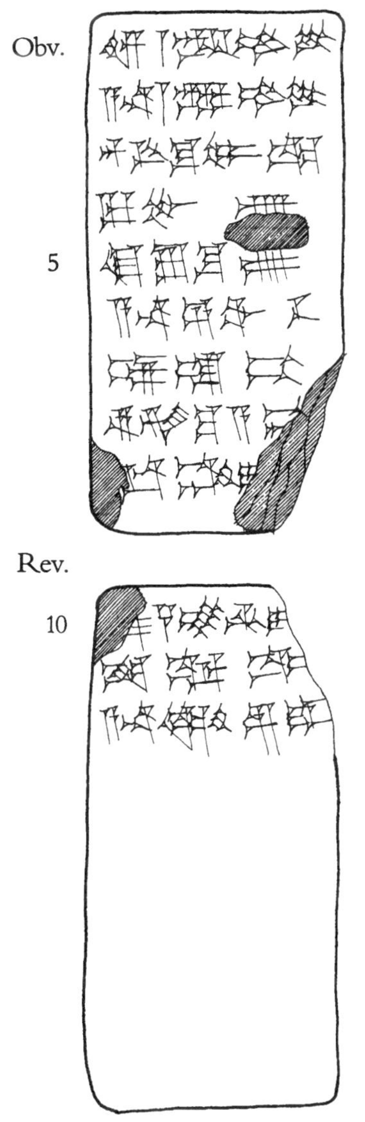

104

Obv.

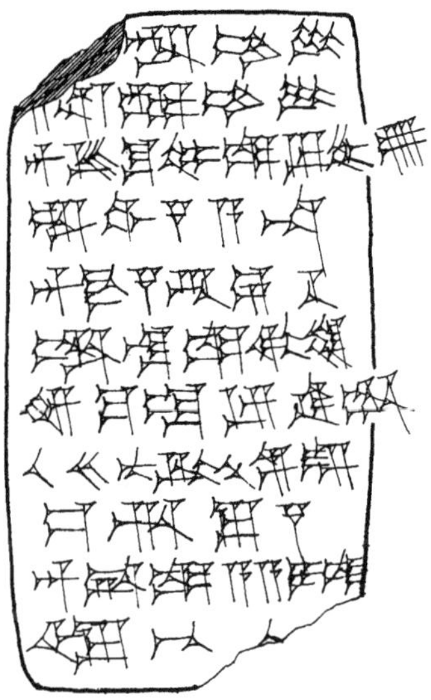

Rev.

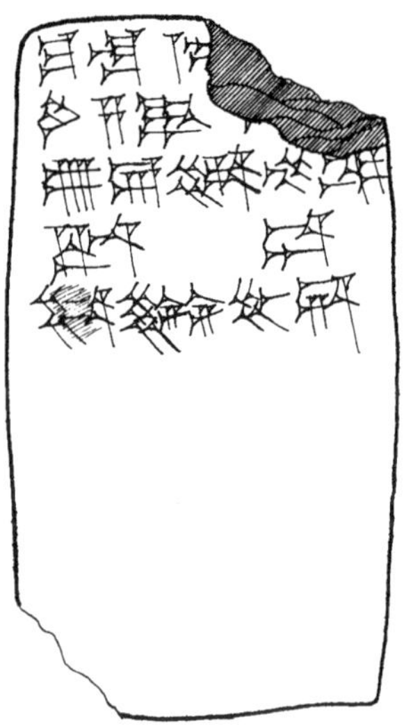

105

Le.E.

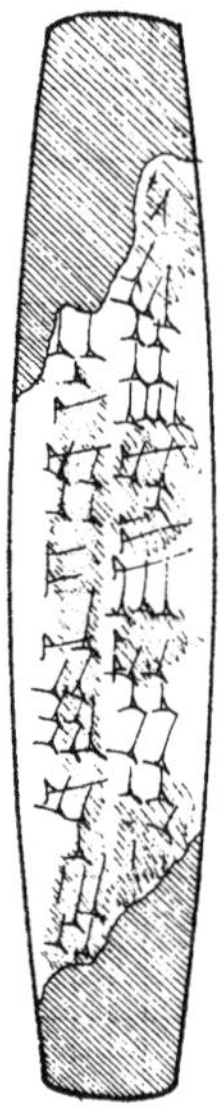

Obv.

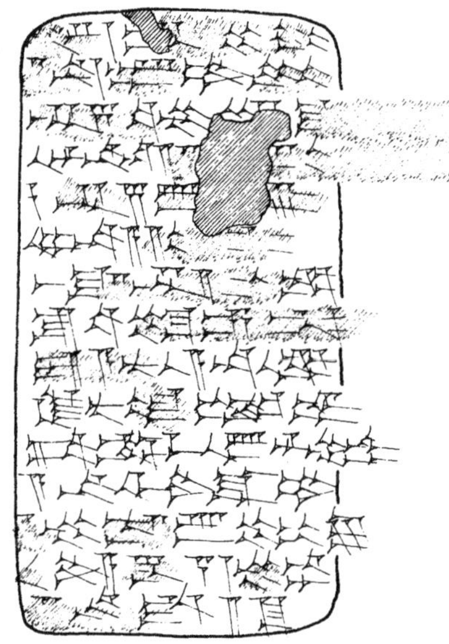

Lo.E.

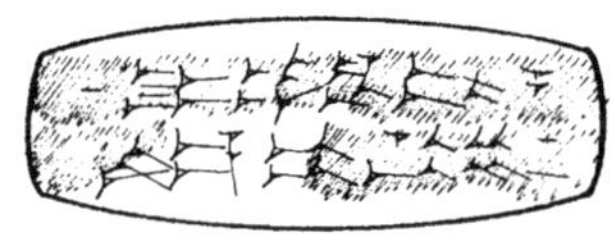

Rev.

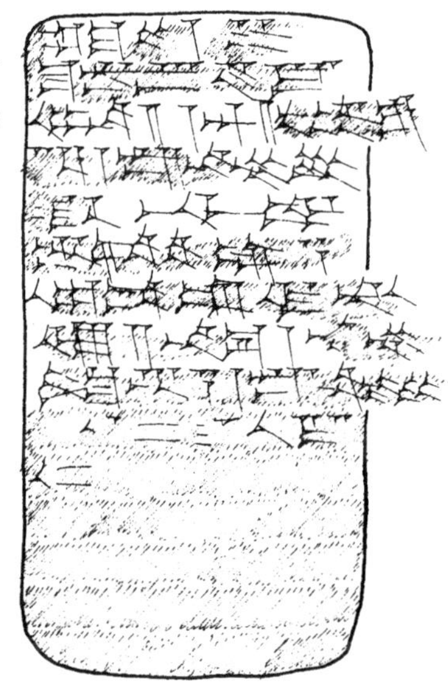

106

Obv.

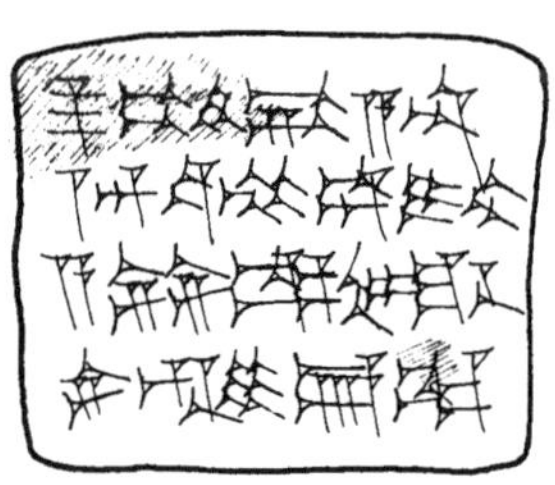

Rev.

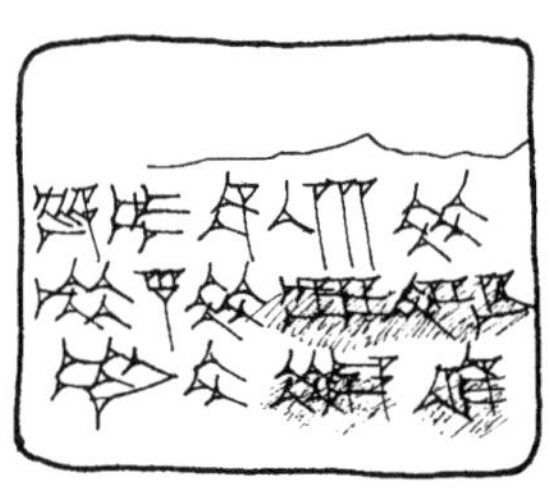

PLATE LIII

107

Obv.

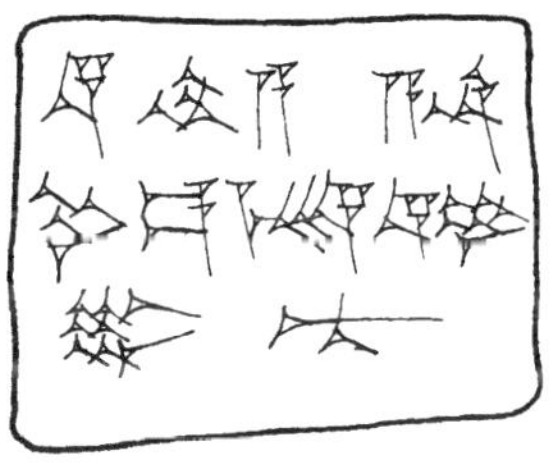

Rev.

108

Obv.

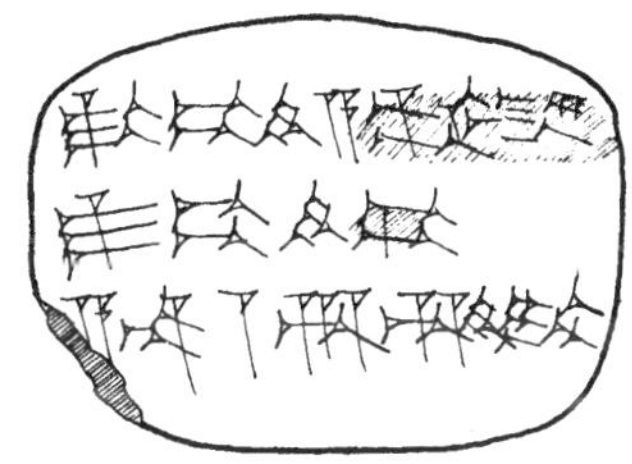

Rev.

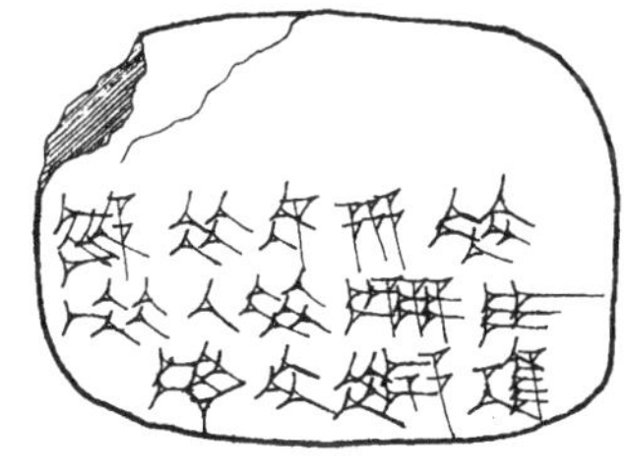

109

Obv.

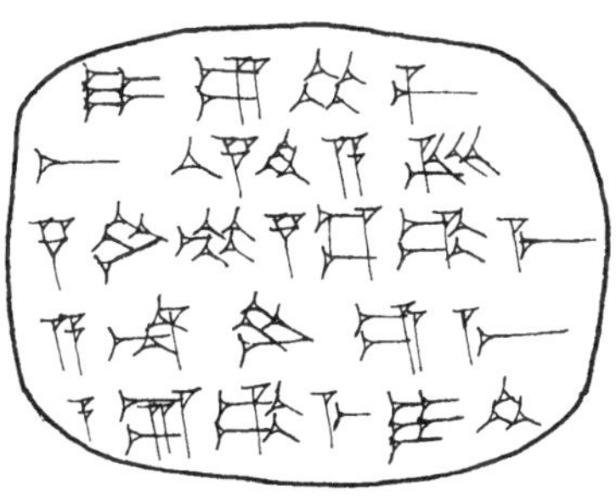

Rev.

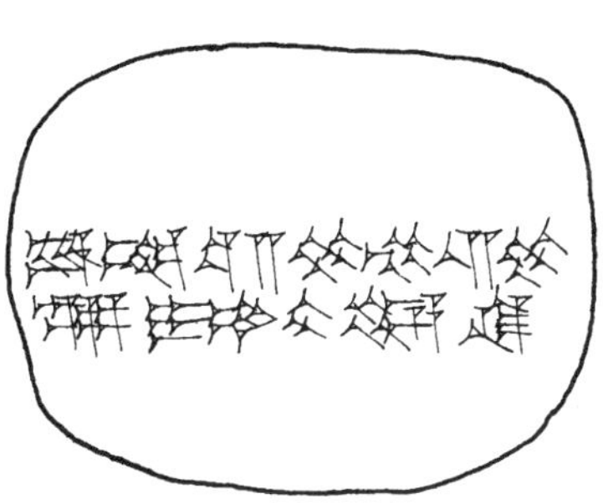

110

Obv.

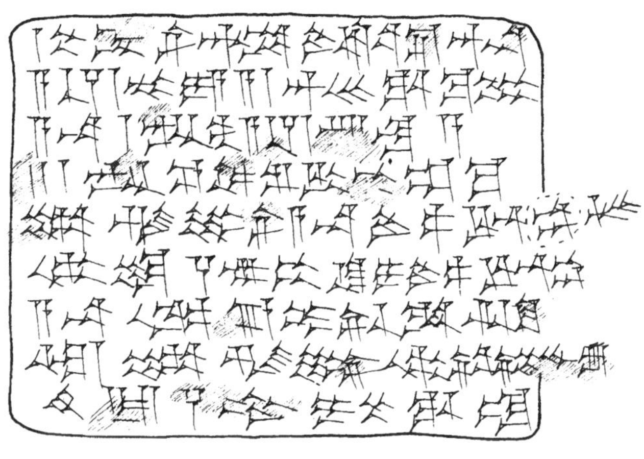

Rev.

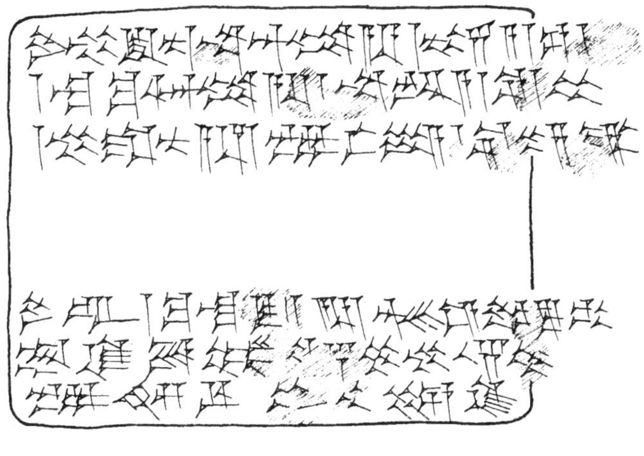

111

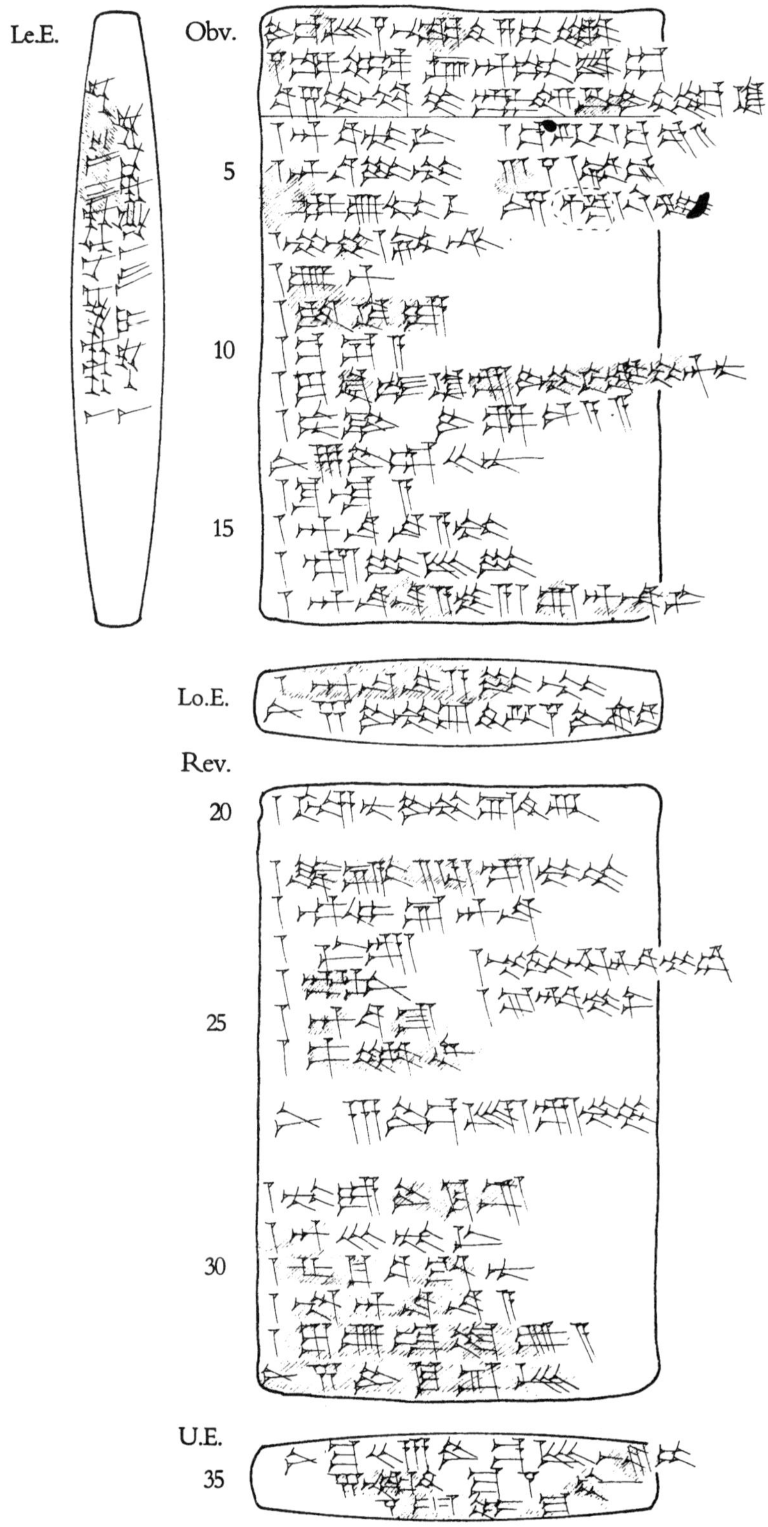

112

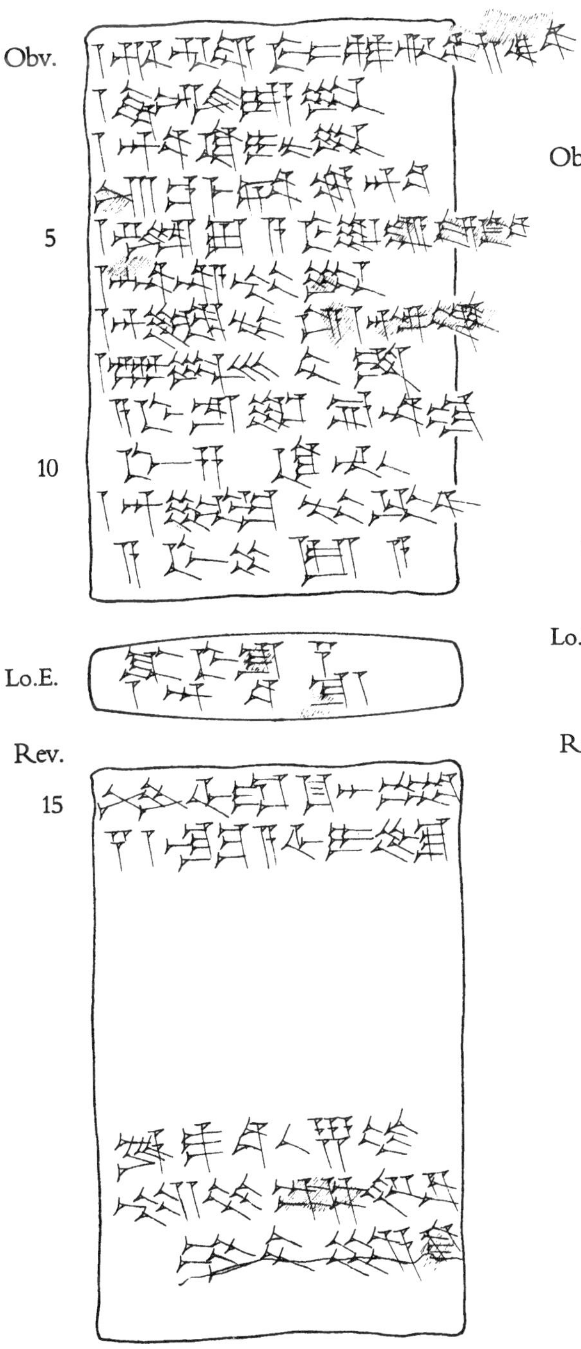

113

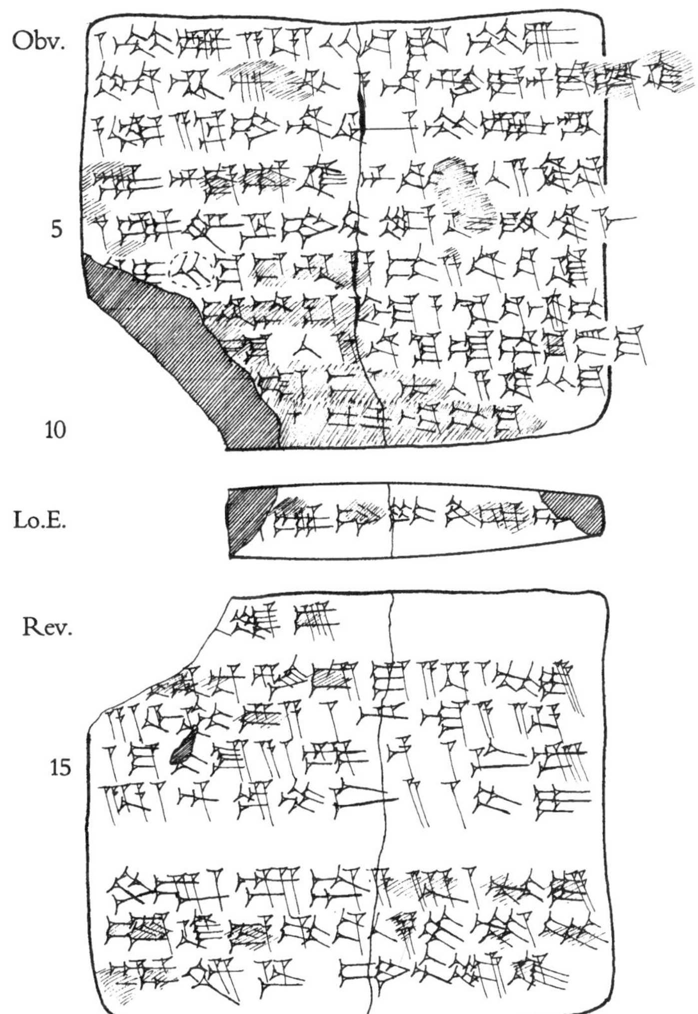

114

Obv.

Rev.

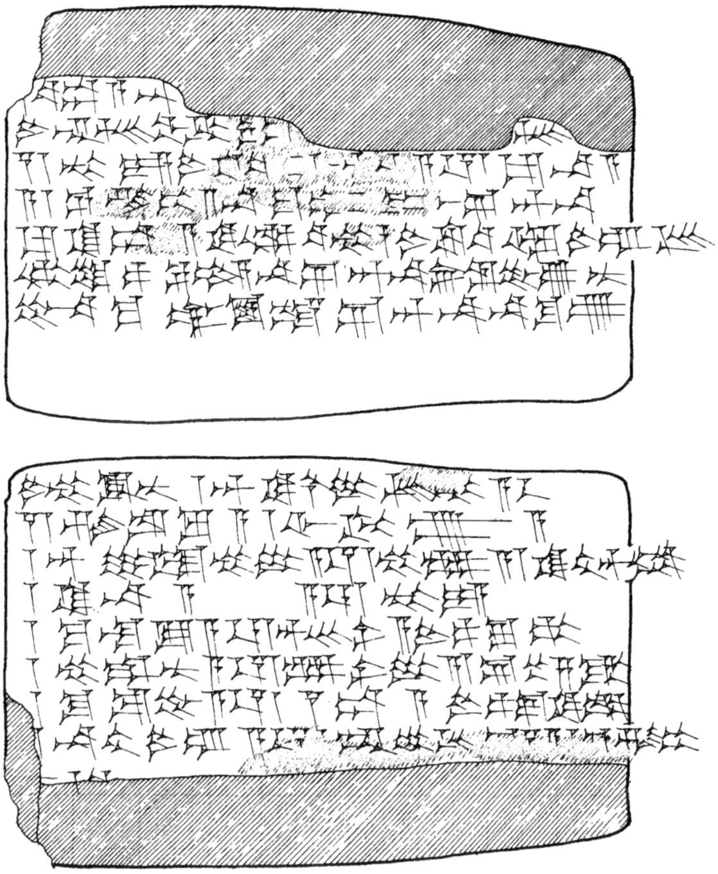

115

rest uninscribed

Rev.

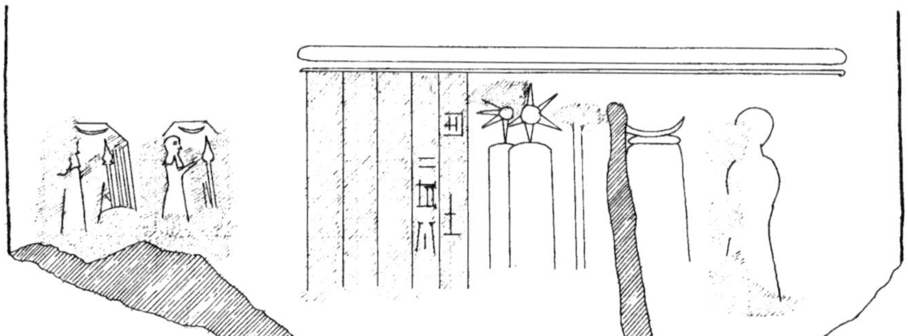

115

Obv.

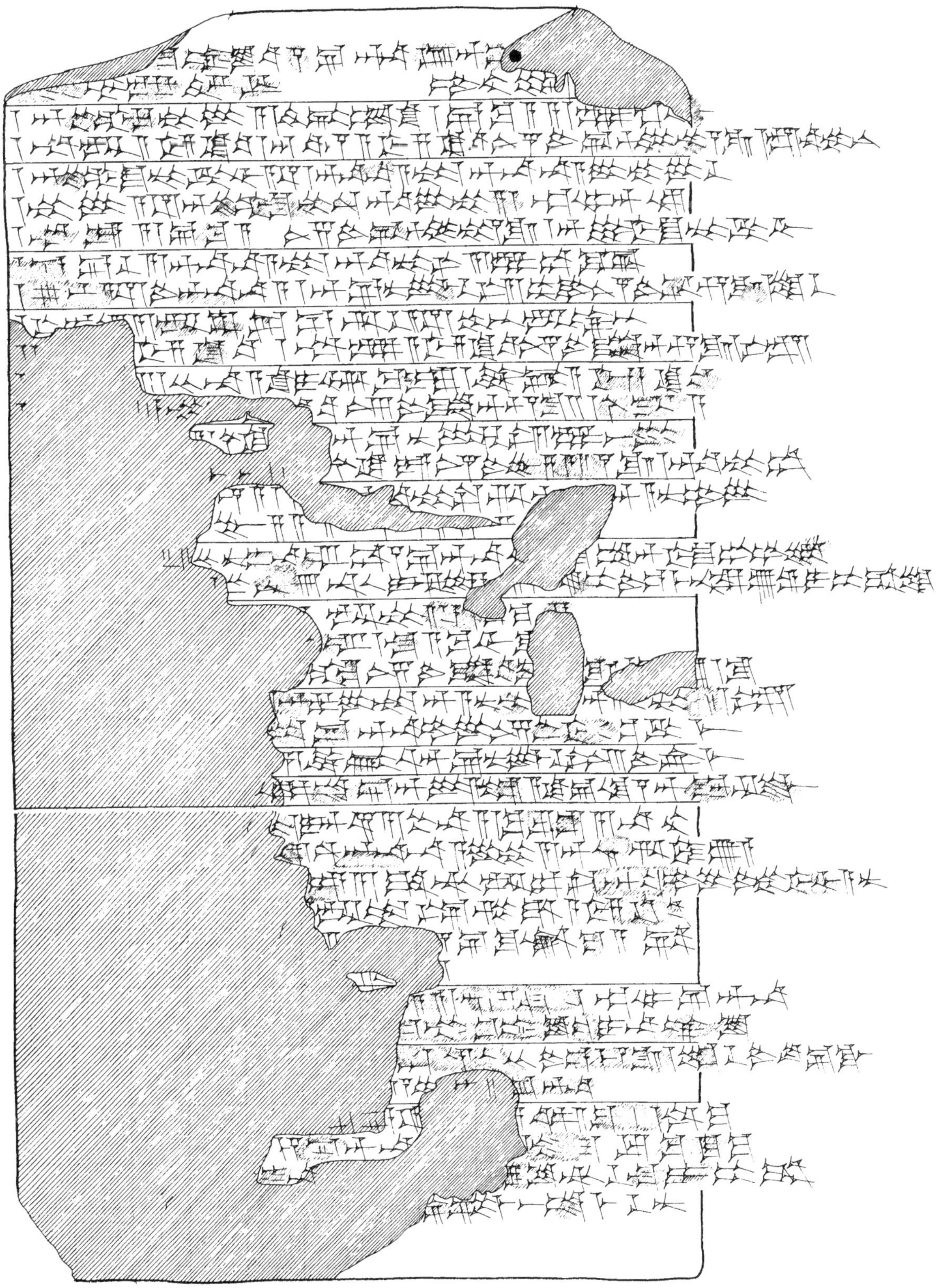

116

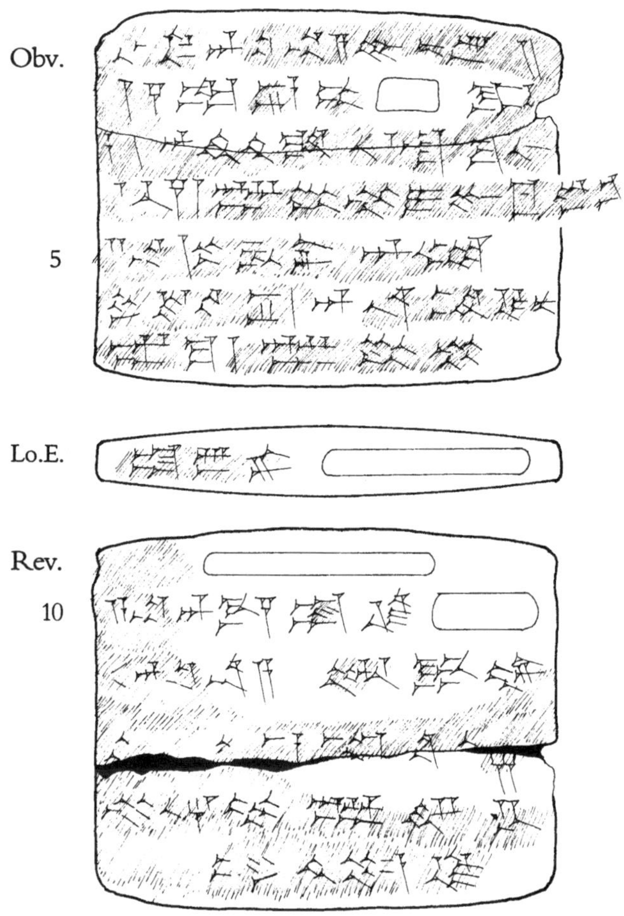

117

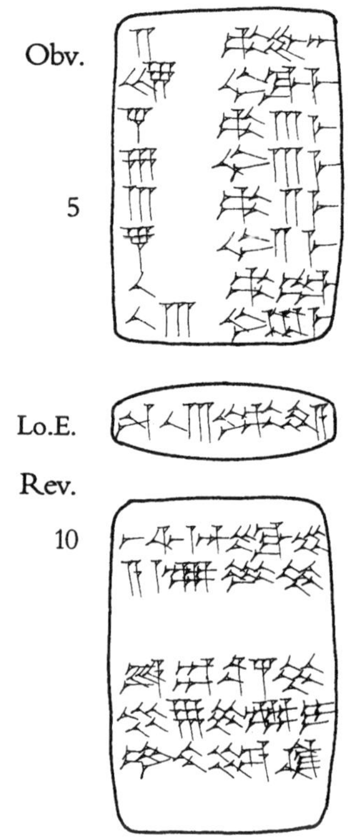

118

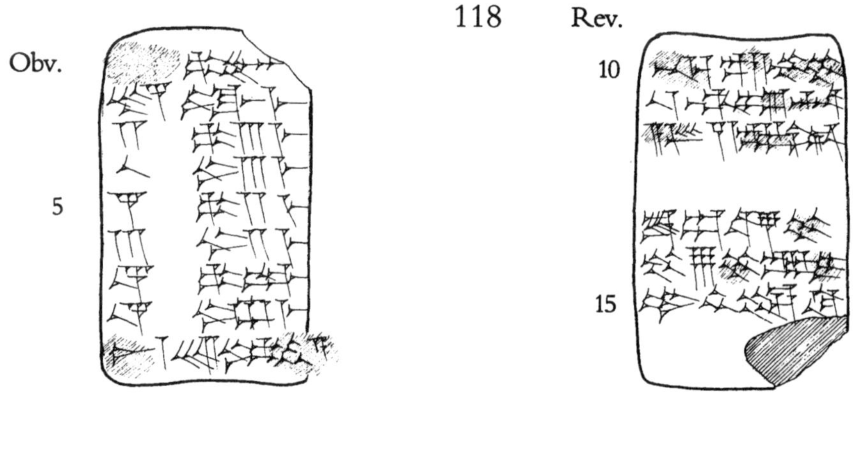

119

Obv.

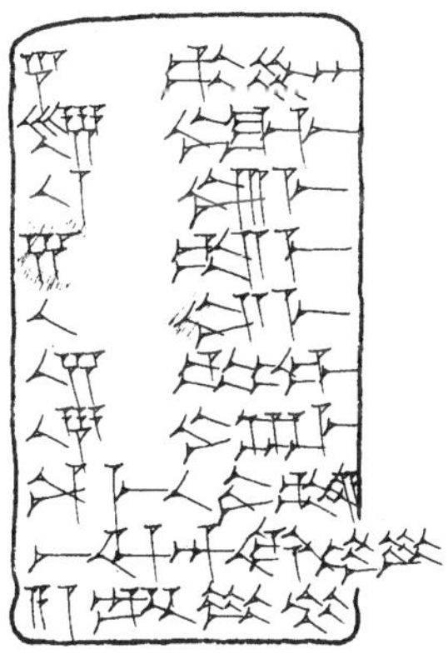

Rev.

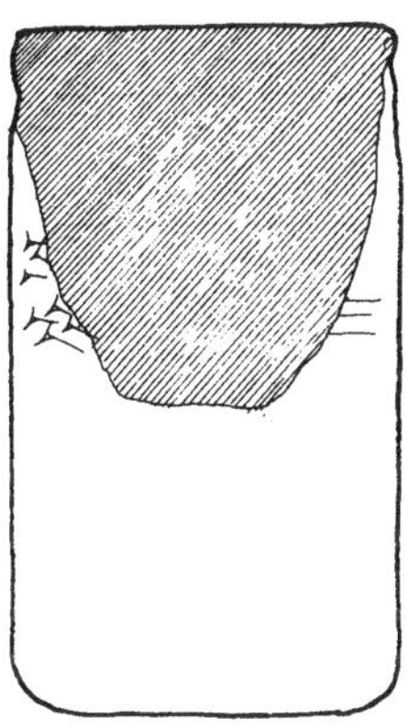

121

Obv.

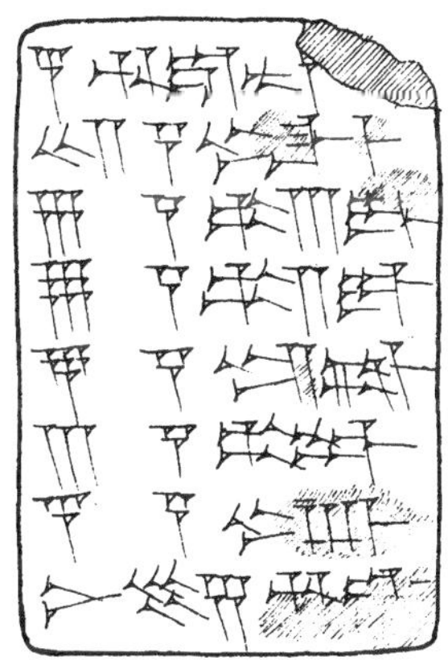

Rev.

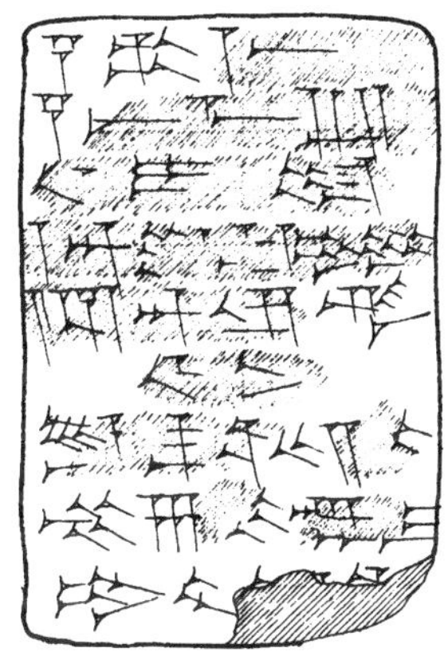

120

Obv.

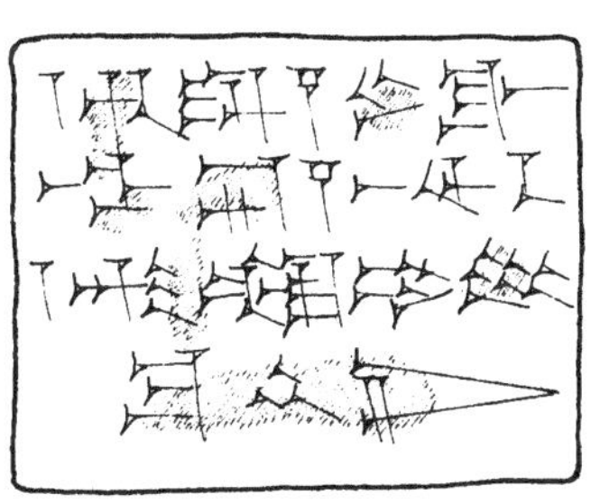

Rev.

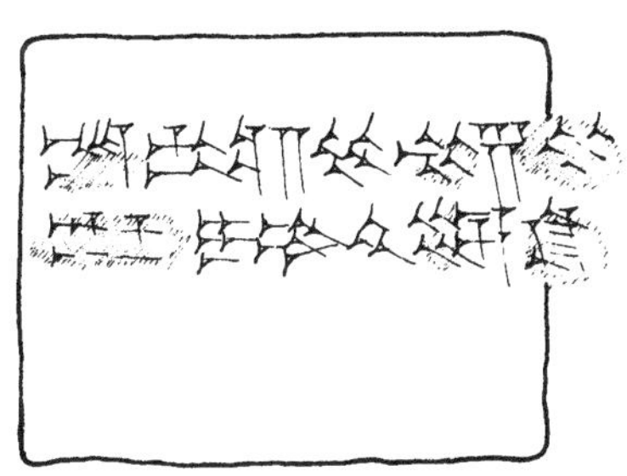

PLATE LX

122

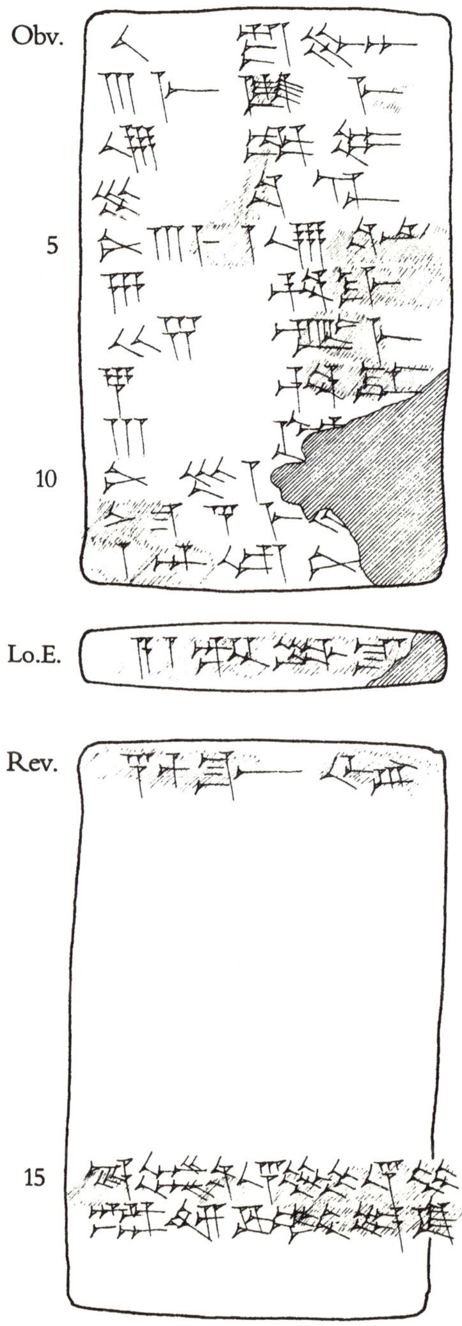

123

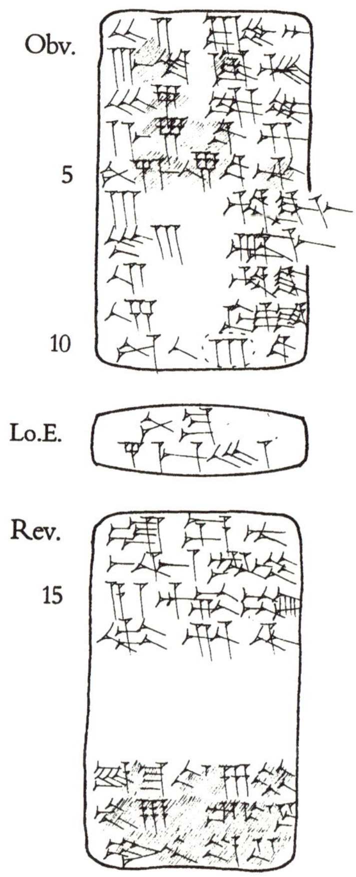

124

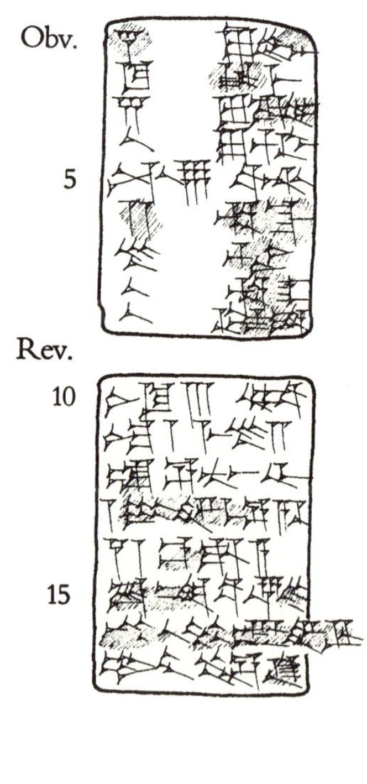

125

Obv.

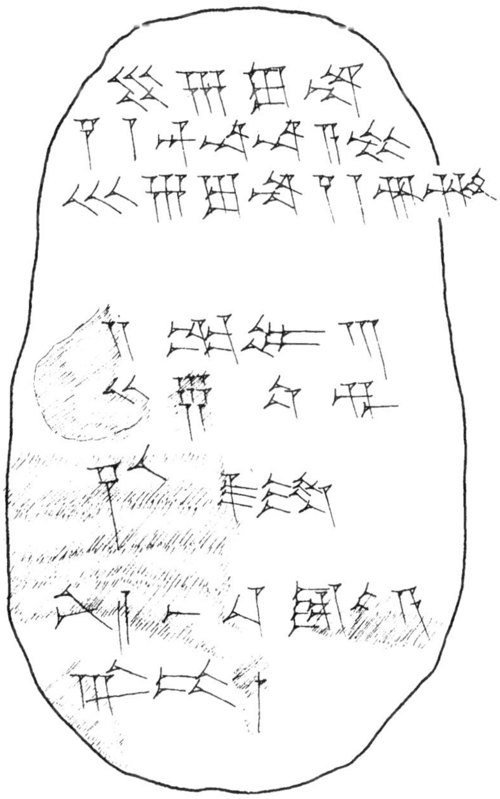

Rev.

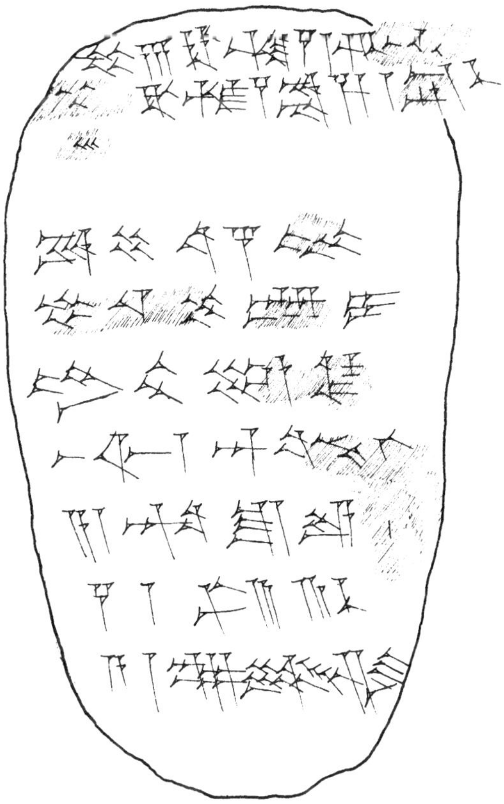

126

Obv.

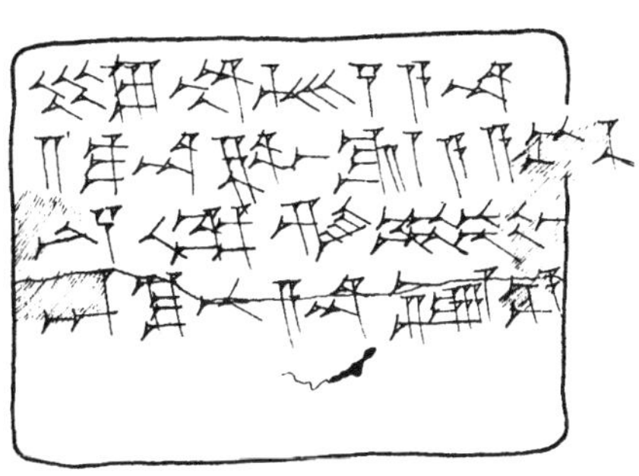

Rev.

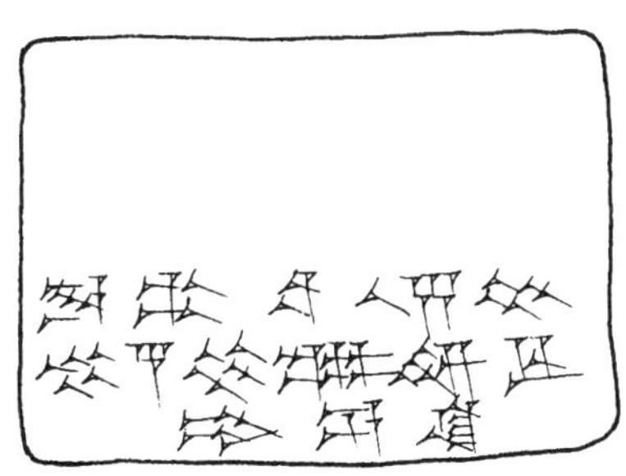

127

Obv.

Rev.

128

Obv.

Rev.

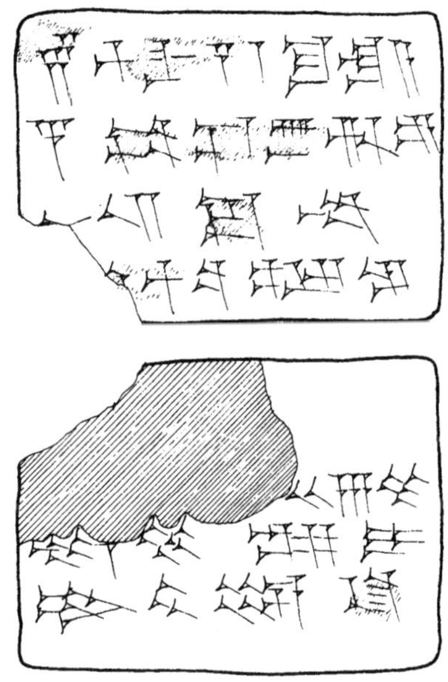

129

Obv.

Rev.

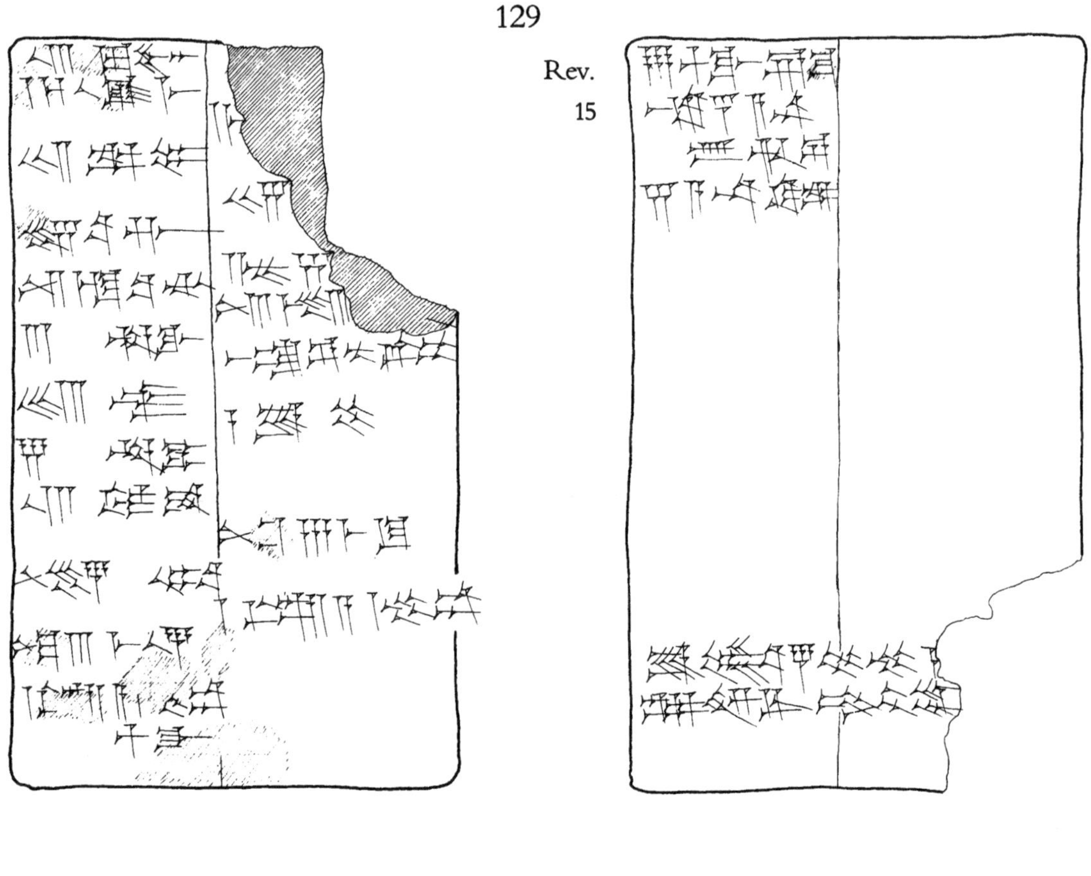

130

Obv.

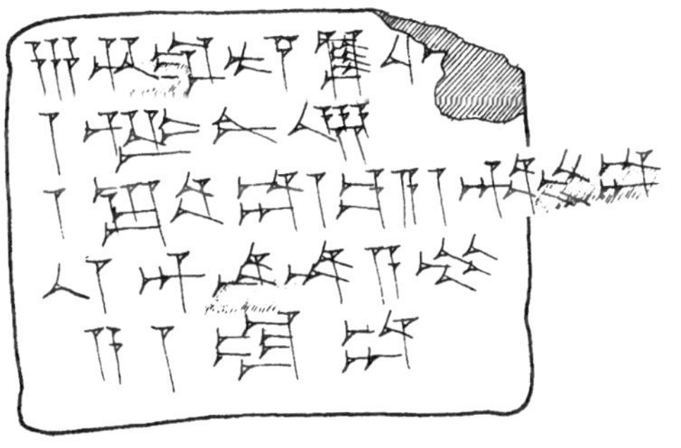

Rev.

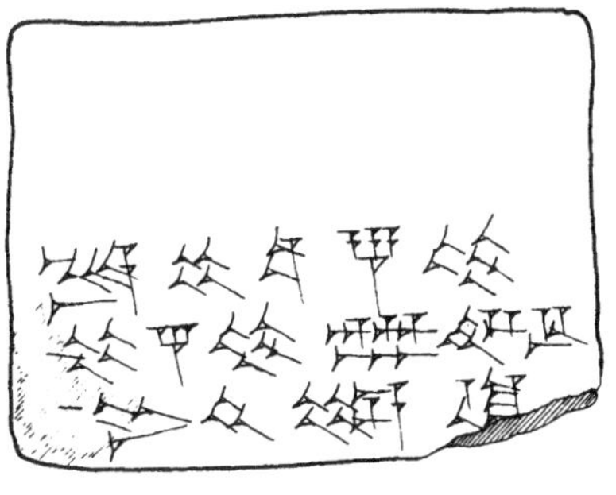

131

Obv.

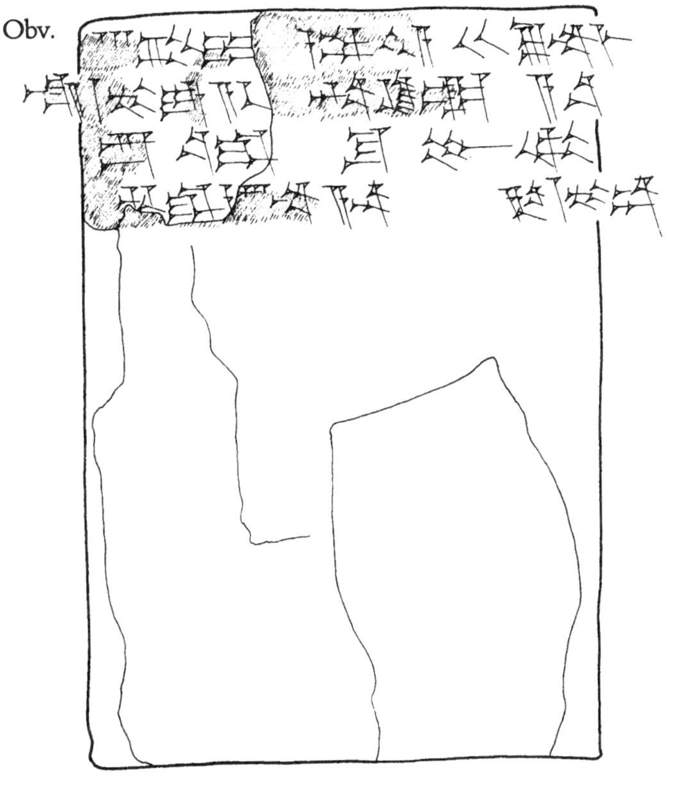

rest uninscribed

Rev.

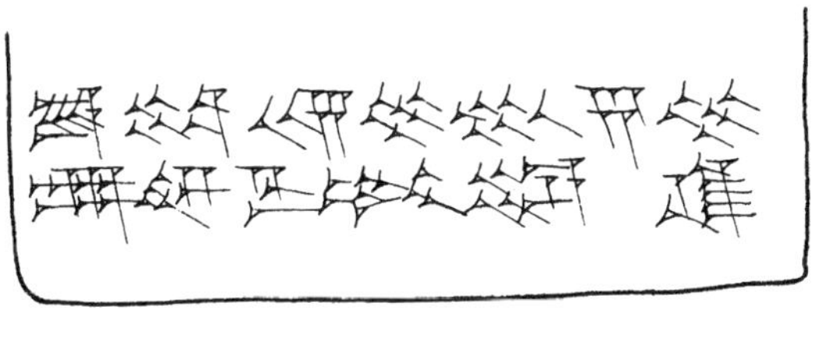

132

Obv.

Rev.

U.E.

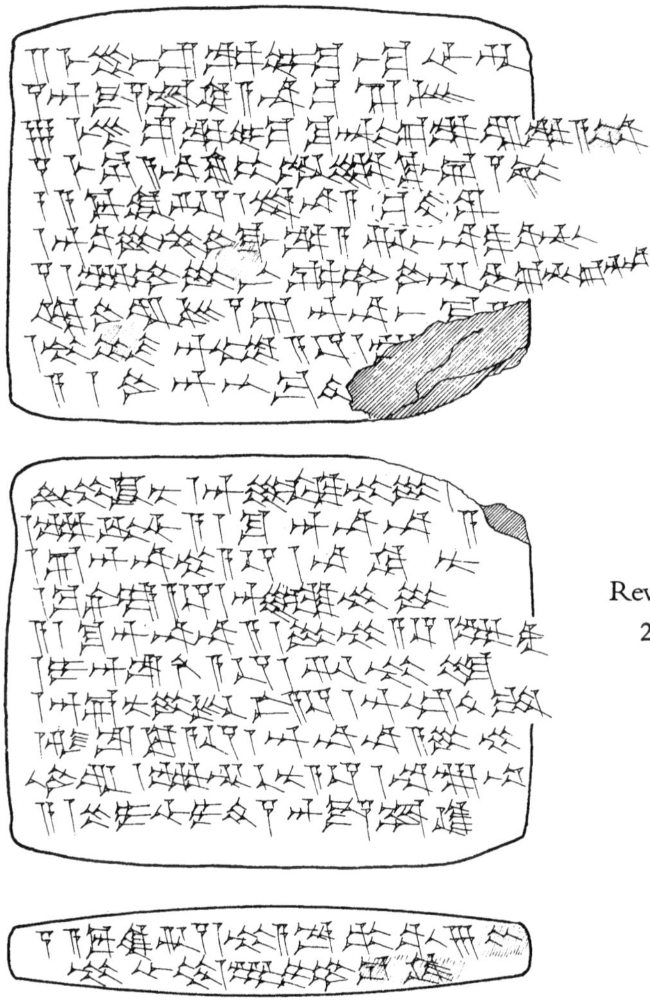

133

Obv.

Rev.

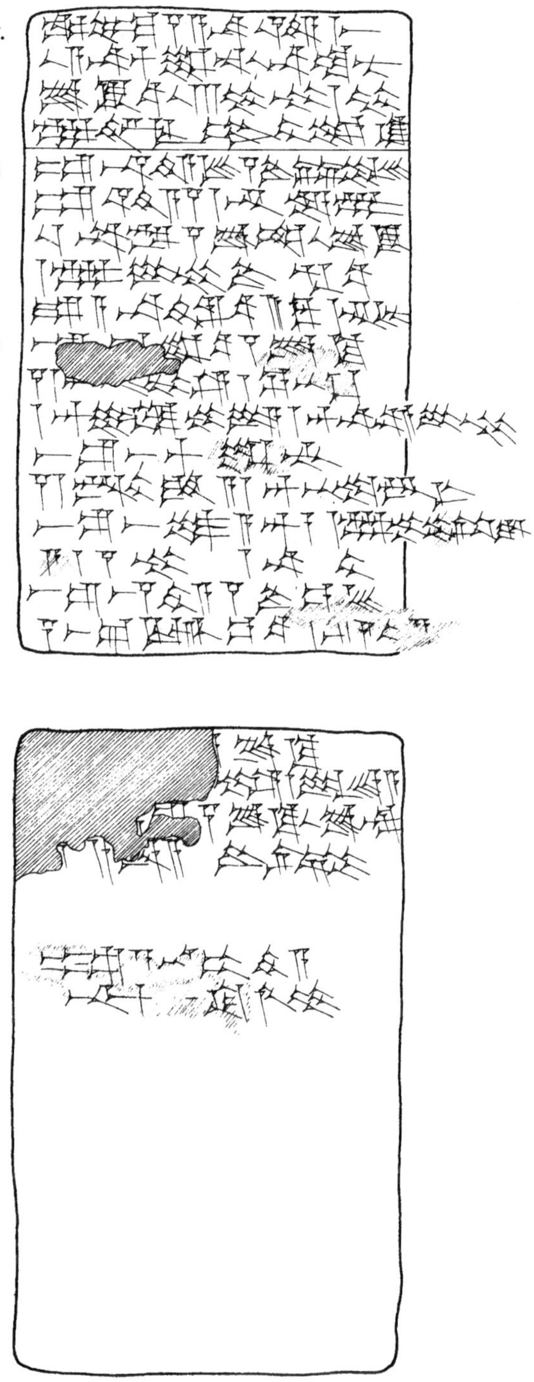

134

Obv.

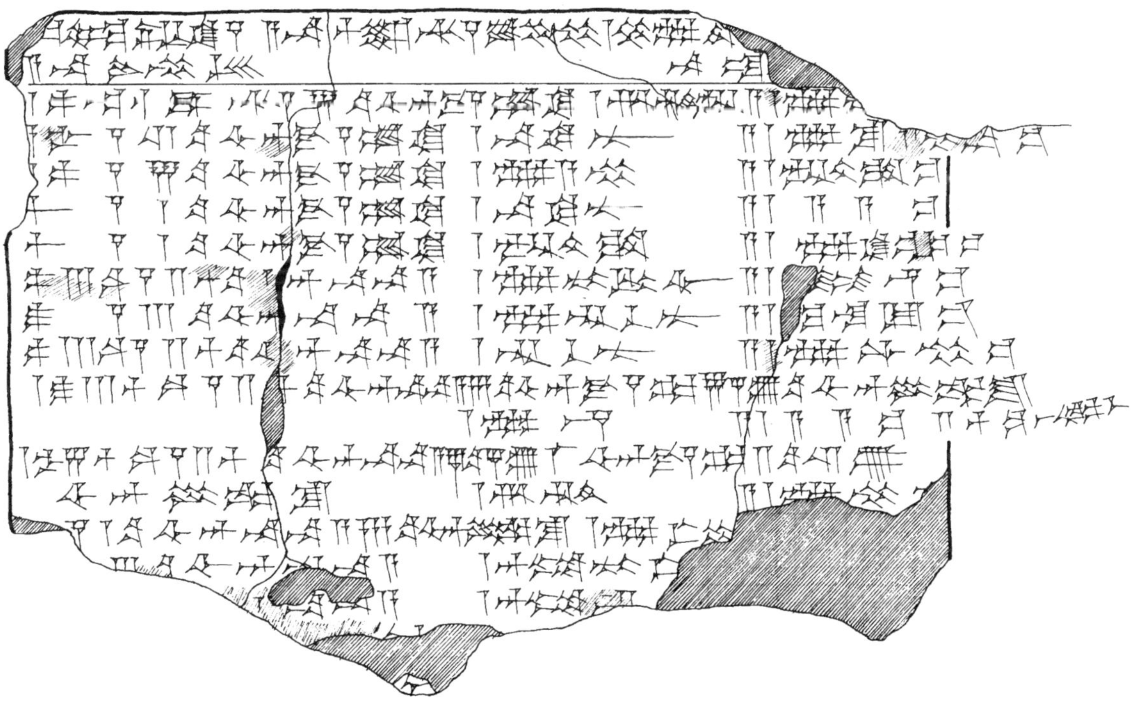

Rev.

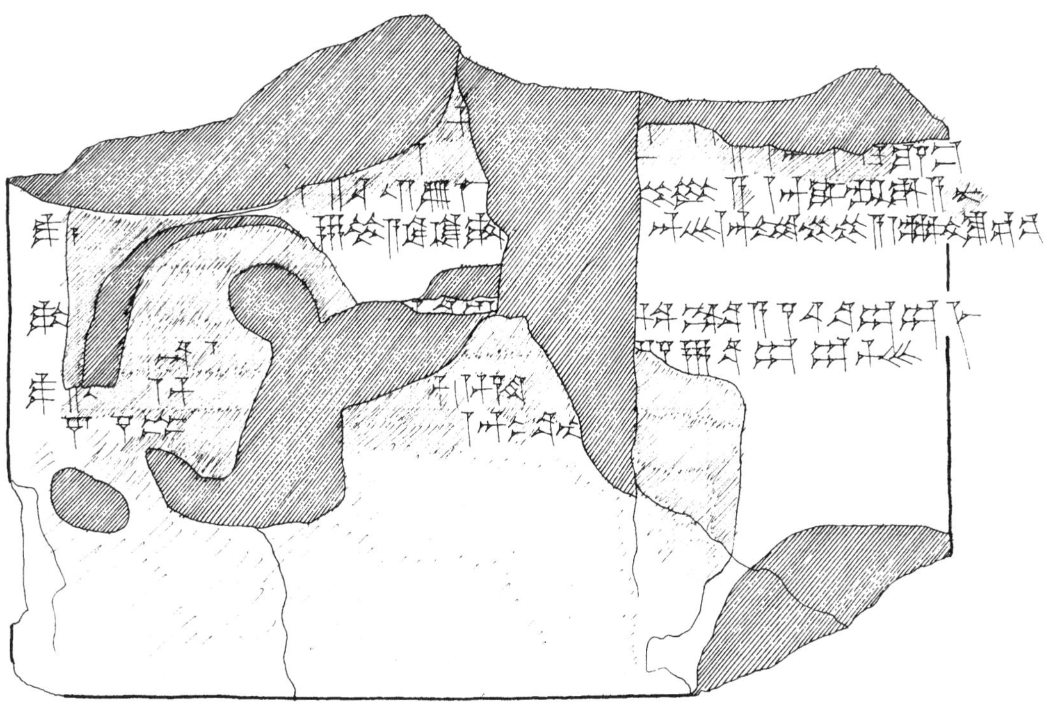

135

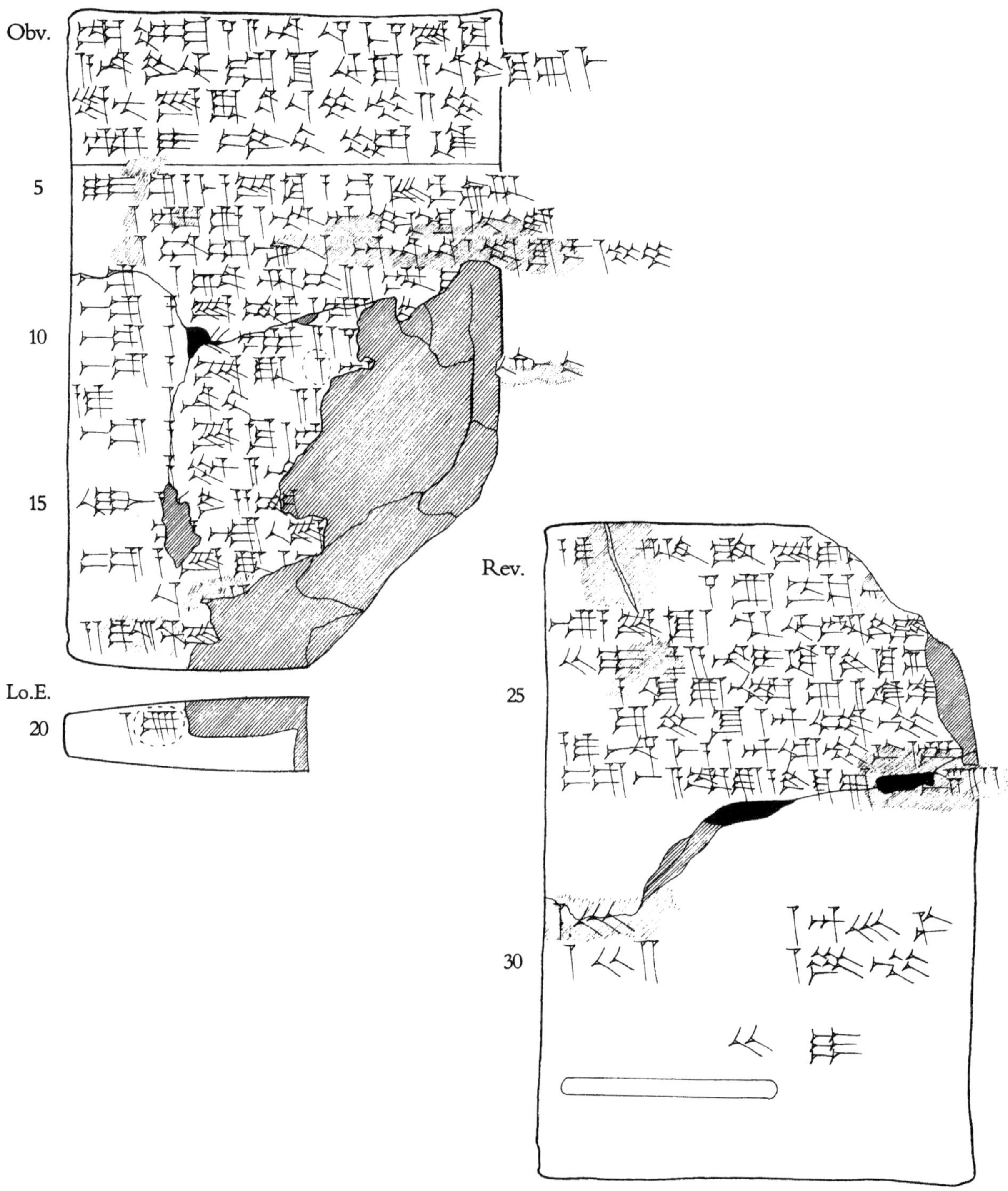

136

Obv.

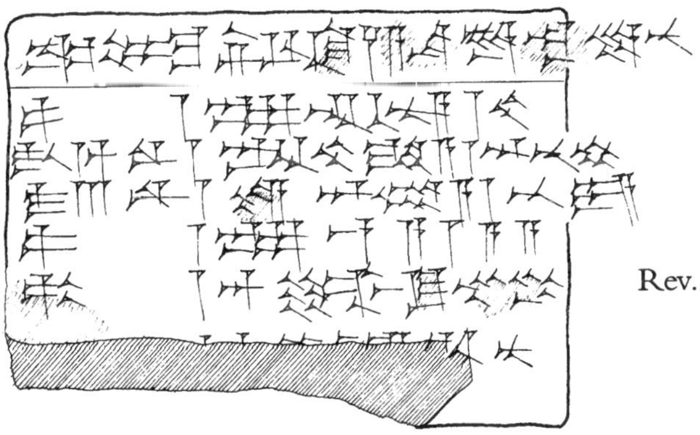

Rev.

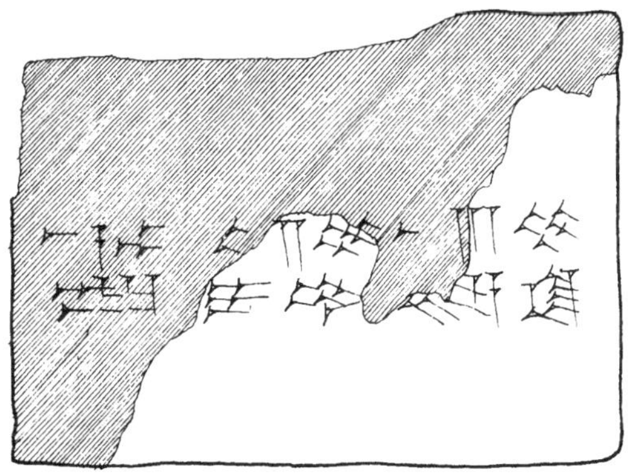

137

Obv.

Rev.

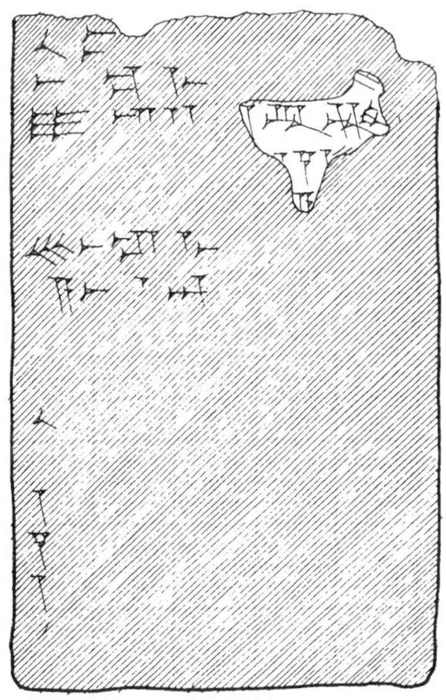

U.E.

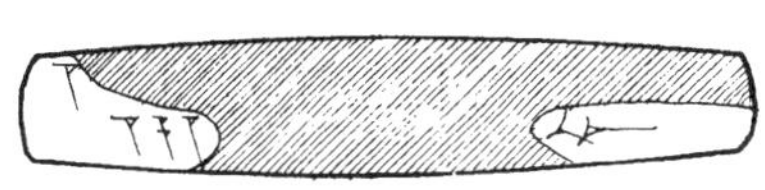

138

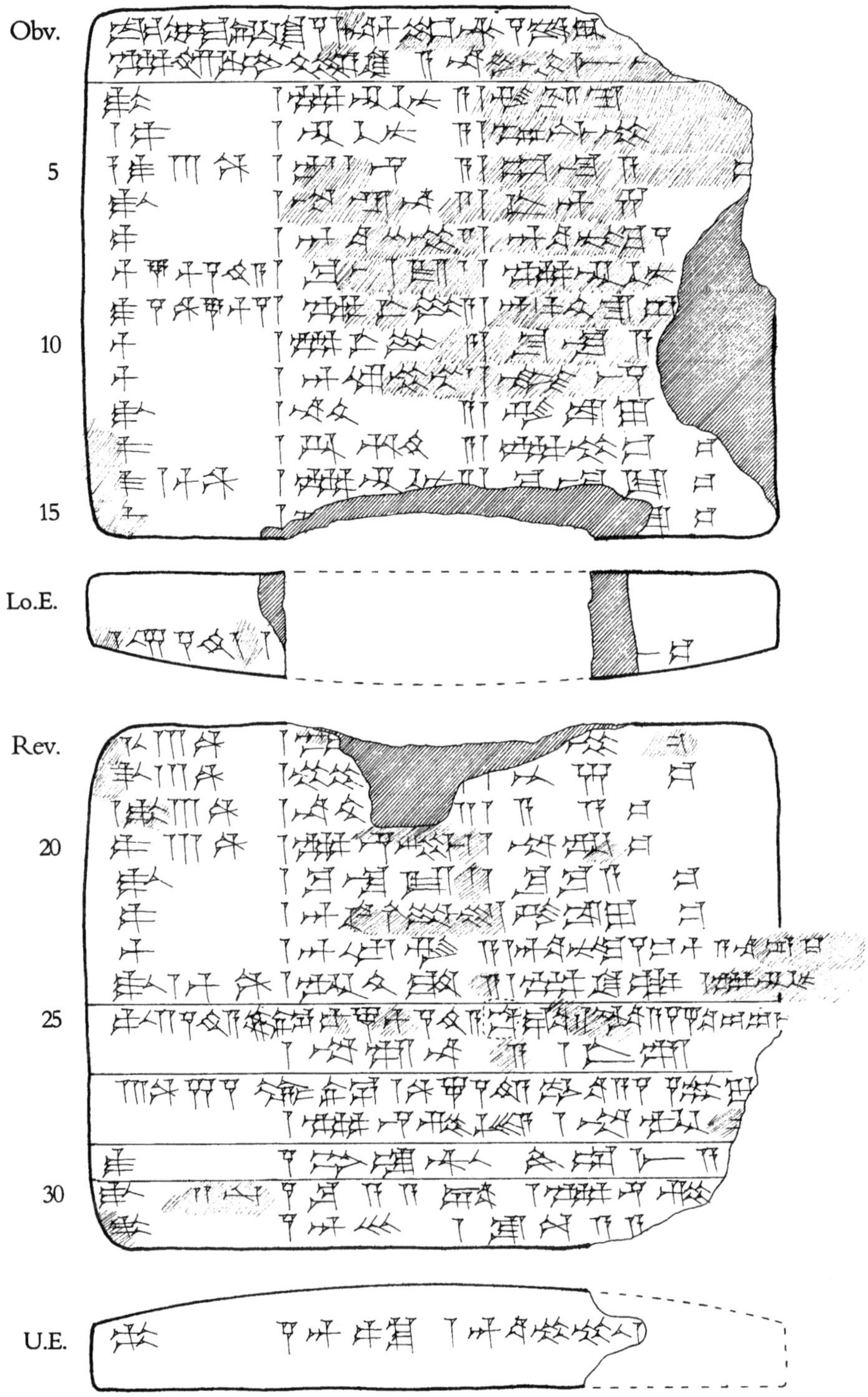

139

Obv.

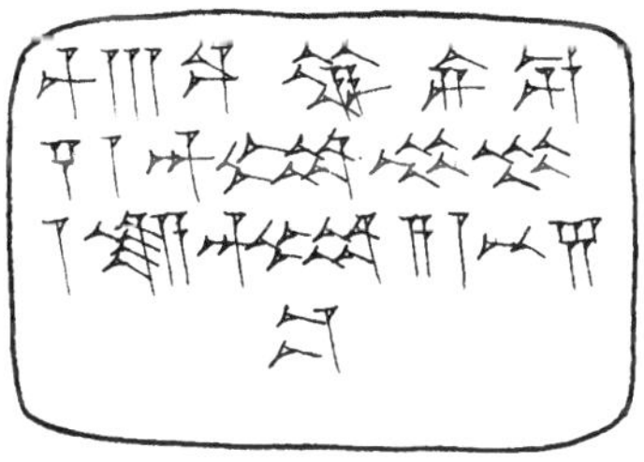

Rev.

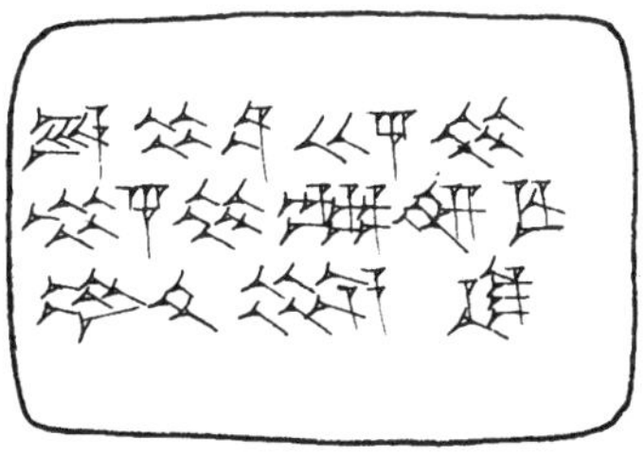

140

Obv.

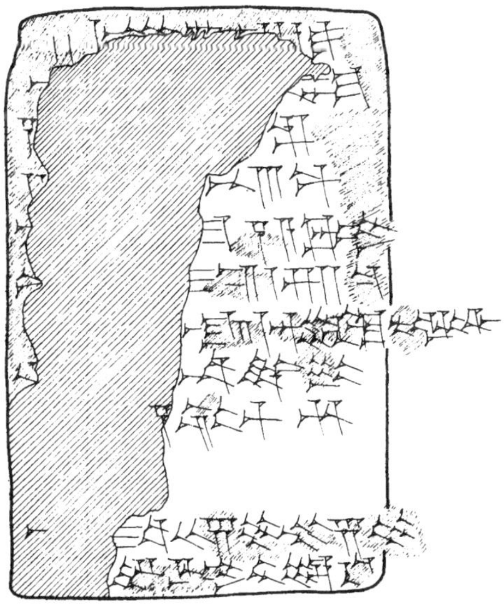

Rev.

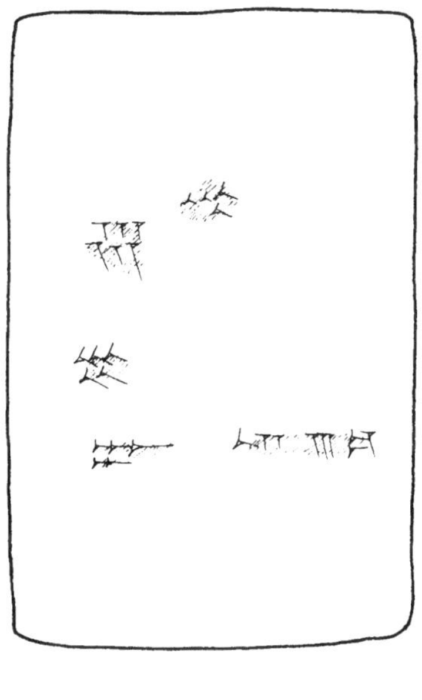

141

Obv.

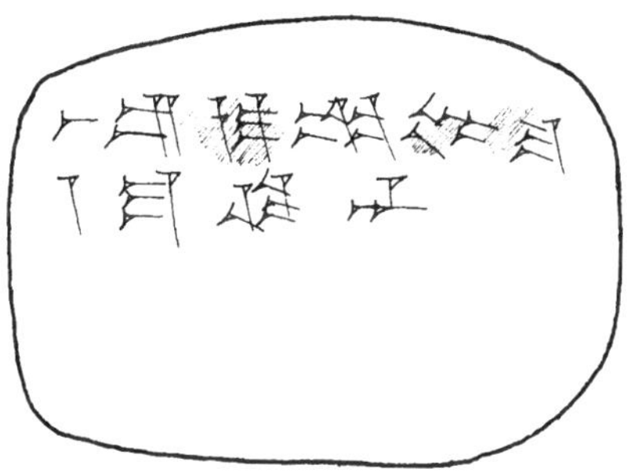

Rev.

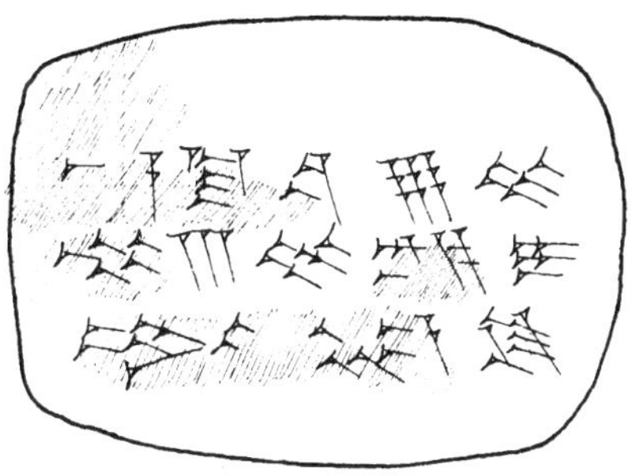

PLATE LXX

142

Obv.

Rev.

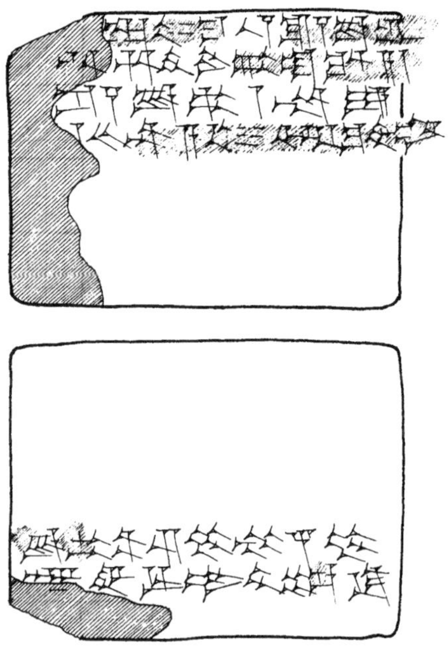

143

Obv.

Rev.

144

Obv.

Rev.

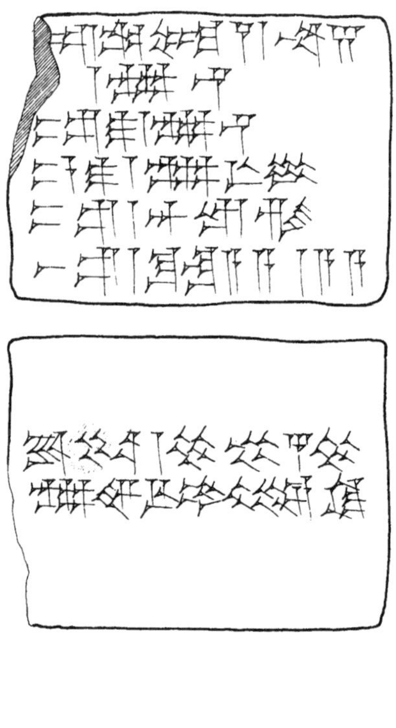

145

Obv.

Lo.E.

Rev.

U.E.

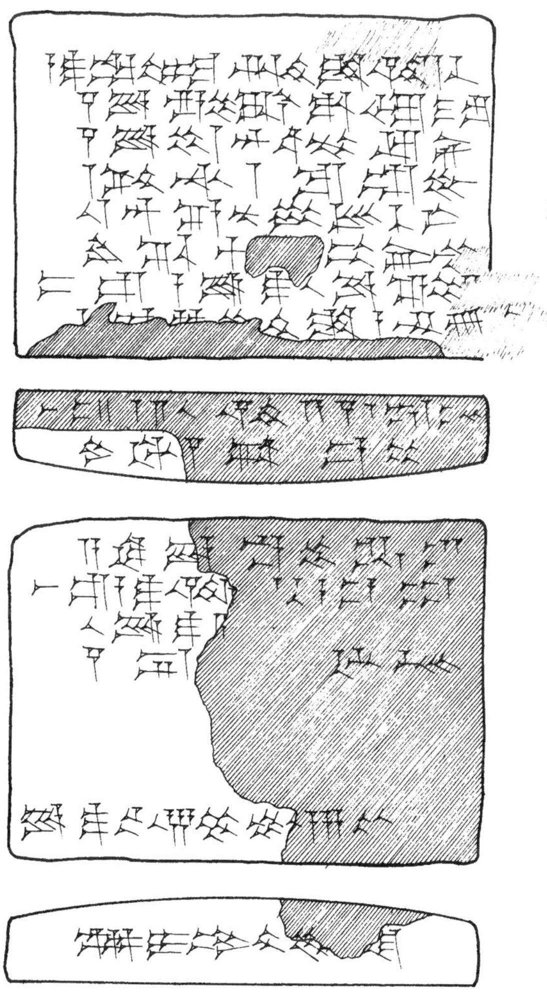

146

Obv.

Rev.

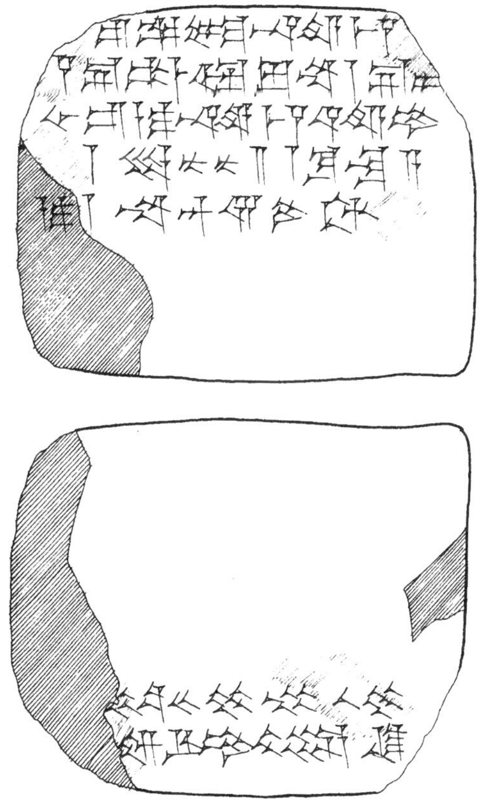

147

Obv.

Rev.

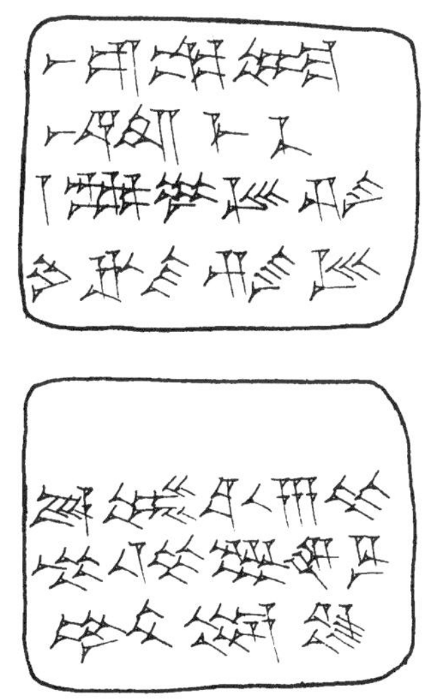

148

Obv.

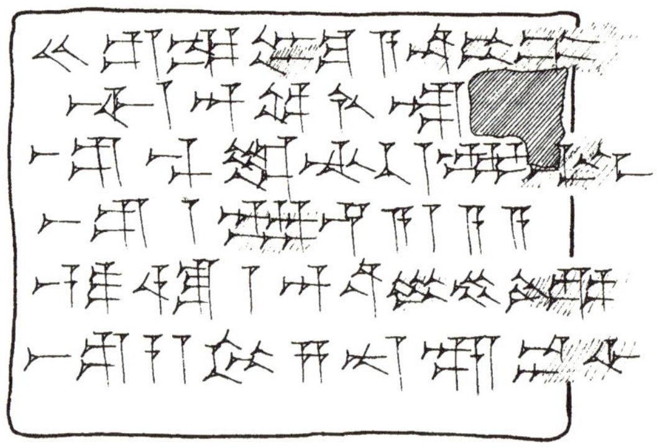

Rev.

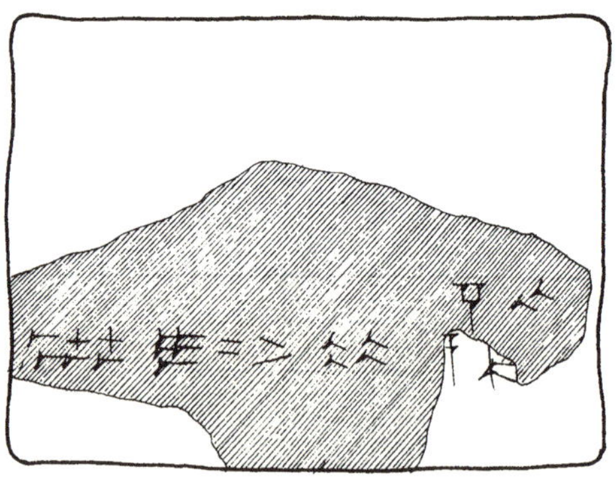

149

Obv.

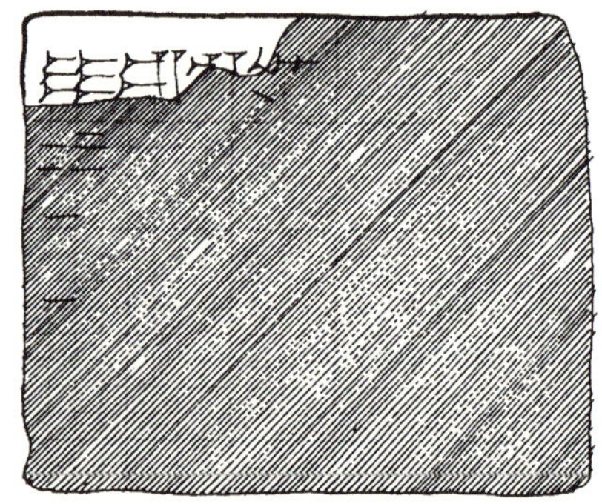

Rev.

150

Obv.

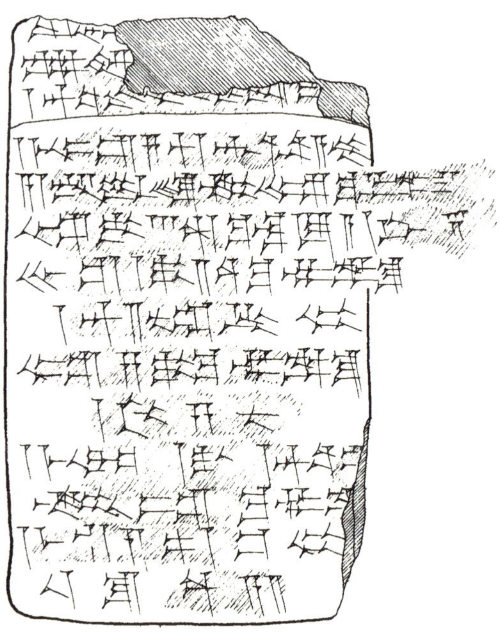

Lo.E.

Rev.

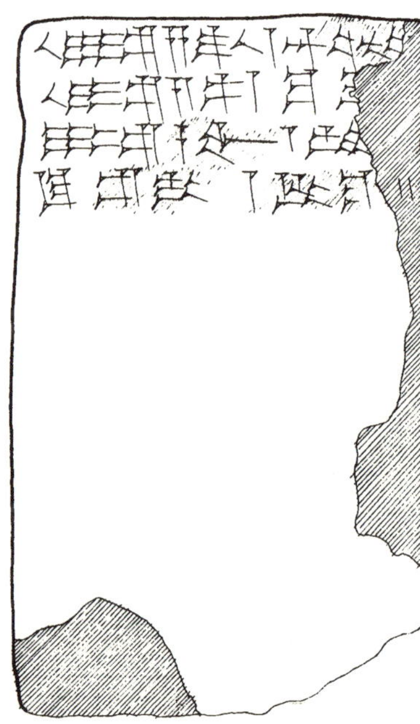

151

Obv.

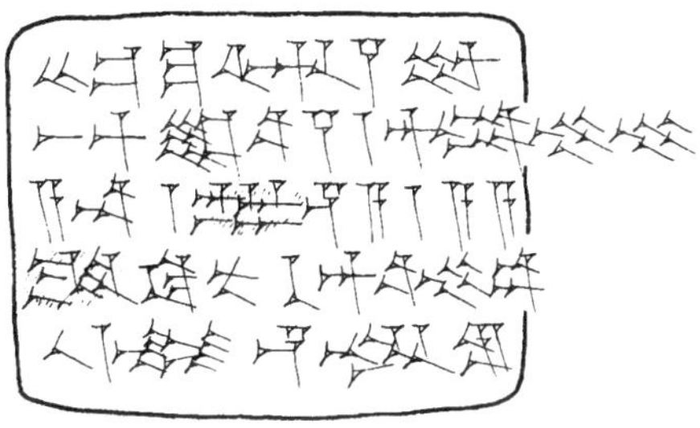

Rev.

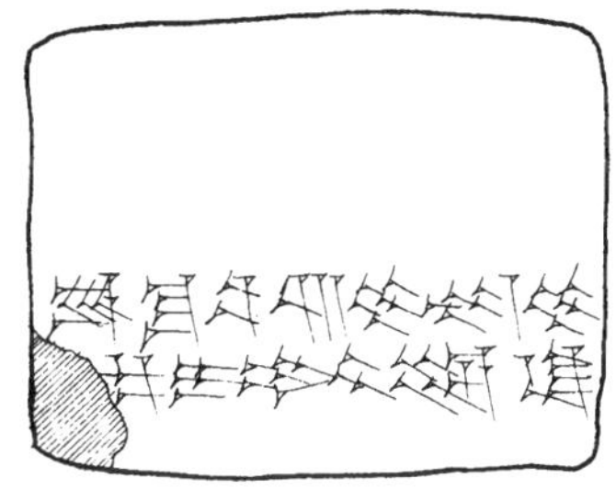

152

Obv.

Rev.

PLATE LXXIV

153

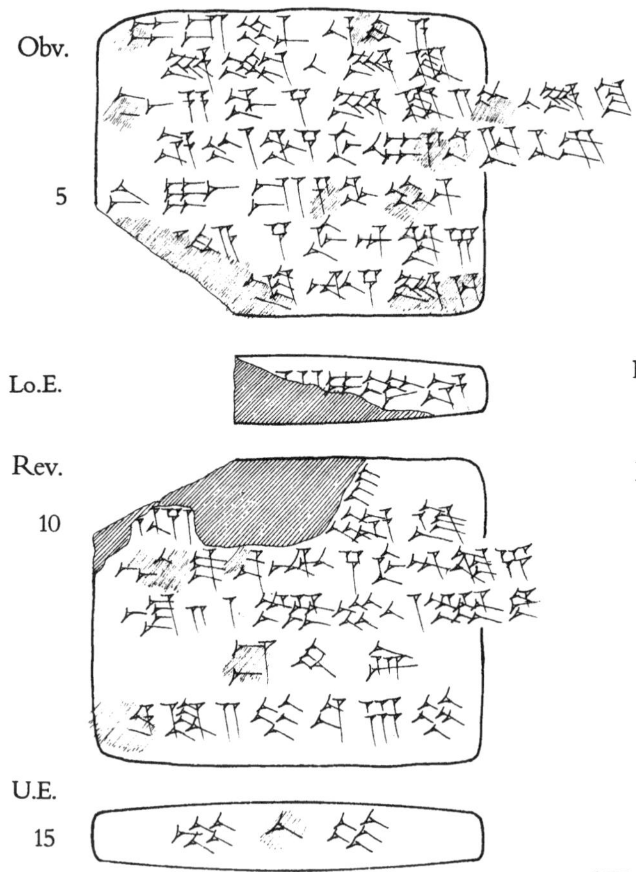

154

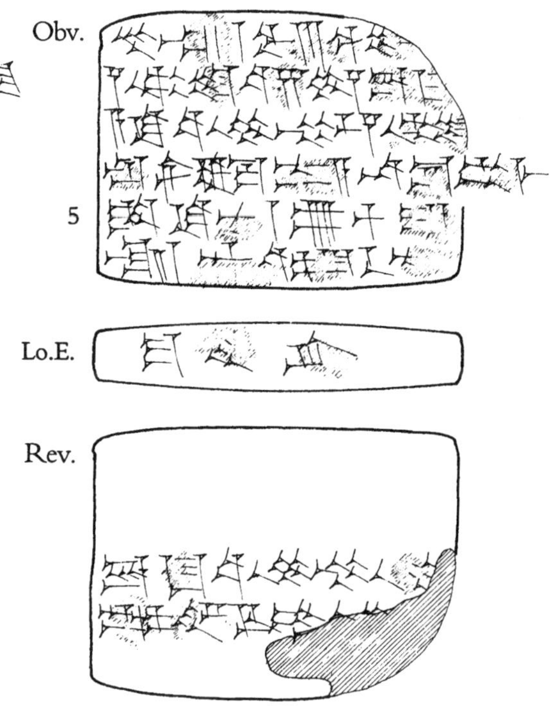

155

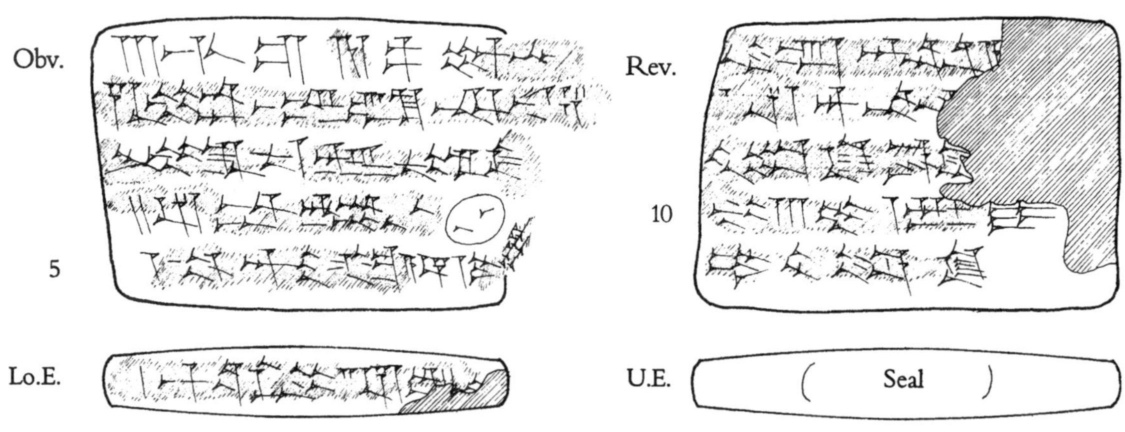

156

Obv.

Lo.E.

Rev.

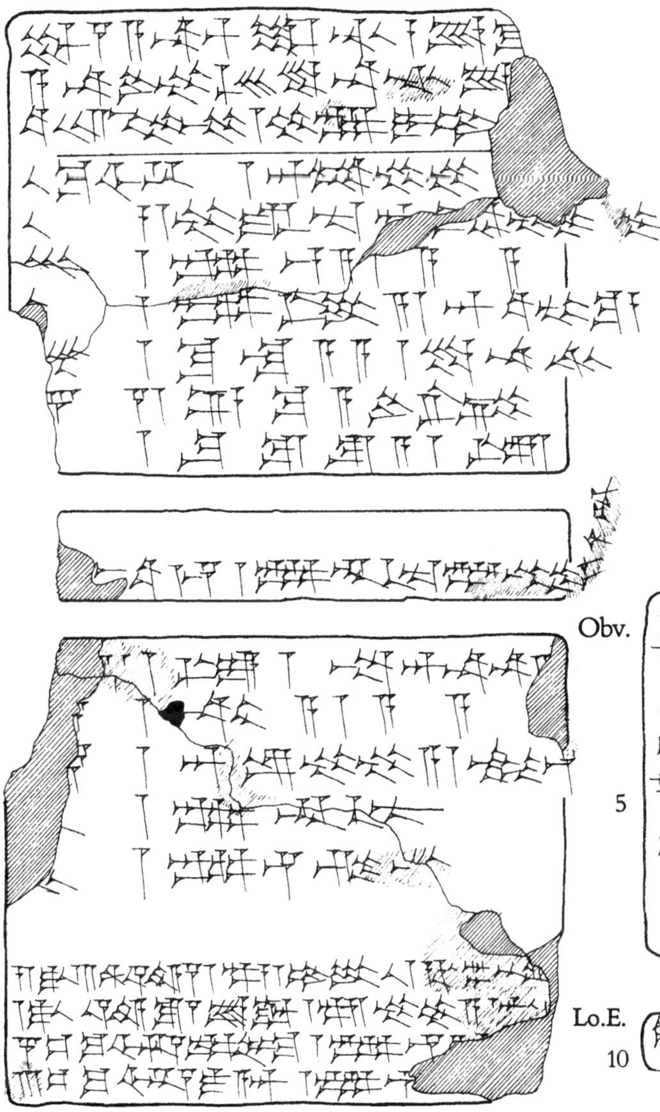

157

Obv.

Lo.E.

Rev.

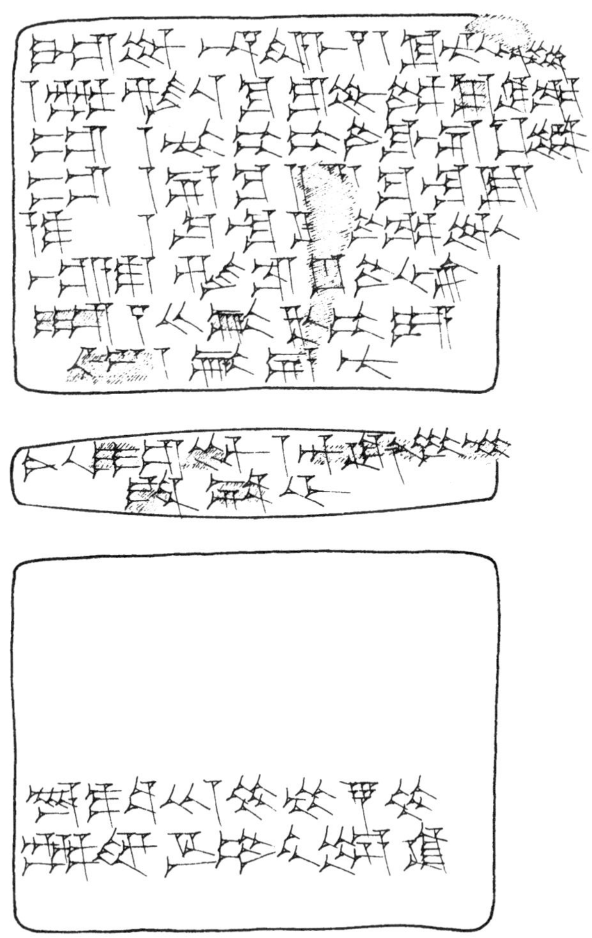

158

Obv.
Rev.
U.E.

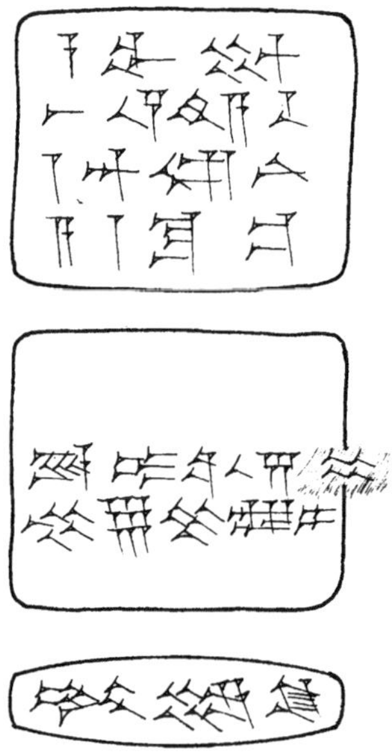

159

Obv.
Rev.

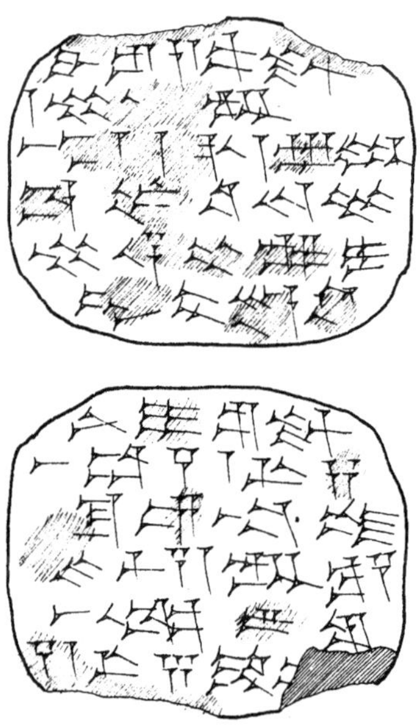

160

Obv.
Rev.

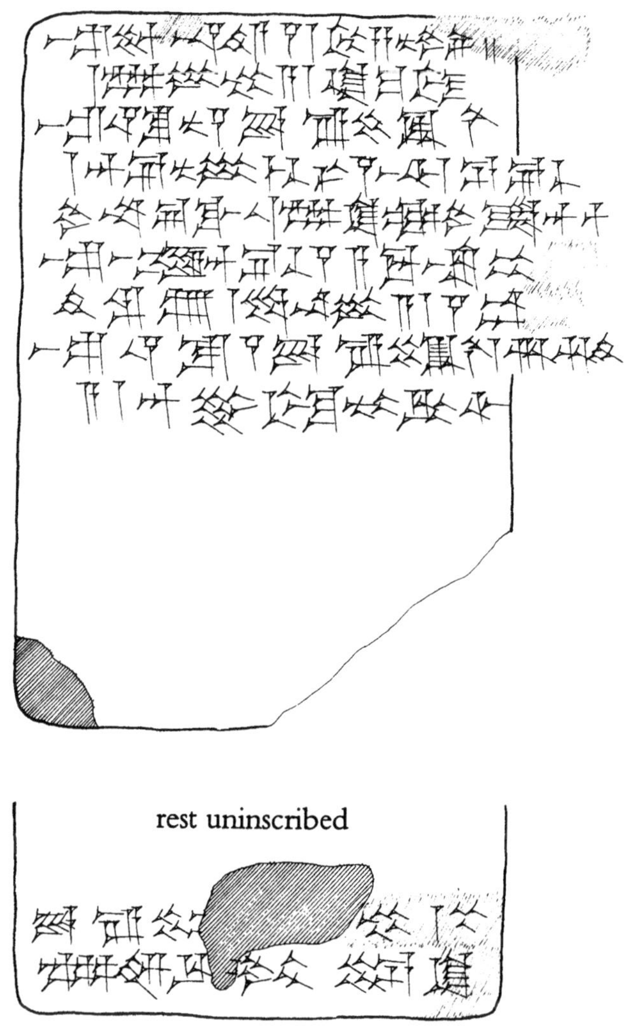

161

Obv.

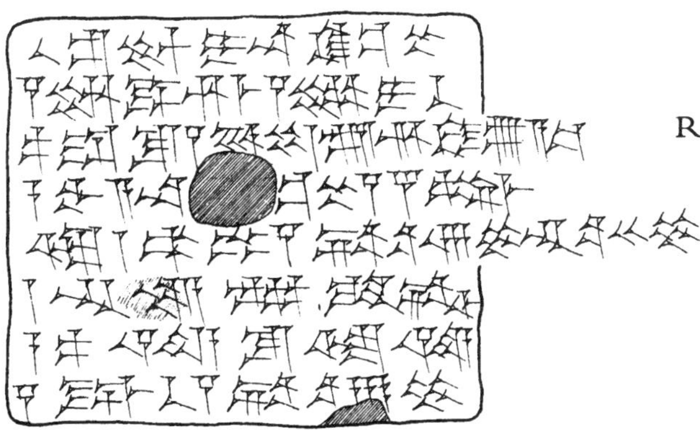

Lo.E.

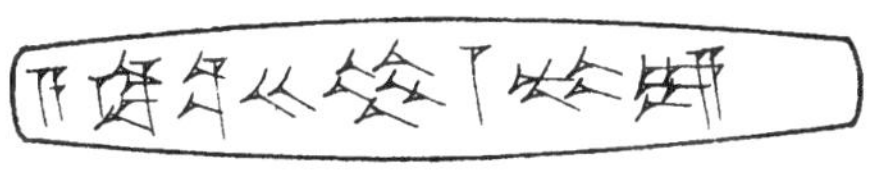

Rev.

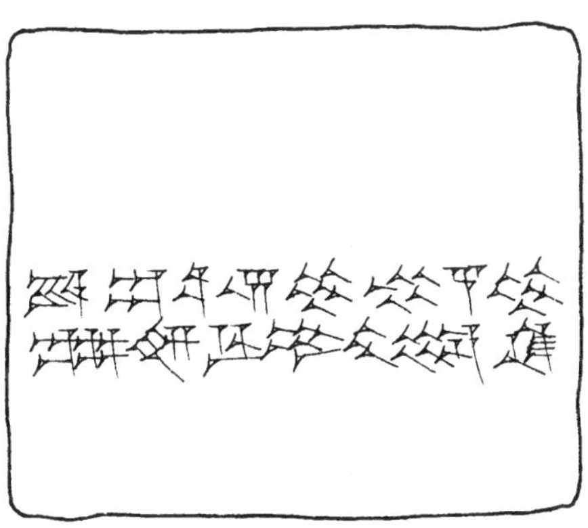

162

Obv.

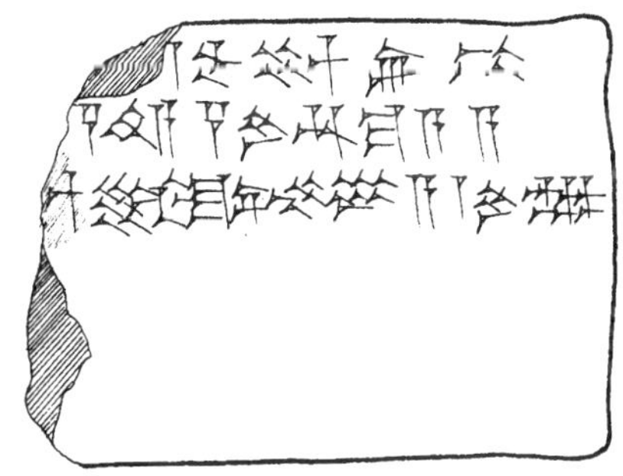

Rev.

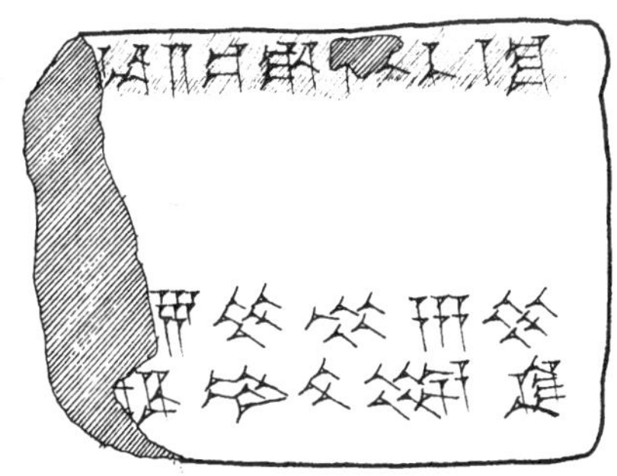

163

Obv.

Rev.

164

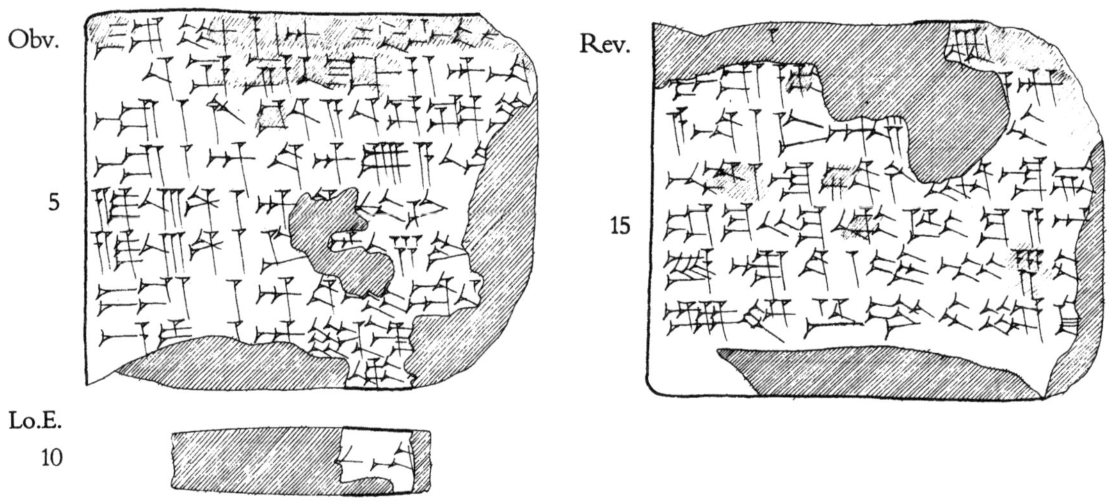

165

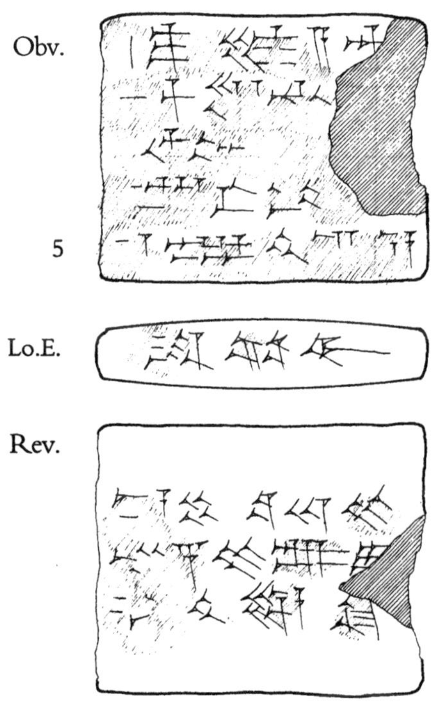

166

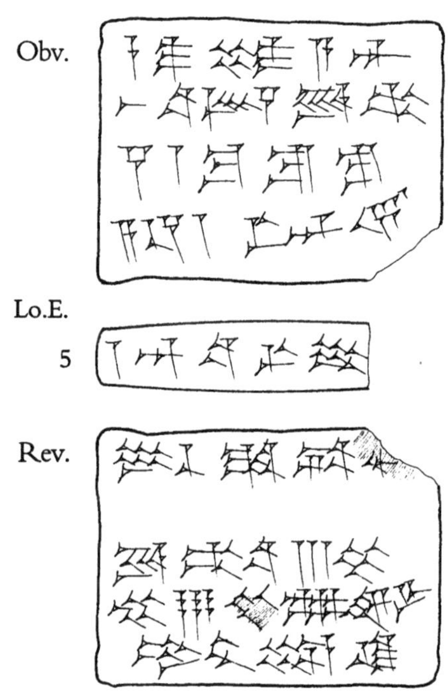

167

Obv.

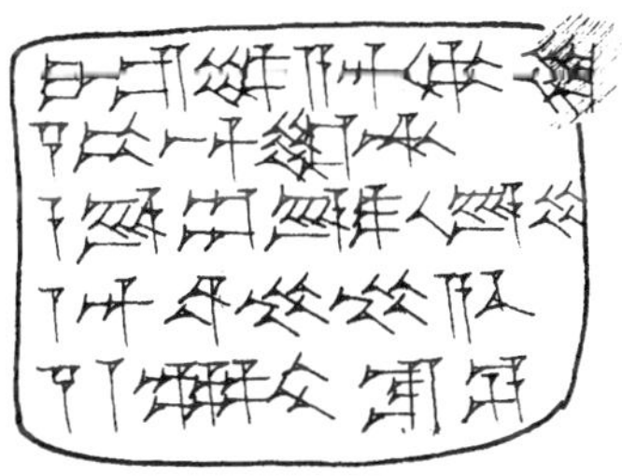

Rev.

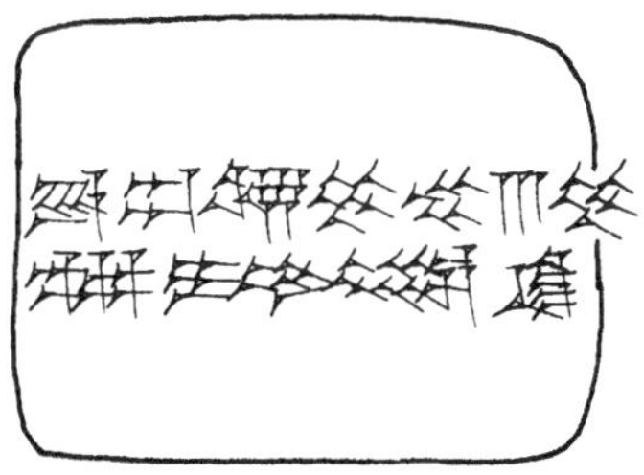

168

Obv.

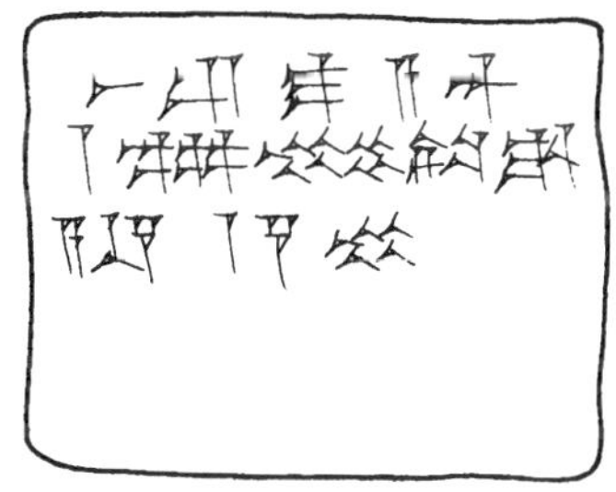

Rev.

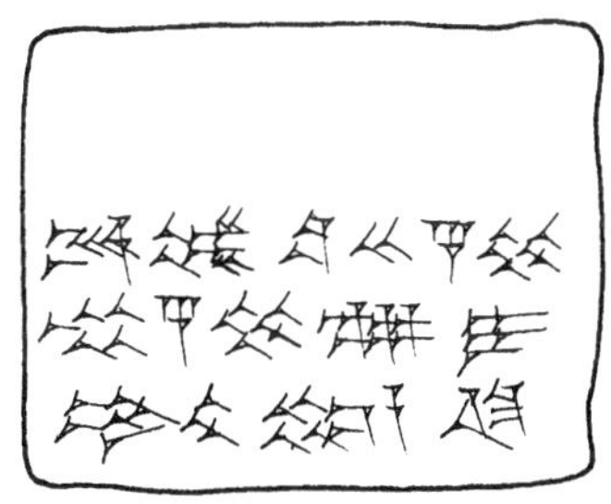

169

Obv.

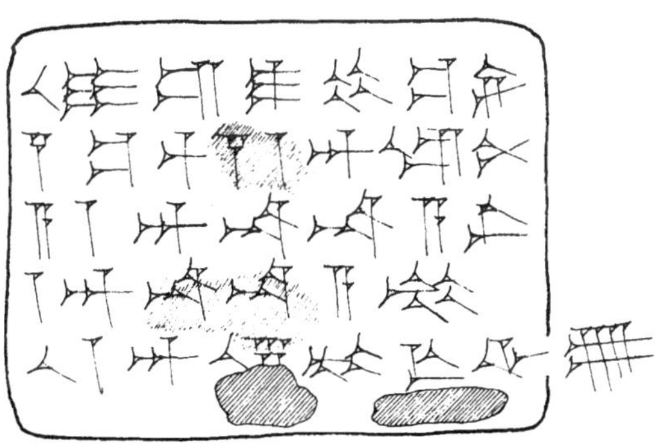

Rev.

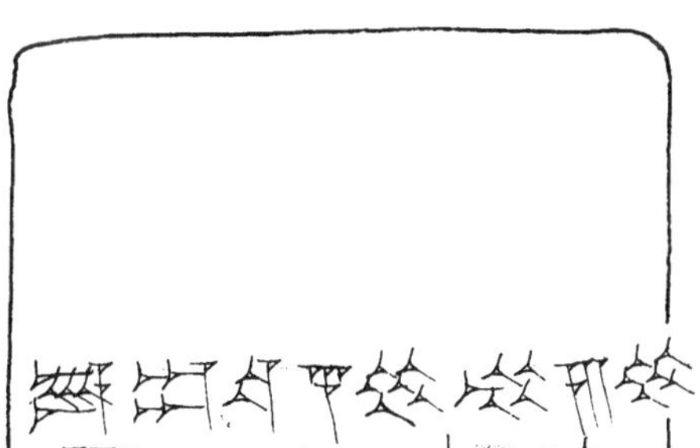

170

Obv.

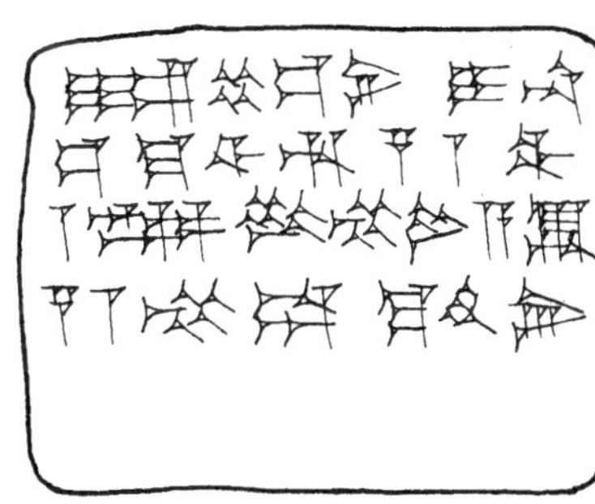

Rev.

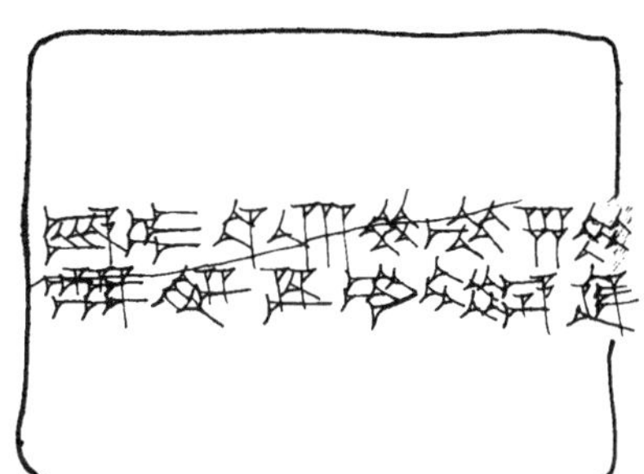

171

Obv.

Rcv.

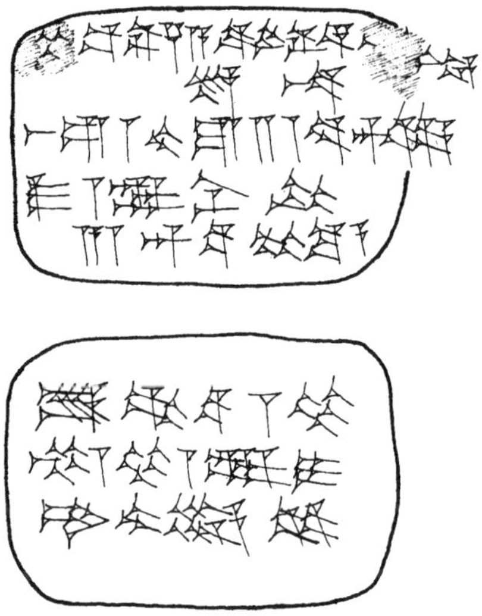

172

Obv.

Lo.E.

Rev.

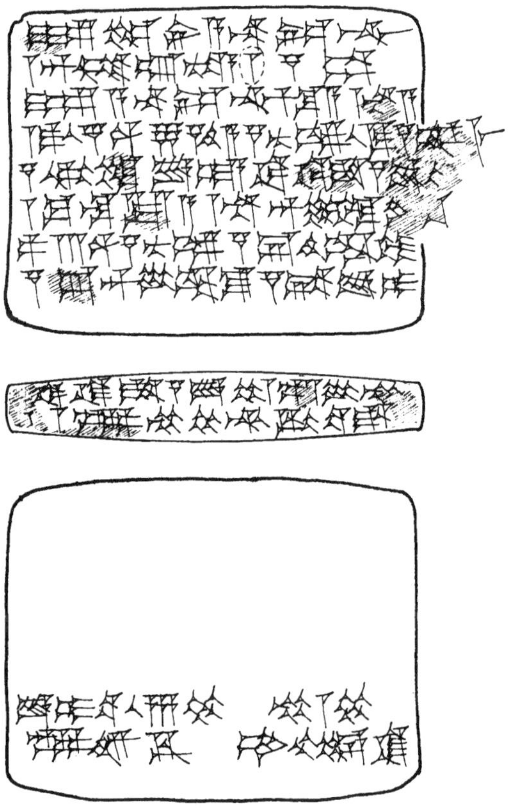

173

Obv.

Lo.E.

Rev.

174

Obv.

Lo.E.

Rev.

U.E.

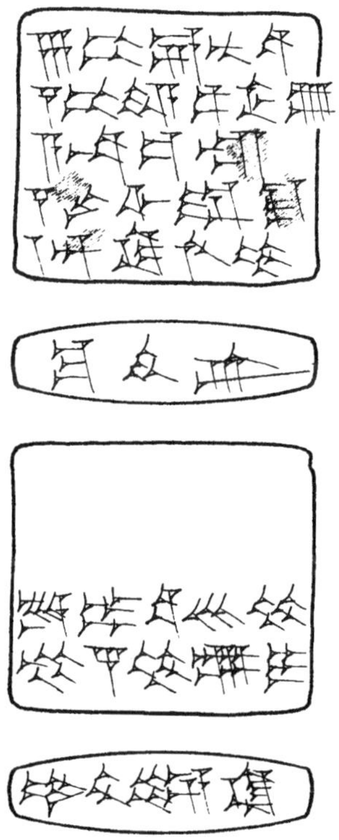

175

Obv. / Rev.

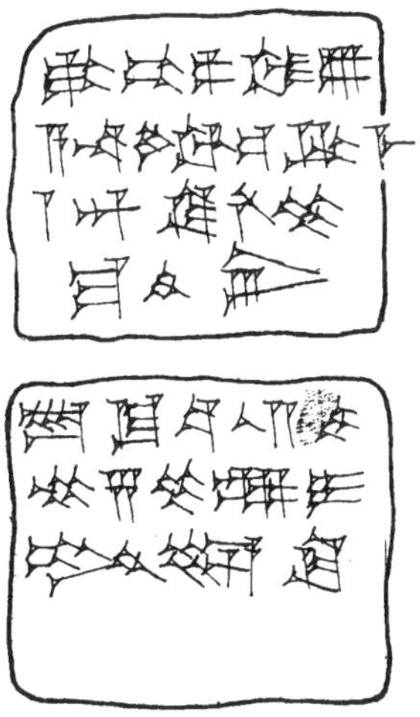

176

Obv. / Rev.

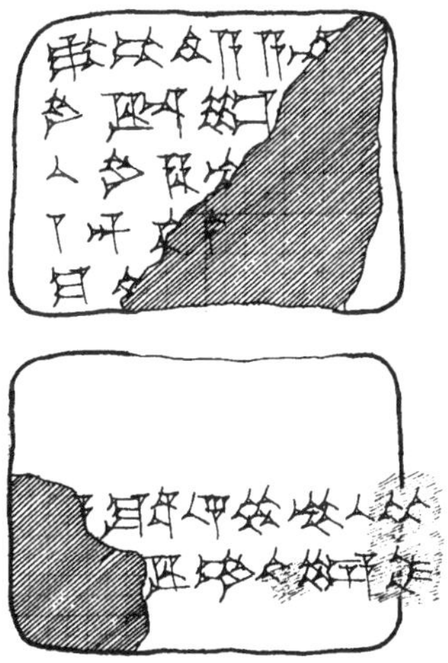

177

Obv. / Lo.E. / Rev.

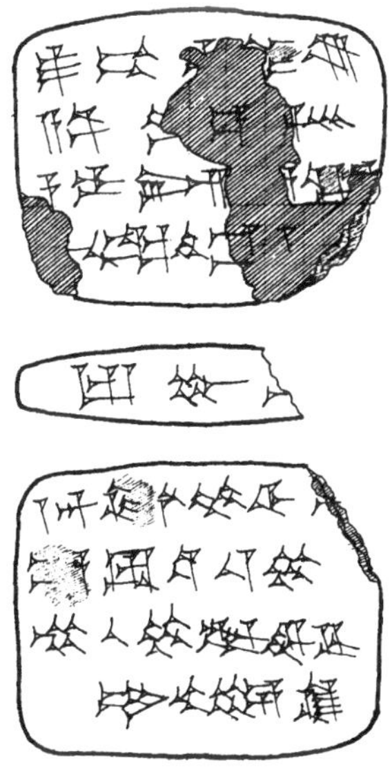

178

Obv. / Rev.

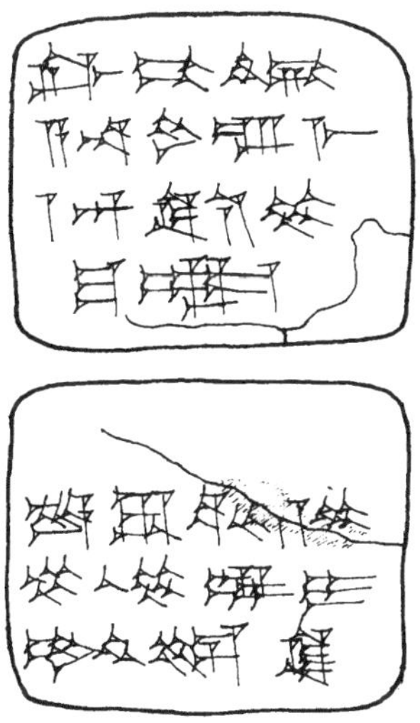

179

Obv. / Rev.

180

Obv. / Rev.

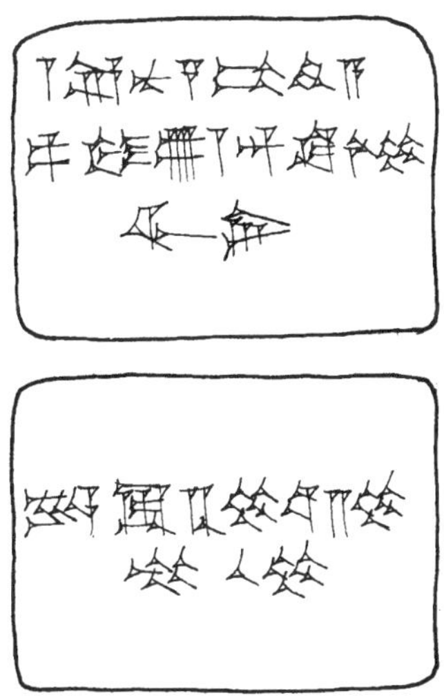

PLATE LXXXII

181

Obv.

Rev.

182

Obv.

Rev.

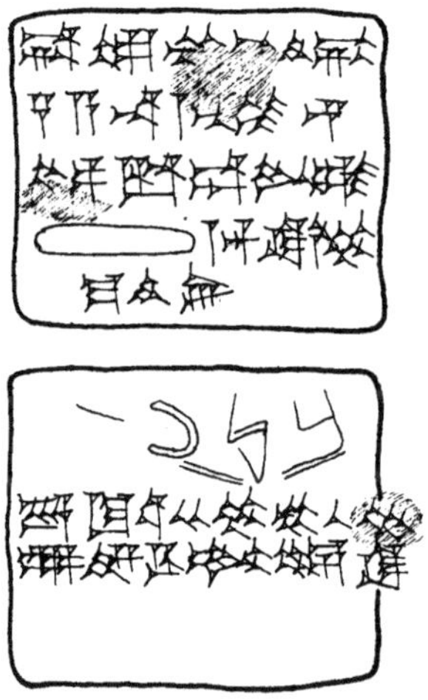

183

Obv.

Rev.

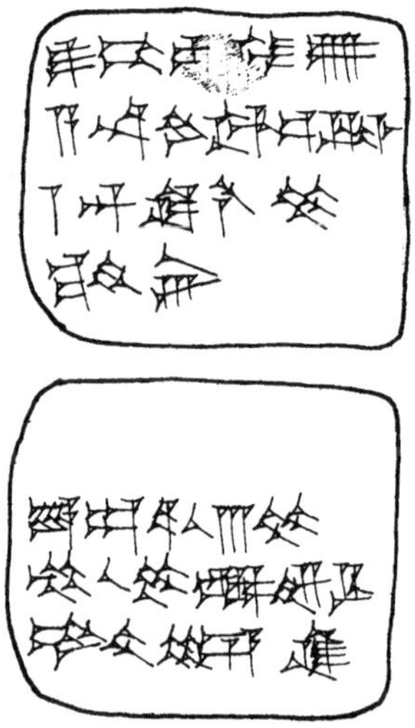

184

Obv.

Rev.

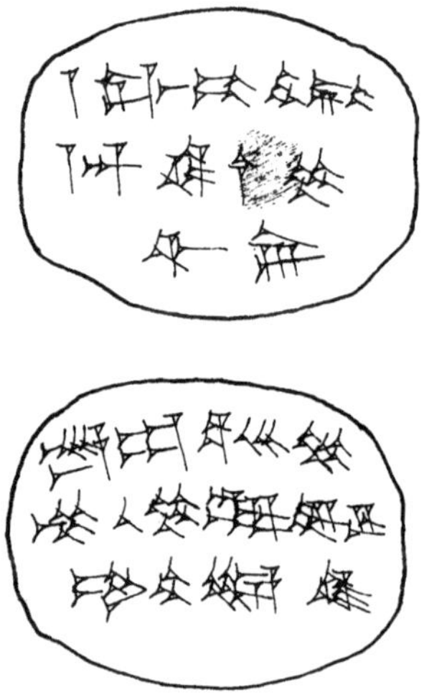

185

Obv.

Rev.

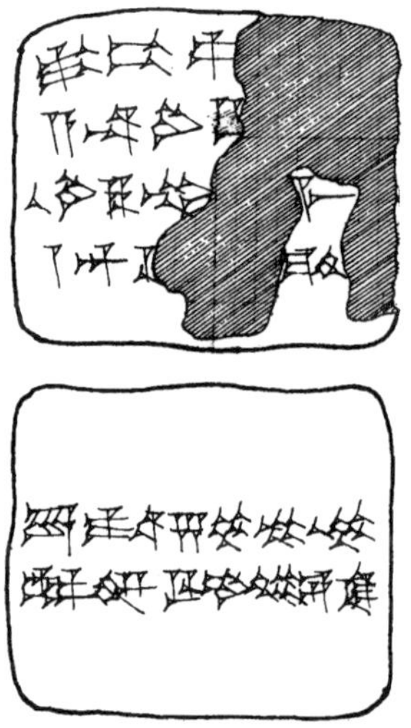

186

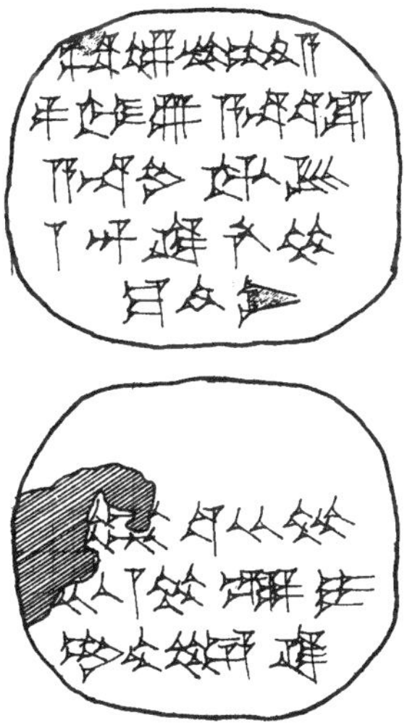

187

188

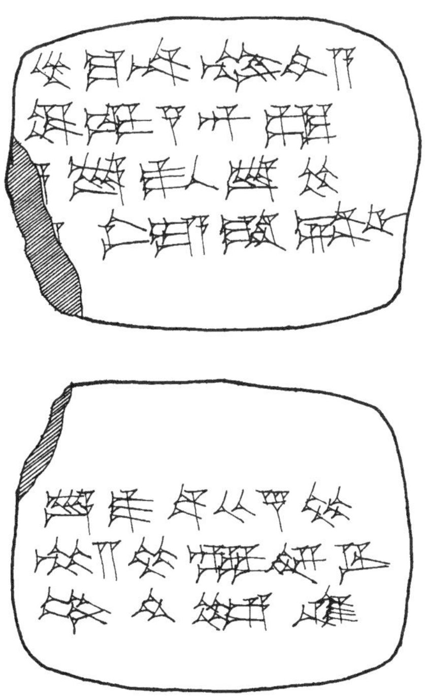

189

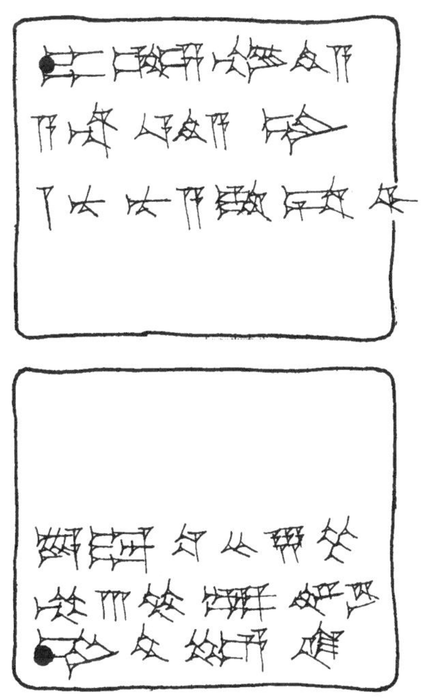

190

Obv.

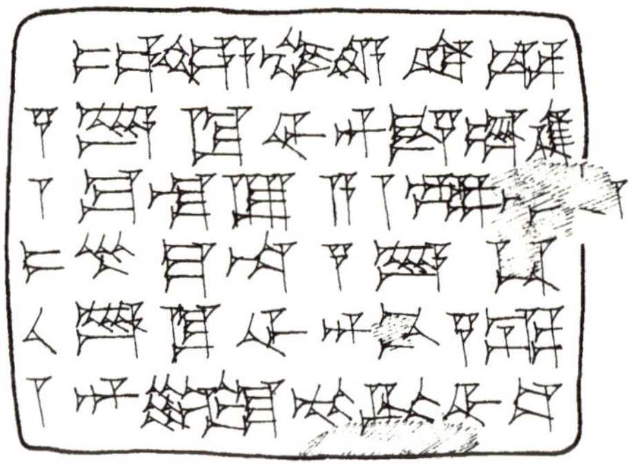

Rev.

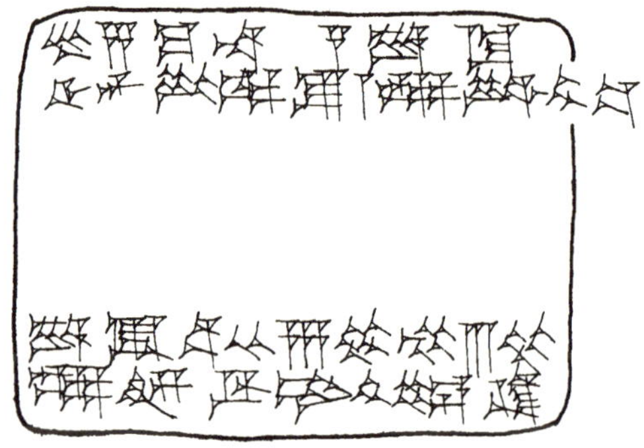

Lo.E.

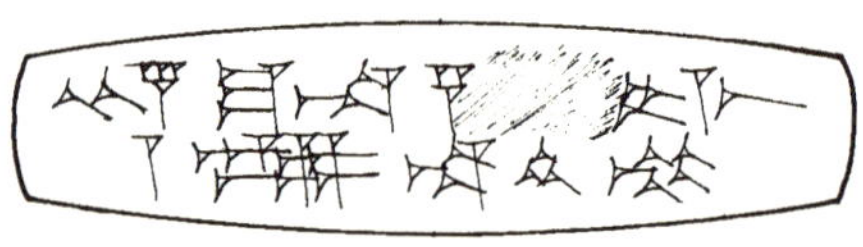

191

Obv.

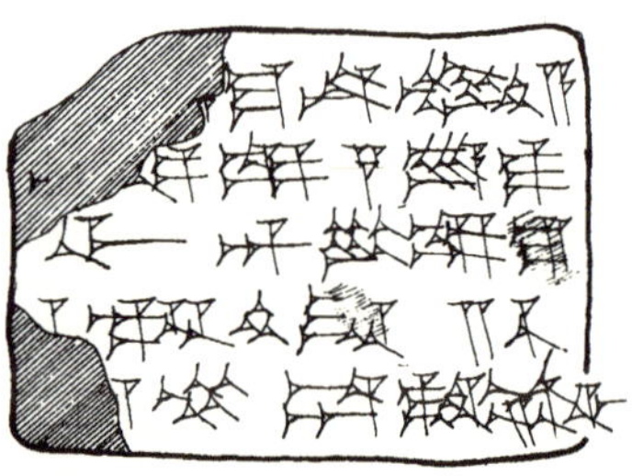

Rev.

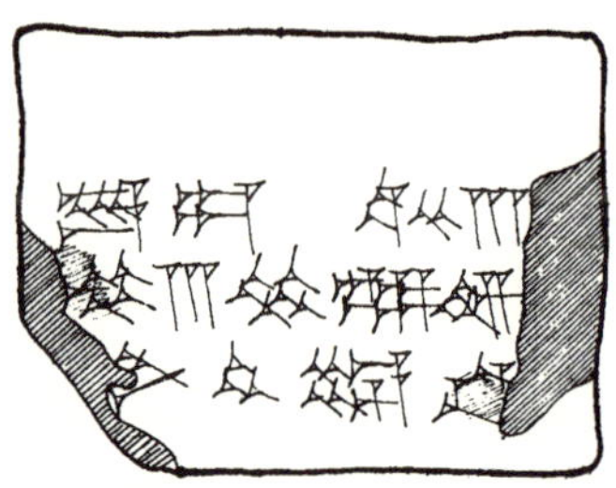

192

Obv.

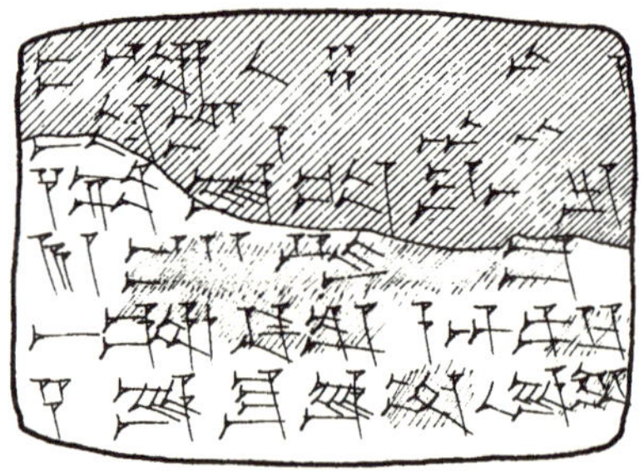

Lo.E.

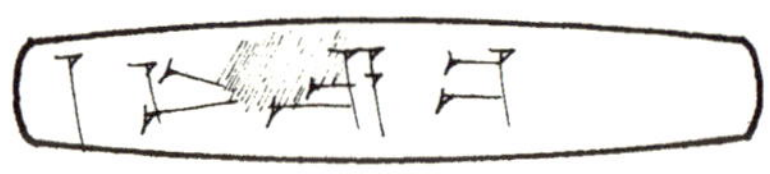

Rev.

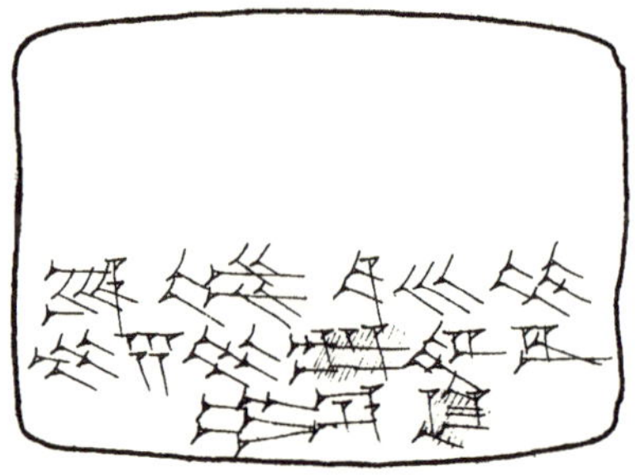

193

Obv.

Lo.E.

Rev.

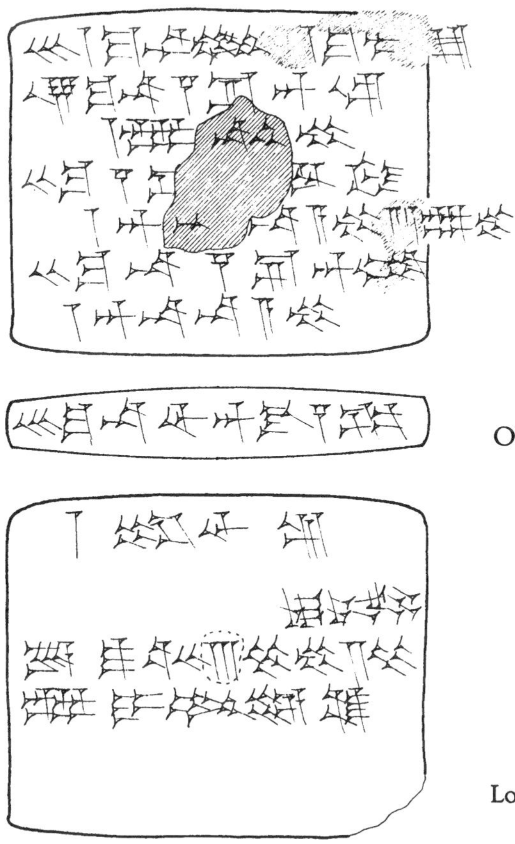

194

Obv.

Lo.E.

Rev.

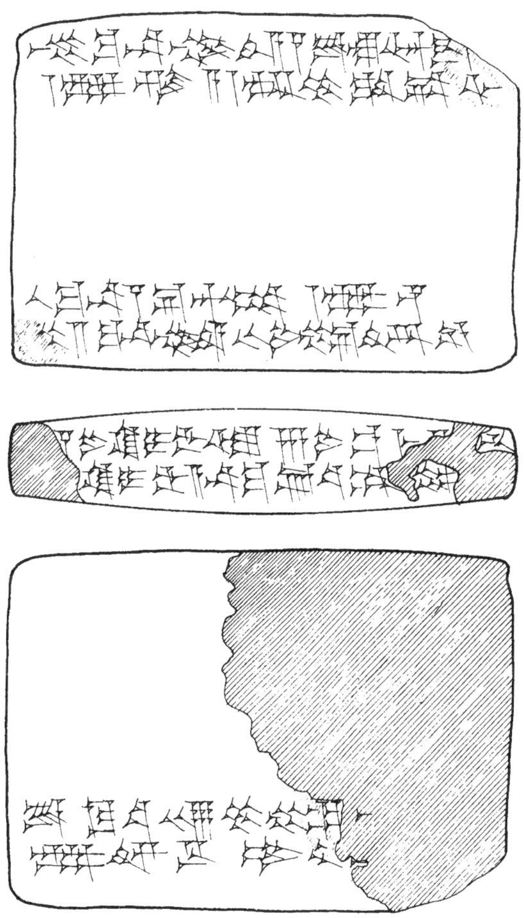

PLATE LXXXVI

195

Obv.

Rev.

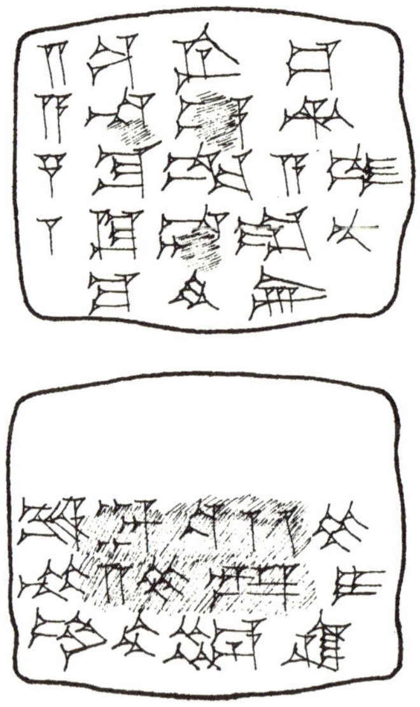

196

Obv.

Rev.

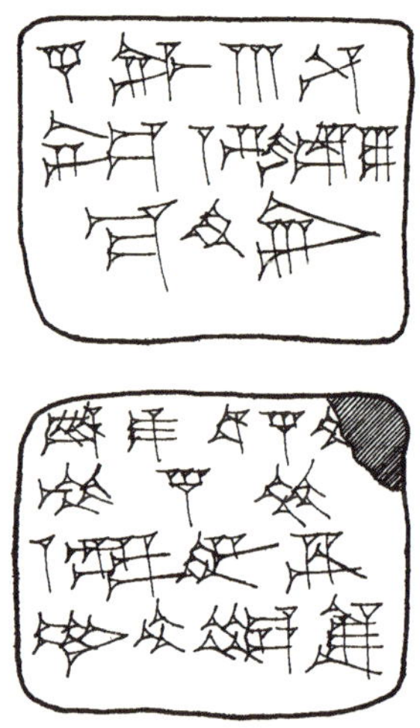

197

Obv.

Rev.

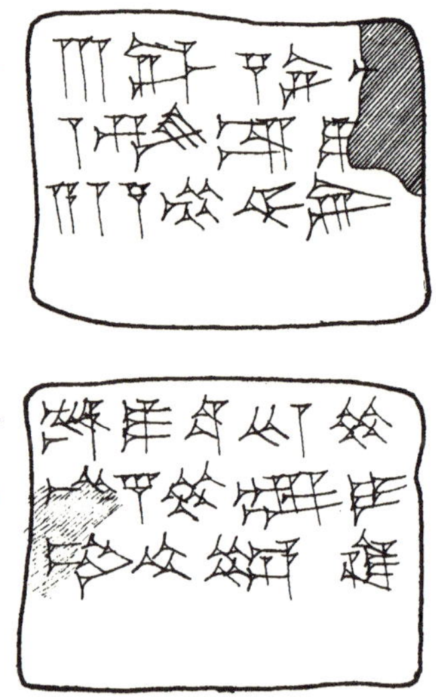

198

Obv.

Lo.E.

Rev.

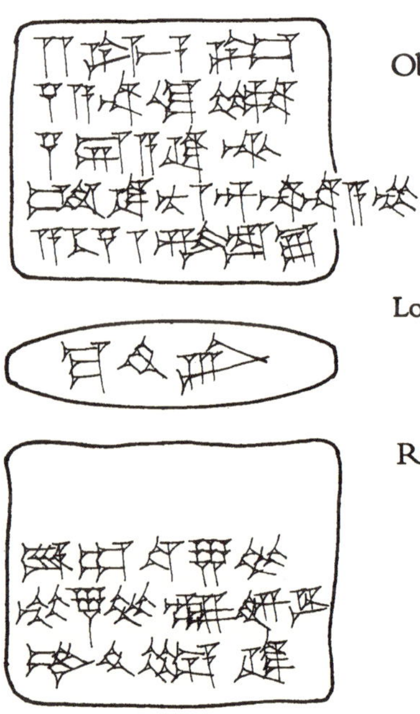

199

Obv.

Lo.E.

Rev.

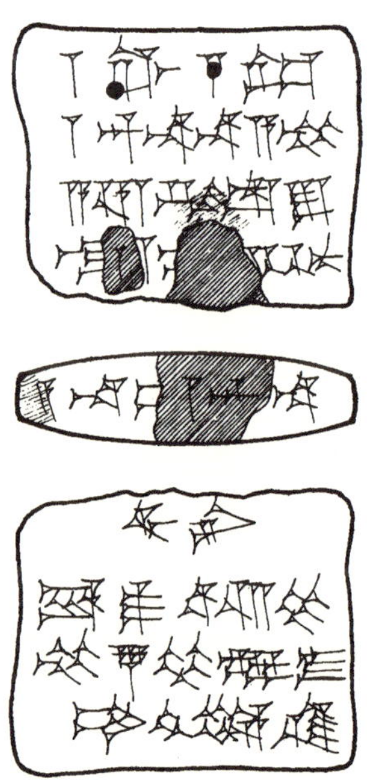

200

Obv.

Rev.

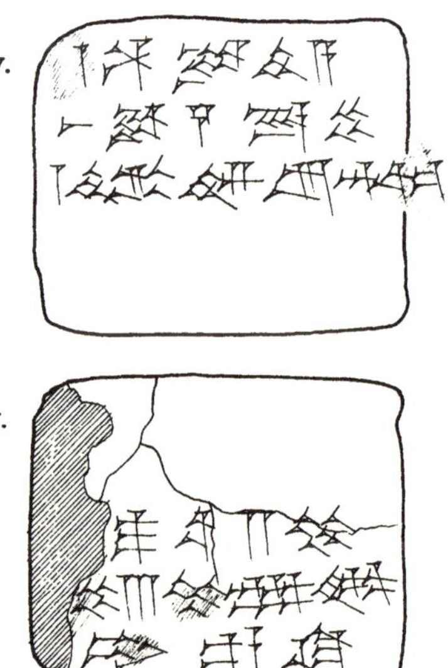

201

Obv.

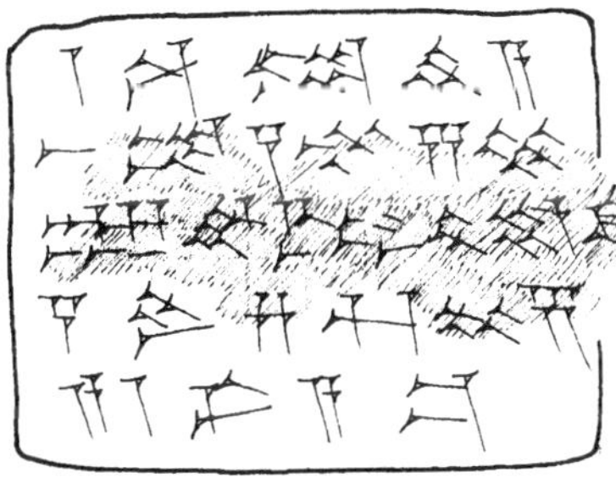

Rev.

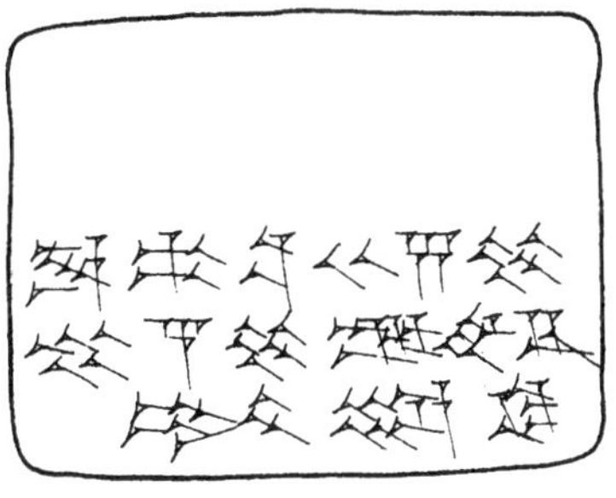

202

Obv.

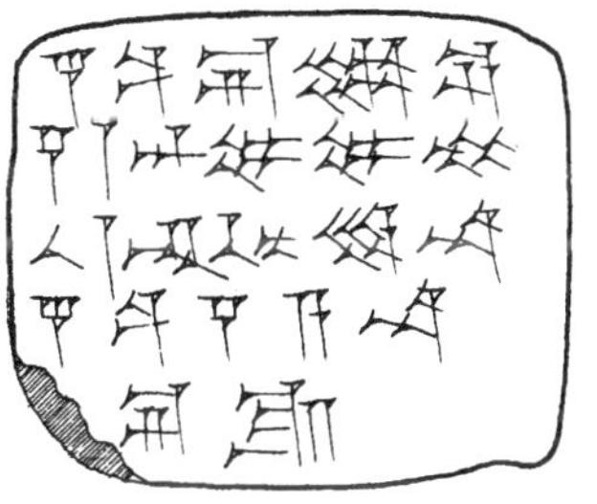

Rev.

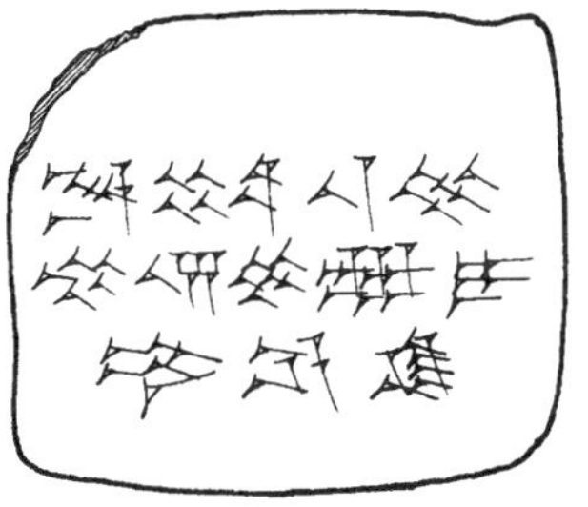

203

Obv.

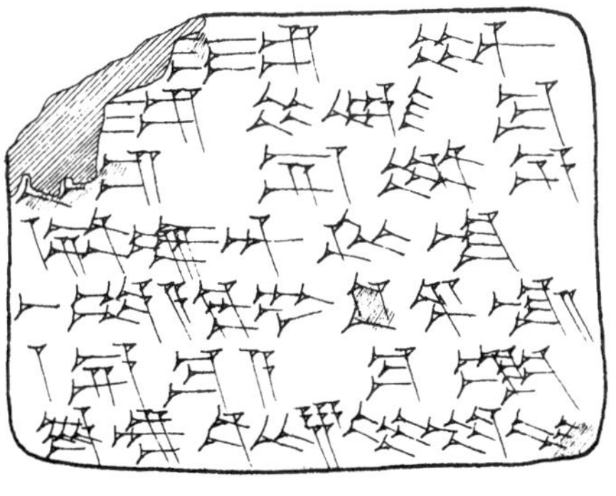

Rev.

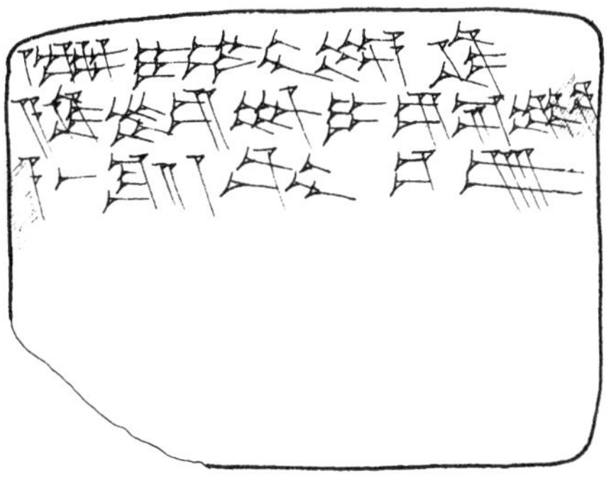

204

Obv.

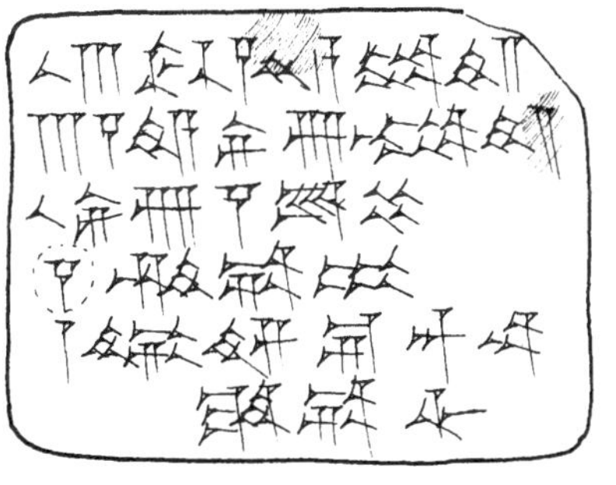

Rev.

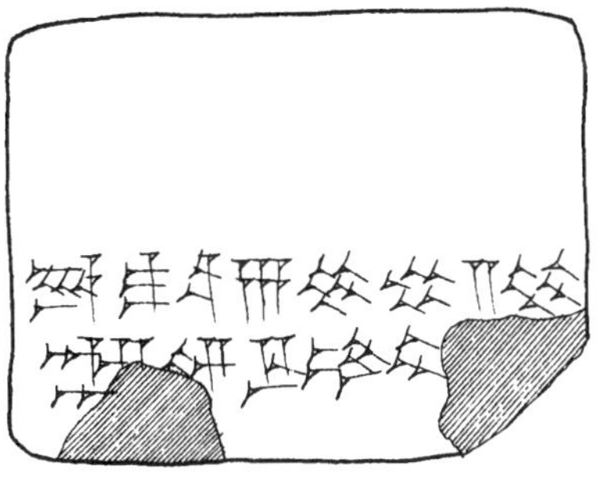

205

Obv.

Rev.

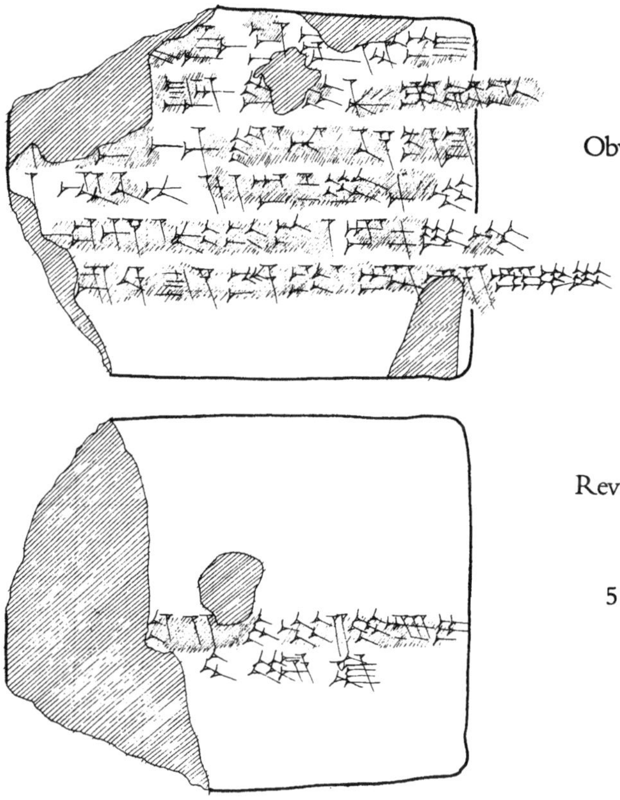

206

Obv.

Rev.

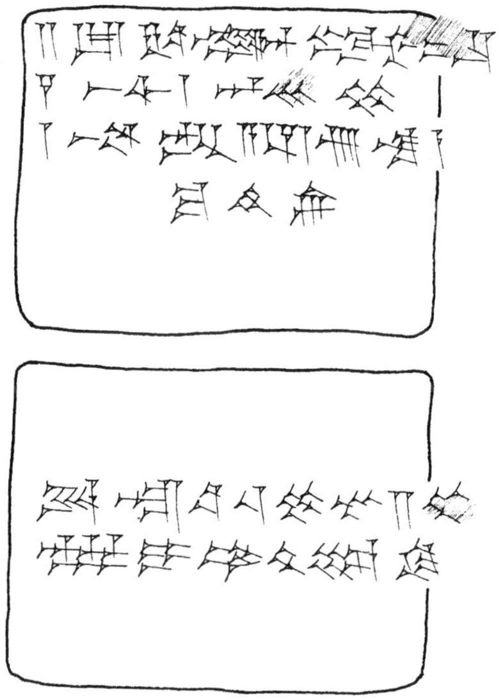

207

Obv.

Rev.

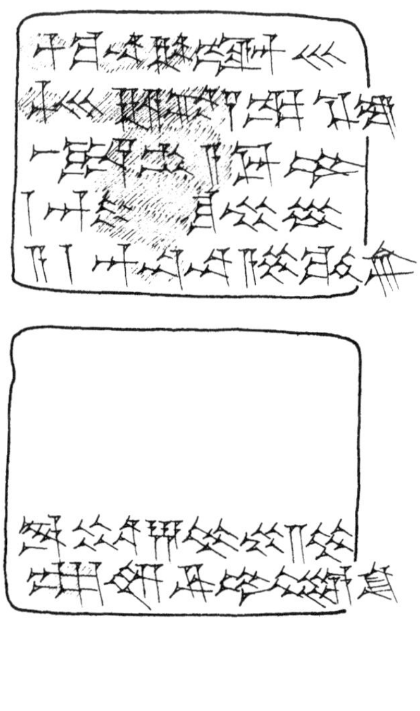

208

Obv.

Rev.

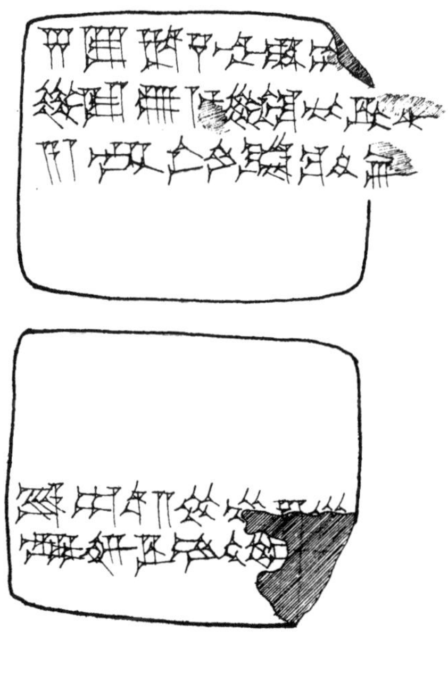

209

Obv.

Rev.

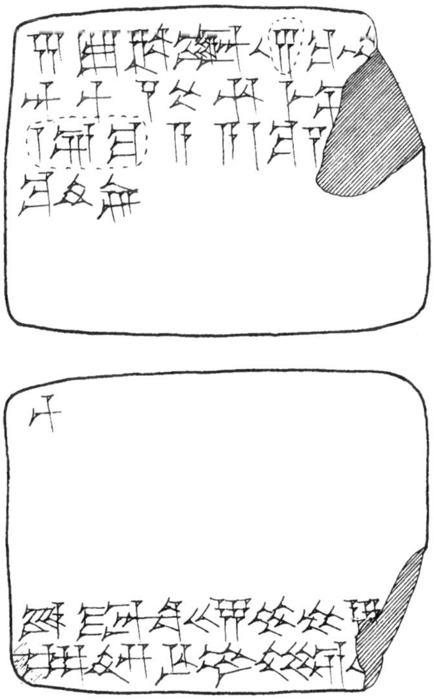

210

Obv.

Rev.

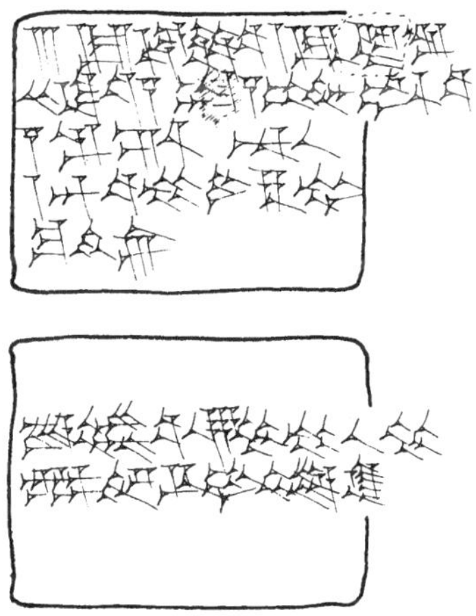

211

Obv.

Rev.

212

Obv.

Lo.E.

Rev.

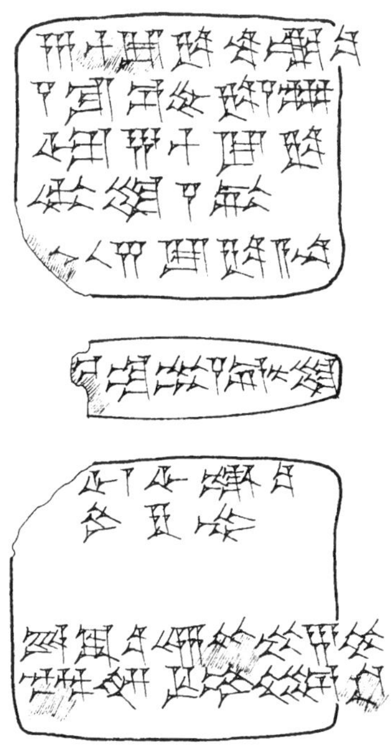

213

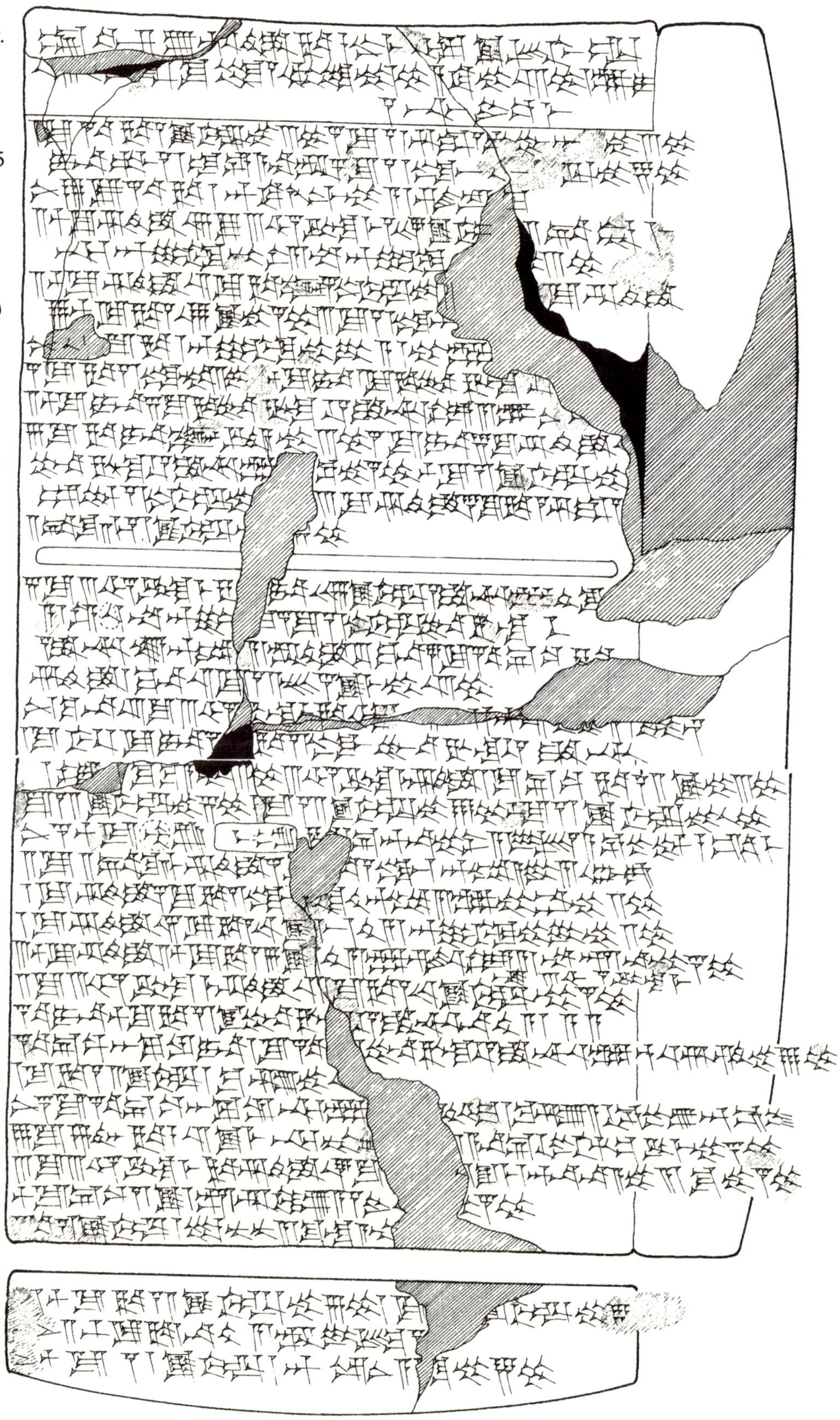

213

Rev.

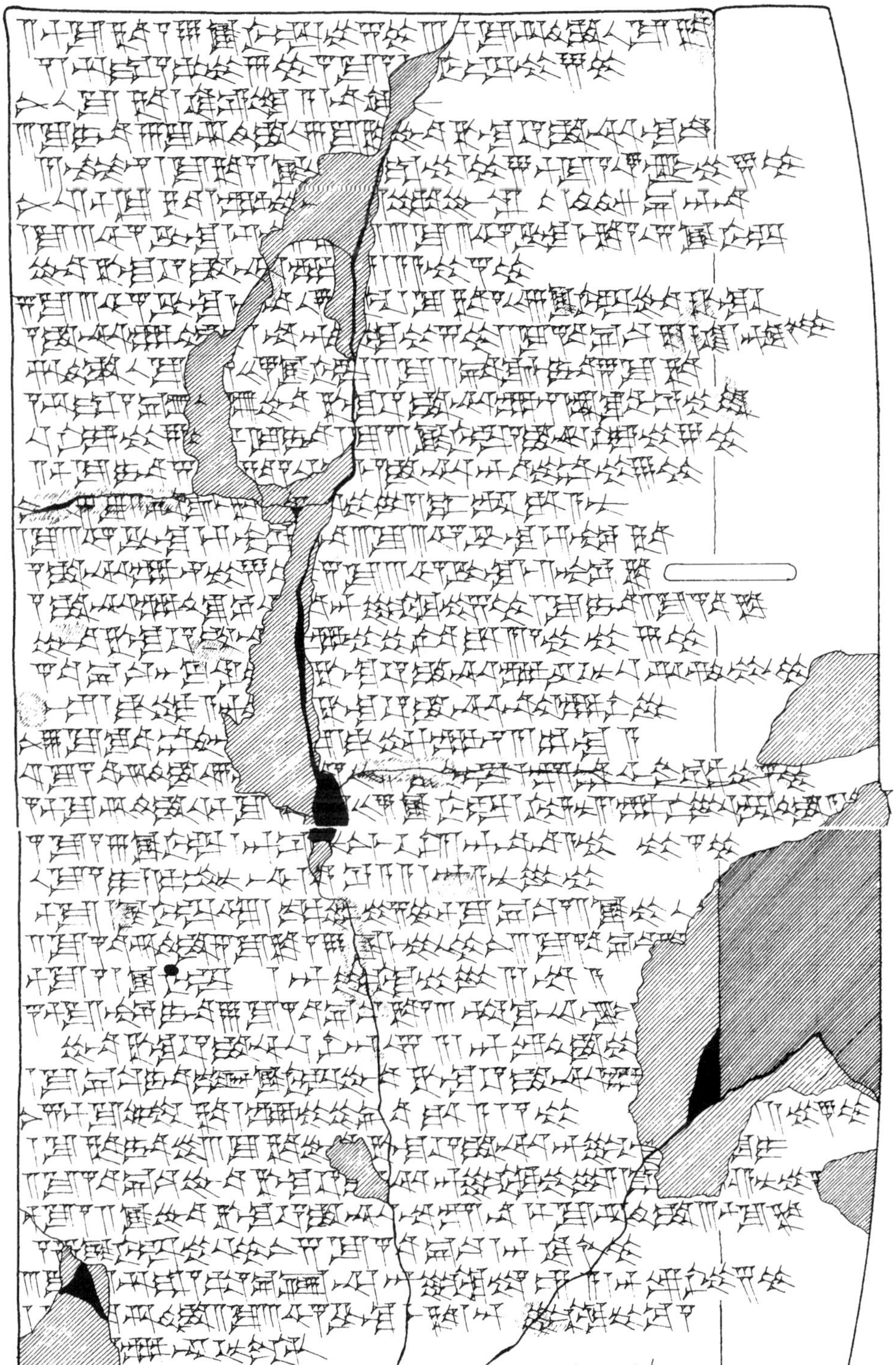

U.E.

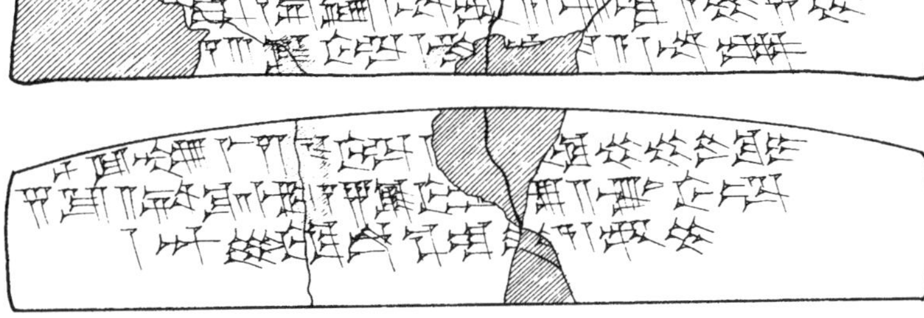

214

Le.E. Obv. Lo.E. Rev. U.E.

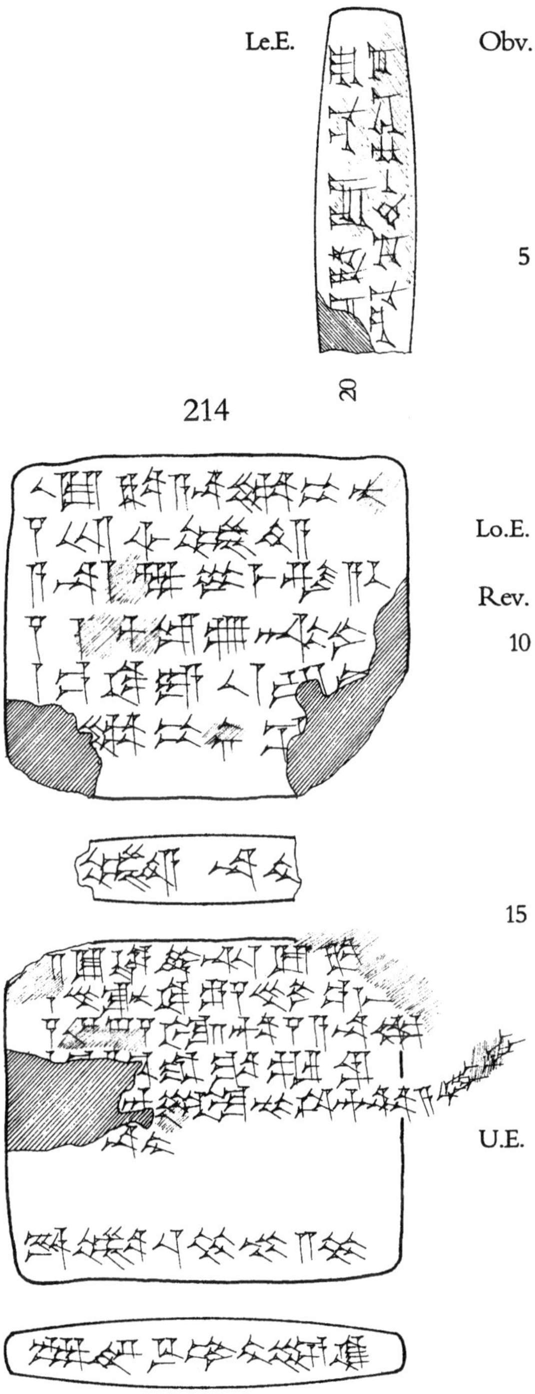

215

Obv. Lo.E. Rev. U.E.

216

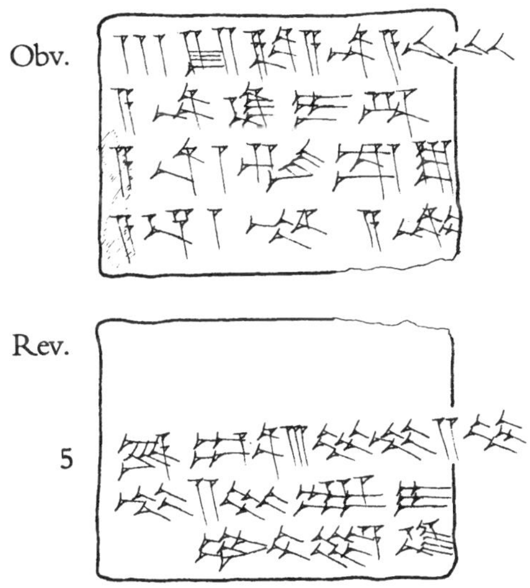

217

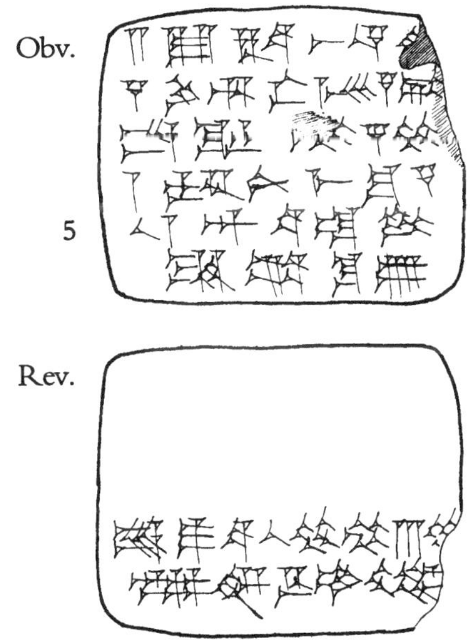

218

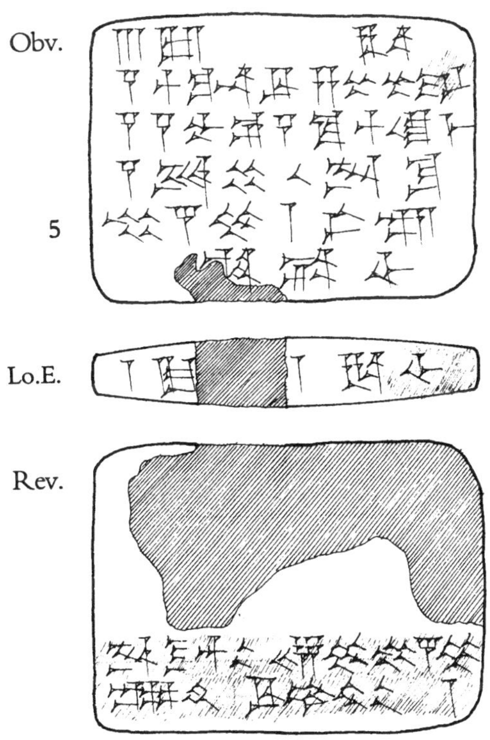

219

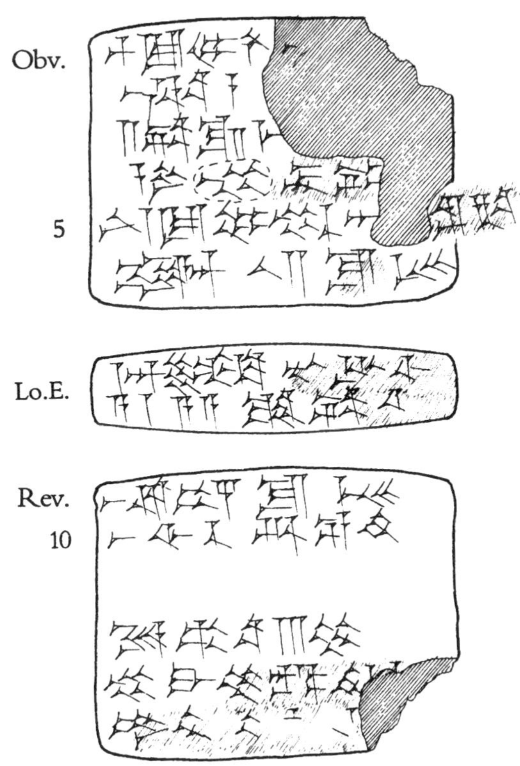

PLATE XCIV

220

Obv.

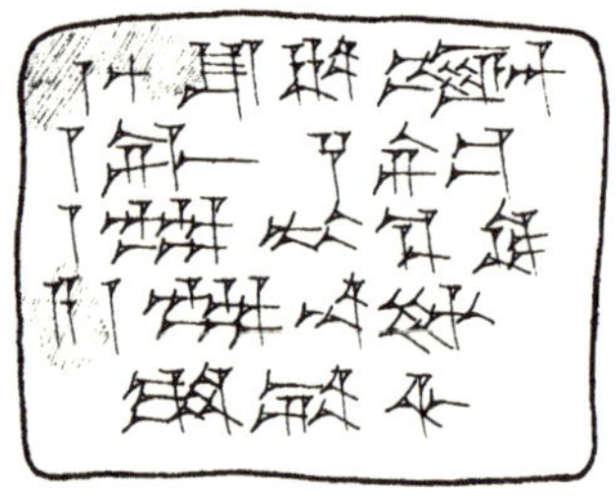

Rev.

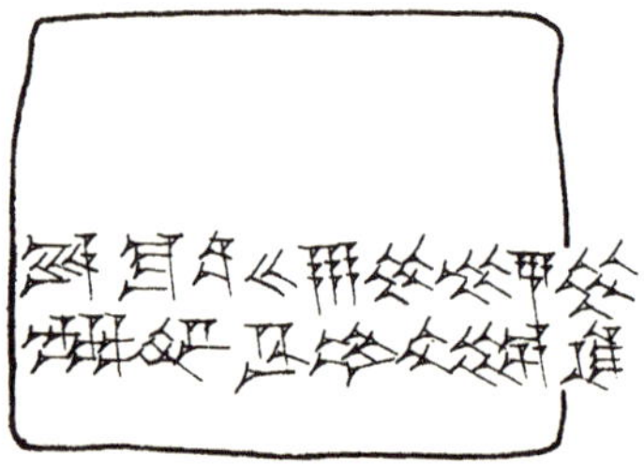

221

Obv.

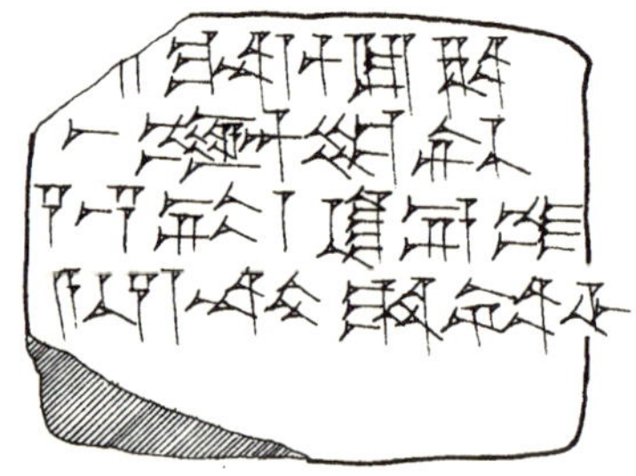

Rev.

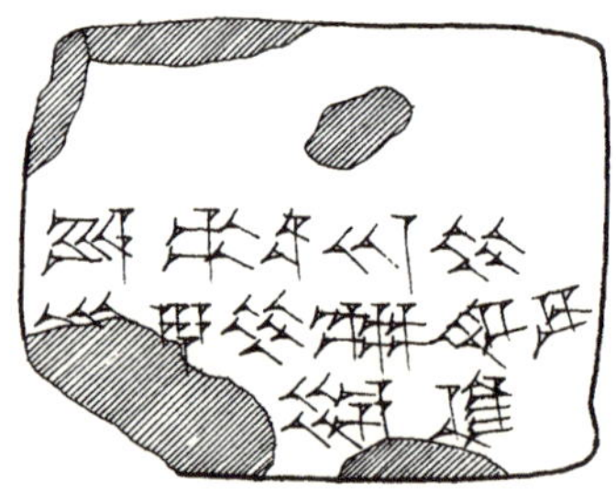

222

Obv.

Lo.E.

Rev.

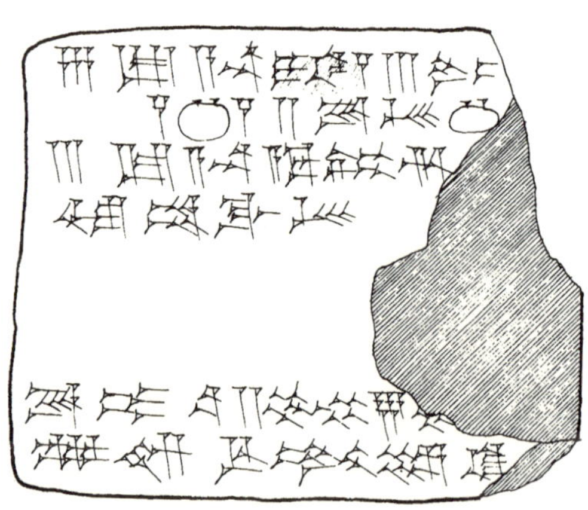

223

Obv.

Rev.

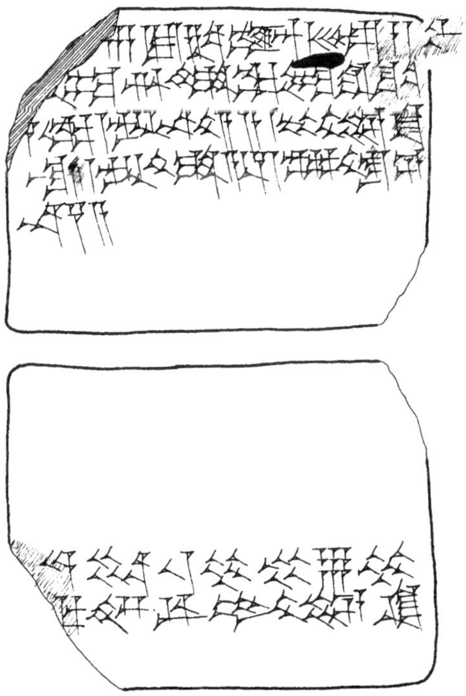

224

Obv.

Lo.E.

Rev.

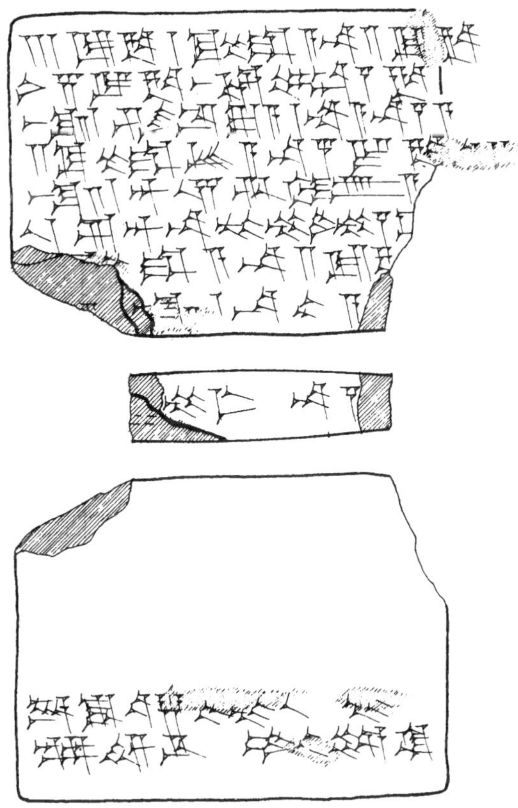

225

Obv.

Lo.E.

Rev.

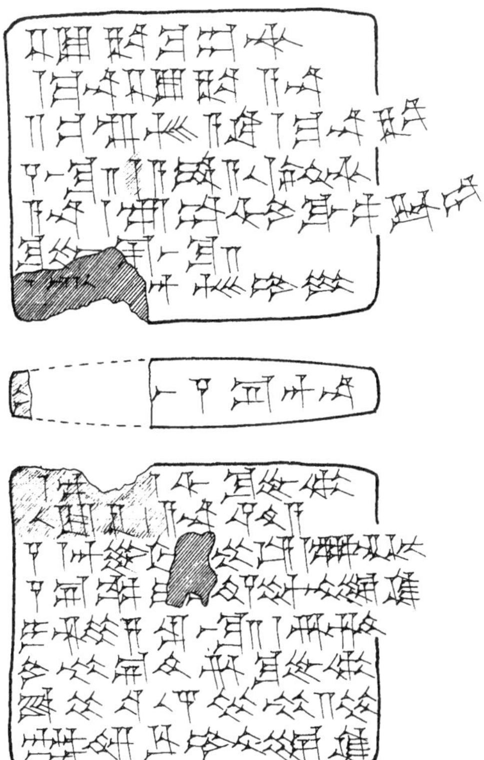

226

Obv.

Rev.

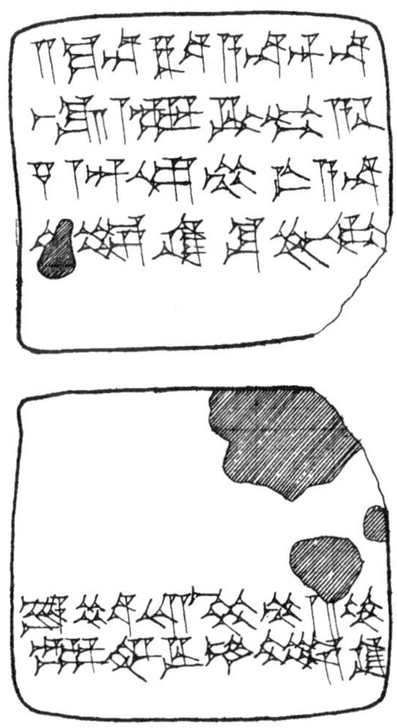

227

Obv.

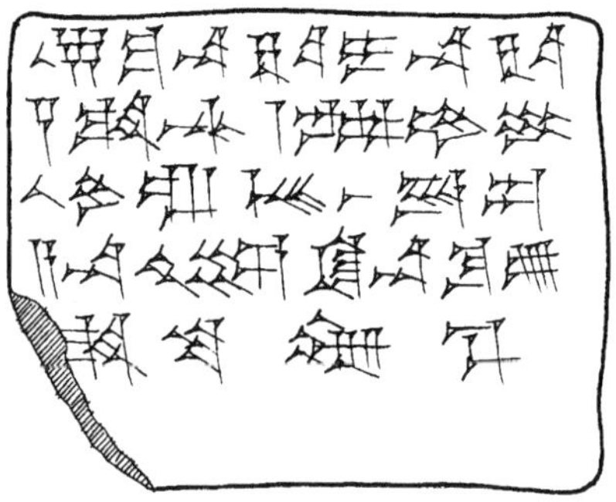

Rev.

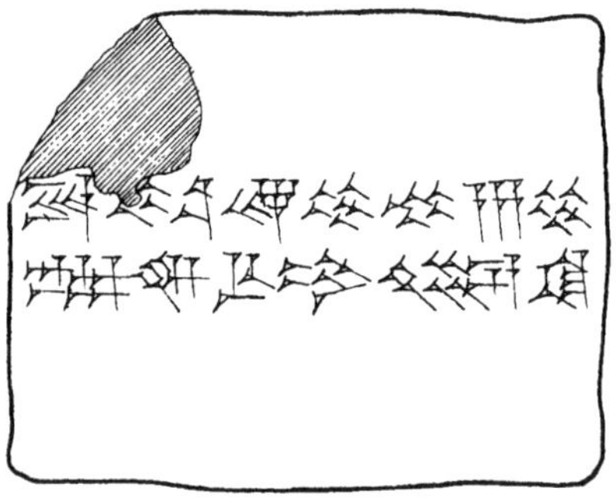

228

Obv.

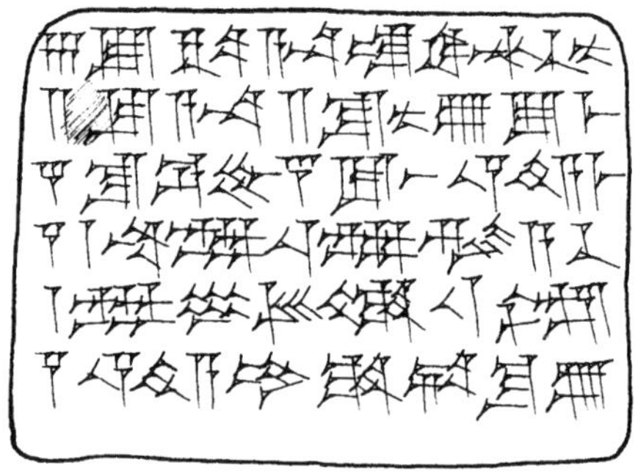

Rev.

229

Obv.

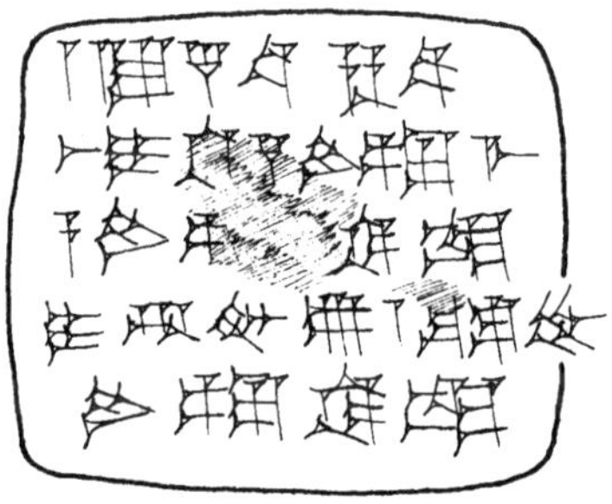

Rev.

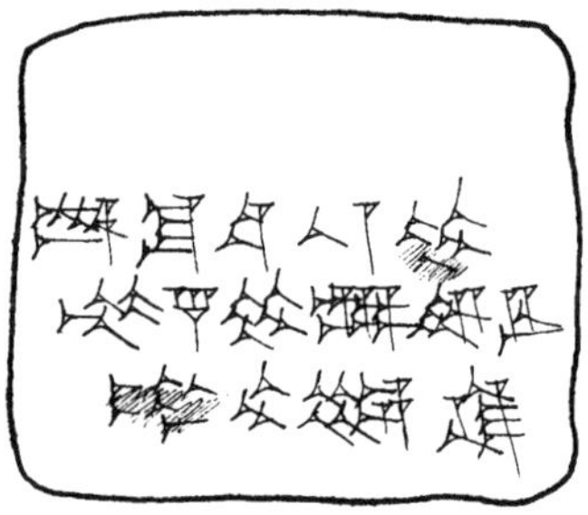

230

Obv.

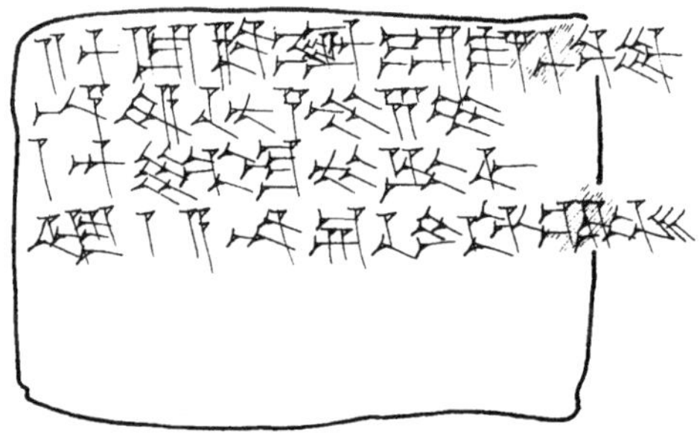

Rev.

231

Obv.

Rev.

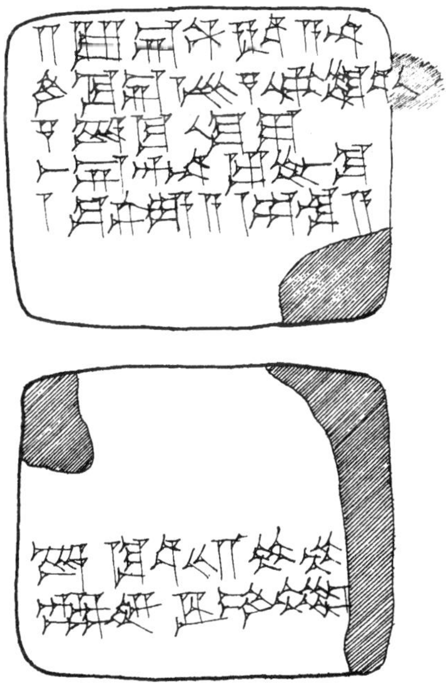

232

Obv.

Lo.E.

Rev.

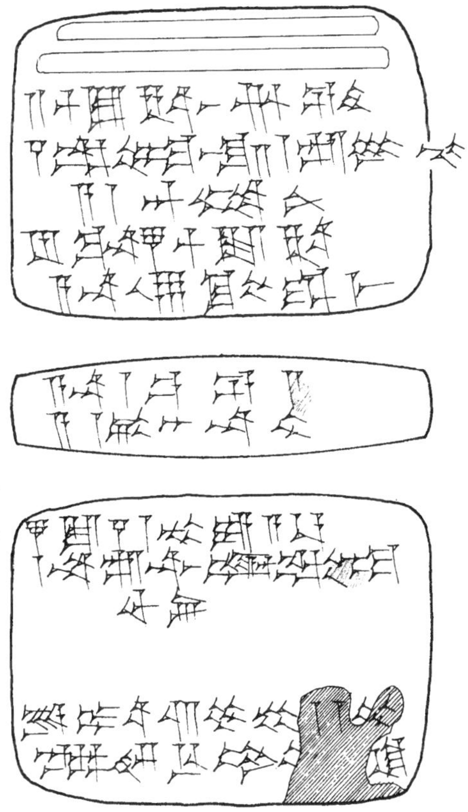

233

Obv.

Lo.E.

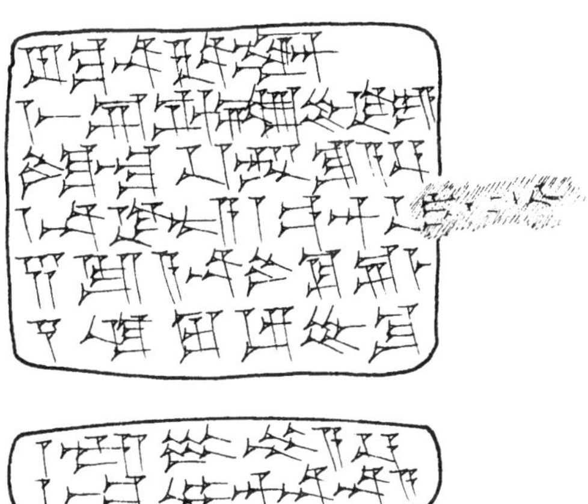

Rev.

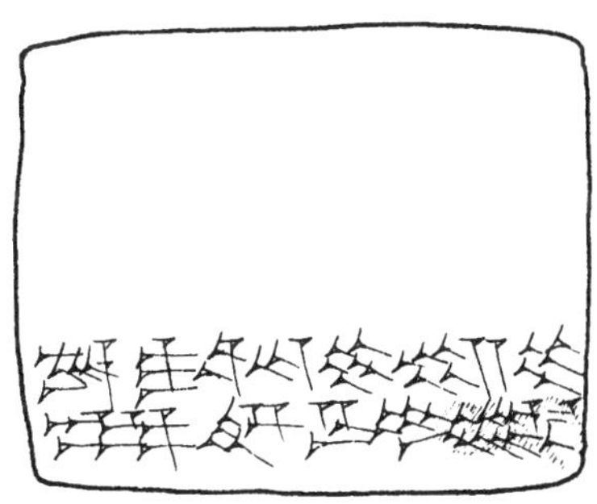

234

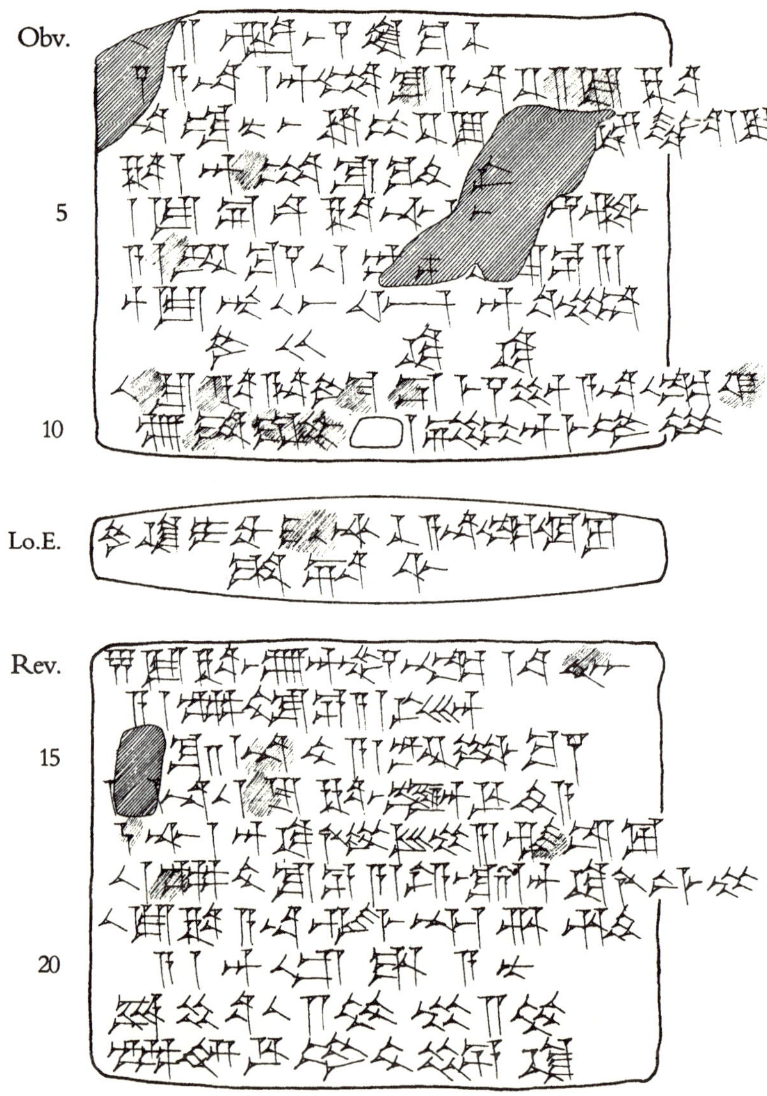

235

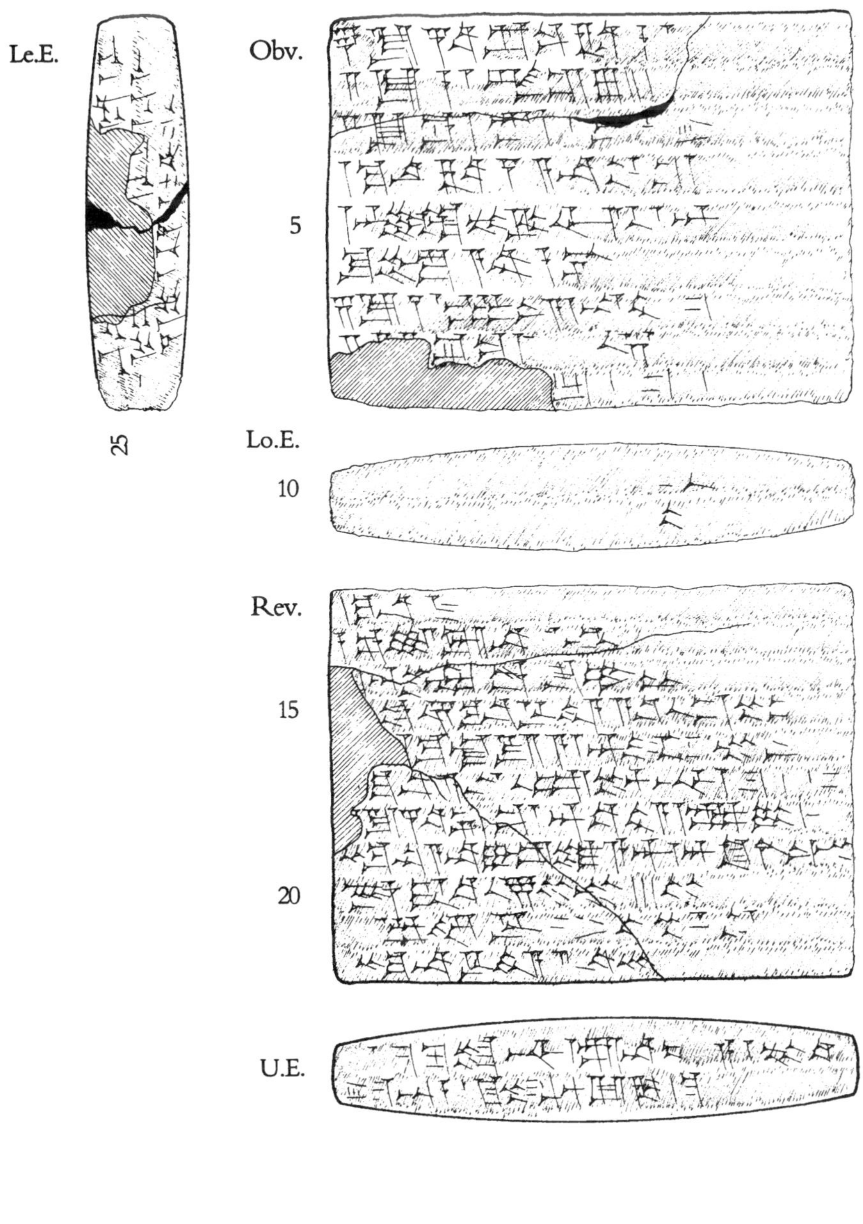

PLATE C

236

Obv.

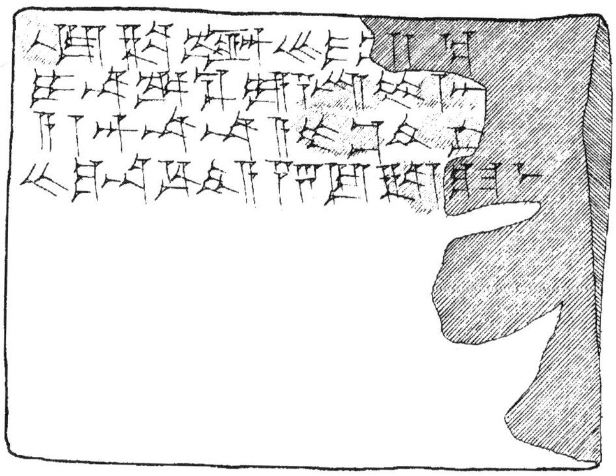

Rev.

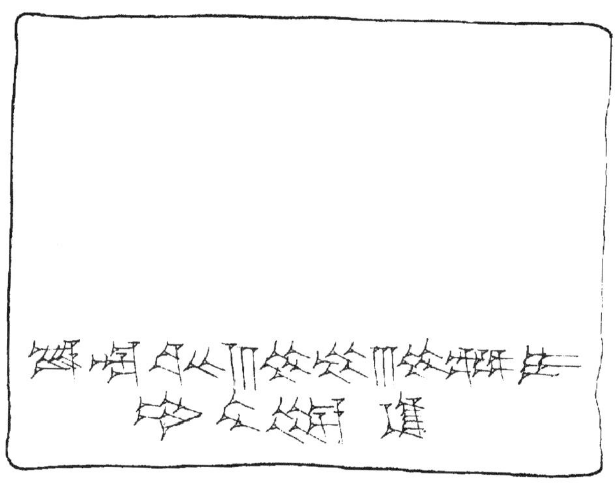

237

Obv.

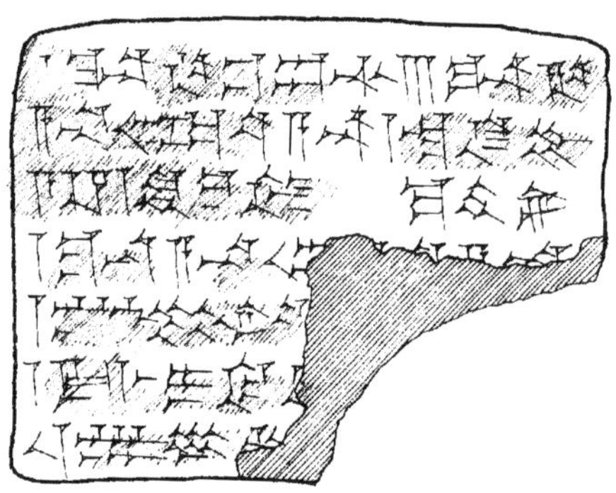

Rev.

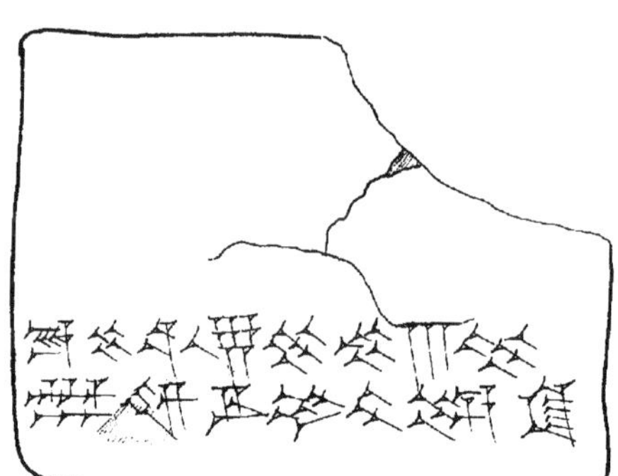

238

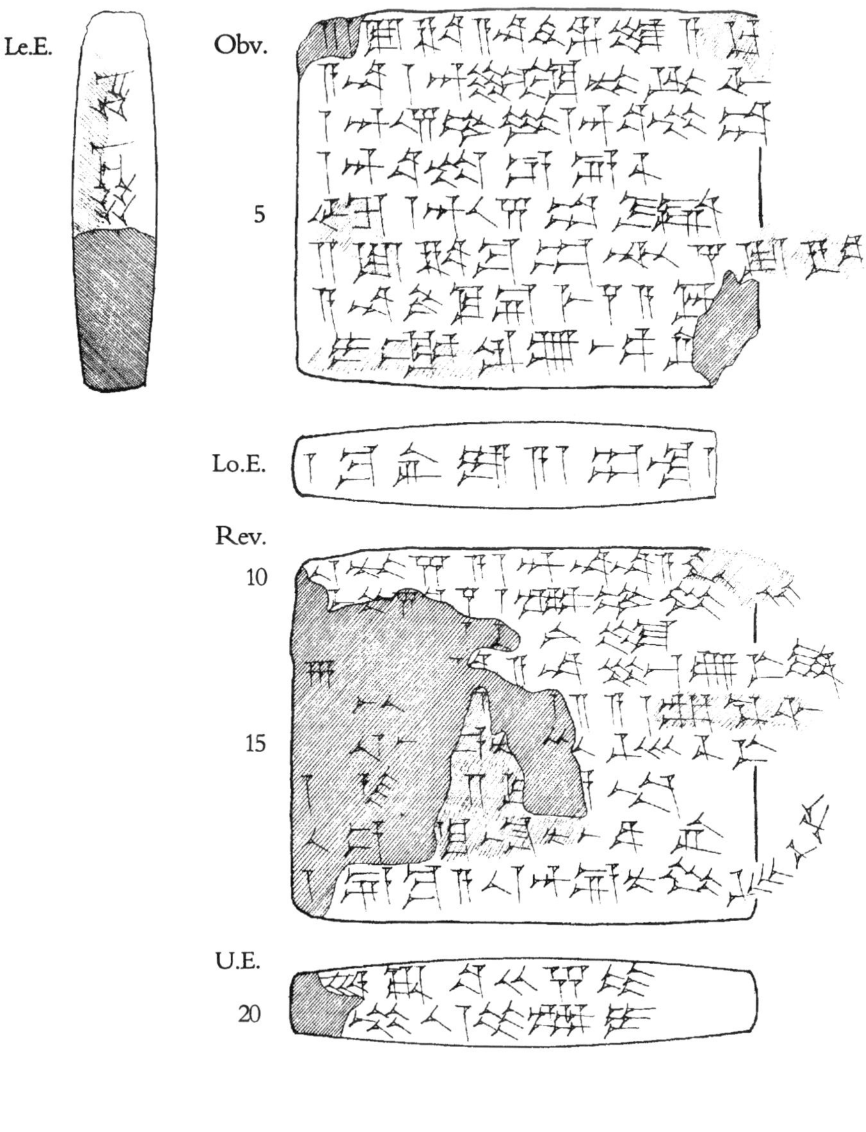

239

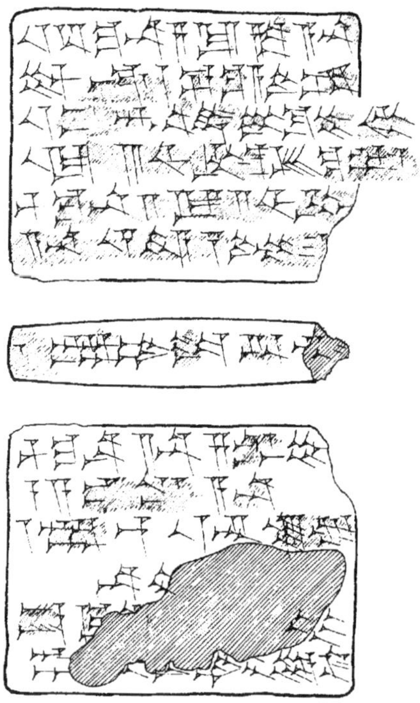

240

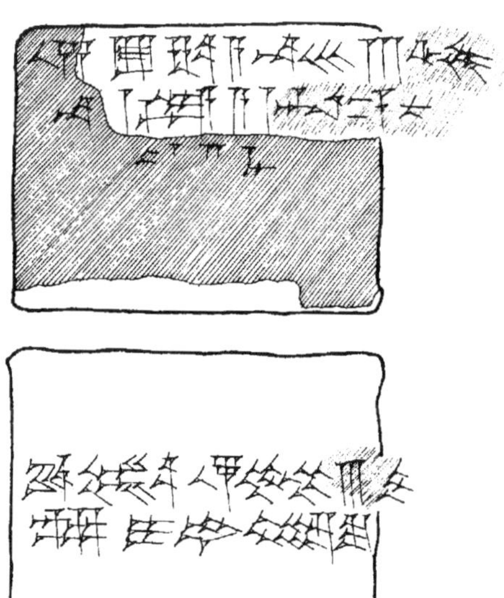

241

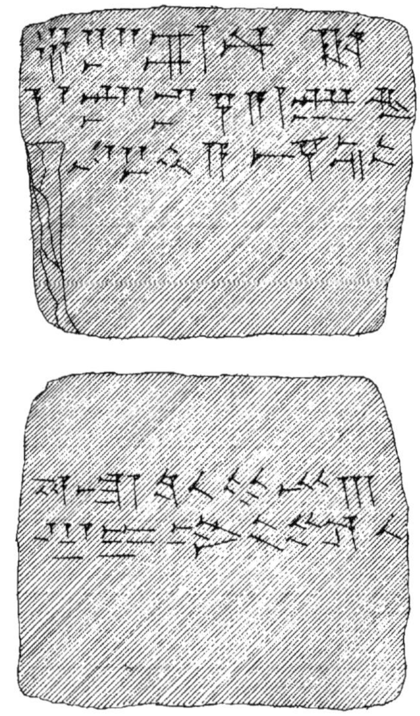

242

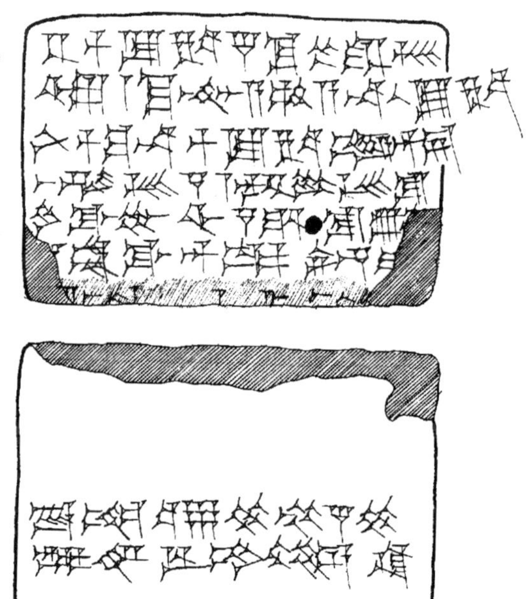

243

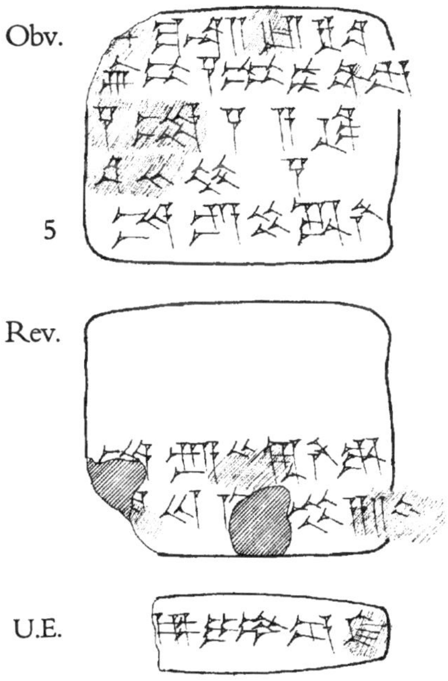

244

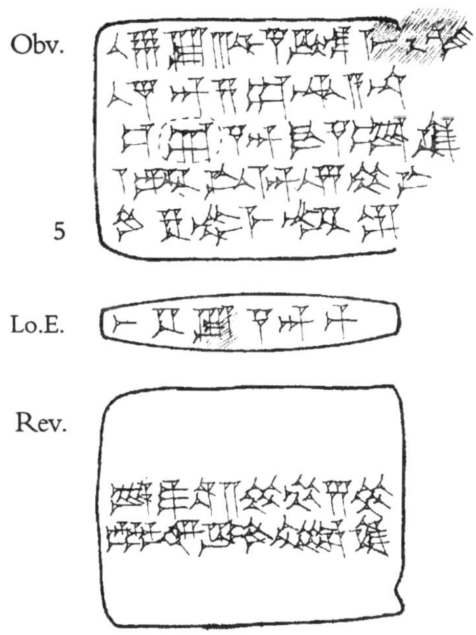

245

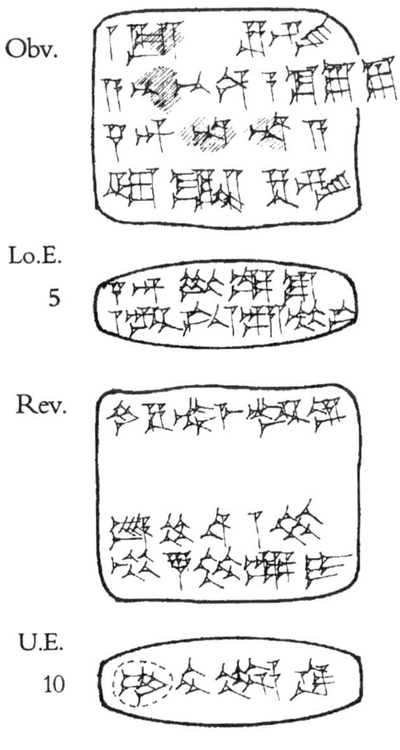

246

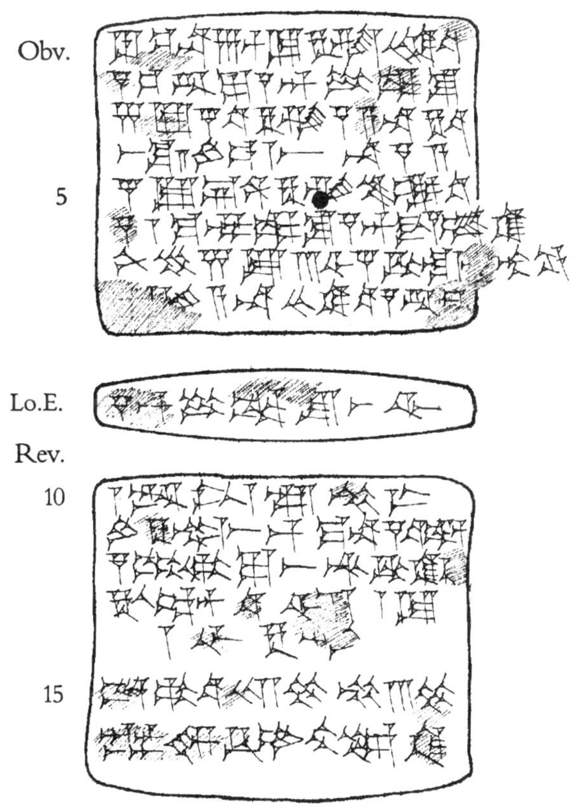

PLATE CIV

247

Obv.
Rev.

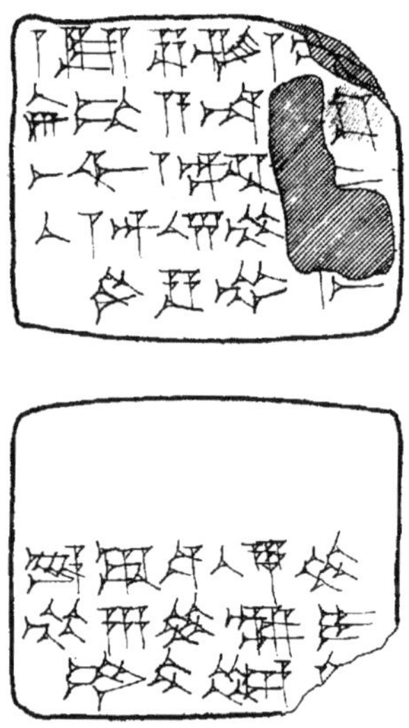

249

Obv.
Rev.

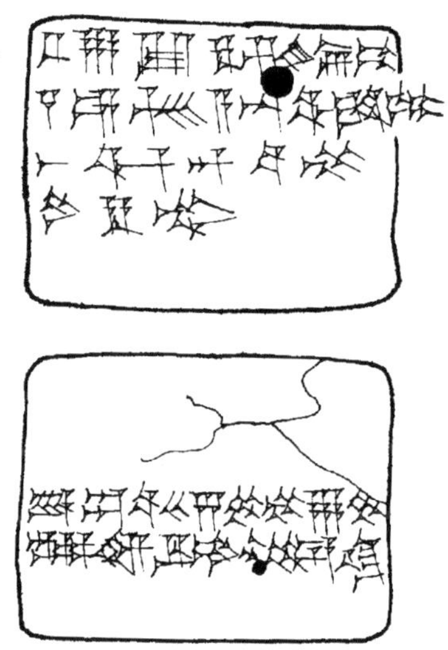

248

Obv.
Lo.E.
Rev.

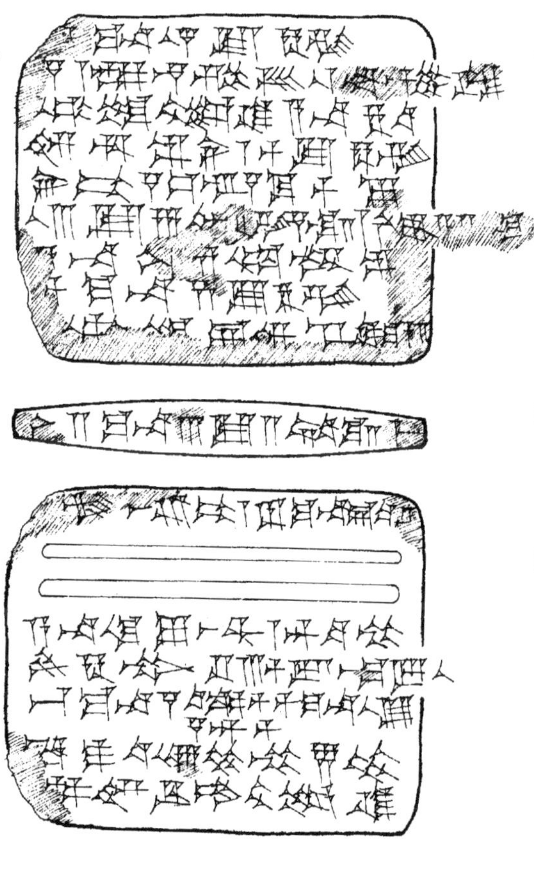

250

Obv.
Lo.E.
Rev.

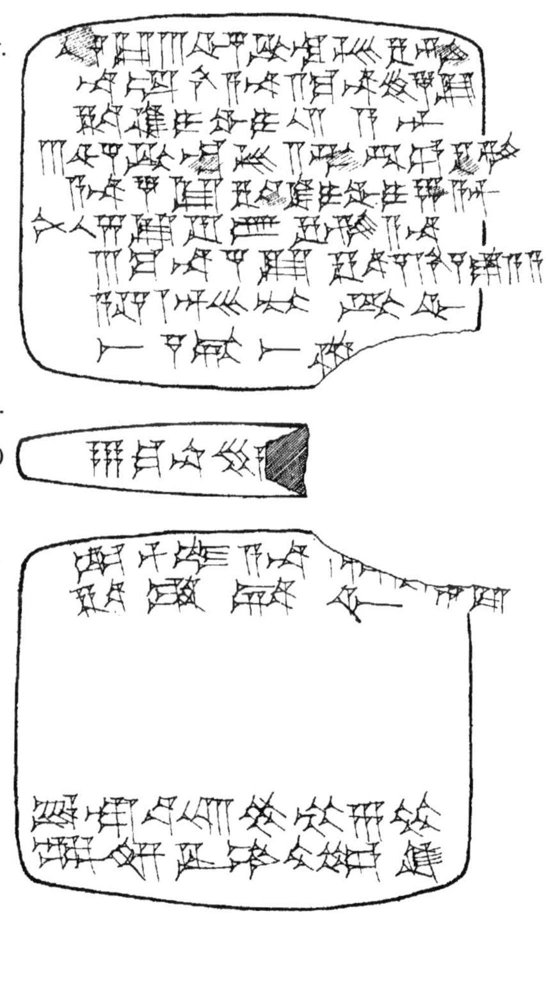

251

Obv.

Rev.

U.E.

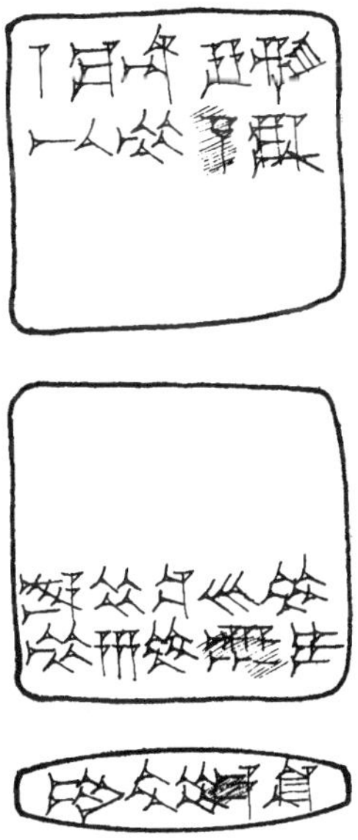

252

Obv.

Lo.E.

Rev.

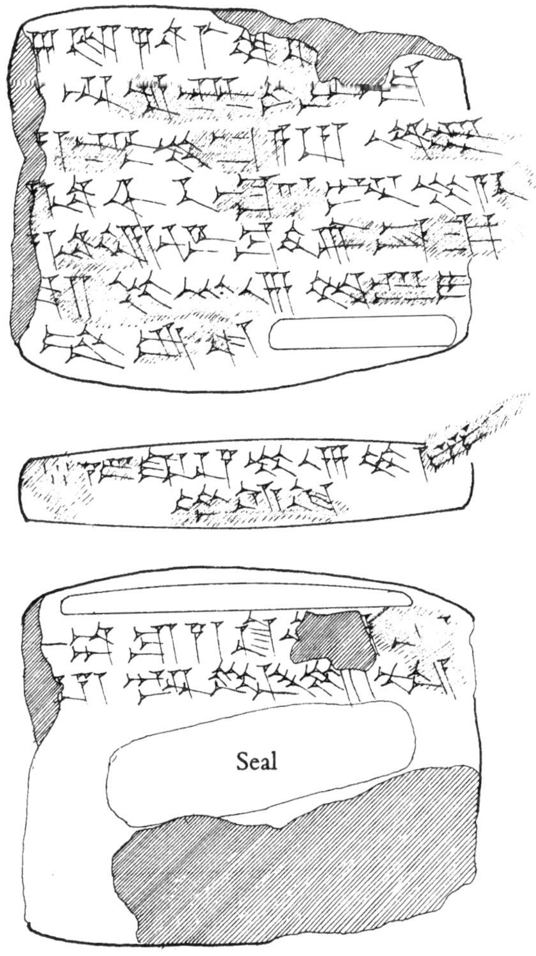

Seal

253

Obv.

Rev.

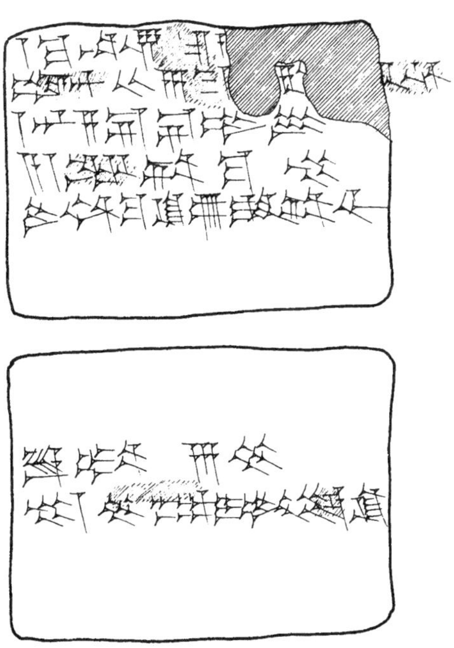

254

Obv.

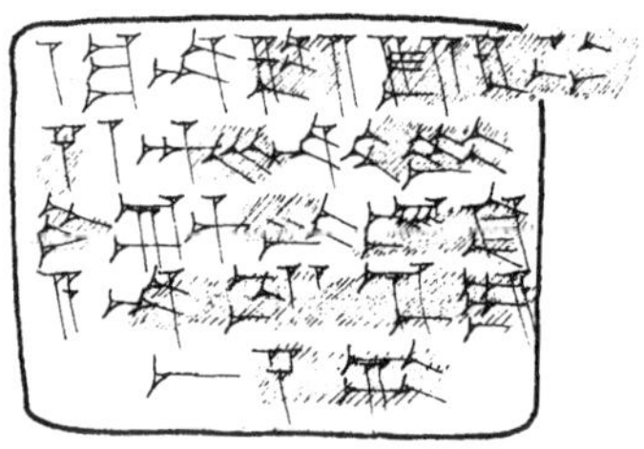

Rev.

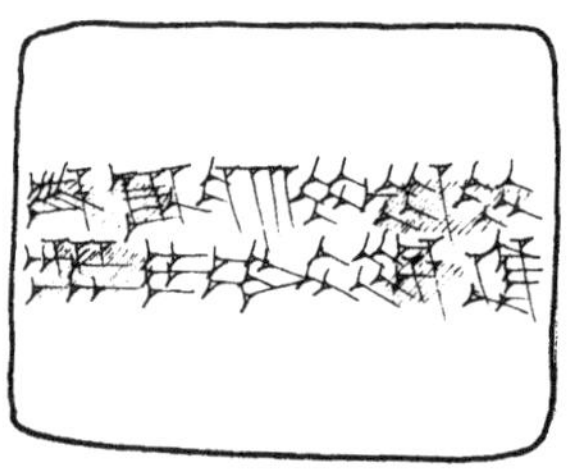

255

Obv.

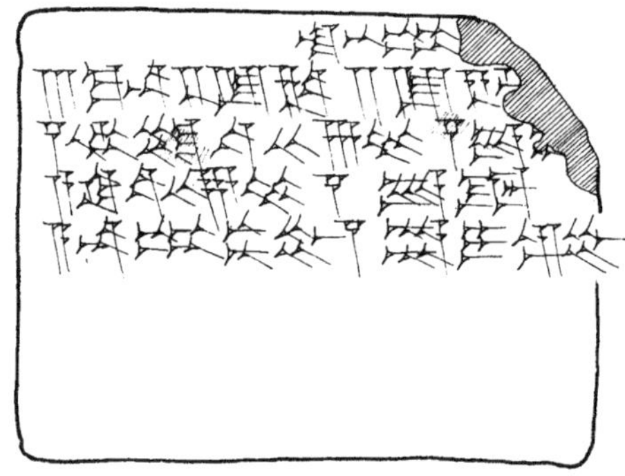

Rev.

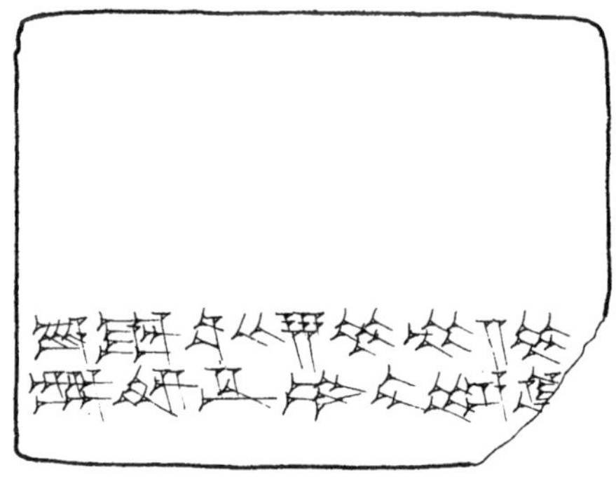

256

Obv.

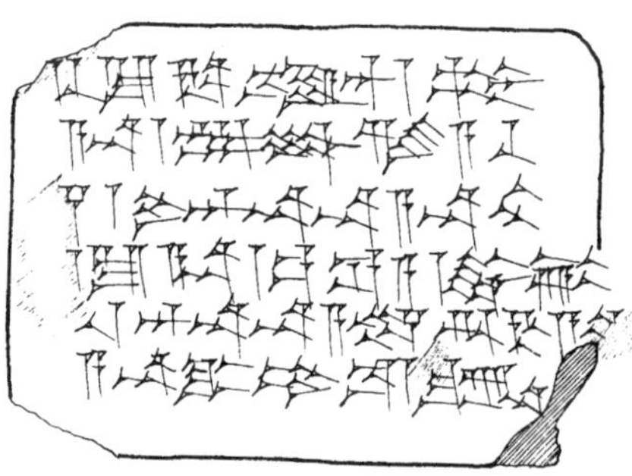

Rev.

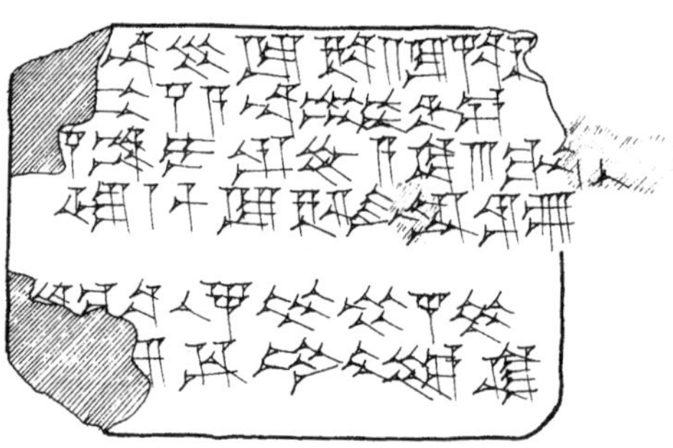

257

Obv.

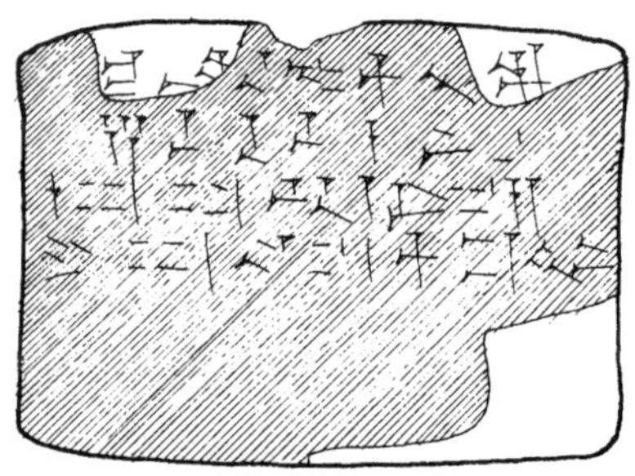

Rev.

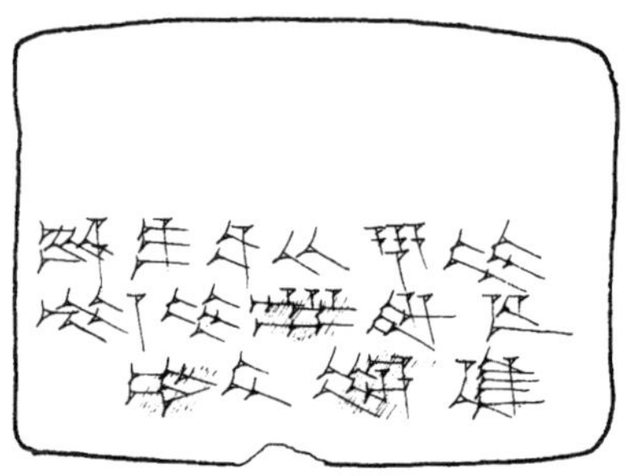

258

Obv. / Rev.

259

Obv. / Rev.

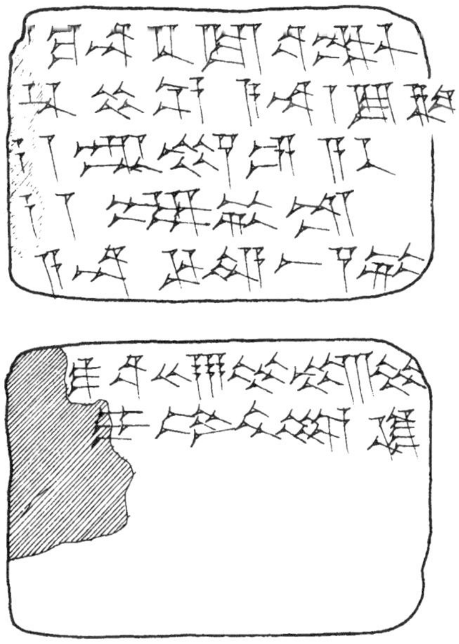

260

Obv. / Rev.

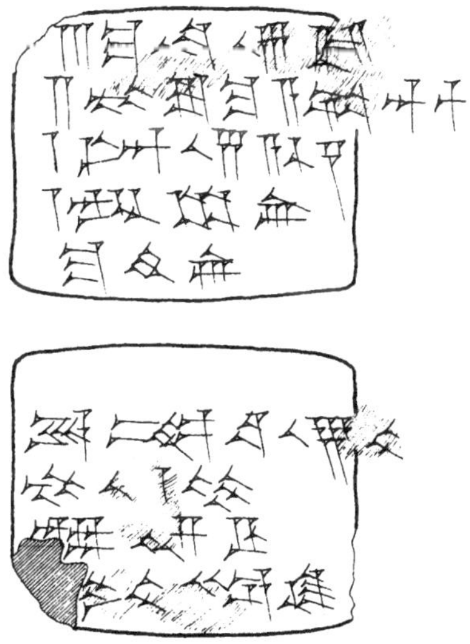

261

Obv. / Rev.

262

Obv. / Rev.

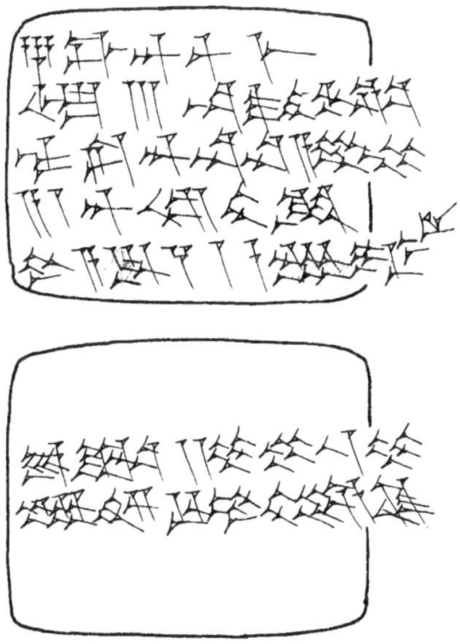

PLATE CVIII

264

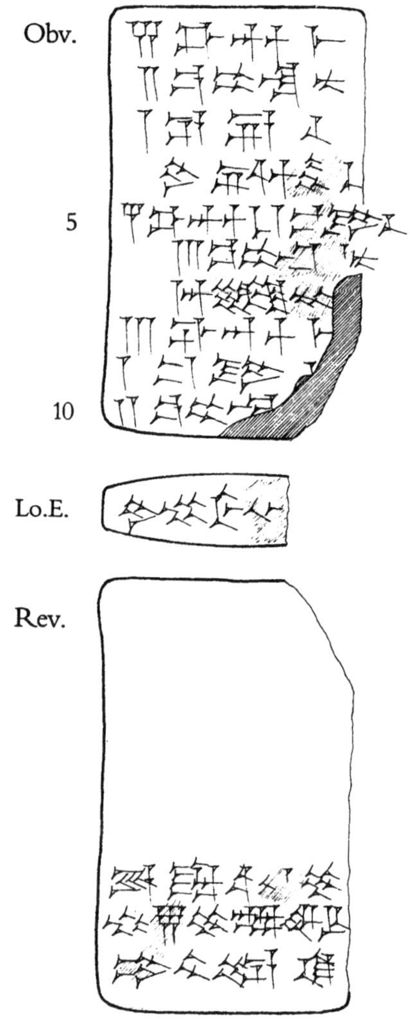

263

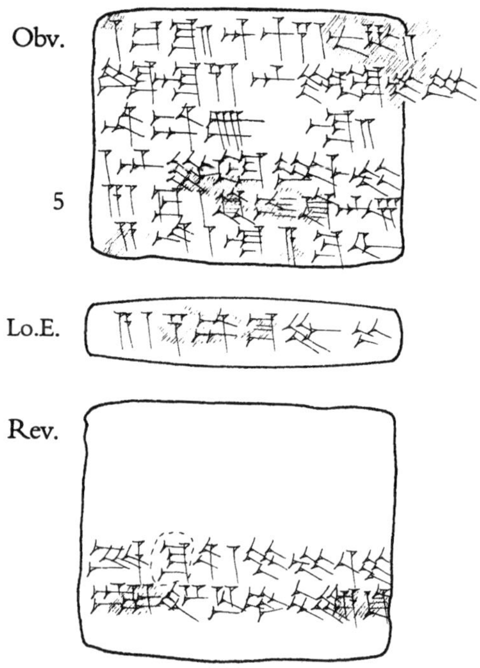

265

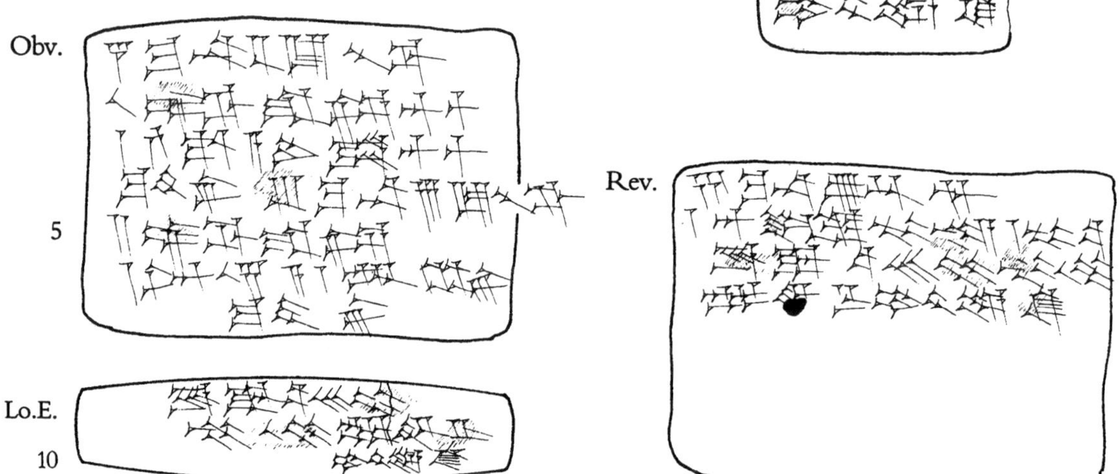

266

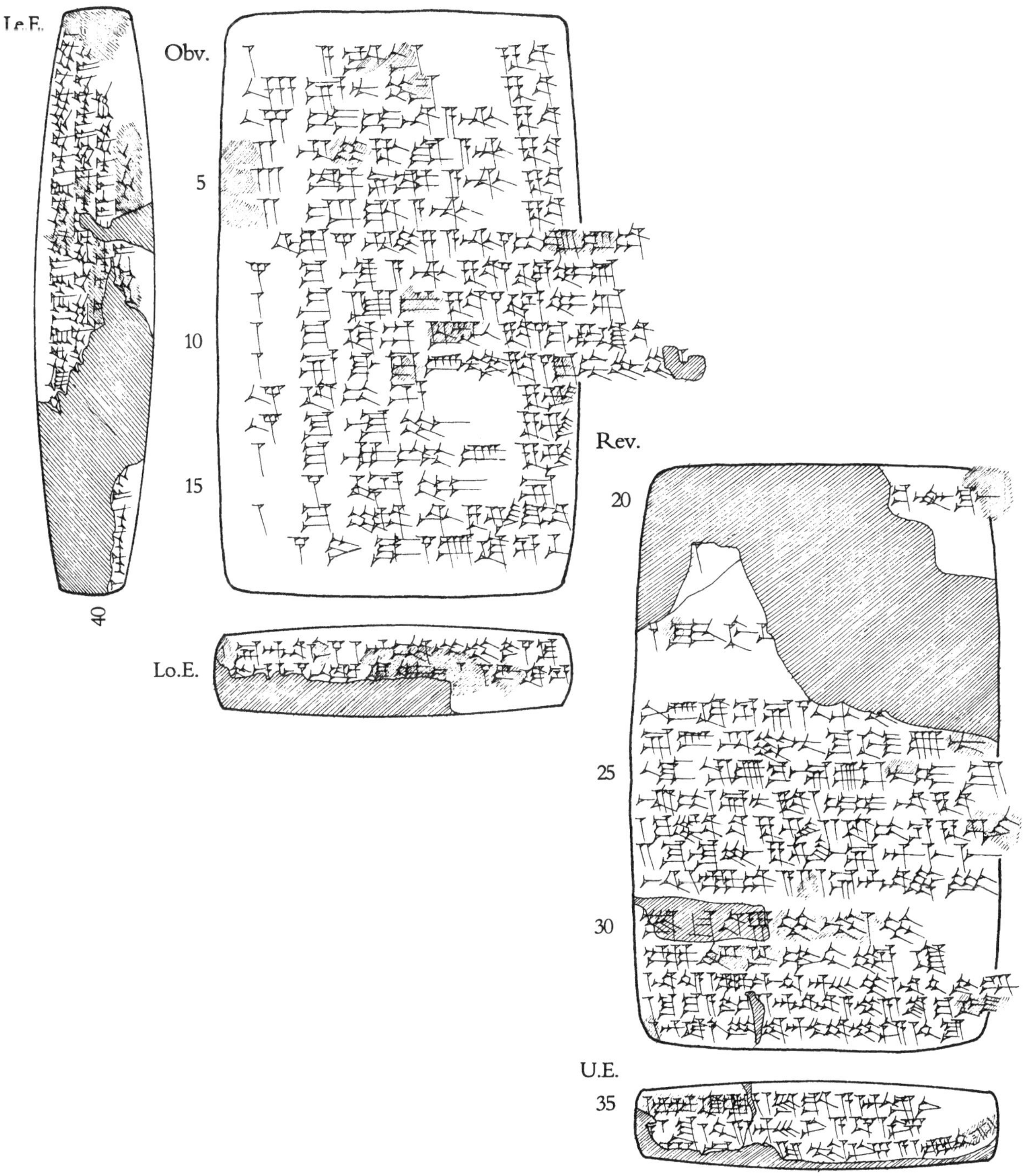

267

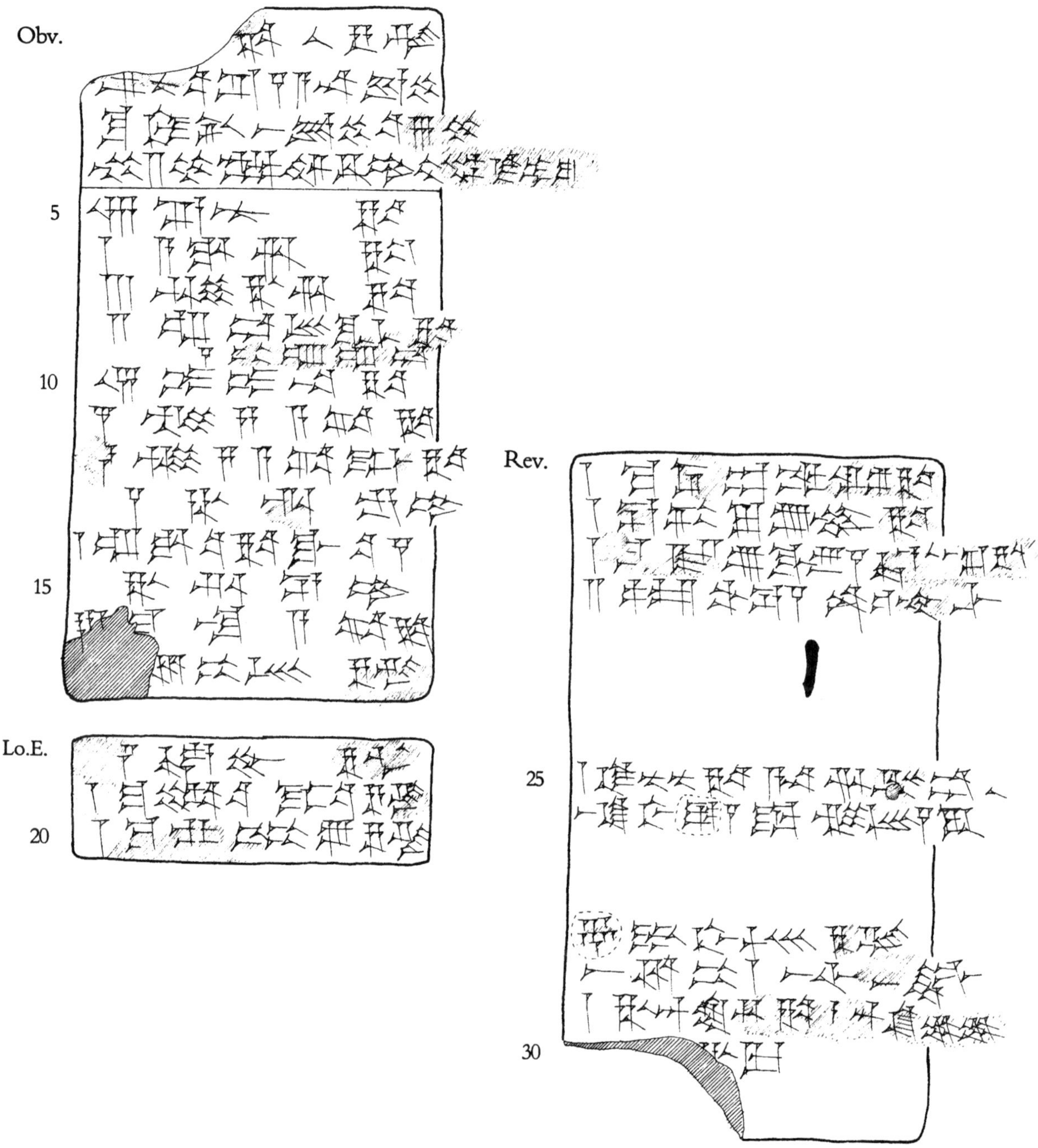

268

Obv.

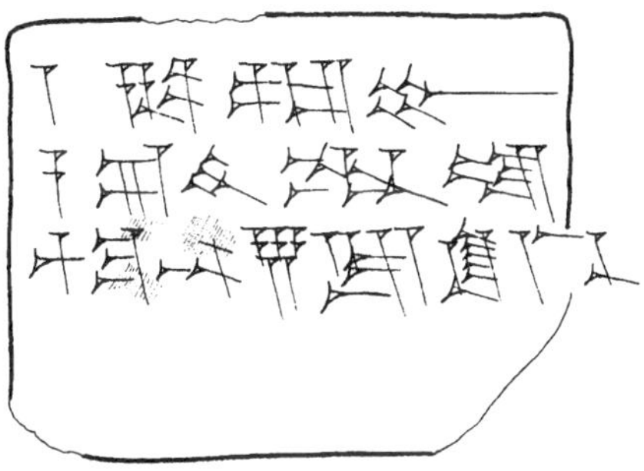

Rev.

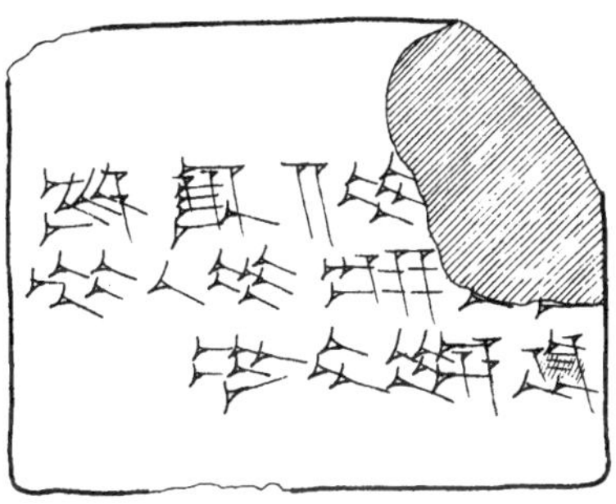

269

Obv.

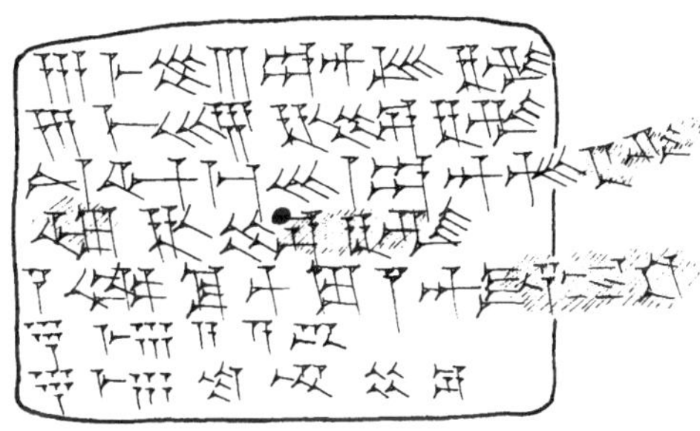

Lo.E.

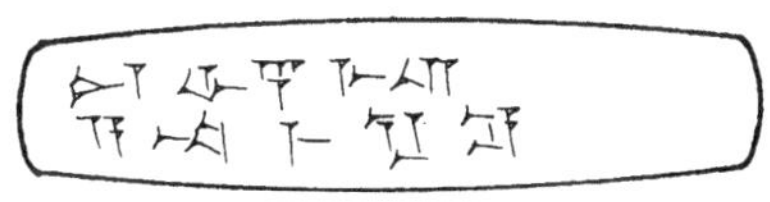

Rev.

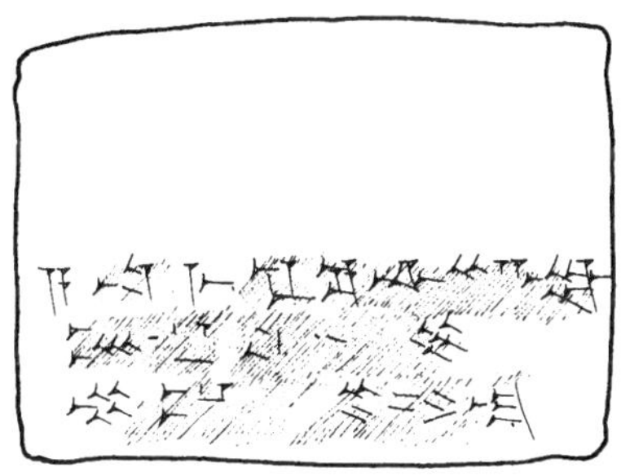

U.E.

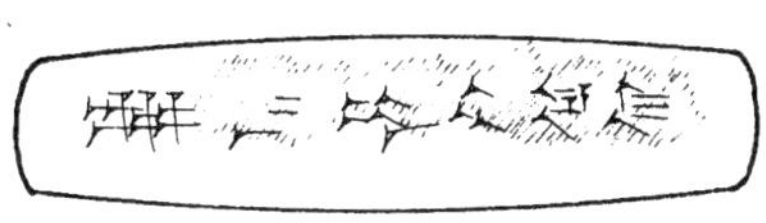

270

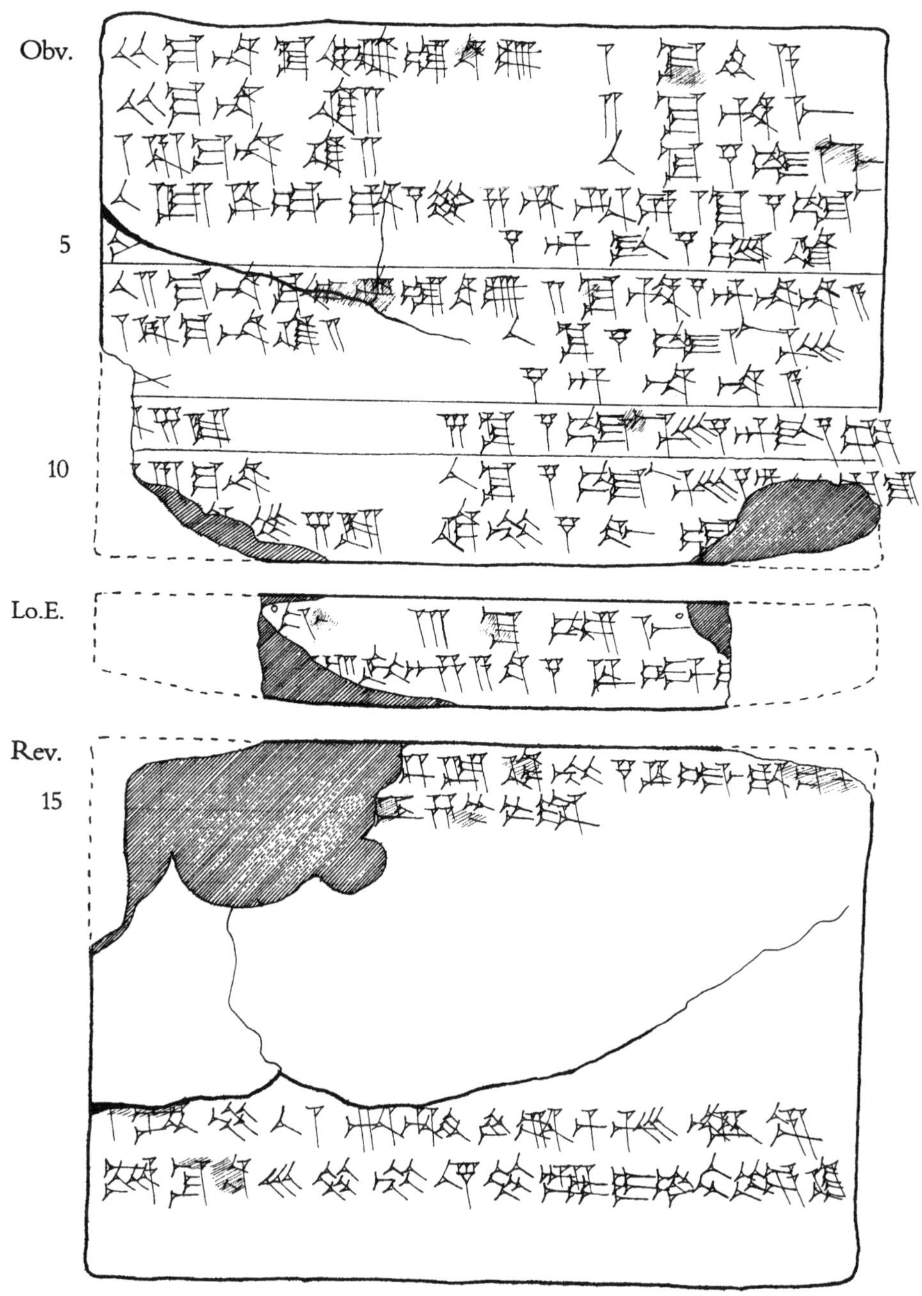

271

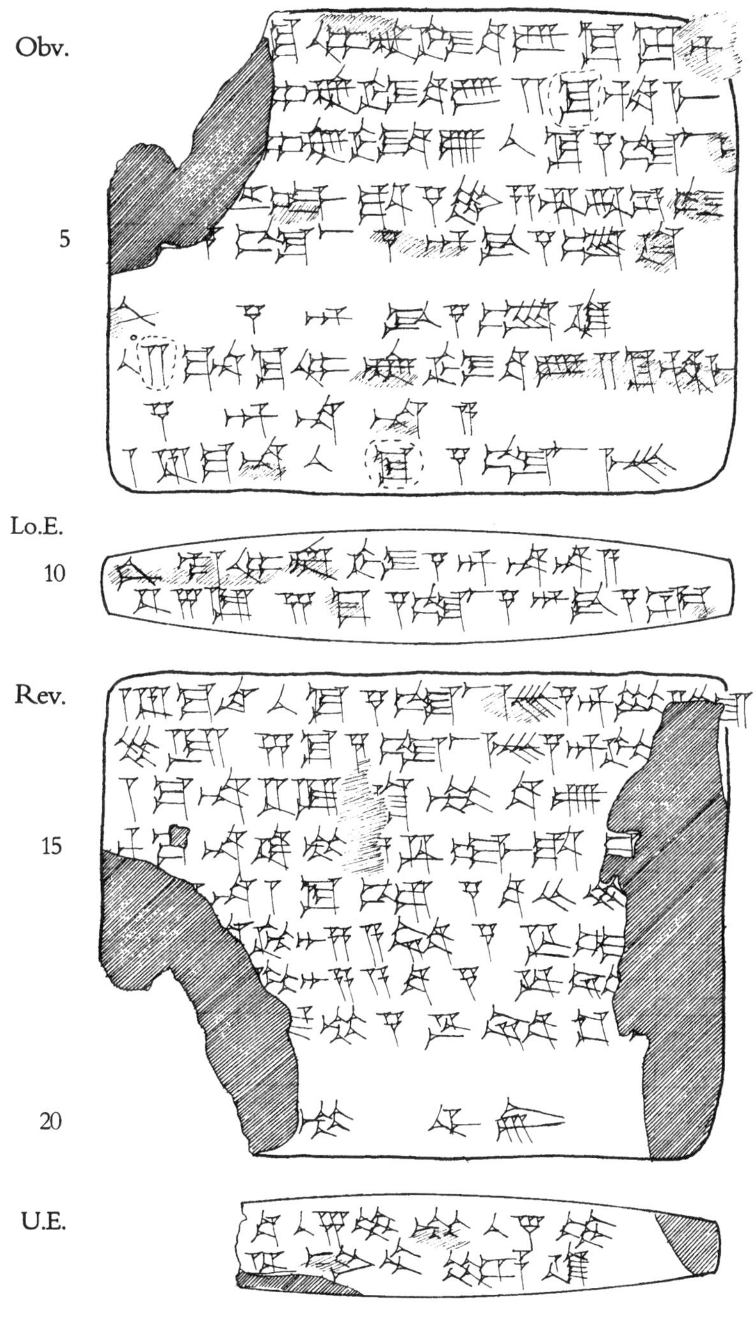

272

Obv.

Rev.

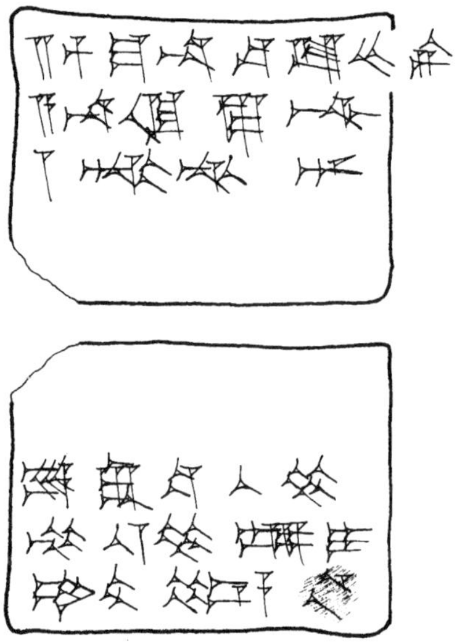

273

Obv.

Rev.

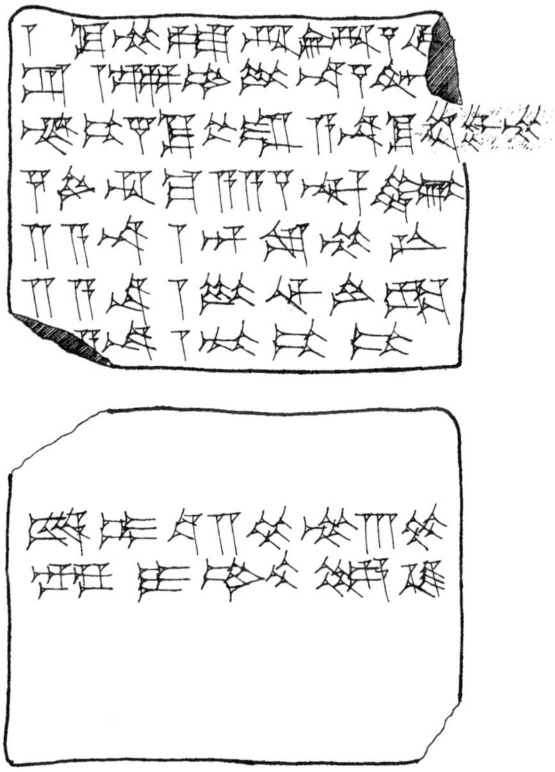

274

Obv.

Rev.

275

Obv.

Lo.E.

Rev.

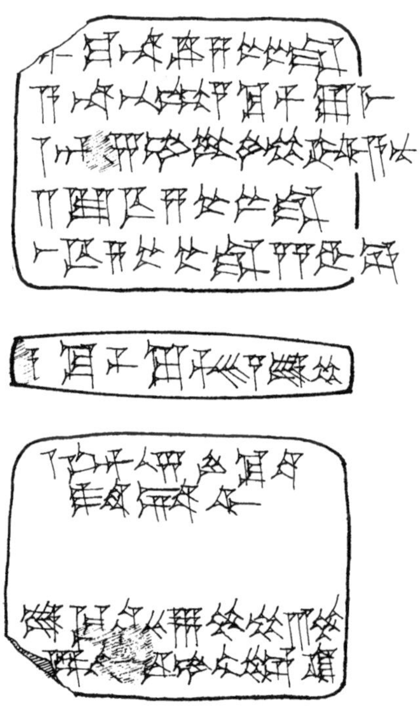

276

Obv.

Rev.

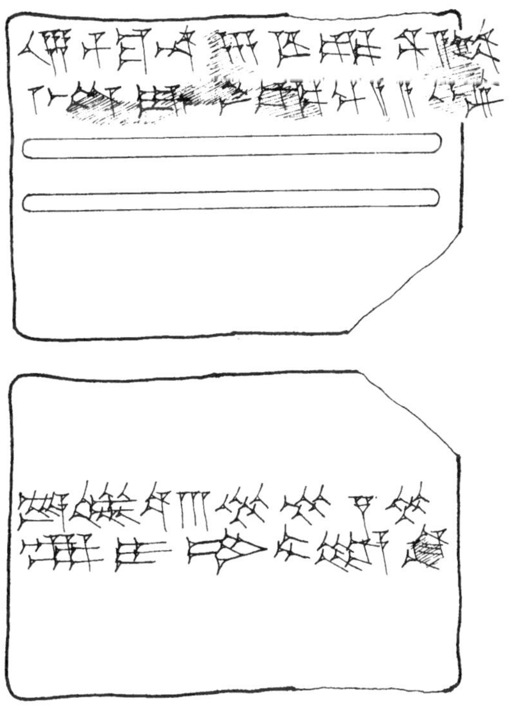

277

Obv.

Rev.

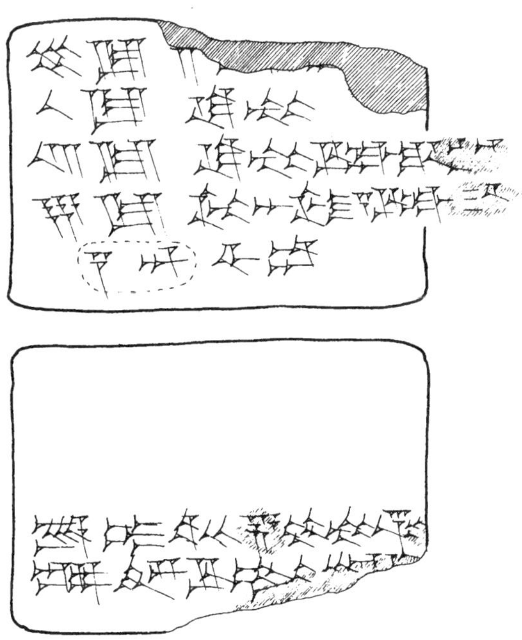

278

Obv.

Lo.E.

Rev.

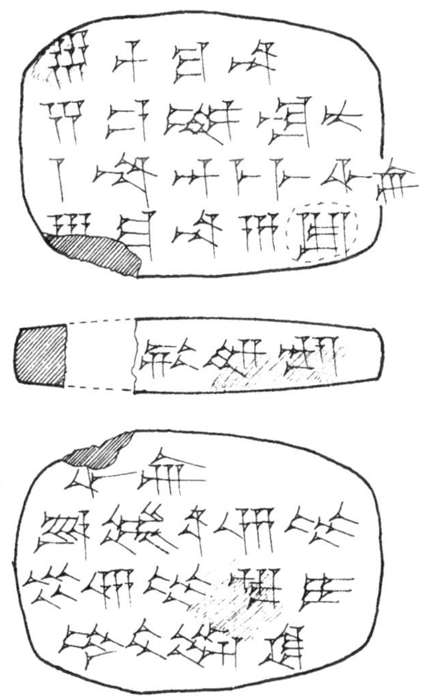

279

Obv.

Rev.

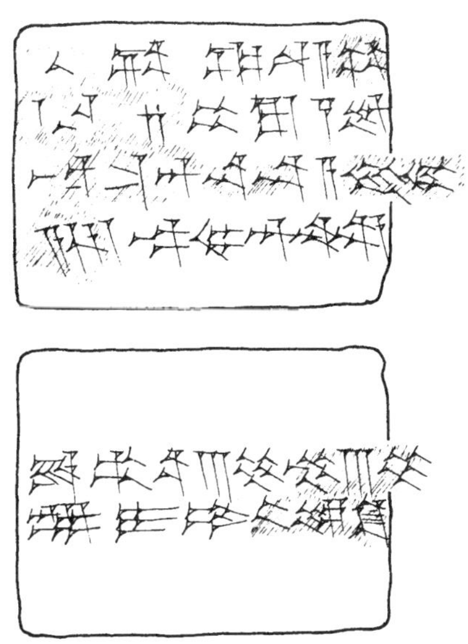

PLATE CXVI

280

Obv.

Rev.

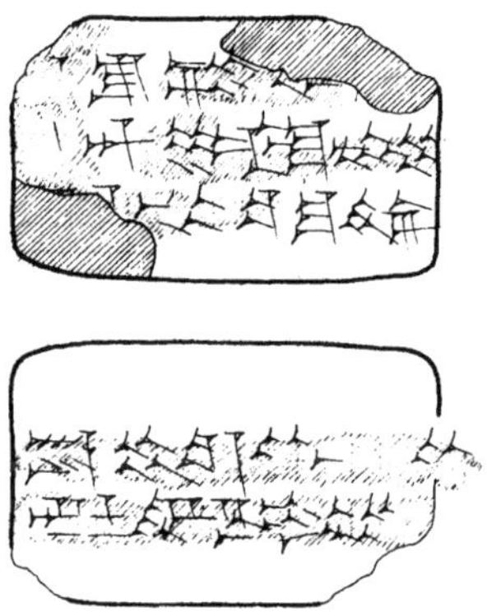

281

Obv.

Rev.

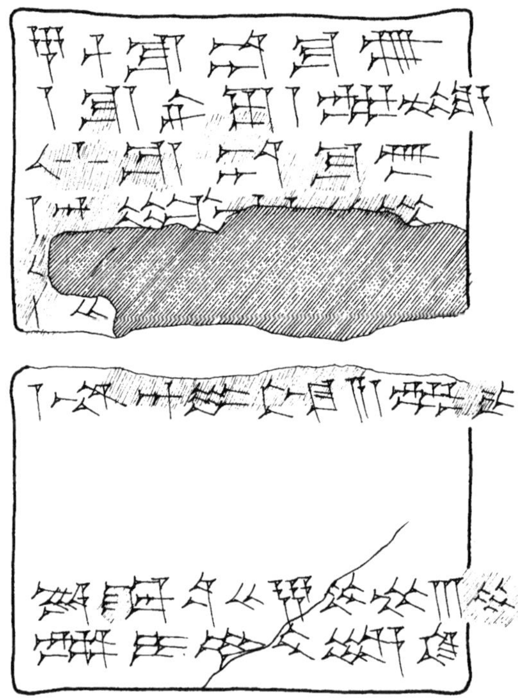

282

Obv.

Rev.

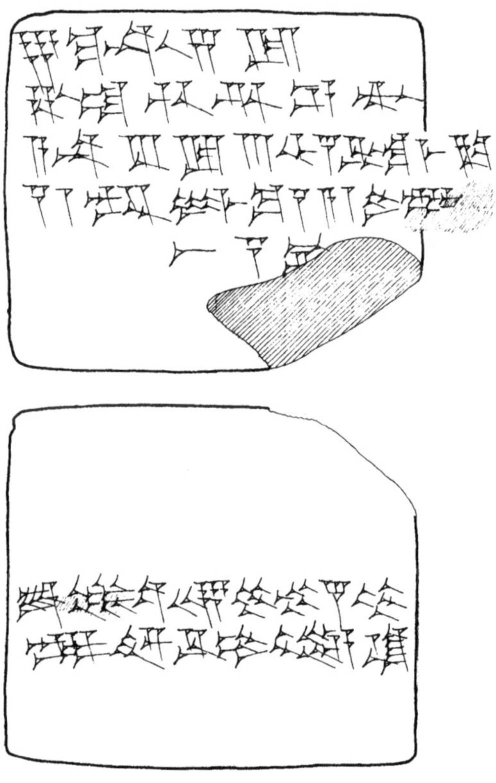

283

Obv.

Rev.

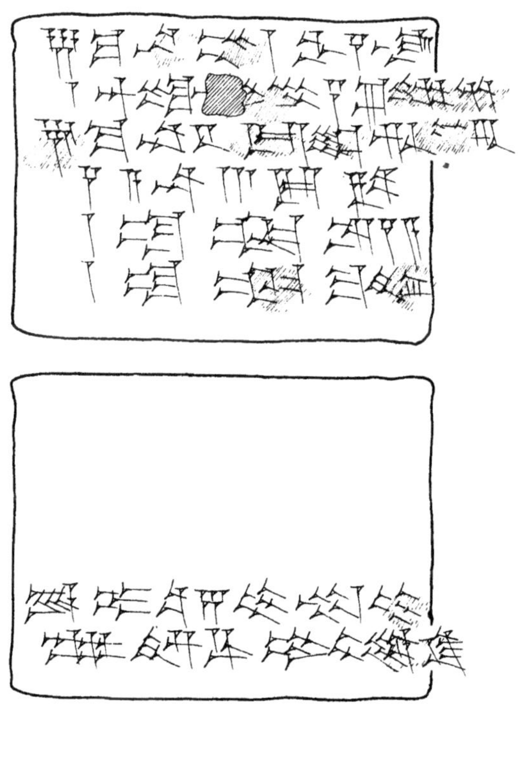

284

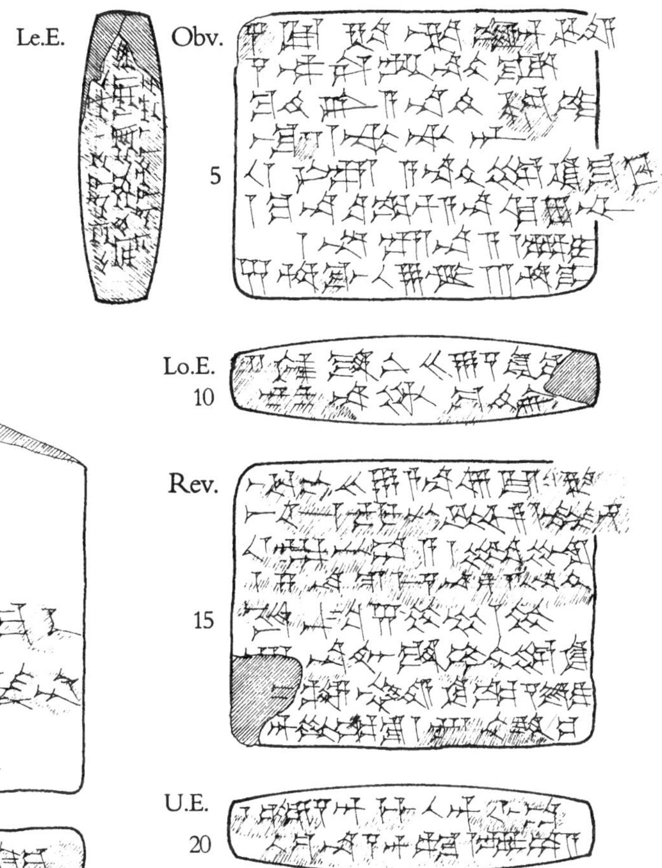

285

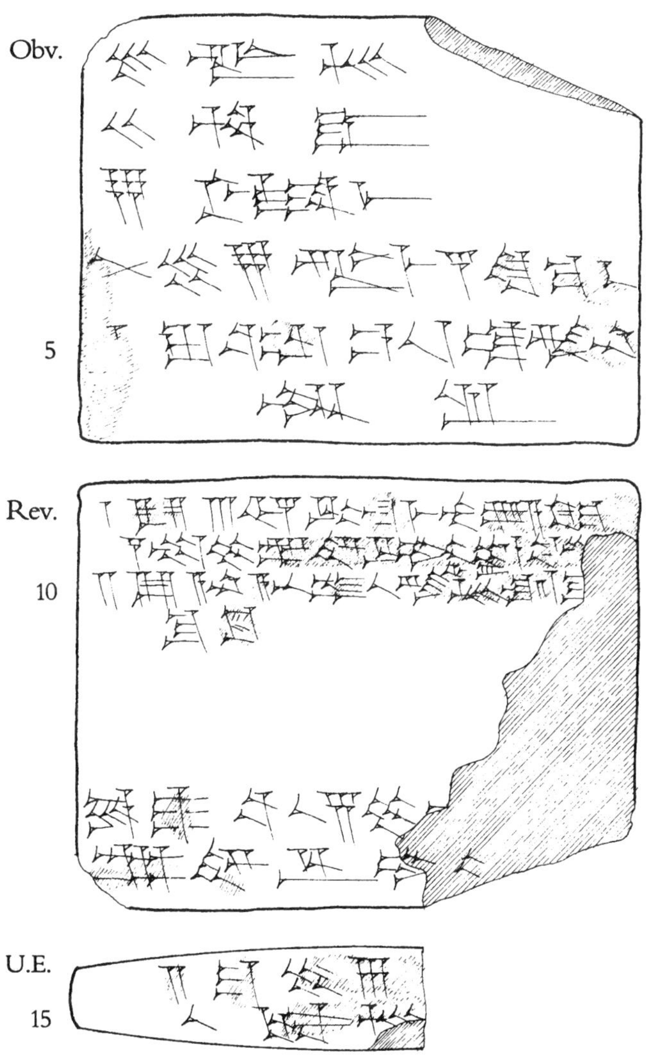

286

Obv.

Rev.

U.E.

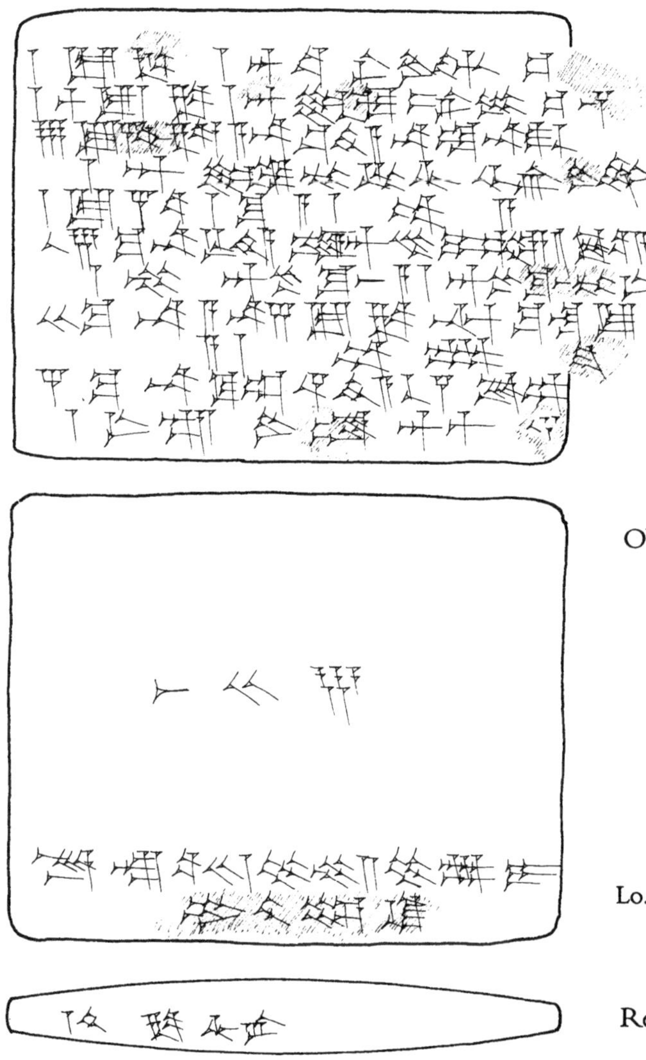

287

Obv.

Lo.E.

Rev.

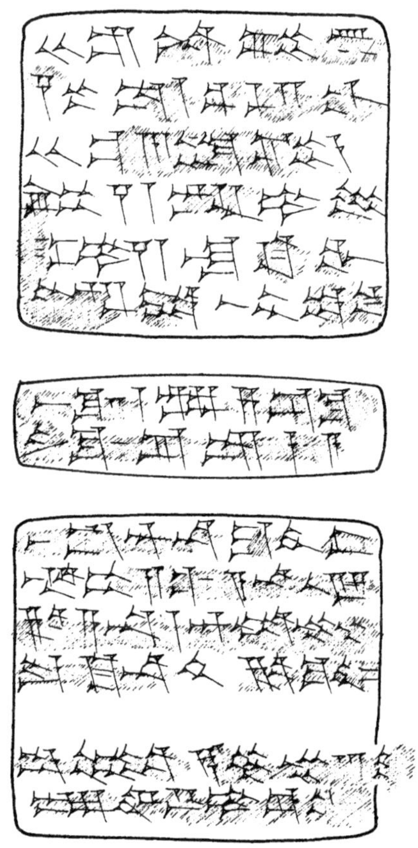

288

Obv.

Lo.E.

Rev.

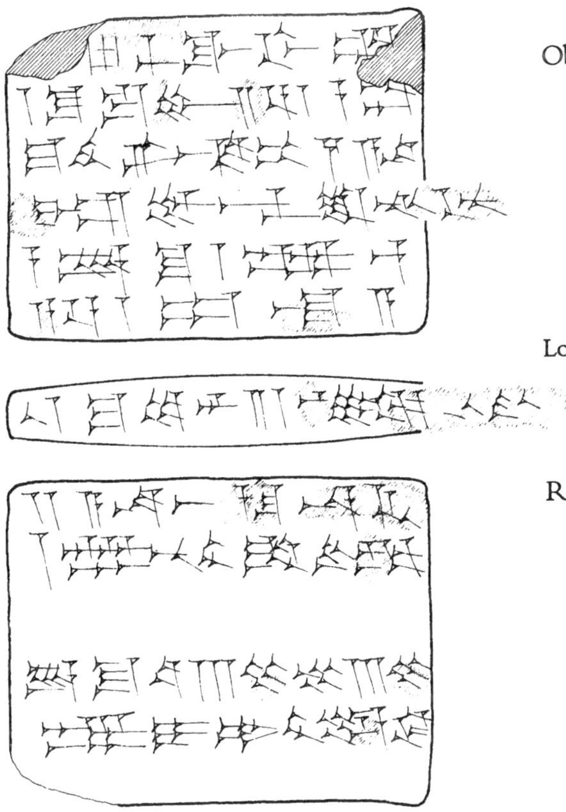

289

Obv.

Lo.E.

Rev.

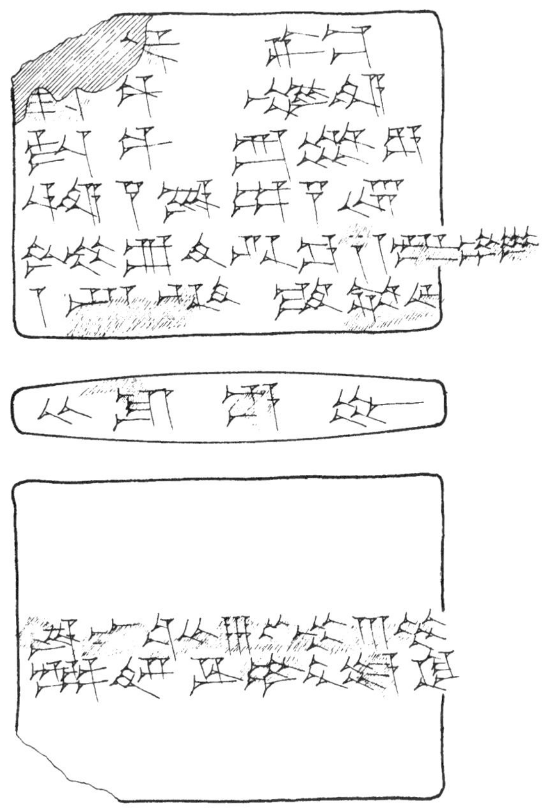

290

Obv.

Lo.E.

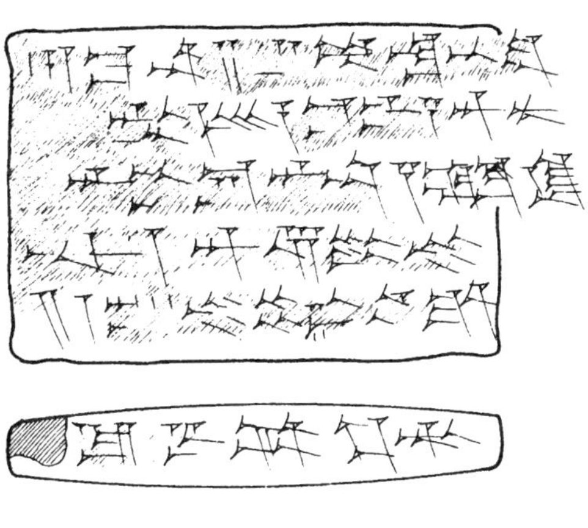

Rev.

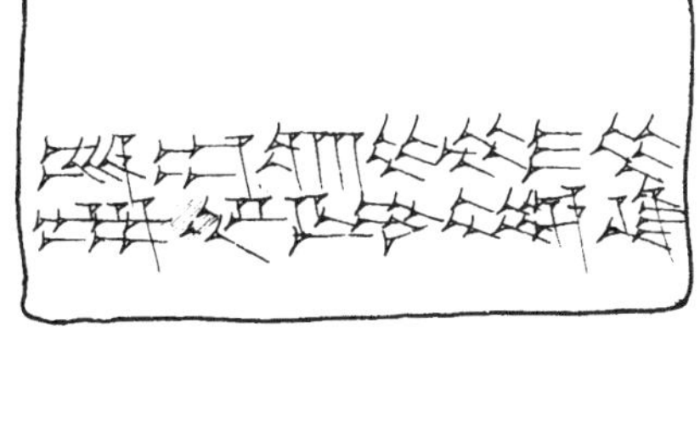

PLATE CXX

291

Obv.

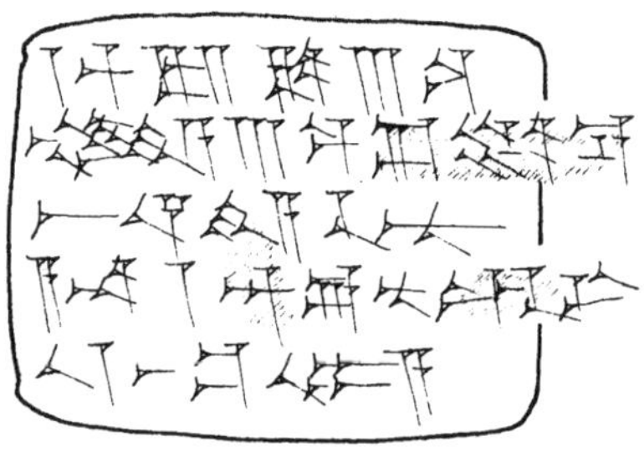

Lo.E.

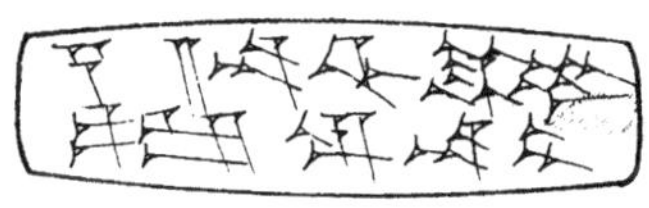

Rev.

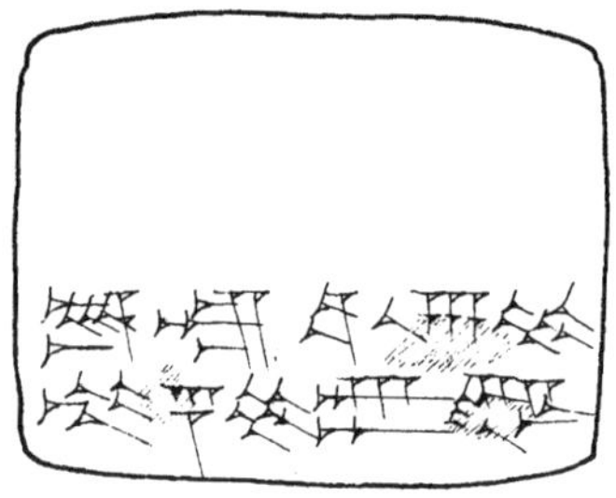

U.E.

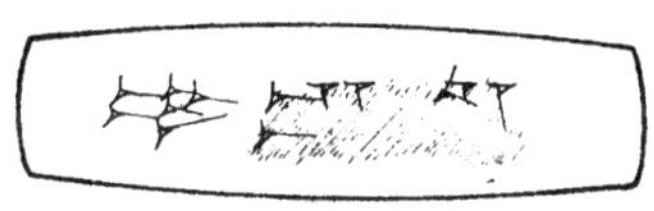

292

Obv.

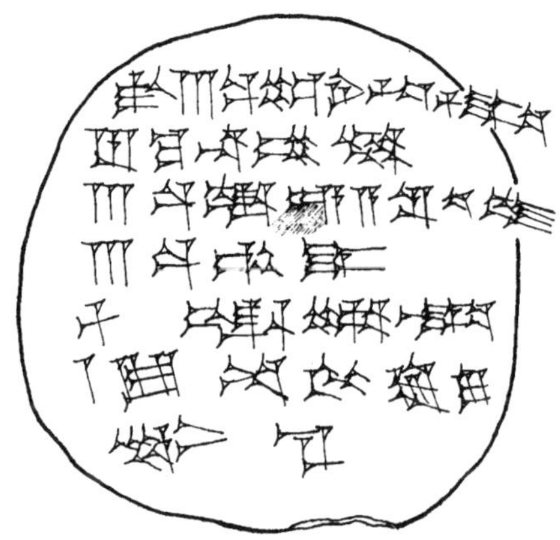

Rev.

293

Obv.

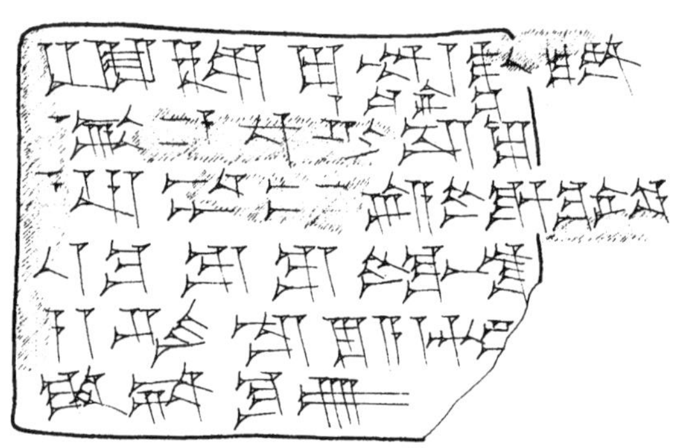

Lo.E.

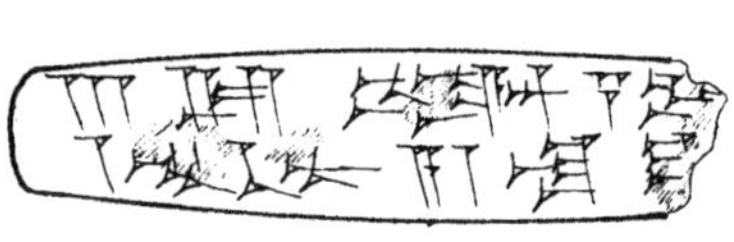

Rev.

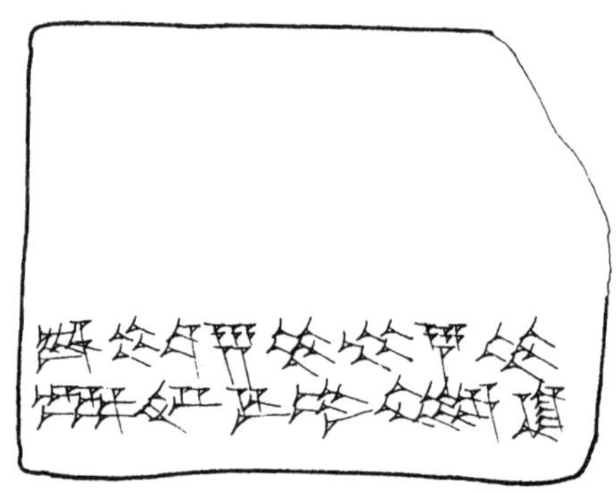

294

Obv.

Lo.E.

Rev.

U.E.

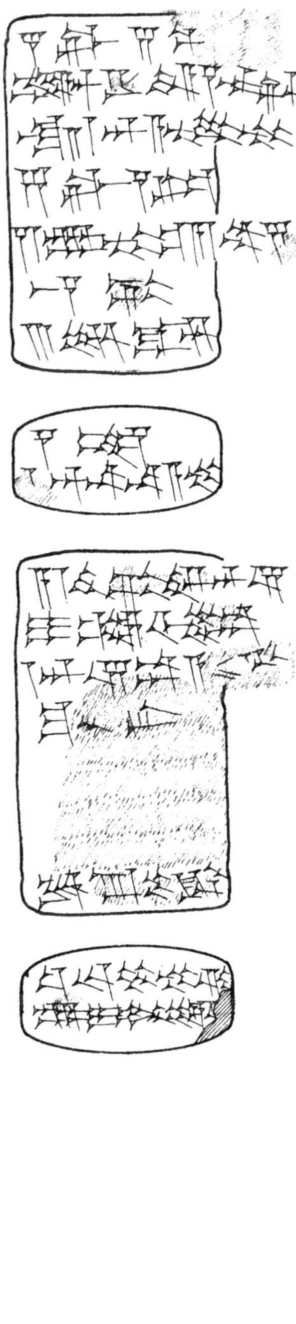

295

Obv.

Rev.

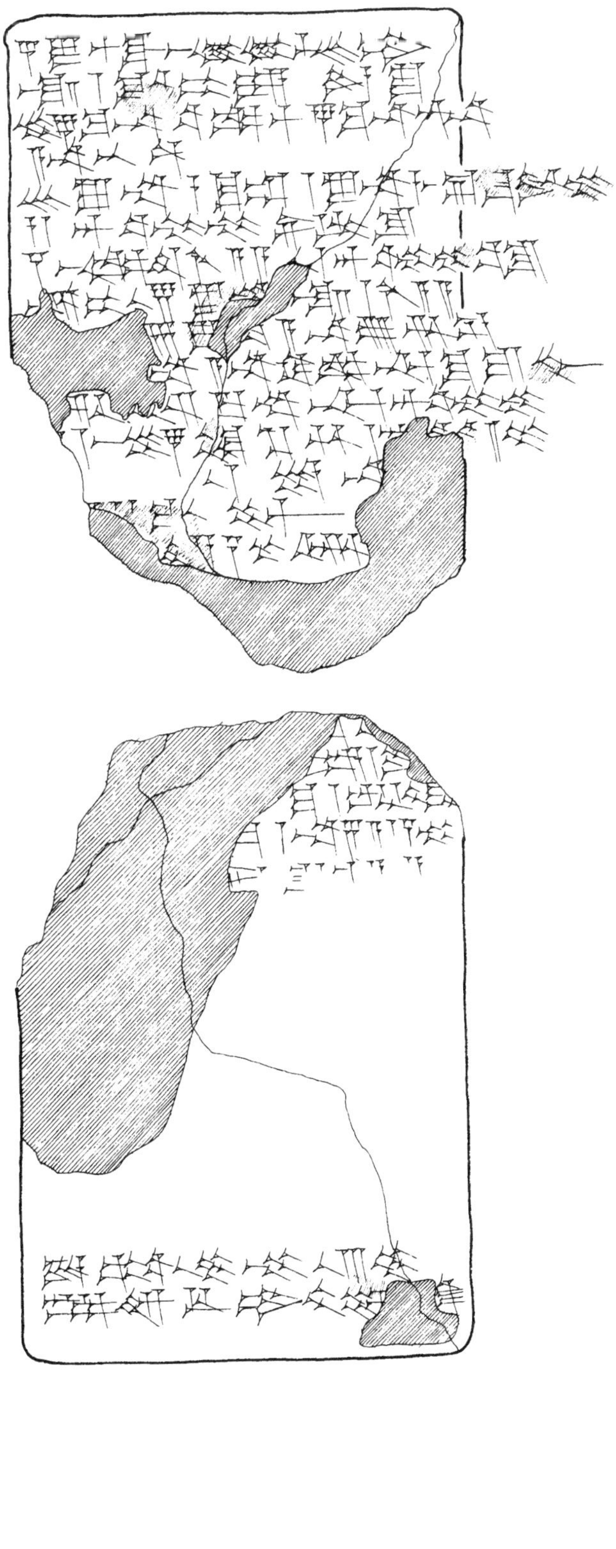

296

Obv.

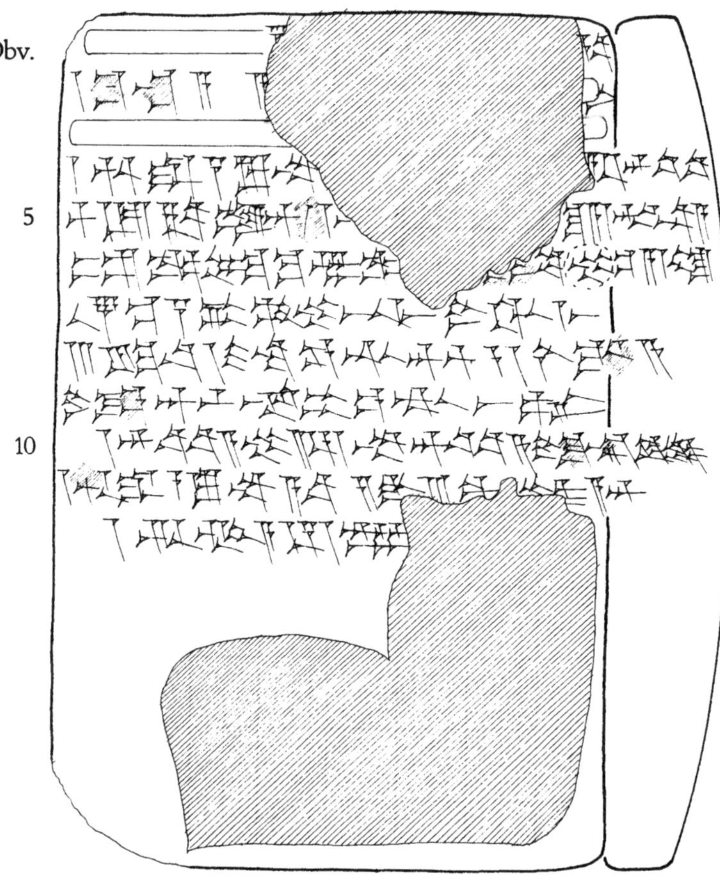

Rev.

rest uninscribed

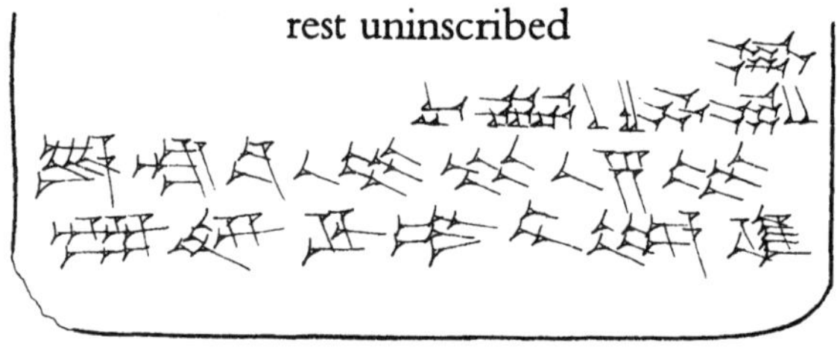

297

Obv.

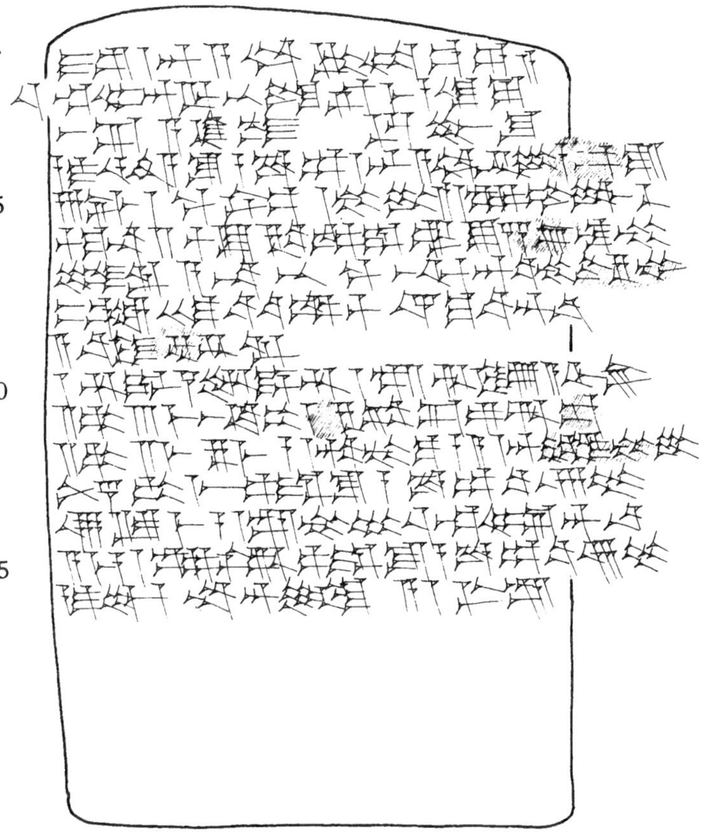

rest uninscribed

Rev.

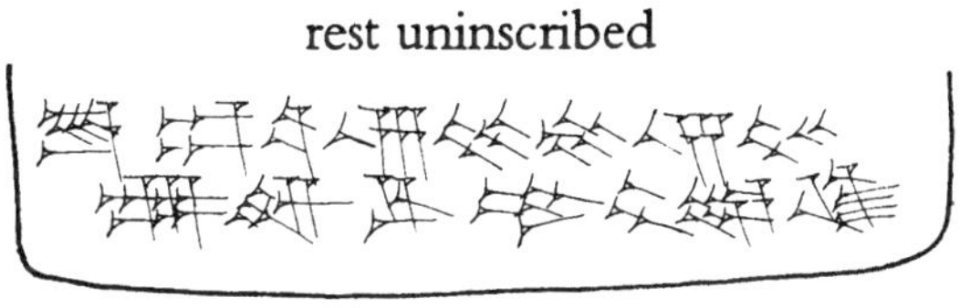

PLATE CXXIV

298

Obv.

Lo.E.

Rev.

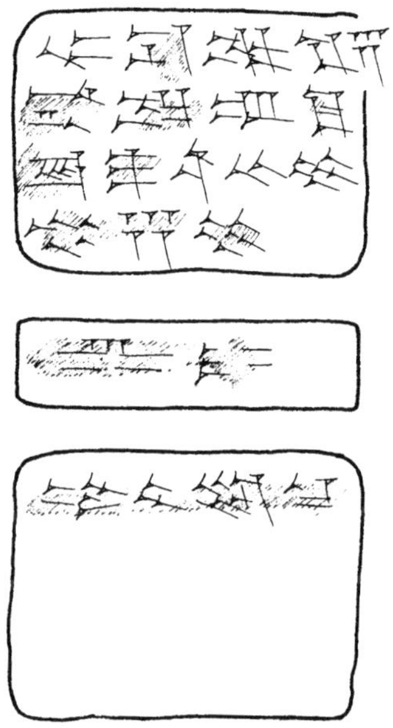

299

Obv.

Lo.E.

Rev.

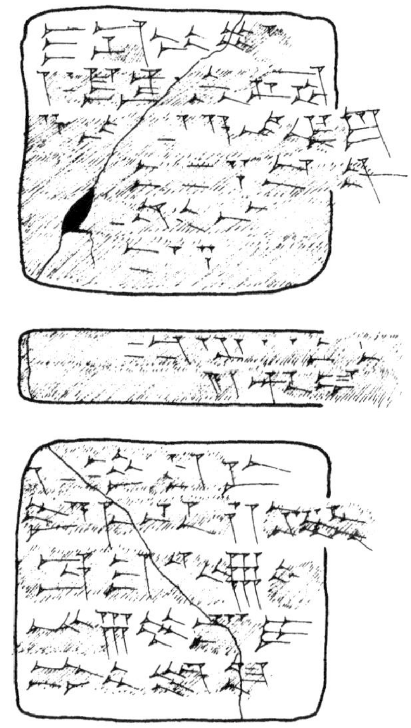

300

Obv.

Lo.E.

Rev.

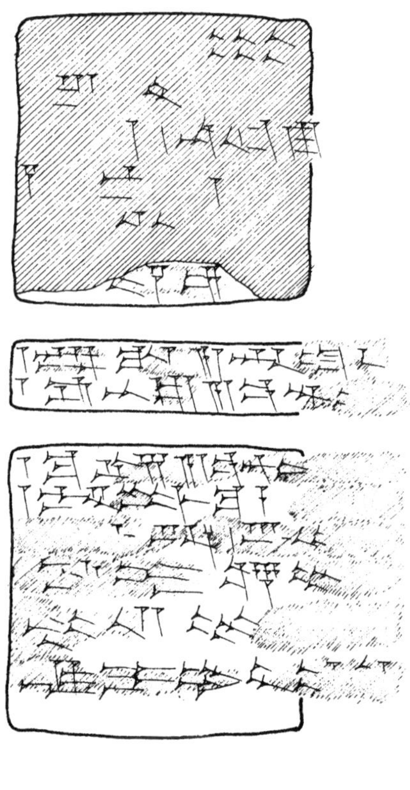

301

Obv.

Lo.E.

Rev.

U.E.

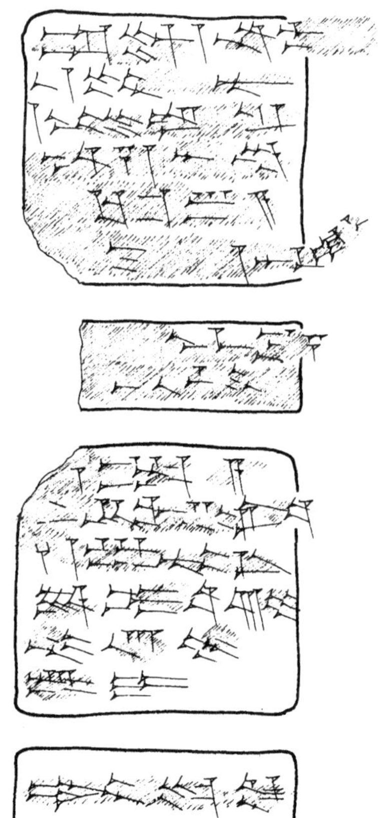

302

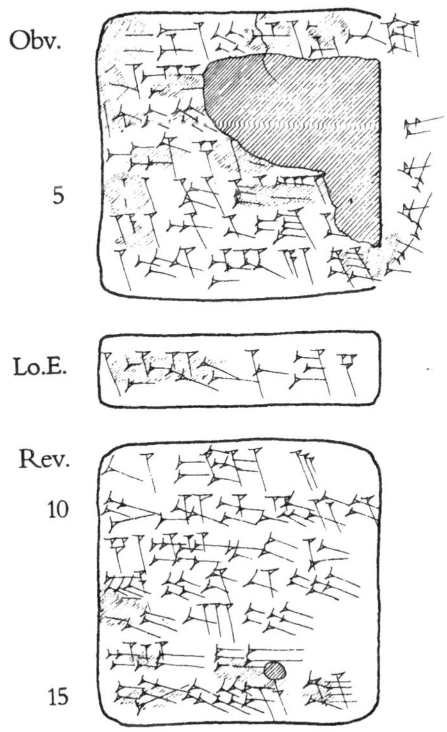

303

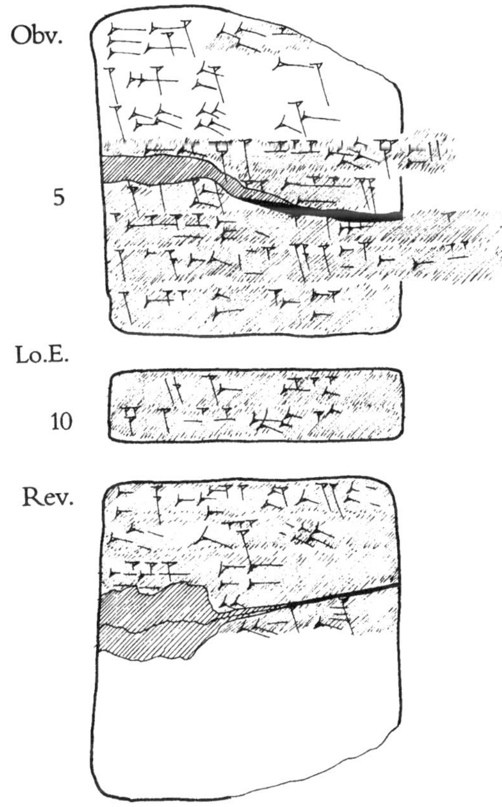

304

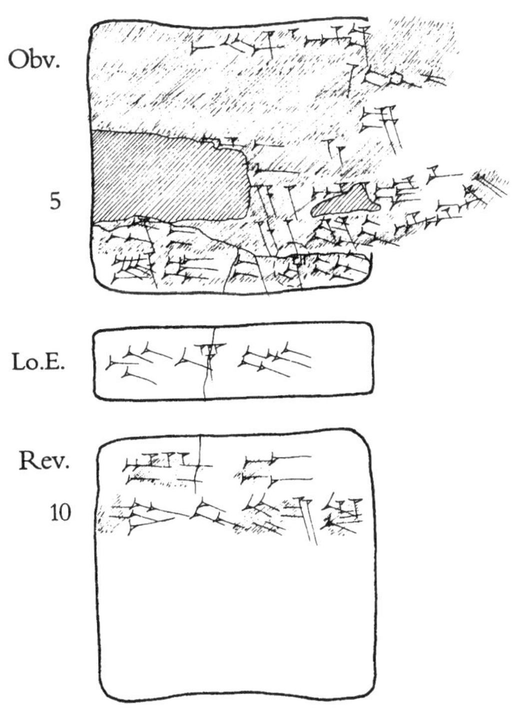

305

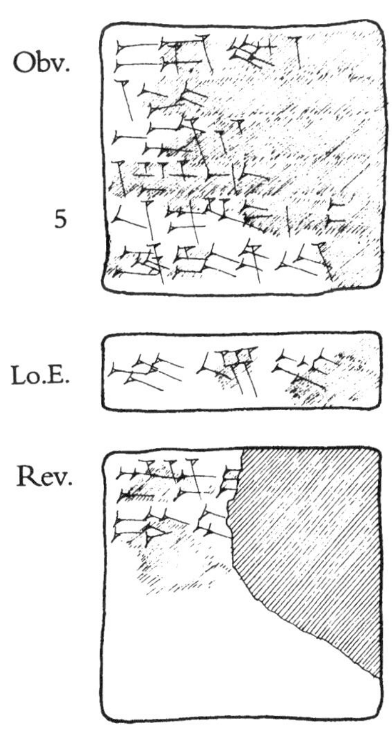

306

Obv.

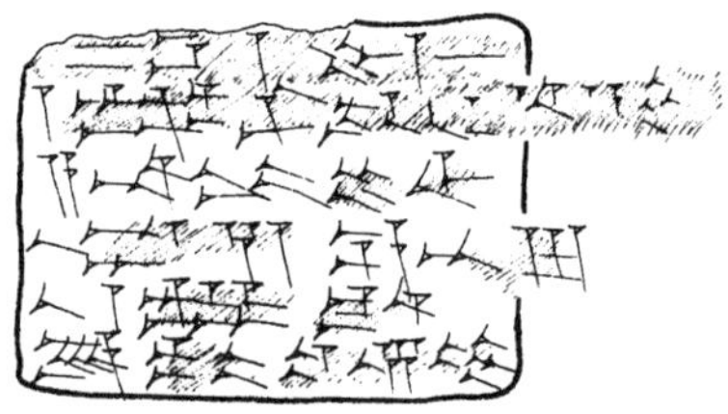

Lo.E.

Rev.

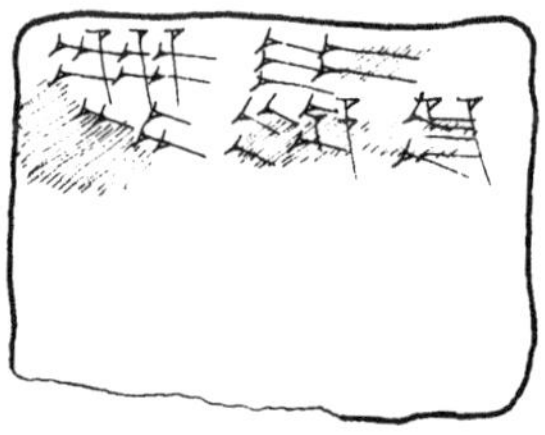

307

Obv.

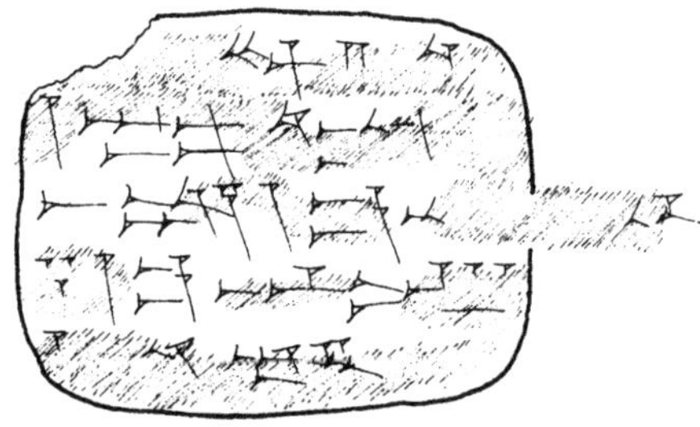

Lo.E.

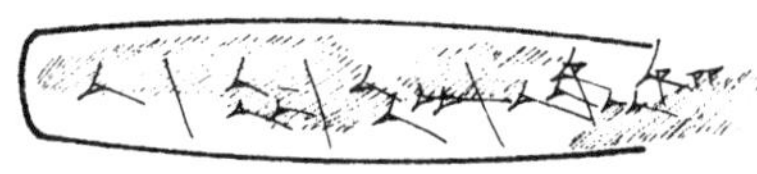

Rev.

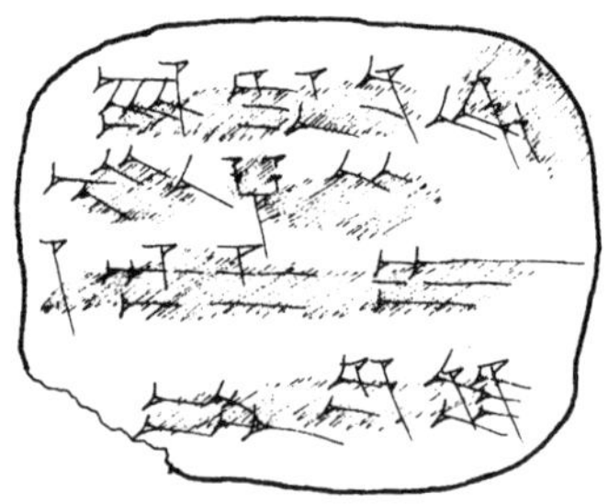

308

Obv.

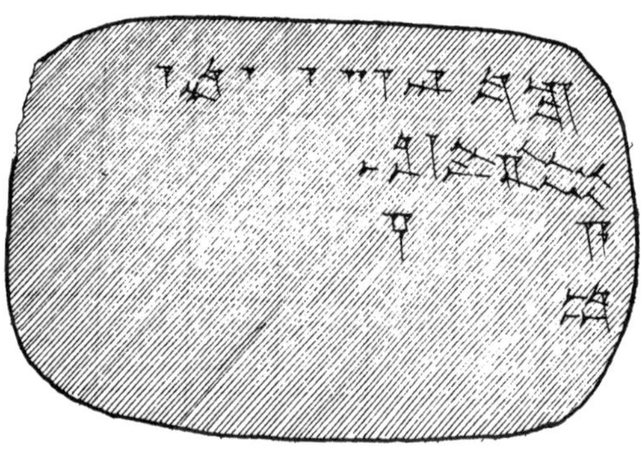

Rev.

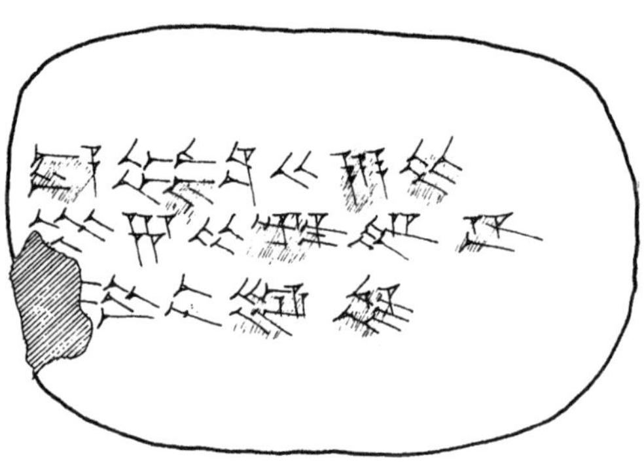

309

Obv.

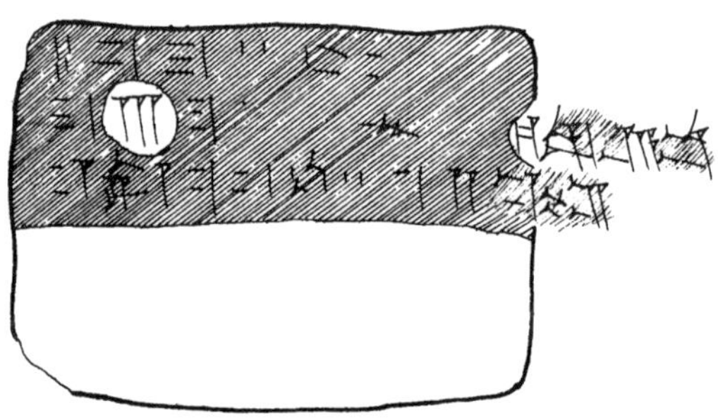

Rev.

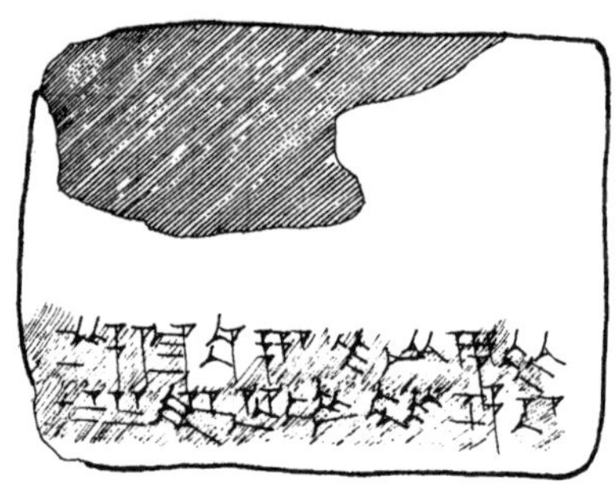

310

Obv.

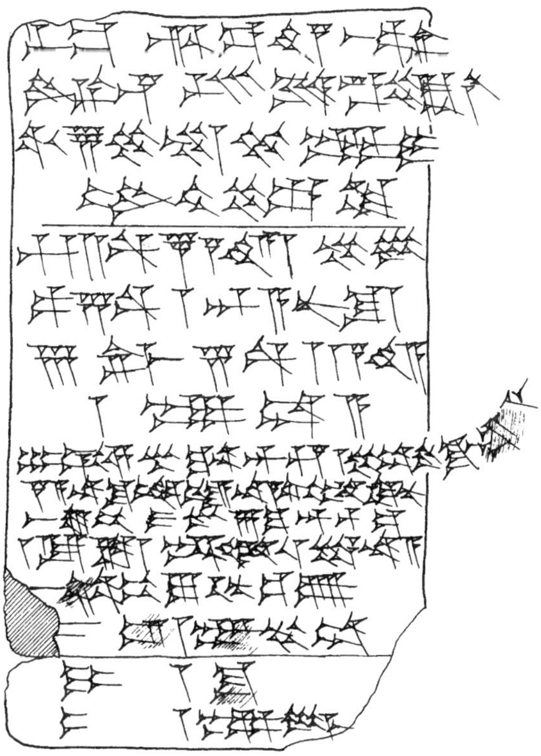

Lo.E.

Rev.

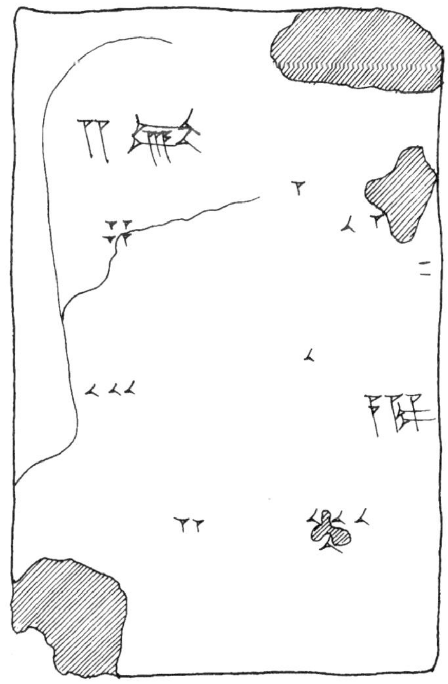

311

Obv.

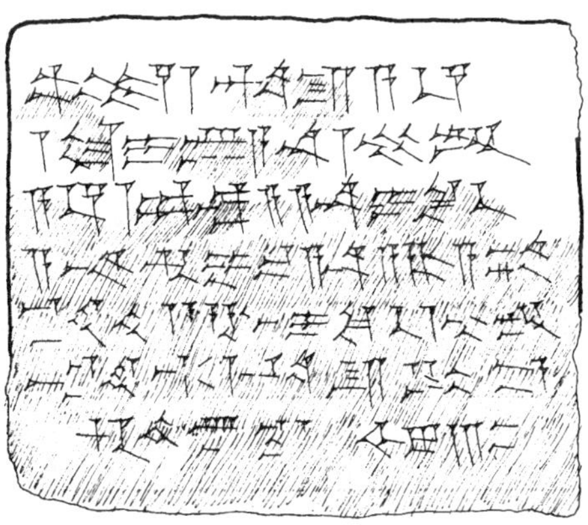

Rev.

Lo.E.

U.E.

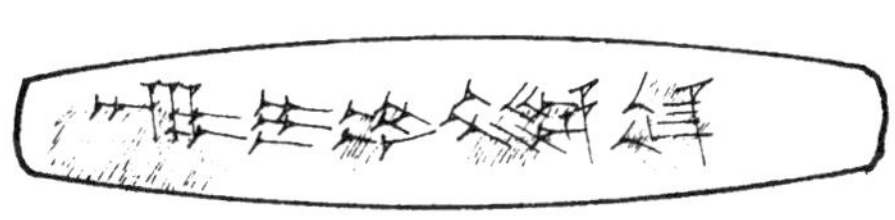

PLATE CXXVIII

312

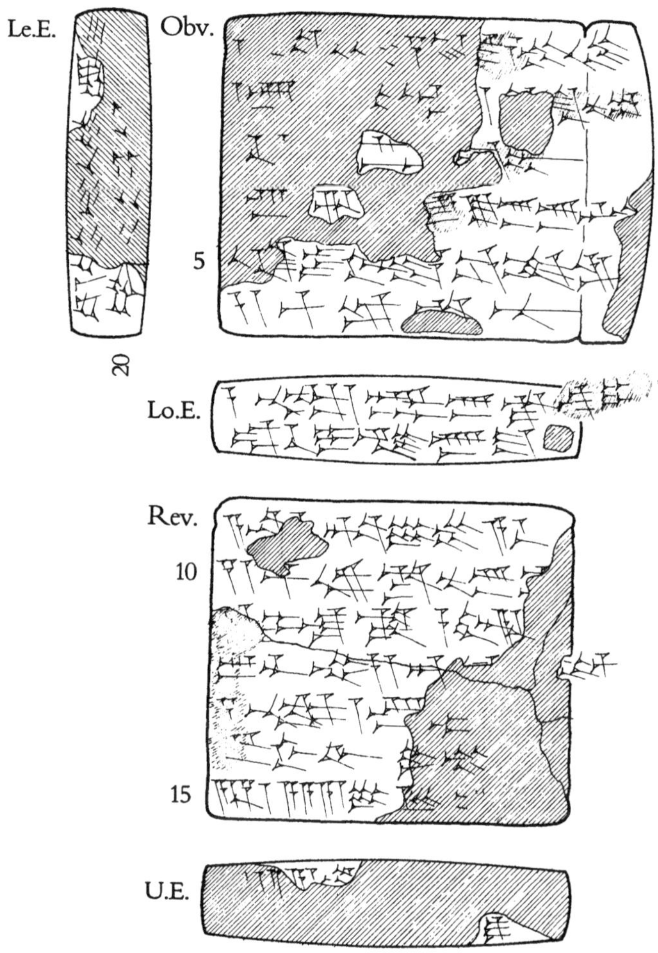

313

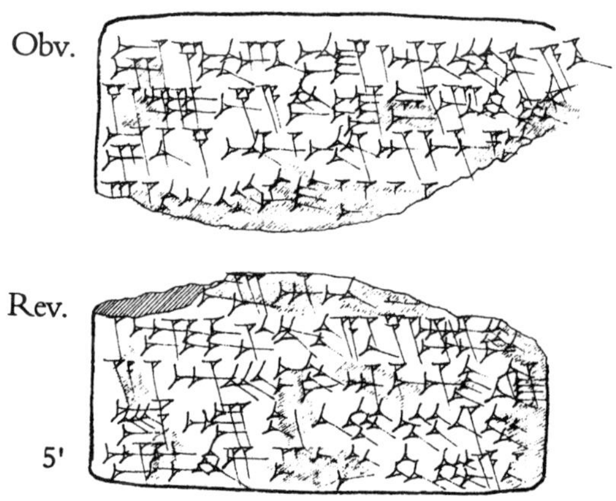